Building Linux® Virtual Private Networks (VPNs)

Contents at a Glance

Building Linux® Virtual Private Networks (VPNs)

Oleg Kolesnikov

Brian Hatch

www.newriders.com

201 West 103rd Street, Indianapolis, Indiana 46290
An Imprint of Pearson Education
Boston • Indianapolis • London • Munich • New York • San Francisco

rtual
(VPNs)

Trademarks

Warning and Disclaimer

Publisher
David Dwyer

Associate Publisher
Stephanie Wall

Production Manager
Gina Kanouse

Managing Editor
Kristy Knoop

Development Editor
Chris Zahn

Project Editors
Christopher Morris
Todd Zellers

Product Marketing Manager
Stephanie Layton

Publicity Manager
Susan Nixon

Copy Editor
Amy Lepore

Senior Indexer
Cheryl Lenser

Manufacturing Coordinator
Jim Conway

Book Designer
Louisa Klucznik

Cover Designer
Brainstorm Design, Inc.

Cover Production
Aren Howell

Proofreader
Sossity Smith

Composition
Marcia Deboy

Oleg Kolesnikov
To Mykola, Tamara, Olya, Andy, and Becky.

Brian Hatch
For Bree and Reegen.

❖

TABLE OF CONTENTS

About the Authors

Oleg Kolesnikov received his B.S. from the Georgia Institute of Technology in Atlanta. He has worked in the industry for more than a decade as a system administrator and a security engineer. Currently, he is focusing on research in computer networks and security. He has been working with the distributed security department at the Berkeley Lab. When he is not busy reflecting on another research topic, he enjoys skiing, rollerblading, playing soccer, and paintball. His web page is available at www.cc.gatech.edu/~ok.

Brian Hatch is chief hacker at Onsight, Inc., where he is a UNIX/ Linux and network security consultant. His clients have ranged from major banks, pharmaceutical companies, and educational institutions, to major California web browser developers and dot-coms that haven't failed. He has taught various security, UNIX, and program- ming classes for corporations through Onsight and as an adjunct instructor at Northwestern University. He has been securing and breaking into systems since before he traded in his Apple II+ for his first UNIX system. He is also co-maintainer of Stunnel, an open-source secure SSL wrapper used around the world to encrypt cleartext protocols.

Chris Davis is currently working as an INFOSEC consultant for Lucent Technologies. He has been active in the fields of information and computer security for four years, with a research concentration in the relationship between artificial intelligence and information security. His current project involves the application of learning algorithms to intrusion-detection systems.

Chris Mongold has worked in the information technology field for nearly a decade, helping to develop enterprise solutions in the auto- motive, financial, and telecommunications industries. Previously, he worked as a consultant providing services such as network engineer- ing and UNIX systems integration. Chris currently holds the position of Senior Security Analyst at NiSource, Inc.

About the Technical Reviewers

These reviewers contributed their considerable hands-on expertise to the entire development process for *Building Linux Virtual Private Networks (VPNs)*. As the book was being written, these dedicated professionals reviewed all the material for technical content, organization, and flow. Their feedback was critical to ensuring that *Building Linux Virtual Private Networks (VPNs)* fits our readers' need for the highest-quality technical information.

Liam Noonan, BSc, CIWMA, CIWCI, MCP is an ICT specialist at the Tipperary Institute in Ireland. He started his career as a Sun OS administrator in 1993 and has since managed Solaris, SCO, Linux, and Dynix systems. He has been using Linux in one form or another since 1996 and has witnessed the rise of its popularity throughout Europe within corporations and universities. A certified security professional, Liam has conducted security audits and training courses for numerous companies throughout Europe in countries such as Norway, Sweden, Germany, Holland, Great Britain, and Portugal. He is conducting ongoing research into the areas of security and location-aware computing. Liam plays traditional Irish music when not troubleshooting firewalls. Liam can be contacted at `lnoonan@tippinst.ie`.

Greg Barnes, CISA, CISSP, CCSA, CCSE, is an experienced organizational and network security architect and senior manager with more than 14 years of computing and networking experience. Greg has spent the last four years with Lucent Enhanced Services and Sales after working for nearly 10 years in the United States Air Force as a communications computer systems specialist. In addition to developing advanced B2B VPN and EDI solutions that are now used as best-practices marketing material within the Lucent Enhanced Services and Sales (ESS) solutions team, he has taught network and host security in a classroom environment, has developed network and host security training material, and currently manages the ESS consulting business for a five-state region. His interests are professional development, reading, art, and team and individual contact sports. Please send any questions to `greg@lucent.com`.

Acknowledgments

Oleg Kolesnikov

I would like to thank Professor Andre dos Santos and Professor Dick Lipton of Georgia Tech—their advice and guidance has been invaluable. I also want to acknowledge Mary Thompson, Keith Jackson, and Vern Paxson of the Berkeley Lab for being my mentors.

I am grateful to Mani Subramanian, Richard LeBlanc, Ellen W. Zegura, and Dan Boneh for their insights and guidance. I also thank Steve Slawsky for being an encouraging and understanding friend for many years. I thank Anne Carasik for introducing me to sushi and helping me to get started on the book.

I would like to acknowledge the team at New Riders for their outstanding participation and professionalism. My special thanks go to Stephanie Wall and Chris Zahn. I would also offer special thanks to the technical reviewers—Greg Barnes and Liam Noonan. I would also like to mention Vicki Harding of StudioB for her help and enthusiasm.

Most importantly, I want to thank my family for believing in me. This book would not have been possible without their love and support.

Brian Hatch

Thanks to Oleg for taking the helm on this project when others had bailed—under his guidance we ended up exactly where we needed to be.

Oleg and Brian

The authors would like to thank all the folks at New Riders, particularly Chris Zahn and Stephanie Wall, for their remarkable support, patience, guidance, and timely remarks. We also thank our tech editors—Greg Barnes and Liam Noonan—for their valuable suggestions, improvements, and constructive criticism.

Tell Us What You Think

As the reader of this book, you are the most important critic and commentator. We value your opinion and want to know what we're doing right, what we could do better, what areas you'd like to see us publish in, and any other words of wisdom you're willing to pass our way.

As the Associate Publisher for New Riders Publishing, I welcome your comments. You can fax, email, or write me directly to let me know what you did or didn't like about this book—as well as what we can do to make our books stronger.

Please note that I cannot help you with technical problems related to the topic of this book and that, due to the high volume of mail I receive, I might not be able to reply to every message.

When you write, please be sure to include this book's title and author as well as your name and phone or fax number. I will carefully review your comments and share them with the author and editors who worked on the book.

Fax: 317-581-4663
Email: stephanie.wall@newriders.com
Mail: Stephanie Wall
               Associate Publisher
               New Riders Publishing
               201 West 103rd Street
               Indianapolis, IN 46290 USA

Introduction

This book is intended to be a practical reference for building virtual private networks (VPNs) on Linux. The book consists of three main parts. Part I describes the essential things you need to know about VPNs, such as choosing a VPN solution, common scenarios, and considerations. Parts II and III focus on techniques and details of VPN packages. These sections should provide you with the information you need to get your VPN up and running as quickly as possible.

The majority of the examples used in this book are based on actual working setups. If you follow our recommendations, you should be able to get your VPN to work quickly. If you are a beginner, you will find step-by-step instructions along with explanations of what is being done. If you already have experience, you can use this book as a reference to deploy a particular VPN solution as well as to find out about possible issues, configurations, and so forth.

This book assumes that you are already familiar with the basics of networking and Linux. We try to explain underlying concepts where appropriate, but our primary focus is on VPNs. If you have not had any prior experience with networking or UNIX systems, we highly recommend that you familiarize yourself with the basics first to make the book serve you more effectively.

Contents in Detail

This book consists of 10 chapters categorized into three parts, plus three appendixes. The following paragraphs provide an overview of the contents of each section.

Part I, "Virtual Private Networks," consists of two chapters. In Chapter 1, "Introduction to VPNs," you will learn what virtual private networks are, when you might want to use them, how you can benefit from them, as well as how you go about choosing a VPN solution that is right for you. Chapter 2, "VPN Fundamentals," gets more technical, explaining possible scenarios, elements you need to consider when building a VPN, routing, interaction with firewalls, and performance.

Part II, "Implementing Standard VPN Protocols," focuses on the standard protocols you can use for your VPN. Chapter 3, "Building a VPN with SSH and PPP," covers how to build a VPN using PPP over SSH. Chapter 4, "Building a VPN with SSL/TLS and PPP," shows you how to create a VPN using PPP over SSL/TLS. Chapter 5, "IPSec," deals with construction of a VPN using the popular IPSec protocol. Chapter 6, "FreeS/WAN," focuses on the free Linux implementation of IPSec, FreeS/WAN, from a practical perspective. All of the chapters in this section concentrate on the essential things you need to know to successfully install, configure, and operate VPNs based on the protocols described. Chapter 7, "PPTP," covers the use of the Point-to-Point Tunneling Protocol in implementing a VPN.

Part III, "Implementing Nonstandard VPN Protocols," covers free VPN packages based on nonstandard protocols. It describes how you can build a VPN using three popular VPN packages available for Linux and BSD. Chapter 8, "VTun," covers the VTun package; Chapter 9, "cIPe," covers the cIPe package; and Chapter 10, "tinc" covers the tinc package. We selected these packages not only because they are widely used but also because they are fairly robust, secure, and well supported. They are also simple and lightweight, so you can deploy VPNs easily and quickly.

The appendixes provide you with information on commercial VPN products (Appendix A, "Commercial Solutions"), how to select a cipher (Appendix B, "Selecting a Cipher"), and definitions of some common terms (Appendix C, "Glossary").

Chapter Characteristics

Each chapter/appendix in this book can be characterized* as follows:

	Level of Technical Detail	Relevance to Decision Makers	Ready-to-Use Material
Chapter 1	###	########	##
Chapter 2	####	####	###
Chapter 3	#######	##	########
Chapter 4	#######	##	########
Chapter 5	#####	#####	##
Chapter 6	########	####	########
Chapter 7	#######	###	#######
Chapter 8	########	##	#########
Chapter 9	########	##	#########
Chapter 10	########	##	#########
Appendix A	#	######	
Appendix B	######	###	#####
Appendix C	##	##	

*The chapter characteristics benchmark is on a scale from 0-9 hash marks. The benchmarks are based on the opinions of the authors.

Conventions

This book follows a few typographical conventions:

- A new term is set in *italics* the first time it is introduced.

- Program text, functions, variables, commands, daemons, and other "computer language" are set in a fixed-pitch font—for example, `pppd`. Bolded fixed-pitch font indicates user input—for example, **yes**.

- Italics are also used to indicate where the user needs to fill in a value in syntax lines. Optional values in syntax are set in brackets [ ].
- Code lines that do not fit within the width of the page are continued on the next line and begin with a code continuation character (➥).

I

Virtual Private Networks

Introduction to VPNs

Y OU'RE READING THIS BOOK BECAUSE YOU have an interest in VPNs and Linux. This interest is perhaps driven by a business decision that needs to be made, research you're doing, or mere curiosity. Whatever the reason, the intent of this book is to give you a detailed description of VPNs and some specific applications that might meet your needs.

As you read this chapter, keep in mind that all the intricacies of VPNs, Linux, and security might not be revealed or discussed all at once. It would be best to read through the entire chapter before you begin to decide on or design a VPN. Otherwise, you might miss some important information that could affect your design and make your implementation insecure.

Because the topic is a bit advanced, some preliminary knowledge will be assumed. You will be expected to be capable of getting around the Linux operating system fairly easily. Where necessary, instructions will be given to configure your Linux system for a VPN, but those instructions will not necessarily include commonly used commands. If you don't feel comfortable on a Linux system, you should read some of the freely available online texts regarding Linux or consult other books such as *Inside Linux* by Michael J. Tobler. If you've used a Linux or UNIX system a decent amount, however, this book shouldn't push the limits of your knowledge too far.

This book will also assume familiarity with basic computer-networking concepts. It seems as though every hard-copy text that skims the surface of computer networking includes a discussion of the OSI protocol reference model. Even though we'll be mentioning the OSI model in this text, a detailed discussion is not needed. If you feel rusty on the subject of computer networking, almost any other networking book on your bookshelf should provide the necessary information.

Finally, this book will assume that you know what cryptography is. Of course, we don't expect you to be able to mathematically prove the weaknesses of a particular cipher or even know any details of a cryptosystem. All you'll need to know is that a cipher makes data unreadable and that it requires keys to lock and unlock data. For more information on cryptography, refer to either *Applied Cryptography* (by Bruce Schneier, John Wiley & Sons, 1996) or *Handbook of Applied Cryptography* (by Alfred J. Menezes, Paul C. van Oorschot, and Scott A. Vanstone, CRC Press, 1996).

When you want to build a VPN, especially if you are using UNIX frequently, you often tend to use simpler, more lightweight packages as low-level tools on which to build. Later, you might want to add scripts, cron jobs, and other neat things, so it is important for the package you select to be highly customizable and simple.

Many of the lightweight packages designed to fill this niche end up leaving important features behind in trying to trade functionality for simplicity. However, many provide more or less the necessary minimum of functions that you need to build a secure private network. Later in this chapter, we will describe one such package called cIPe.

That's it for the preliminaries. Now let's move on to VPNs.

What is a VPN?

To answer this question, the best place to start is with a general definition. We will then move into some of the technical details that will really flesh out the definition.

Definition

VPN stands for virtual private network. The network part is obvious, but the other terms might evade intuitive understanding, so let's use a couple of familiar examples.

Let's first begin with the "virtual" part of a VPN. Hypothetically speaking, let's say you're the IT manager for a small publishing company. You've yet to connect to the Internet, so there aren't any restrictions placed on your network. All the computers in the office are connected via a single ethernet backbone. About one-third of the computers are Macintosh, doing most of the graphics and layout work, and the rest are MS Windows PCs, providing basic productivity applications.

Now let's say you designed this network before TCP/IP became the de facto standard for electronic communication. Thus, you have two protocols operating over the same ethernet network: Appletalk and NetWare's IPX/SPX. These protocols are not compatible, but they also don't interfere with one another.

Because both protocols co-exist peacefully and are mutually exclusive, you could say that you have *two* networks, even though they both use the single ethernet network. Each network, the Mac network and the NetWare network, are logical, or *virtual*, networks. Hence, you have two virtual networks.

So, in the sense of a VPN, you're effectively running a separate protocol apart from the TCP/IP protocol suite. The separation in protocol provides a virtual network. You can run a VPN over the same network you have right now. You can even run a VPN over the Internet so that you can connect multiple, distant networks without severe infrastructure investment and reconfiguration.

Virtually Virtual

Technically speaking, this isn't entirely true because VPNs rely on the TCP/IP protocol. However, the data is abstracted to the point where the raw VPN data is not compatible with the TCP/IP protocol. Hence, it's a veritable virtual network. As you will find with all technically oriented scripture, a little bit of inaccuracy can save a lot of explanation.

Now for an explanation of the contextual meaning of "private." A big concern on the Internet is privacy. When we send an email to an acquaintance, we don't want everyone else in the world to read it, just the intended recipient. We can use tools such as PGP or PKI to encrypt the information and make it private so that only the recipient can read it.

The "private" part of VPN works much the same way, although it's handled a little differently. Communication over a VPN is encrypted so that only the recipient, or the recipient network, can understand the information. This provides the desired privacy.

The "network" part of VPN should be intuitive, so we won't discuss it. Therefore, a VPN is a virtual (not needing separate hardware) private (using cryptography to make information confidential) network (an infrastructure over which computers communicate).

VPN Elements

In the preceding section, we explained why VPNs are called VPNs. In this section, we'll discuss the different parts of a VPN and why they're needed.

Encrypted Tunnel

These days, privacy comes in many forms. We put up fences to give ourselves privacy, we rely on our employers and healthcare organizations to keep our medical secrets, and some of us masquerade around with alter egos on the Internet just to keep people from learning who we are. Sometimes we're justified in keeping things private, and sometimes we're not. Luckily, we're not going to bore you with a discussion of social dynamics. That's not what this book is about.

From a business perspective, privacy is crucial to a business's continued operation. The Internet also plays a vital role in business. But the Internet is a public network. So how do we keep things private? Data is data and, if I can read it, so can someone else, right?

Cryptography asserts quite simply that if we cannot guarantee that no one else will read the message, we *can* guarantee that it will be really difficult for other people to understand it, as long as we keep the key a secret. Caesar was one of the first people to come up with this idea. He would write messages to his generals using a very rudimentary cryptosystem (known as the Caesar or shift-key cipher). He would first write the message in Latin and then rotate each of the letters three characters down the alphabet. Thus, the message "ATTACK ATHENS" would become "DWWDFM DWKHQV." The generals would then use the same process but backwards. The messenger couldn't read it, but the general could. Although Caesar could not guarantee that his messengers would go unmolested by the enemy, his cipher had the effect of increasing the security of his military intelligence. It was almost like he was talking to his generals face to face.

Fortunately, cryptology has come a long way, and VPNs use encryption to protect data. Data is encrypted upon transmission and decrypted upon reception. This gives the impression that the two hosts are communicating directly rather than having to pass unprotected data from node to node along the way. Therefore, it's like having data directly tunneled from one place to another.

Authenticated Endpoints

One thing that Caesar wasn't able to determine was whether or not the intended generals were actually the ones reading the messages. If the enemy intercepted the message and knew how to decipher it, then the enemy could read the message. The only thing protecting the message was ignorance.

In a VPN, messages are authenticated to ensure that they are coming from valid users. Valid users are granted access, whereas invalid ones are denied. Some VPN protocols, such as IPSec, authenticate each packet to ensure integrity of communication.

At this point, you might be saying, "But the data is already encrypted! Why do I need to authenticate the data!?" The reason is simple: replay attacks. An attacker might not be able to read the data, but if the attacker grabs a communication session, then he or she can begin a variety of cryptanalysis attacks that can reveal the keys of the cryptosystem. One method is to alter the payload slightly and send the payload to the VPN device. When the VPN device responds, the attacker now has a much better idea of what the original packet contained. After many attempts like this, the attacker might be able to determine the keys being used by the in-place cryptosystem.

VPN authentication uses standard authentication protocols, which usually employ a hashing algorithm. If any part of a message changes, even just one bit in the whole packet, the output of the hashing algorithm changes. If the hash is different than what was expected, the VPN device simply drops the packet. The attacker is then left to guessing keys at random, which in some cases could take millennia to guess correctly.

Underlying Transport

The beauty of a VPN is that it uses the network connection you already have. VPN technologies utilize the TCP/IP protocol that holds the Internet together. A secure packet is built by one VPN device, and then the VPN device sends the packet to another VPN device using the underlying transport mechanism. Thus, you can stick a VPN device anywhere on your network or anywhere on the Internet. This equates to savings, as we'll discuss in the next section.

Why Use a VPN?

Okay, we now have some idea of what a VPN is. Now the question becomes, why would we want to use it? This section provides you with a number of clear reasons as to why you might want to implement a VPN.

Savings

Using a VPN is an inexpensive way to connect physically distant networks together. Because the Internet carries the traffic between these networks, it is unnecessary to pay for dedicated WAN links.

Central Office

The root of the feelings of "security" with dedicated WAN links, be they satellite, long-haul Plesiochronous Digital Hierarchy (PDH), or Synchronous Digital Hierarchy (SDH) links, lay in the physical security of the Central Offices (COs) that house them. Every CO is physically secured and usually is monitored in some way by the carrier that owns the space in which it lays. In the case of either copper or fiber links, it is unlikely that an attacker would be determined (or savvy) enough to vampire-tap the link to extract passing data. It is not unlikely, however, that a determined attacker would be able to collect meaningful data over time without being detected. This is particularly true if the attacker makes the attempt on an intermediate telephone pole, or junction. Even with costs to the purchasing organization being equal, the security offered by a VPN can be of demonstrably greater value than those WAN links commonly referred to as "private" or "leased" lines.

To demonstrate, consider the following. The fictitious company Exemplify Technologies, Inc., has three offices across the world: one in Washington D.C., one in Munich, and one in Tokyo. The company executives have decided that information is too scattered amongst these offices and that consolidation is desperately needed. Also, a report from an efficiency consultant stated that employees were spending too much time tracking down information and connecting to the scattered resources. So, the edict from on high is to consolidate information and resources while making access to that information transparent to the end user. This can be quite a formidable task.

Using a VPN, the company resources can be easily consolidated and used more efficiently. Because the VPN can operate over the Internet, there won't be high equipment or leased-line costs. Leased lines can easily drive costs into the hundreds of thousands of dollars, which can be a difficult expense to justify.

Transparency

Here are some big questions when deciding whether or not to implement a new piece of software or hardware: How difficult will it be to train our users on this new stuff? How long will it take? How much will all the training and migration cost? Unfortunately, the answers to these questions are guesstimates at best.

One of the main advantages of VPNs is the transparency by which they operate. This means that users do not need to be trained on how to use the VPN: It just happens. In addition, software doesn't need to be modified to use the VPN. The software will operate the same as it always has. This equates to not needing to upgrade or replace the software in which you've already invested.

Security

A Little Security History

Prior to the release of the Morris worm in 1988, concerns regarding computer security had not yet been evinced in practical application. Tens of thousands of hosts were connected to the then-infant Internet, mostly in research institutions, large companies, and the government. When Robert Morris released the Internet worm—the first known computer virus—it infected many of these interconnected hosts. Since then, the study of computer security has developed so much that whole conferences are devoted to it, universities are developing programs that deal specifically with the topic, the government is subsidizing college-level computer security coursework, and books like this are being written.

A major advantage of a VPN is being able to secure multiple communication streams through a single mechanism. Over the VPN connection, web, email, file transfers, Internet-based videoconferencing, and any other traffic that uses TCP/IP for transport is secured from prying eyes. More specifically, the traffic is cryptographically secured and indecipherable by unintended recipients.

From a business perspective, a VPN is an extremely cheap and quick way to secure communications between two endpoints. Otherwise, each protocol would need to be secured individually, which can be costly and time consuming because each service would need to be replaced or heavily modified.

Keep in mind that the VPN doesn't secure *all* Internet traffic, only that which flows over the VPN link. The security that a VPN provides only protects what it carries, and it only protects it within the bounds of the VPN. Basically, the traffic from one VPN device to another VPN device is protected, but it isn't protected anywhere else (unless, of course, you've protected it through another mechanism).

Trust Your Mobile Users

It goes without saying that the Internet has brought about a major shift in the way people and businesses operate. Instantaneous communication from any Internet access point has enabled organizations to have a mobile workforce, a workforce unhindered by lack of proximity to the office. Through the Internet, employees can access company resources just as easily as if they were sitting at an on-site terminal. Unfortunately, this can have negative consequences.

As previously discussed, some Internet protocols are insecure, passing messages in the clear. This situation is complicated by the fact that, by their very nature, mobile computers appear to be no different than rogue Internet hosts. By default, no assurance exists that mobile hosts are actually part of your organization.

Secure That Mobile Computer!

Not only is communication between a mobile employee's computer and company resources insecure, mobile computers themselves are insecure. Many companies have been the victims of industrial espionage, not by failing to secure the controlled infrastructure but by failing to properly secure mobile computers. If hackers want a company's trade secrets or intellectual property, why go through the trouble of hacking the corporate infrastructure? Just hack an employee's laptop!

A VPN can only protect information on the wire, so be aware that a VPN will not offer protection against stolen laptops or industrial espionage. Other protections must be employed to mitigate those risks.

VPNs can protect your mobile infrastructure and make mobile users part of your trust domain. Transmissions between mobile computers and intranet resources can be authenticated and encrypted, effectively providing an extended security perimeter between the Internet and your organization. Some protocols, such as PPTP, have specifically been developed for this purpose. Using a VPN for mobile-user-to-intranet connectivity can ensure that your intellectual property isn't compromised in transit.

A Sample VPN

At this point, with all this high-level, abstract discussion of VPN technologies, specific applications might seem elusive. So here we'll present a concrete description of a VPN within a corporate environment. This example is complicated but will be as closely mapped to the real world as is practical to include discussion of business justification and design details.

We'll continue with the previous example, Exemplify Technologies, Inc. Exemplify's three offices (Washington D.C., Munich, and Tokyo) are each connected to the Internet, as shown in Figure 1.1.

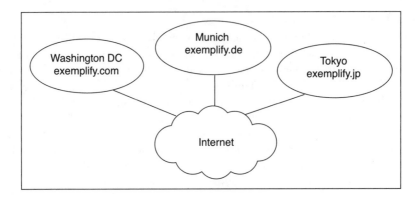

Figure 1.1   Exemplify, Inc.'s world map.

Thus far, each office has been relatively independent of one another, each focusing exclusively on its region of operation. Each office operates its own email gateway and has its own web presence, resulting in the topology for each office looking like Figure 1.2.

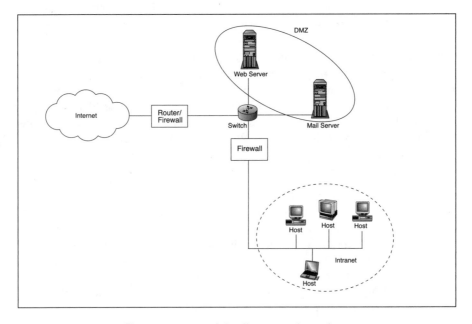

Figure 1.2   Exemplify office network topology.

Fortunately for Exemplify, information security has always been a concern, hence the DMZ at each site.

Exemplify has recently experienced a boom in the growth of its business, encouraging the company to expand its points of presence for more global saturation. The company has deployed sales staff to multiple points in North America, Europe, and Asia. Also, because of this growth, it has employed efficiency and branding consultants to assist with the restructuring of the company's global presence.

The consultants found many disparities in Exemplify's structure and provided the following three recommendations:

- There is too much separation between the offices, making it difficult to consistently express a corporate identity. The recommendation is to consolidate the global presence into a single web site and email infrastructure.

- The global sales staff finds it difficult to access corporate resources, requiring them to travel more frequently to one of the three main offices. The recommendation is to provide remote access to intranet resources.

- Administration of Internet-accessible computing resources is redundant and inefficient. The three main offices should not be under separate administrative control. The recommendation is to consolidate Exemplify's Internet resources under a single administrative umbrella.

Exemplify's executives asked a working group to explore how these recommendations could be implemented. After a month, the working group presented an analysis. Each recommendation was presented in turn, with advantages and disadvantages for each design option. The following sections contain a discussion of each item.

Recommendation 1: Consolidation of Corporate Identity

All offices should have access through the exemplify.com domain. exemplify.de and exemplify.jp will be renamed to de.exemplify.com and jp.exemplify.com, respectively, and WWW requests will be redirected from `www.exemplify.com` to either `www.de.exemplify.com` or `www.jp.exemplify.com` upon the user's request. All email addresses will follow the form `<addr>@exemplify.com`. Externally, SMTP server selection will be based on DNS MX records, with mail.exemplify.com listed with a priority of 10 and mail.de.exemplify.com and mail.jp.exemplify.com listed each with a priority of 20. This will cause the North American email server to be chosen first and the other email servers to be failover servers in case the North American server is unreachable. Internally, employees of each office will use their local email server, and that server will forward the email to the appropriate server for delivery.

When the North American SMTP server receives an email message, it is analyzed and passed on to the appropriate POP server for that address. For instance, if the North American server receives an email addressed to an employee in Japan, the email server then forwards the email to pop.jp.exemplify.com, where it is delivered to the intended recipient.

After some analysis of this design, it was discovered that, on average, one-third of all emails would be forwarded to the servers in Germany or Japan. (The offices in Germany and Japan are much smaller than the North American office.) The bandwidth use and latency are acceptable, but the insecurity of the model is not: Emails are forwarded in the clear without any protection against modification or eavesdropping.

The following options were considered:

- Purchase leased lines that connect the offices in Germany and Japan to the North American office.
- Set up a VPN to protect traffic between the three offices.

A cost-benefit analysis of the two options showed that the recurring cost of leased lines is not affordable, not to mention that the leased lines would be underutilized. However, the one-time cost of the VPN is very reasonable. In both situations, hardware and long-term support are needed, and those costs are comparable.

Recommendation 2: Remote Access to Company Intranet Resources for Mobile Employees

Currently, employees dial in to an ISP of their choosing for Internet access when they're not at one of the offices. Providing them access to intranet resources can be done through one of the following mechanisms:

- Open the intranet firewalls to allow access to intranet resources from the Internet.
- Implement RAS access at each office.
- Set up a VPN gateway at each of the three offices.

The first mechanism was thrown out immediately due to security reasons. Opening up the intranet to the Internet would make the internal firewall almost useless.

After the cost-benefit analysis of implementing a RAS solution, the working group found that the company would actually be paying more for mobile employees to access intranet resources as compared to the present costs. Not only would the RAS equipment be expensive, the long-distance calls would be extremely high! That kind of recurring expense would not be possible to justify.

The VPN gateway solution was the most attractive option of the three. Mobile users could continue to use the ISP service they presently use, and the only thing they would be required to do is install some software on their mobile computers. The only needed hardware would be the VPN gateway, which would be a one-time cost that is significantly less than RAS hardware.

Recommendation 3: Consolidate Administration of Internet Computing Resources

For this recommendation, security is the biggest issue. If malicious attackers were to gain administrative access to these resources, intellectual property could be compromised and Exemplify's reputation could be sullied.

It was decided that administrative access could only come from Exemplify's intranet and that most of the administration should originate from the North American office. Because of this, three options were considered:

- Purchase leased lines connecting the North American office to the offices in Germany and Japan. The leased lines would connect to the intranet firewall, and access would only be permitted to dedicated administrative interfaces on the Internet resources.
- Install secure remote access software on the Internet servers.
- Set up a dedicated administration VPN.

Purchasing leased lines solely for administrative access is an extravagant expense for the same reasons found in the cost-benefit analysis of recommendation 1.

The installation of secure remote access software on the Internet servers, such as SSH, was the cheapest option because no added hardware was needed. However, recent studies had shown that, even though the software was more secure than cleartext alternatives, it was still vulnerable to various attacks (such as traffic analysis and cryptanalysis attacks). That alternative also did not scale very well because key management issues could not be easily resolved.

The dedicated administration VPN quickly became the most attractive option because of the savings involved. In addition, administration of Internet resources used so little bandwidth, comparatively speaking, that the small cost justified itself.

Recommended Solution

The working group then recommended the design shown in Figure 1.3.
This design enforced the following security policy:

- Email can be delivered from anywhere on the Internet.
- Email can only be retrieved via Exemplify's VPN intranet.
- The POP server located on each office's LAN enables each office to function independently of the others. It also reduces the number of externally available services.
- When email is received at the SMTP server, it is checked for validity and forwarded via the VPN intranet gateway to the appropriate POP server.
- All administrative access must flow through the administration VPN.
- All remote access to intranet resources is required to pass through a VPN gateway.
- The firewalls separating the intranets from the DMZ will block all incoming connection requests.
- Connection attempts originating from the SMTP or WWW servers will not be allowed to traverse any firewall.

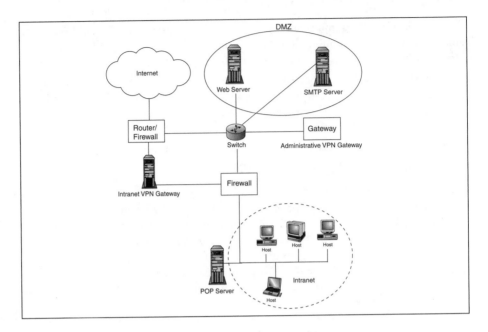

Figure 1.3   Exemplify office VPN design.

Unfortunately, SMTP could not be secured. The design of the protocol itself and the need for it to be accessible to all Internet hosts made it impossible to secure without the addition of an application-level protocol such as SSL. However, because the SMTP server could be accessed through the intranet VPN, internal emails would be secured through the VPN.

Social Engineering Considerations

It is entirely possible for employees to bypass VPN-encapsulated SMTP mail delivery. If a user disables his or her VPN client, the user will be able to deliver emails in cleartext. However, this scenario would clearly be an attempt to circumvent security and could be logged and dealt with procedurally, as described in Exemplify's security policy.

At this point, you might be thinking, "Could you have thought of a more complicated example!?" The answer to this question is yes. A more extravagant example is entirely possible, and companies and consultants create them every day and then turn around and implement those designs. The purpose of this example was to represent a real-world scenario as closely as possible.

VPN Topologies

In this section, we'll present the three basic varieties of VPN topologies: host-host, host-network, and network-network.

Host–Host

The simplest implementation of a VPN is from one host to another. For the purposes of simplicity, we'll assume that the hosts are connected via ethernet to a LAN that then connects to the Internet. Figure 1.4 illustrates the host-host topology.

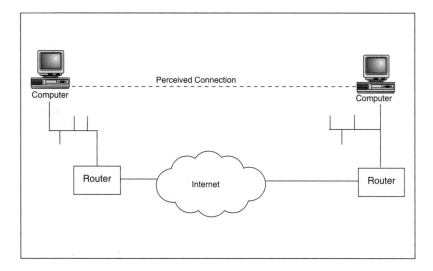

Figure 1.4   A host–host VPN.

Of course, in a real-life situation, communication would probably go though hubs, switches, routers, and WAN clouds. In addition, if hosts are directly connected via a CAT5 ethernet cable, the only risk you'd be mitigating with a VPN is wiretapping: a skill that's rare to find and difficult to execute.

In a host-host scenario, two hosts are connected to the Internet at their innermost point by either a dedicated line or a dial-up connection. Communication between these two hosts is insecure and is subject to the wilds of the Internet. By implementing a host-host VPN, all communications between these two hosts are secured by the authenticated and encrypted VPN transport.

The application for this type of configuration is not readily apparent, so we'll provide an example of how it could be effectively implemented. An instance of where a host-host VPN might be appropriate is where you have two servers, each protected by a firewall, responsible for financial accounting. These servers need to communicate infrequently to synchronize data. The servers are connected to each office's ethernet LAN, with the Internet gateway being a 128K ISDN connection. Building a network-network VPN would be overkill because there is no LAN-to-LAN traffic except for the financial servers' synchronization, and the network-network VPN would require dedicated hardware. Therefore, a host-host VPN, being a software-only implementation, is the best solution.

Host–Network

An easy way to provide mobile users with the capability to connect to the company network is via a secure virtual network, or a host–network VPN. Such a topology is shown in Figure 1.5.

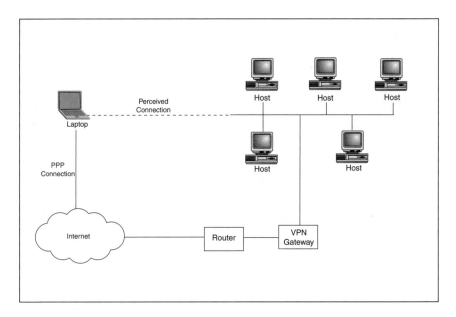

Figure 1.5   A host–network VPN.

In this configuration, each host independently connects to a LAN via a VPN gateway. Each host is authenticated, and VPN tunnels are initiated for each host. The mobile host can connect via any connection, be it dial-up, a LAN connection, or a wireless link.

Host-Network VPNs are found in remote-access situations. A mobile user can have VPN software on his or her laptop and connect to the intranet through the VPN gateway. This VPN topology can also be used for employees that work from home. The slow but steady growth of DSL and cable-modem customers makes working from home an attractive option. Unfortunately, these situations can make company information more vulnerable. For instance, because some cable-modem providers used shared-access methods, thousands of cable-modem subscribers all exist on the same segment, meaning that many users have visibility to other users' traffic. A simple packet sniffer can reveal usernames, passwords, email, and so on. A VPN can make the traffic private and unreadable until it hits the corporate VPN gateway.

Network–Network

The third topology found in VPNs is network-network. In this configuration, each gateway sits on the edge of a network and provides a secure communication channel between the two (or more) networks. Figure 1.6 provides an illustration of this topology.

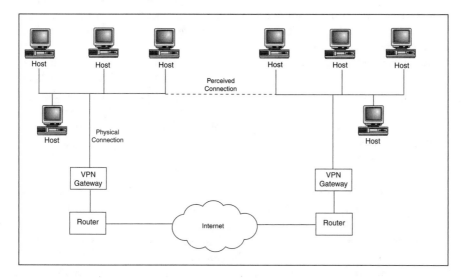

Figure 1.6   A network-network VPN.

This type of configuration is best suited to connecting geographically separate LANs. A major advantage of this configuration is that the remote LANs in the VPN are transparent to the end user. As a matter of fact, the VPN gateways appear to the users to be conventional routers.

Network-to-network VPNs can be used to connect intranets, making the networks appear to be adjacent. The data transferred between the intranets is kept confidential during transit. This topology is also useful for extranets between multiple companies, with each company sharing particular resources with only the partner businesses.

Advantages and Disadvantages of VPNs

Although this is a book about VPNs, it wouldn't be fair if we didn't point out the disadvantages to VPNs as well as the advantages. Both are discussed here.

Advantages

Advantages discussed in the following sections include those related to security, consolidation, transparency, cost, and administration.

Improved Security

First and foremost, a VPN provides multiple elements of security to your networks. A VPN mitigates external risks such as IP spoofing, passive sniffing, loss of confidentiality, and packet injection. In addition, a VPN can protect your intranet from Internet-born viruses such as the CodeRed worm, which infected Internet-accessible hosts at a phenomenal rate.

However, a VPN should *not* be implemented to defer a good and thorough approach to security because a VPN does not necessarily protect hosts from malicious users *inside* the network. The annual CSI/FBI survey has shown that, on average, insider attacks can be more costly overall, more costly per incident, and more frequent, especially when you count unauthorized use and internal fraud, waste, and abuse results. Disgruntled or bored employees can sometimes pose a greater threat to your organization than the rogue cracker.

Consolidation of Scattered Resources

Having multiple offices and multiple office networks means you probably have resources scattered amongst them. These scattered resources signify a few things: increased administration, multiple pieces of hardware and software, duplication of effort, and so on. This all equates to a higher total cost of ownership (TCO).

A VPN is an easy way to consolidate these resources, which, in turn, can reduce your total cost of ownership. In addition, the hardware and software that remain after consolidation can be applied to increase the availability of those resources.

Transparency to Users

One of the major advantages of VPNs is transparency. Users, applications, and in most cases even hosts need not know that a VPN is in use. Thus, adding new software or hardware to your network does not require any more configuration than usual.

Reduced Cost

Because a VPN is implemented using a local Internet connection, the need for dedicated lines and internal dial-up infrastructure is removed. The cost of a dedicated circuit, whether it's a frame-relay or ATM link, can be a significant initial expense and recurring cost for a company. Maintaining telephone lines and RAS equipment can also be cost prohibitive. A VPN can become very attractive when the options are weighed.

Ease of Administration

Because the most common VPN configuration, the network-network topology, is transparent to users, applications, and hosts, relatively nothing is added to the administration or training efforts for these components of your organization.

Disadvantages

The disadvantages of VPNs are related to implementation, troubleshooting, trust, and Internet availability.

Implementation Can Be Time Consuming

Implementing a VPN can sometimes be difficult and time consuming. Configuration planning, management of keys, and troubleshooting can easily turn what seems to be a simple task into weeks of labor. If the option is available, it might be helpful to use consultants or contractors experienced with VPNs to assist in these matters. An experienced individual should be able to fully design, implement, troubleshoot, and document a network-network or host-host VPN in about two weeks. This assumes that the individual implementing the VPN has a detailed and accurate network design and that there are minimal network elements (that is, two firewalls, two routers, two switched, and two VPN devices). Any inaccuracies in the network design could require more time for VPN implementation because those inaccuracies would need to be troubleshot first. If these inaccuracies do not exist, the majority of the time will be spent on implementation and troubleshooting/testing. Design and documentation should only require a couple of days apiece. Host-network VPNs can require more time because the number of components involved is much greater than for the other configurations.

Troubleshooting Problems

Because, in a VPN, data enters a gateway unencrypted and leaves the gateway encrypted, it can be very difficult to troubleshoot a VPN. Problems such as key desynchronization, failures in authentication, dropped packets, and gateway load and stress can all make pinpointing problems in the VPN a difficult task.

To make your VPN reliable, make sure the VPN administrators clearly understand the underlying software architecture and have a thorough understanding of Internet protocols.

Network + Network = Huge Trust Domain

Because you're connecting two networks transparently, trust between the two networks becomes an issue. Do you trust the users on the other network to use the resources on your network responsibly? Also, do you trust the security of the other network? If a malicious hacker gains access to the other network, he or she might also have gained access to your network.

Planning a network-network VPN should involve close coordination with administrators and IT managers from all networks. Make sure that everyone has a good understanding of the security risks associated with the software and hardware you're using and that they've considered the option of authentication to mitigate the risks associated with blanket trust.

Internet ≠ 99% Availability

With all the advantages of a VPN, one thing it does not ensure is high availability. Because the VPN relies on the Internet for transport, VPN service might sometimes be disrupted during Internet outages. Outages can originate not only from your ISP but also from the networks in between. If a node or link in the path from one network to another goes down, it might take a while for service to be restored. If uptime is a critical requirement for your VPN, you might want to consider using only ISPs that offer service-level agreements (SLAs) to their customers.

This situation differs from a dedicated line because the dedicated line has many fewer points of failure than a VPN does. Furthermore, many ISPs these days support some form of QoS. However, you won't get an assurance from your ISP that you'll be able to connect to anywhere in the world 99% of the time; if they do tell you that, you're probably talking to someone in sales. Have a talk with someone in operations and you'll get a different story. ISPs only have control over the lines they own and manage.

If uptime and bandwidth availability are a huge factor, be sure to weigh your options carefully. In some cases, leased lines might be more appropriate.

Vendor Interoperability

With many vendors offering VPN solutions, along with the complex nature of VPN protocols such as IPSec, it can be difficult to get different vendor solutions to interoperate. The first step in attempting to connect two vendors' VPN devices is to check the VPNC web site (www.vpnc.org) and check for your vendors' interoperability. The second thing to do is to make sure you have the configuration right between the two, (that is, SA parameters, crypto parameters, ESP/AH parameters, and so on, assuming the connection will be IPSec). Other than that, research the products as best as you can to discover their eccentricities.

Comparison of VPNs to Conventional Technologies

Another way to look at VPNs is by comparing them directly to other technologies. In the following sections, we compare VPNs to RAS and leased lines.

VPN vs. RAS

These days, many businesses are trying to be flexible when it comes to employees' schedules. Being able to work from home is an attractive option for many people, especially if they're single parents or live a decent distance from the office. Also, many companies need a mobile workforce: Salespeople and support engineers need to travel the globe to conduct business.

Traditionally, there have only been two options available: either open the intranet resources to the outside world or maintain a pool of modems through which users can connect. Both of these solutions have severe disadvantages.

Providing resources over the Internet means those resources are accessible to *everyone* on the Internet, not just the intended users. This can pose serious security risks. If the resources are compromised, you could be susceptible to unauthorized disclosure of trade secrets, proprietary information, and intellectual property. Not only that, if there are trust relationships between servers, one compromised server can cascade into other compromised servers. From a business perspective, this can translate to exponential financial losses.

If you instead choose to maintain a modem pool, your costs can quickly skyrocket. PPP servers, modems, multiport serial boards, telephone lines, long-distance calls, and administration costs can add up. In addition, you could be a victim of war dialing, a method still practiced that could compromise your internal network. Again, this could constitute financial losses for your company.

VPN vs. Leased Lines

When connecting together geographically distant networks, it is commonplace to use dedicated lines for the connection. Although the name can be misleading, dedicated lines can be anything from traditional T-carriers (T1, T3, or the European analogue, E-carriers), DS-lines (DS1, DS3), OC-lines (OC3, OC12, OC48, OC192), or wireless links (microware, RF, line of sight, or satellite). The lines are "dedicated" because the bandwidth provided is devoted to the owner of the line.

Dedicated lines are good for some applications. If you have a database that is mission-critical and needs a lot of throughput, a dedicated line would be a good choice because it provides a guaranteed bandwidth. Also, you can purchase dedicated lines based on how much throughput you need. If you were in New York, you probably wouldn't even notice that the database server was in San Francisco if it was on an OC-3!

Another benefit of dedicated lines is that they are (or should be) always available. Because you control the equipment that maintains the connection, you're reasonably in control of the connection. This isn't always the case because the dedicated lines usually pass through a WAN cloud; however, the WAN cloud is closely monitored and usually has redundant links with automatic failover capability. The probability that you'll experience downtime as a result of WAN-cloud failure is relatively low. If your database is regularly replicated, requires continuous queries, or requires regular updates over a 24-hour period, you'll probably want a dedicated line.

Even though a dedicated line is advantageous in certain situations, it can be very cost prohibitive. Depending on where you are, a simple T1 can cost upwards of $5,000 for installation, $2,500 per month for service, and $5,000 for customer premise equipment (CPE). For the first year alone, this can add up to $40,000, and it doesn't count personnel costs, equipment costs, and so on. That's in addition to your current Internet connection! Keep in mind that this calculation only takes into account connectivity between two networks. More networks equate to higher cost.

We rely on ISPs and telcos for our Internet connectivity, but we shouldn't always trust them. They have full access to the data that traverses their lines. What prevents one of their employees from sniffing the data? Many service providers have sniffers attached to their networks for troubleshooting purposes, but are the sniffers operated ethically, keeping customer confidentiality high on the list of priorities? If you need absolute trust in communications between two endpoints, your service provider does not belong in the loop.

Using a Linux VPN solution, you can reduce the first year's cost to about $5,000 with only administrative costs in following years. Also, with a VPN, you won't have to factor in other dedicated lines in future migration or expansion efforts.

Making VPNs Secure

Although a VPN helps strengthen the computer and information security of your organization, it cannot mitigate all risks that your organization could face. Security, no matter which type, requires a comprehensive approach to be effective. This section will present other factors that are relevant to overall VPN security.

The Importance of Planning

As mentioned in previous sections, the proper operation of a VPN depends on many factors. If VPN design isn't planned carefully, vulnerabilities could appear on your network that previously didn't exist. That would defeat the purpose of the VPN!

First of all, be sure that everyone involved in the design and implementation of a VPN is communicating. VPN planning and implementation will probably require two or more people working together. If those people are not communicating, timely implementation of the VPN is at risk. The VPN design should also be reviewed by peers from different teams, such as networking administrators, system administrators, DBAs, and other related parties. This will help flesh out some of the bugs or potential pitfalls before they happen.

Also make sure that the design is well documented and that the documentation is maintained as things change. All too often, companies make changes to their infrastructure, and those changes are not consistently documented. Fortunately, discovery tools exist and are commonly employed to map a network.

One of the major pitfalls people run into when dealing with VPNs is a comprehensive key management strategy. It seems trivial, but experience has shown that it's actually a lot more difficult than one might realize. In most VPNs, multiple keys are used to secure the communication path. There's the seed key that allows the initialization of the VPN, and then more keys are negotiated as the VPN operates. There are also host keys and gateway keys, and they should be different. Do you want to only have a single key protecting all your information and give that same key to all your mobile users? What if their laptops are stolen? Your entire infrastructure could be easily compromised.

There's also the decision of manual versus automatic key management. In either case, how often should keys be changed? What cipher is the VPN using? How vulnerable is that cipher to traffic analysis or cryptanalysis attacks? Encryption only buys you time, it doesn't protect your information forever. What if a key is compromised? Are there key revocation methods in place? If you don't revoke and change keys, you will continue to be vulnerable.

What about failover protection? What if the VPN stops operating as it should? It could be days before service is restored. Be sure to include a failover mechanism when designing your VPN. Otherwise, downtime could result is financial loss.

Worms and Failover Protection

The need for redundancy, or failover protection, was evinced by the Nimda and CodeRed Internet worms. These worms consumed massive amounts of bandwidth with their activity, which had the side effect of a DoS attack in many sections of the Internet. Your VPN is not immune to this phenomenon.

Because VPNs can be complex, VPN management is not strictly a technical issue. Be sure that procedural and administrative safeguards are in place for the things that can't be managed automatically.

Using Firewalls

If you're planning to implement a VPN, you're probably already using a firewall to protect your systems. If the VPN traffic will be traversing that firewall, the firewall ruleset needs to change to allow the VPN traffic. When the ruleset changes to accommodate the VPN, the firewall policy should be updated to reflect the current configuration.

Firewalls should be as protective as possible, only allowing access to particular resources. For instance, if you have a VPN gateway that forwards traffic from company LANs to the company's intranet, and you have a separate VPN gateway that forwards traffic from mobile users to the company intranet, do you want to allow everyone the capability to reach both gateways? The answer should be no. Mobile users have no reason to communicate with the LAN VPN gateway, and LANs have no reason to communicate with the mobile VPN gateway. By allowing everyone to connect to both gateways, you could be vulnerable to traffic analysis, cryptanalysis, and replay attacks.

One last note about firewalls: Many times, when implementing and testing a VPN, the firewall ruleset will change. Unfortunately, the ruleset isn't always restored to a secure configuration. If the ruleset isn't restored, it's not doing anything except introducing latency and risk to your network. Change control is critical when you're dealing with your security architecture.

Proper ID Required

When choosing a VPN, be sure it includes a decent authentication mechanism. What good is a VPN if you can't tell who's using it? Some VPN software, particularly IPSec-compliant derivatives, has built-in authentication that uses hashing functions such as MD5 or SHA1. Other VPN implementations rely on external authentication services such as SOCKS.

Are authentication attempts encrypted? Does it employ a challenge-response mechanism that changes for each authentication attempt? If not, usernames and passwords might be transmitted in cleartext, or attackers might be able to guess the sequence and grab vital information. If an attacker can decipher an authentication stream, the attacker might be able to use that information to gain access to other resources on your network such as email or shell accounts. Poor authentication can lead to security breaches on other parts of your network.

Whatever the authentication mechanism, it needs to be robust. Lack of proper authentication can leave your network vulnerable to a variety of attacks. Be sure to thoroughly understand the authentication services your VPN provides.

Keeping Your Secrets Safe

One of the major reasons you've decided to implement a VPN is because it protects your information from prying eyes. However, just because it uses encryption doesn't mean it is secure. RFC 2401, the RFC that describes the IPSec protocol, specifies that the default cipher that should be included in all IPSec implementations is 40-bit DES. DES has been cracked in as little as two hours! IPSec supports other algorithms, but when implementing your VPN solution, be sure to take the strength of the cipher you're deploying into consideration. Make sure your cipher is able to provide adequate protection for your information over a sufficient period of time to make the information useless to an attacker.

Fortunately, common sense has prevailed, and most VPN packages include other, stronger cryptosystems. Then again, some VPN software will default to DES encryption unless otherwise specified. So it would be wise to understand which ciphers are supported by your VPN of choice and select the one that's appropriate for your application.

Key Generation

To ensure confidentiality and authentication, keys must be generated in a correct manner. Some cryptosystems are vulnerable to cryptanalysis attacks because keys are not generated in such a way as to make them secure and not easily discernable. Because VPNs rely on the underlying cryptosystem, the implementor(s) must be knowledgeable about the cryptosystem being used so that they can effectively implement the VPN.

This recently became an issue with the commonly used OpenSSL libraries. It was discovered that, previous to OpenSSL 0.96b, the pseudorandom number generator in the OpenSSL package did not generate enough entropy when generating random numbers for keys. This made it easier for a cracker, with access to the right resources, to guess the keys and subvert the cryptosystem. This problem was resolved in the OpenSSL 0.96b release, but what if your VPN had keys generated by one of the vulnerable versions, and what if you didn't upgrade OpenSSL? You might be vulnerable to an attack that exploits this vulnerability.

Be sure your keys are generated using a robust mechanism. In addition, it is good practice to change your keys frequently, with the change interval depending on the cryptosystem you're using. Depending on your requirements, you might need to change keys once daily, once per month, or never. It is difficult to say, exactly, what this interval should be; if you are connecting many hosts via a VPN, replacing keys could become very time-consuming and therefore costly. On the other hand, if you have only a few hosts on a VPN, keys can be changed quickly and easily. Weigh all the factors of key management before selecting a VPN solution.

Distributing Keys Securely

Because both ends of a VPN link need a key(s) to encrypt and decrypt data, the keys need to be transmitted between sites securely. If transmitted manually, it can easily take an hour or two to implement the new keys and test the configuration. This process is made easier by using commonly used privacy protocols such as PGP or PKI.

If your VPN uses a public-key cryptosystem, you'll need two pairs of keys. This becomes another area of concern because a third party is needed to establish trust of the keys. How is the third party controlled? Where are the keys stored? What happens if a private key is compromised? Be sure that the third-party certifying authority operates at a higher security level than the VPN itself. If not, the public-key trust model becomes lopsided.

Are You Sure It's Working?

In this ever-complex world of information technology, we must constantly rely on assumptions. We assume that everything is working between us and our email servers, and we very rarely check to see that it's actually working as we expect. What if you set up your VPN and assume it's working and then later find out that it hasn't been doing a darn thing?

A VPN is one of those things you don't want to make assumptions about. Make sure your VPN is working by sniffing the outbound connection every once in a while to make sure it's encrypting the communication stream. Also try breaking the authentication mechanism every so often to ensure that it's actually checking users' credentials. Try to authenticate using invalid credentials and see if it rejects you.

What VPNs Do Not Secure

Information security is not a single-sided issue. Good security involves many layers and many protections. A VPN is only one of those layers, and even with a VPN, your infrastructure could still be vulnerable.

As stated earlier in this chapter, laptops are a common oversight when it comes to computer security. Employees carry proprietary information all over the world, many times without any security safeguards. The laptop could be stolen, or it could be hacked while connected to the Internet through an ISP, regardless of whether the employee is using a VPN connection or not. A VPN cannot protect mobile users from these threats. However, a VPN combined with a host-based firewall could prevent the laptop from being hacked, and some commercial VPN software includes this firewall.

What about hacking attempts from within your organization? As stated earlier, the annual CSI/FBI survey shows that, on average, almost half of hacking attempts originate from inside the organization, where restrictions and auditing are usually lax. When using a VPN, your network trust domain automatically becomes larger than before. Do you trust the security of the remote networks? A successful hack of a remote network could result in your own network being cracked.

It is important to understand what a VPN protects and what it does not. Failing to do so could result in a breach of security.

Making the Decision On Using a VPN

Sometimes it is appropriate to use a VPN, and sometimes it isn't. This section will discuss some different situations to help you decide whether a VPN is right for your application.

When to Use a VPN

Everything has its time and place, and VPNs are no exception. It can take time and cost money to install a VPN, so you need to be sure that the VPN addresses a specific business need and that it's more cost effective than the alternatives.

If you need a significant number of resources secured between multiple networks and the privacy of the information traversing those networks is at issue, a VPN can be a good choice. That's the beauty of a VPN. With one sweep, you can secure whole networks from the outside world.

If you need hosts to appear as though they're on the same network, a VPN is the way to go. This can really come in handy when you have mobile clients that need transparent access back to headquarters or if you want to have full and secure access to your home network. Why bother with all the fuss of multiple IP address spaces? Why change your infrastructure if you change service providers? If you're using a VPN, all you'll need to change is the gateway configuration.

If all the hosts on your different intranets operate at the same trust level, why should they be on different networks? Of course, there might be glaring conventional or technical reasons, but a VPN can make it seem as though everyone's on the same network. If everyone needs access to the same MS Windows shares or other intranet resources, you can address this need with a VPN without opening your network to IP spoofing and session hijacking attacks.

When Not to Use a VPN

Simple measures need simple means. If you only want to secure one protocol or service between a couple of hosts, do you really want to spend all the time setting up a VPN? To some, the answer is undoubtedly yes, but to those who have specific business justification guiding their rationale, this doesn't necessarily equate to a cost-efficient use of resources.

There are much easier ways to secure a protocol or two than a VPN. The most common way of doing this is to use freely available tunneling software that can tunnel one port to another through an encrypted and authenticated pipe. SSH can do this, as can a program called `stunnel`. These things are a cinch to set up, requiring less than an hour from start to finish.

Setting up a secure tunnel is really, really simple. Here's a quick how-to:

1. Let's say you're running a VNC server on your web server for remote administration. VNC is insecure in and of itself, so you want to set up a secure pipe between your workstation and the web server.

2. Using `stunnel`, you type the following commands:

   ```
   server$ stunnel -d server:4000 -r localhost:5900
   client$ stunnel -c -d 127.2:5900 -r server:4000
   client$ vnc 127.2
   ```

And there you have it! A secure pipe just for VNC. Painless, no?

Another reason you might not want to set up a VPN is if you're thinking about connecting networks of different trust levels. That's like a military organization connecting a top-secret network to an unclassified one. You would actually be making your network *less* secure by doing this because the users operating at the lower trust level could now access all the resources at the higher trust level. Seems a little counter-productive, don't you think?

VPN Groups

There are two major active groups in the world of VPNs: VPNC and open source. Each group offers significant contributions to the constant development of VPN technologies, and each will be briefly discussed here.

VPNC

VPNC (the VPN Consortium) is a group of vendors that analyze and certify commercial VPN products. Technically, VPNC provides compliance checks and interoperability reports, thereby promoting its members' products. VPNC has been very influential in encouraging VPN vendors to cooperate and to design their products based on Internet standards.

When planning a commercial VPN implementation, be sure to check `www.vpnc.org` for details about each VPN solution.

Open Source

There are many open-source VPN projects available. Because Linux is one of the most popular open-source projects, we would be remiss in excluding discussions of open-source VPNs from this book. As a matter of fact, this book deals almost exclusively with open-source VPNs. (You probably already knew this.)

One of the advantages of open-source projects (tongue firmly planted in cheek) is the capability to completely ignore Internet standards. Some open-source VPN projects have done this very well. It is important to note that the decision to ignore standards is usually based on sound reasoning or fundamental design considerations. Despite their obvious advantages, standards can sometimes become cumbersome and difficult to work with, thereby causing protocol bloating and inefficiency. One of the main underlying concepts of a sound approach to security is simplicity, and it's important to be aware of how standards can sometimes fall short in this area.

Another advantage of open-source projects is that you'll usually be able to find one that fits your needs almost perfectly. Open source is driven by someone's need or interest and the desire to fill that quickly, whereas you might need to wait for a commercial vendor to release an upgrade to a product or a new product altogether.

The downside of open-source projects is the lack of support and, occasionally, documentation. Basically, you're left to figure it out for yourself. When using open-source programs, be sure to have a person experienced with the operating system and the open-source paradigm working on the implementation.

VPN Protocols

Lastly, we'll present a brief summary of some of the common protocols used in VPNs. For a detailed discussion of each protocol, refer to the corresponding chapter later in this book.

Standard VPN Protocols

Over the past decade, a number of secure protocols have been developed and accepted by the Internet community. In this section, we'll be discussing some of those protocols, namely secure tunnels over PPP, PPTP, and IPSec.

Layer-2 PPPoE

Probably the easiest way to implement a VPN is by way of tunneling traffic over an encrypted connection. Usually, this is accomplished by using PPP (the Point-to-Point Protocol) or PPPoE (PPP over ethernet). Because the traffic going into this connection has already passed through the TCP/IP stack, it is relatively simple to encrypt this traffic before it is sent over the wire.

Although this implementation seems somewhat complex, we actually use the encryption methods quite frequently. One way to encrypt this traffic is by using SSL, the protocol used in "https" connections. This protocol was developed for the Defense Messaging System (DMS) initiative in the early 1990s. Netscape had a suite of products that could transfer web traffic, email, newsgroups, and directory services all over SSL connections. Even though it's very rudimentary, this type of communication system could be considered a VPN.

Luckily, this type of VPN is somewhat cryptosystem independent. The SSH protocol could easily replace SSL and reduce much of the administrative burden at the same time because tools exist that can create secure tunnels using both protocols. However, using SSH comes with its own pitfalls. SSHv1 has a vulnerability that allows effective execution of a man-in-the-middle attack, which can compromise all communications flowing over the stream. Both SSHv1 and SSHv2 are susceptible to traffic analysis attacks, which can reveal passwords and other sensitive information. No matter which encryption protocol is used, each has its advantages and disadvantages, and those factors should be taken into consideration before a decision is made.

Individual secure tunnels over PPP or PPPoE can be very cumbersome. Each protocol must have its own "wrapper" or encryption channel. In addition, this configuration can be closely tied to PKI, which can be a beast in and of itself. This type of VPN approach is good for securing one or two protocols at most. Anything more becomes a huge administrative burden.

PPTP

Microsoft independently developed a protocol intended for VPN-like communications. PPTP (the Point-to-Point Tunneling Protocol) is a proprietary protocol that produces a secure PPP pipe between MS Windows hosts. Fortunately, Linux also supports PPTP.

Using PPTP might be a good choice if you have a large installation of mobile Windows users. The ease of configuration can also help reduce the administration costs of maintaining a PPTP-enabled VPN: To a certain extent, users can administer their own connections.

PPTP is not a very flexible protocol, however, and most vendors do not support it. If the VPN needs to interoperate with other VPN products, such as Checkpoint FW-1 or Cisco PIX, a PPTP VPN is not a good idea. PPTP has also been shown to not be that secure. For more information on the strength of PPTP security, refer to "Cryptanalysis of Microsoft's PPTP Authentication Extensions (MS-CHAPv2)," by Bruce Schneier and Mudge, 1999, `www.counterpane.com/pptpv2-paper.html`.

The best application of PPTP is for securing traffic between MS Windows hosts and an intranet. If broader-based connectivity is needed, an IPSec-compliant system is probably the best approach.

IPSec

Many net–years ago, the IETF realized that the critical mass of the Internet had been reached and that the TCP/IP protocol could not be secured. It then began work on developing a protocol that could be layered on top of the existing TCP/IP protocol and provide decently secure communications. The end result was IPSec (IP security).

> **IPSec Spellings**
>
> The spelling of IPSec differs depending on who is writing about it. Variations on the theme include IPSec and Ipsec. None is more or less correct than the other. For the purposes of this text, we'll stick with IPSec.

IPSec consists of three major components: the Internet Key Exchange (IKE), Authentication Header (AH), and Encapsulating Security Payload (ESP). Each component can be implemented separately, although it wouldn't make much sense. The model outlined in the RFCs provides a great deal of flexibility, but its lack of specificity in some areas causes some implementations to differ to the point of noninteroperability.

As with any cryptosystem, there must be a way to exchange keys. That is the role the IKE algorithm plays. IKE manages and distributes keys between many security associations (SAs). Until recently, IKE was considered a secure mechanism. However, vulnerabilities have been discovered that dispute this claim.

The AH provides another level of security. With any secure model, authentication is an absolute must. What good is it to trust something if the source cannot be verified? That is the capability the AH provides. In IPSec, communications are authenticated using the AH. In addition, if confidentiality is not a concern, the AH can be used to verify communications.

The third part of IPSec is the ESP. This part takes the payload (the meat) of each packet and encrypts it based on the cryptosystem being used. This ensures confidentiality through the underlying cipher.

For a pointed analysis of IPSec, refer to "A Cryptographic Evaluation of IPsec," by Niels Ferguson and Bruce Schneier, 2000, `www.counterpane.com/ipsec.html`. As you read this paper, try to remember that, despite its limitations, IPSec remains the best-bet solution for most VPN applications. Its wide support base and standardized approach also makes it the choice for interoperability. As Mr. Schneier aptly points out, it's also a very complex system that depends on many relatively interdependent factors. However, many implementations have effectively reduced the impact of that complexity on administrators by simplifying their exposure to it.

Nonstandard VPN Protocols

In addition to the "standard" VPN protocols, there exists a number of nonstandard VPN protocols (or "hacks," colloquially speaking). This section will introduce three of them: VTun, cIPe, and `tinc`.

VTun

VTun is another open-source VPN package. It operates on Linux, the BSDs, and Solaris, and it supports a wide variety of protocols. It relies on the TUN/TAP driver and can theoretically operate on any platform that supports this driver.

VTun is highly configurable. Not only does it support TCP/IP, it also supports IPX/SPX, Appletalk, and other protocols. Like other VPN packages, VTun has compression and encryption engines. In addition, VTun also has a traffic shaping mechanism. VTun is described in Chapter 8, "VTun."

cIPe

cIPe (Crypto IP Encapsulation) also is an open-source VPN package. It operates very similarly to the PPP method previously described but with some differences. The main difference is that it can encapsulate IP datagrams either within UDP datagrams or within TCP packets. This encapsulation includes IP headers, so the packet is unchanged. cIPe then relays the packet through the network interface to another cIPe gateway, where the IP datagram is removed from the UDP datagram or TCP packet. The full IP datagram is then sent on its way.

For purposes of confidentiality, cIPe encrypts the full IP datagram with either Blowfish or IDEA ciphers. Because these are symmetric ciphers, keys must initially be exchanged via a secure mechanism. After the tunnel is established, new keys are generated and exchanged.

> **Note**
>
> IDEA is a patented cipher, so using it in a commercial environment might require the payment of license fees. If in doubt as to whether or not this applies to you, just use Blowfish.

cIPe also supports SOCKS5, which can make firewalling much easier. The UDP datagrams that cIPe produces can be passed to a SOCKS5-enabled gateway, where they can be authenticated. Thus, the CIPE gateway can easily be placed behind the firewall for added protection.

For simplicity, cIPe relies on UDP for datagram transport. Although this simplifies configuration and tunnel establishment, it also allows for dynamically changing carrier addresses. Thus, if one end of the tunnel changes addresses during operation, cIPe will recover gracefully.

If you decide to use cIPe, it is suggested that you use it in conjunction with a SOCKS gateway because VPN utilization will be authenticated using a proven mechanism. A detailed description of cIPe, its installation, and its use is provided in Chapter 9, "cIPe."

tinc

tinc also relies on the universal TUN/TAP driver. It's easy to implement and configure, can be reconfigured during operation, and has extensive documentation. Also, because it relies on the TUN/TAP driver, it is supported on Linux, the BSDs, and Solaris.

tinc currently supports only the Blowfish cipher. It uses UDP tunneling for ease of operation and configuration. tinc could best be applied to small networks in which efficiency and speed are key. See Chapter 10, "tinc" for details.

Summary

At this point, you should have a high-level understanding of VPN theory, an understanding of the business justification relating to VPNs, and a general knowledge of the different players in the VPN community. The next chapter will delve deeper into the technical aspects of VPNs, the VPN design process, and how the services within your network are affected by a VPN.

2

VPN Fundamentals

THIS CHAPTER COVERS THE IMPORTANT ISSUES you need to be aware of before choosing and deploying a VPN solution. It describes the conventions used in the examples throughout this book. It also describes various related concepts in the context of VPNs, such as firewalls, routing, and netmasks.

Our Conventions

In this book, we describe a number of VPN technologies and packages. For each specific VPN package or setup, we provide examples corresponding to the following three basic VPN scenarios you might have: network–network, host–network, and host–host.

In the *network-network* scenario, two subnets are connected using a VPN tunnel. Each subnet should consist of a gateway/router and a host. The gateway for each subnet should have two network interfaces: one to the outside world and one to the gateway's internal subnet. You can use this scenario to securely connect to your company's branch overseas, for example.

The *host-network* scenario can be interpreted as a degenerate case of the network–network scenario. The *host-network* scenario is used when one of the subnets to be connected consists of just one host. To illustrate, you use the host-network scenario when telecommuting or when you want to securely connect to a corporate network while on the road.

The *host-host* scenario is formed by further reducing the host-network scenario so that it consists of only a pair of hosts that want to connect to each other. For example, you might want to use this scenario to establish a secure tunnel between two hosts that belong to different networks. This scenario is different from others in that only these two hosts can send secured traffic to each other. If more machines need to communicate securely, a host-network or network-network setup would be more appropriate.

Gateways vs. Networks

In this book, we say that VPNs have the capability to connect networks, for example the host-network or network-network VPN scenarios. All VPNs have two hosts that handle the encryption/decryption of the VPN traffic, the endpoints of the VPN. When one or both of these hosts allows access to a network of machines rather than to just the single host, we call the host a *gateway*.

The concept of a gateway is already standard networking terminology. For example, the router that connects a business to its ISP is a gateway, as could be a firewall through which all traffic passes. In VPN terminology, a gateway is simply a VPN endpoint that sits in front of a network that has access to the VPN.

In other literature, you might see our three VPN senarios referred to as host-to-host, host-to-gateway, and gateway-to-gateway. The former explicitly mentions the endpoint of the VPN—be it a host or gateway—while the latter two describe what you want to connect—a host or a network. The two forms of terminology are functionally equivalent, but we prefer the "network" form because it is easier to see what you are trying to connect—one or more networks—instead of specifying how this connection is implemented.

For instance, if we use a VPN package and configure it to connect 192.168.1.0/24 and 192.168.2.0/24, we are connecting two networks. Each of the networks will have a gateway (say, 192.168.1.1 and 192.168.2.1) that will forward traffic for its respective network.

Sample Scenario

To help you understand the scenarios just described, we will consider a simple network-network scenario (see Figure 2.1), which is similar to those used in the examples throughout the book.

As you can see, the network-network scenario shown in Figure 2.1 consists of two networks, one in Chicago and one in Atlanta.

The Chicago network is 192.168.1.0/24, with the VPN server/gateway (Bears) located on the internal network on IP address 192.168.1.1. Several hosts, such as Cubs, Bulls, and Blackhawks, are on the internal Chicago network. Atlanta has a similar configuration, with Falcons as its VPN server/gateway.

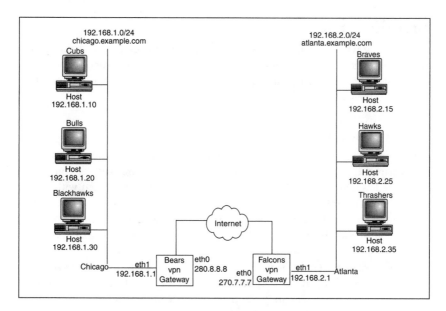

Figure 2.1   A network-network scenario example.

Both networks use addresses in the private-network range, as specified in RFC 1918. (We detail the RFC 1918 networks later in this chapter.) The IP addresses on the outside (280.8.8.8 and 270.7.7.7) are fictitious Internet-routable IP addresses that the two machines will use for their actual communication.

Our External IP Addresses

You might notice something fishy with our two external IP addresses: 280.8.8.8 and 270.7.7.7. These addresses are not legal; the legal range for any byte in an IP address is 0 to 255. We did not want to use actual routable IP addresses, lest you accidentally type them in and attempt to establish a VPN between you and some unsuspecting party. The examples we provide will do one of the following:

- Use private IPs as external IPs, explicitly stating that you should replace them with real routable Internet IPs.

- Use w.x.y.z addresses as external IPs, where w is greater than 255 and is thus illegal on the Internet.

Our network-network scenario can be converted into the host-network one by removing the eth1 interface and the entire 192.168.1.0/24 network from Bears and connecting Bears to Falcons. Similarly, the host-network scenario can be converted into host-host by removing the eth1 interface and the 192.168.2.0/24 network from Falcons and having Falcons and Bears be the only two machines involved in the VPN.

Considerations

Before deciding what kind of VPN is right for you, you need to first define your requirements, conduct a risk analysis, and review collateral issues such as long-term support and operational management needs. In the next few sections, we will describe various issues for you to consider.

Key Distribution

Key distribution among your VPN clients and servers should be one of the first security concerns you review. If your keys are compromised, the security of your system is compromised. When we talk about key distribution, we are concerned with two types of keys: symmetric and asymmetric.

It is crucial to be able to distribute symmetric keys securely. Ideally, you should use a secure out-of-band channel or physically access both systems and set keys up yourself.

In most cases, however, this is not an option. If you have to distribute symmetric keys remotely, make sure you at least use SFTP, SCP, or SSL/TLS. (Telnet and FTP are insecure. If you use them, you are potentially giving your keys away to attackers.) You could even go so far as to hire a professional courier or have one of your employees travel to the remote site with the keys on a floppy disk.

Asymmetric keys (which consist of both a public and private key pair) are a different matter. The public key can be transmitted without secrecy, such as with FTP or even email. Public keys by themselves do not offer an attacker anything that can be leveraged to break into your VPN. The secret key should not be transmitted to the remote end at all because it is only needed for decryption.

Although it is completely fine to transfer public keys in nonsecure manners, it is crucial for you to verify that the keys have not been tampered with when they are received. This can be done simply by installing the key as appropriate to your VPN software and then calling up the administrator at the other end of the VPN link and reading the key aloud. If you transmit your key in a way that allows an attacker to modify it, the attacker could perform a man-in-the-middle attack, defeating the security of your VPN.

In short, reliable transmission of the public key is important, though secret transmission is irrelevant. A secret key should never be stored on the remote endpoint of the VPN. If you are not familiar with asymmetric cryptography, see our glossary (Appendix C) for explanation.

Scalability

VPNs, like all pieces of your network infrastructure, must be able to support the traffic you have and be able to scale with the traffic you will support in the future. If you are implementing a VPN only to connect central and branch offices and have a limited growth plan, you are probably not concerned much with scalability because most VPN technologies will provide what you need. If you are rolling out an enterprise-wide VPN service and are supporting many dial-in users, scalability will be near the top of your list of VPN requirements.

Three main issues help define scalability:

- Capability to handle more connections
- Ease of maintenance and support
- Cost

All three of these issues will depend on the VPN you choose and its design. The topology you use can also greatly affect scalability.

Star Topology

We will now examine a sample network-network VPN that has been built using the star topology (see Figure 2.2).

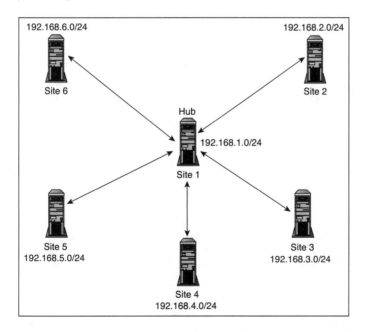

Figure 2.2   The star topology for VPNs.

In the star topology, you have a VPN connection from each remote site to the main VPN hub, Site One. The VPN hub must be able to support n VPN connections, where n is the number of remote sites. Each remote site that wants to communicate securely must send its traffic through the VPN hub in the center.

The main benefit of this model is that adding new sites is straightforward because all configuration changes are made at a central location, the VPN hub. The drawbacks are as follows:

- There is a single point of failure. If the hub goes down, all the spokes can no longer communicate.
- If performance on the hub suffers, performance for all VPN traffic suffers.
- Two nodes that might be geographically close still have to route through the hub to communicate.

Most of the drawbacks can be mitigated by adding more hubs to distribute the load and provide fault tolerance.

Full Mesh Topology

Next, we will review a VPN built using the full mesh topology. In the fully meshed design, each site communicates directly with every other site. Figure 2.3 shows our sample network built as a fully meshed VPN.

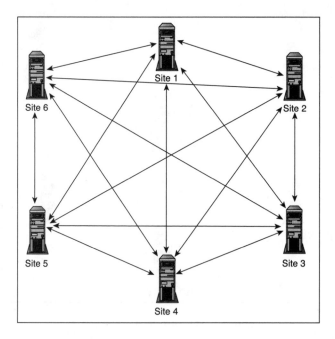

Figure 2.3   The full mesh topology.

Again, this VPN model has several benefits and one main drawback.
The benefits are as follows:

- There is no more single point of failure. Sites do not rely on a hub for intra-VPN communication. VPN connectivity is lost to the problematic network, not all networks.

- Overall performance is not limited to a single system.

- Geographically close sites can now communicate directly.

The drawback is increased maintenance. If you add a new node, you would typically create VPN associations with every other node.

Although this topology has only one drawback, it is a big one. Instead of managing your keys at a central site, you must now manage them on every node. Again, if you have 1,000 nodes, this can be a formidable task.

Note

Some VPN solutions, such as `tinc` (see Chapter 10, "*tinc*"), handle routing for you automatically. This probably will not help much with a 1,000-node setup, but it can still save you a lot of time and effort.

Issues

From both of the preceding examples, we see that adding nodes can be a lot of work. Both star and fully meshed topologies need a scalable way to distribute keys in a secure fashion.

Instead of placing keys on each server, one solution some VPNs have implemented is retrieving key information from a centralized source. FreeS/WAN (see Chapter 6, "FreeS/WAN") supports what is called "opportunistic encryption" and is able to pull key information from DNS.

Another issue that might be a problem is routing. You need to be able to propagate routing information (perhaps by running a common IGP routing protocol such as RIP or OSPF within your networks) or be stuck hard-coding routes manually.

Interoperability

VPN software—even products based on open standards and RFCs—has notoriously had problems with interoperability. For example, administrators frequently find that different standards-compliant commercial solutions don't actually work well together or at all. Your interoperability needs can make or break your VPN decision.

First, you must decide whether you will be connecting to VPNs not controlled by you. If you are connecting to devices over which you have no control, it is best to choose a VPN that is standards based for maximum interoperability.

FreeS/WAN is a good choice for interoperability. IPSec is an industry standard for traffic encryption and has been implemented by many different vendors. Although some of the implementations have only partial support for some of its features, usually both sides of the VPN can be configured to use a set of commonly shared features.

FreeS/WAN itself does not use 56-bit DES for encryption; it supports only triple (168-bit) DES as it is currently bundled. Although this was done by the developers to make FreeS/WAN more secure, it can cause compatibility issues with other implementations. Fortunately, most vendors have implemented IPSec to include support for triple DES as well. This is just one example of the possible snags you will find as your try to connect one protocol implementation to another.

Overall, the issue of interoperability boils down to this question: "Will I ever need to communicate with VPN implementations not under my control?" If so, stick with a standards-based solution. If not, interoperability becomes a nonissue. Just make sure to plan far enough ahead so that you are not constantly rethinking your VPN.

Cross-Platform Availability

Another thing to consider is whether your VPN package will need to run on multiple platforms.

Some VPN packages rely on a common interface that is available for many platforms. For example, the universal TUN/TAP driver provides such an interface, which is used by cIPe (see Chapter 9, "cIPe"). As a result, cIPe is less coupled to the underlying architecture, and as soon as the driver is ported to a new platform, cIPe can then be added relatively quickly.

Cost

Fortunately, because Linux is a free OS, costs incurred from building a Linux-based VPN are usually smaller than for other commercial solutions. The costs you will encounter are for the hardware and the Linux installation media, although the installation can be downloaded free from a distribution mirror.

Other operating systems require licensing for the OS as well as per-seat licensing for the VPN software. Linux has none of these licensing requirements. Not only is Linux VPN software free, a number of free firewall and security packages can be used in conjunction with the VPN software to further secure your site. If you were using similar software on commercial OSs, it could get expensive very quickly.

Although Linux VPNs are cheap, client VPN packages for WinTel platforms are scarce, and as a result, they might not be the best choice for end user VPNs (unless your end users are UNIX savvy, which might rule out all but your engineers). Linux VPNs do provide a great solution for network-network VPNs, where end users and their inferior OSs are not directly involved.

VPN and Firewall Interaction

VPNs enable you to set up secure communications between endpoints and are just one weapon in your security arsenal. Firewalls, an older and more established security technology, are common in almost every environment. A VPN should be integrated into your security policy and that means making sure your VPN and firewall play nicely with each other.

Types of Firewalls

Three main types of firewalls are in common use today: packet filters, application gateways, and stateful inspection firewalls. They are described in the following sections.

Packet Filters

A packet filter is the simplest form of firewall. A packet filter firewall will compare any IP packet that attempts to traverse the firewall against its access control list (ACL). If the packet is allowed, it is sent through. If not, the packet filter can either silently drop the packet (DENY in ipchains speak) or send back an ICMP error response (REJECT).

Packet filters only look at five things: the source and destination IP addresses, the source and destination ports, and the protocol (UDP, TCP, and so on). These tests are very fast because each packet contains all the data (in the packet headers) necessary to make its determination. Due to its simplicity and speed, a packet filter can be enabled on your routers, eliminating the need for a dedicated firewall.

One problem with packet filters is that they generally do not look deeply enough into the packet to have any idea what is actually being sent in the packet. Though you might have configured a packet filter to allow inbound access to port 25, the Simple Mail Transfer Protocol (SMTP) port, a packet filter would never know if some other protocol was used on that port. For example, a user on one system might run his Secure Shell (SSH) daemon on that port, knowing that the traffic would be allowed by the packet filter, and be able to SSH through the firewall against policy.

Another problem with packet filters is that they are not effectively able to handle protocols that rely on multiple dynamic connections. The FTP protocol, for example, opens a command channel on which the various commands such as USER, RECV, and LIST are sent. Whenever data is transferred between the hosts, such as files or the LIST output, a separate connection is established. You would need to have an ACL that would allow these data connections through for FTP to work. However, packet filters do not read the FTP command channel to know when such an ACL should be permitted.

Application Gateways

An application gateway goes one step beyond a packet filter. Instead of simply checking the IP parameters, it actually looks at the application layer data. Individual application gateways are often called *proxies*, such as an SMTP proxy that understands the SMTP protocol. These proxies inspect the data that is being sent and verify that the specified protocol is being used correctly.

Let's say we were creating an SMTP application gateway. It would need to keep track of the state of the connection: Has the client sent a `HELO`/`ELHO` request? Has it sent a `MAIL FROM` before attempting to send a `DATA` request? As long as the protocol is obeyed, the proxy will shuttle the commands from the client to the server.

The application gateway must understand the protocol and process both sides of the conversation. As such, it is a much more CPU-intensive process than a simple packet filter. However, this also lends it a greater element of security. You will not be able to run the previously described SSH-over-port-25 trick when an application gateway is in the way because it will realize that SMTP is not in use.

Additionally, because an application gateway understands the protocols in use, it is able to support tricky protocols such as FTP that create random data channels for each file transfer. As it reads the FTP command channel, it will see (and rewrite, if necessary) the data channel declaration and allow the specified port to traverse the firewall only until the data transfer is complete.

Often there is a protocol that is not directly understood by your application gateway but that must be allowed to traverse the firewall. SSH and HTTPS are two simple examples. Because they are encrypted end to end, an application gateway cannot read the traffic actually being sent.

In these cases, there is usually a way to configure your firewall to allow the appropriate packets to be sent without interference by the firewall. You might hear this called a *plug*, which comes from the `plug-gw`, a part of the Firewall Toolkit (FWTK) that was used to connect a client and server directly when the protocol was not supported.

It can be difficult to integrate application gateways into your standard routing hardware due to the processing overhead. Some newer high-end routers are able to function as application gateways, but you'll need a lot of CPU power for acceptable performance.

> **Note**
>
> Even application gateways can be fooled if you are crafty enough. For example, you could tunnel any arbitrary protocol over SMTP: The client could send data as the DATA portion of the transaction, and the server could respond in the resulting error/success code message. The nature and ubiquity of the HTTP protocol makes it even easier; SOAP and .NET are just two "accepted" examples of tunneling other protocols across HTTP. Httptunnel, available at www.httptunnel.com, is a good freeware tool capable of tunneling any protocol across HTTP.

Stateful Inspection Firewalls

Stateful inspection firewalls are a middle ground between application gateways and packet filters. Rather than truly reading the whole dialog between client and server, a stateful inspection firewall will read only the amount necessary to determine how it should behave.

Take the SMTP DATA command, for example. When this command is sent, the client will send the data (the text of the email) ending with a line containing a single ".". The server then responds with a success or error code. An application gateway will need to be reading all the data that is sent and looking for the "." and error code. A stateful inspection firewall, however, will realize that the client is sending data until the server responds. Thus, it will simply forward the client's packets without inspection until the server responds. Simply put, a stateful inspection firewall understands the manner in which stateful protocols must conduct themselves and manages that traffic accordingly within the confines of its rulebase.

By not reading all the data sent, a stateful inspection firewall achieves a significant performance gain over an application gateway while maintaining the higher level of security and protocol support. Our VPN traffic, however, will be encrypted end to end. As such, there will be very little that a stateful inspection firewall will need to look at in our VPN datastream—it can't inspect the actual data anyway. Because of this, there is no functional difference between a stateful inspection firewall and an application gateway for our VPN traffic. There is, however, a solid performance boost from using a stateful inspection firewall. Because our VPN is already introducing latency due to the overhead of encryption, the more performance you can get with your firewall, the better.

Stateful Inspection Concerns

Stateful inspection firewalls have suffered from occasional faults. For example, to support the FTP protocol, stateful inspection firewalls would look at the beginning of a packet to see whether a data channel was requested. An attacker could trick the server into sending a large error message containing a data channel request that aligned perfectly at the beginning of a second packet. The firewall would then open a channel dictated by the attacker. A program called `ftpd-ozone` (available at www.monkey.org/~dugsong/) can exploit this vulnerability. This particular problem has been fixed by firewall vendors, but there might be more lurking around.

Common Linux Firewalls

Several firewalls can run on Linux. We will briefly describe them here, but it is beyond the scope of this book to cover them in depth. See New Riders' *Linux Firewalls, Second Edition* by Robert Ziegler (2002) for more information on firewalls.

- **The Firewall Toolkit (FWTK).** This was the first publicly available application gateway suite and was the basis of the commercial firewall Gauntlet. It is a set of userland applications that support various protocols such as STMP, HTTP, `telnet`, and X11. It is still available at www.fwtk.org, though it has not been officially supported in years.

- **IPF.** A Linux packet filter for 2.0 kernels. If you are still using a 2.0 kernel, you should really upgrade.

- **IPChains.** The Linux packet filter for 2.2 kernels. Though it is a simple packet filter, you can support some protocols via kernel modules. The `ip_masq_ftp` module enables you to support the FTP protocol, for example. The problem with IPChains is that the kernel packet filters are handled before the modules can see packets, meaning you must allow inbound access to ports that potentially could be required by the kernel modules.

- **IPTables.** The Linux firewall software for 2.4 kernels, also known as Netfilter. IPTables supports both packet filtering and application gateway support together. Taking the FTP protocol as our example, the data channels that are used are accepted as `RELATED` packets. This makes your firewall much cleaner because you do not need to leave holes in your firewall for packets that might or might not be used by modules.

- **IPFilter.** Created by Darren Reed, IPFilter is the default kernel packet filter of NetBSD and FreeBSD, it and runs on many other UNIX-like systems. IPFilter only runs on the very old Linux 2.0 kernels, so if you want to use IPFilter, we suggest that you use a BSD machine instead. It is available at `http://coombs.anu.edu.au/~avalon/`.

Note

Darren Reed modified the IPFilter license (or clarified it, depending on your position) to deny modifications to the source, rendering it not completely open source. Because of this, it was removed from OpenBSD. Reed later allowed modifications when used as part of NetBSD and FreeBSD. OpenBSD is creating a new packet filter, PF, from scratch to replace IPFilter. Yes, now and then there doth be strife in the open-source community ...

- **Dante.** Though normally included as part of a larger commercial firewall system, Dante is available as open source under a BSD-style license. It is a circuit-level firewall/proxy that is largely transparent to users. It is available at `www.inet.no/dante/`.

- **T.REX.** Open sourced in April 2000, T.REX is a sophisticated application gateway firewall that includes intrusion-detection features, strong authentication support, and extensive logging. Version 2 of T.REX was not yet available at the time this was written; though precompiled versions are available on CD. You can obtain T.REX at `www.opensourcefirewall.com`.

Placing Your Firewall

We strongly suggest that you use a firewall as part of your security infrastructure. Using a VPN in conjunction with your firewall, however, requires careful planning and configuration. Several different configurations are available when using both a firewall and a VPN server. Each has its pros and cons, and we'll do our best to help you pick the option that makes sense for you.

VPN Server on a Firewall

The solution that feels most natural is to install your VPN software on your firewall itself. Many commercial firewalls include VPN components as an extra option. If you are working in a mixed commercial and freeware VPN environment, you will likely end up supporting this configuration.

As seen in Figure 2.4, we have a single point of entry into our network, which serves three purposes:

- The firewall allows outbound access to the Internet.
- The firewall prevents inbound access from the Internet.
- The VPN service encrypts traffic to remote clients or networks.

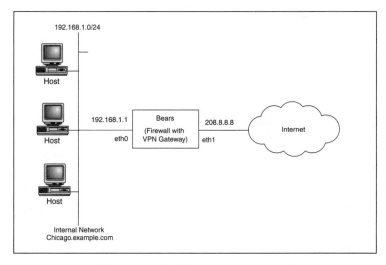

Figure 2.4   The VPN server on a firewall.

The pros of putting your VPN on your firewall are as follows:

- You have one place controlling all your security, meaning fewer machines to manage.
- You can create firewall rules that apply to your VPN traffic using the same tools you already use to manage your firewall.

The cons of putting your VPN on your firewall are as follows:

- You have one place controlling all your security. You'd better make sure this machine is extremely secure.

- You must configure your routes carefully to make sure the traffic goes through the appropriate interfaces (eth0 vs. vpn1, for example.)
- Improper configuration in your firewall rules could allow traffic from the Internet to get through to the inside by slipping through using VPN addresses.
- Your Internet and VPN traffic will compete for resources on the machine, so a larger machine is likely necessary.

VPN Server Parallel to Firewall

Another topology that seems logical is to use your VPN parallel to your firewall. Your internal machines will still point to the firewall as their default route. The firewall will have a route to the VPN-accessible networks via the VPN server and will inform clients to send packets to the VPN machine when appropriate. (The "Routing" section later in this chapter discusses how this works.) You can see this topology in Figure 2.5.

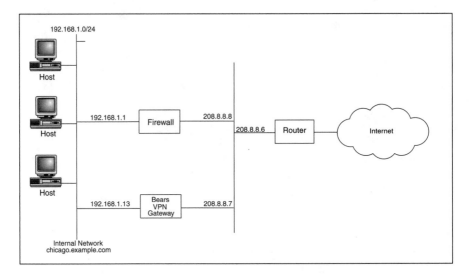

Figure 2.5   The VPN server parallel to a firewall.

If you prefer, you can place a router between the internal network and the VPN and firewall machines. You would configure the router to know the networks accessible through the VPN and would set up your routing rules there instead of on the firewall.

The pros of putting your VPN server parallel to your firewall are as follows:

- Your VPN traffic is not going through the firewall at all, so you do not need to modify your firewall configuration to support the VPN packets. Because some VPN protocols are not supported by all firewalls, this might be your only option.
- You can scale much easier. If you find that a VPN server is under too much load, you can add machines and distribute the VPNs that can be established

between them. If you are connecting multiple remote networks, you can have one VPN machine per network.

- If you are supporting roaming users in a host-network configuration, you can simply add VPN servers and use round-robin DNS to distribute the load between the VPN servers.

The cons of putting your VPN server parallel to your firewall are as follows:

- Your VPN server is directly attached to the Internet. You had better be very sure that it is well secured; otherwise, an attacker could break in and have direct access to your internal network.

- You now have two machines that communicate with the Internet, and you must make sure that both are correctly configured to only pass legitimate traffic, thereby increasing the support workload and associated costs.

- Cost, of course, increases incrementally with the addition of new servers and related support staff.

VPN Server Behind Your Firewall

Another location for your VPN server is to put it behind your firewall completely, attached to the internal network. As shown in Figure 2.6, our VPN server is not directly reachable from the Internet at all, and all packets must reach it through our dedicated firewall.

As with the previous topology, you will need to add a route to your firewall that redirects VPN traffic from internal machines to the VPN server. You will also need to configure your firewall to pass the encrypted VPN traffic directly to your VPN server.

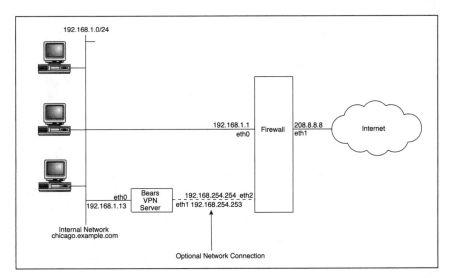

Figure 2.6. The VPN server behind a firewall.

The pros of putting your VPN server behind your firewall are as follows:

- The VPN is completely protected from the Internet by the firewall.
- There is only one machine controlling all access to and from the Internet.
- Network restrictions for VPN traffic are located only on the VPN server, which can make writing rulesets easier.

The cons of putting your VPN server behind your firewall are as follows:

- All the VPN traffic must travel through the firewall as well, adding a degree of latency.
- The firewall will need to shuttle VPN traffic from the Internet to the VPN directly. Because it cannot inspect this traffic (it is encrypted, after all), it will require a simple packet filter ACL or application plug proxy.
- Getting your firewall to pass the encrypted VPN traffic to the VPN server is sometimes tricky. Some firewalls do not know what to do with IP protocols other than ICMP, TCP, and UDP. This means it might be harder or impossible to support VPNs that use different IP protocols, such as ESP packets for IPSec VPNs or GRE packets for PPTP VPNs.
- All the VPN traffic travels through the same LAN wire twice, once from client to VPN server in the clear and once from the VPN to the firewall encrypted. This can degrade LAN performance.

One option to decrease latency would be to connect a second network card (eth1) on the VPN server directly to a network card on the firewall (eth2) with a crossover cable. You could use a hub or switch and create an actual network segment if you prefer, but because you'd only have the two hosts here, a crossover cable would work as well and would be faster because no extra equipment is involved. This enables you to route the encrypted VPN traffic directly over this wire and through the firewall rather than backtracking over the existing LAN segment. This means the VPN traffic won't be competing for LAN resources.

The direct VPN-to-firewall link will need to either be a point-to-point link or be given its own network segment. If you prefer the latter, we suggest a small network such as a /252, which can hold only two hosts, plenty for our purposes. We could allocate 192.168.254.254 to the firewall and 192.168.254.253 to the "external" VPN interface, and the network itself would be 192.168.254.252/252.

Configuring Your VPN with Its Own Firewall

In any of the configurations previously described, it is possible to restrict what traffic can traverse the VPN connection. This might be desired when the networks or hosts you are connecting are not of the same trust level.

For the case in which your Internet firewall and VPN server are the same machine, this can be achieved simply by adding new rules to the firewall using your existing firewall software.

For cases when you have a separate VPN server, you might either install a separate firewall machine in front of your VPN server or simply rely on Linux kernel packet filters on the VPN server itself. For example, if you want to allow only mail-related traffic to traverse your VPN, you might implement kernel restrictions on your VPN server, such as the following:

```
# Allow only SMTP, POP, IMAP and POPs/IMAPs through our VPN:
for port in 25 109 110 143 993 995
do
   ipchains -A output —destination-port $port -i vpn1 -j ACCEPT
   ipchains -A  input      —source-port $port -i vpn1 -j ACCEPT
done
ipchains -A output -i vpn1 -j DENY
ipchains -A  input -i vpn1 -j DENY
```

These rules assume that your VPN traffic goes through the virtual interface vpn1. This is a very simple example. You can create ACLs tailored for your VPN using whatever tools (IPchains, IPtables, IPfilter, and so on) you are comfortable with.

Networking Issues

You will need to address a fair number of issues when designing your network topology. If you do not plan, you will have a good deal of trouble getting things working correctly. A solid network topology map, complete with all the machines, business functions by IP address, routes, other network settings, and the driving business need are critical to establishing a successful VPN setup.

Dedicated vs. Dynamic IP Addresses

Because you are connecting machines across the Internet, the IP addresses of these machines are dictated largely by your Internet service provider. Your ISP will allocate to you one or more IP addresses that you will have available for Internet access.

If you have a dedicated connection such as a T1 or greater, you will likely be given an IP subnet by default. On the other hand, if you have DSL or a dial-up modem, most ISPs prefer to dole out IP addresses with the Dynamic Host Configuration Protocol (DHCP). This means your machine might have a different IP address each time you connect to the Internet.

It is not too much trouble for roaming clients to be given nonstatic IP addresses. When they dial up from their hotel, for example, they will simply point to the VPN server—say, bears.example.com—and establish a connection. Unfortunately, supporting roaming users with nonstatic IP addresses means your VPN server cannot restrict the IP of the connecting machine.

Your VPN server, however, must certainly have a dedicated IP address; otherwise, your remote networks and users will never be able to find it. In our example, bears.example.com must resolve to the IP address on which your VPN server is listening. Although you could survive by changing your DNS entries each time your VPN server gets a new IP address, this is largely a hack. It also introduces an unnecessary level of complexity, and is time consuming.

Unless you want to spend a lot of time maintaining your DNS records, we highly suggest that you get a dedicated IP address from your ISP for all of your VPN servers.

Internal Subnets

If you are creating a host-network or network-network VPN, you will need to have different network IP ranges for each network you want to connect. In our sample network described at the beginning of this chapter, we have two interconnected networks. Chicago is 192.168.1.0/24 and Atlanta is 192.168.2.0/24.

We did not pick these networks entirely at random. These are a set of networks reserved for private internal use, specified in RFC 1918. By using only these networks, you are guaranteed not to have a conflict with a network that exists on the Internet. The "private" networks are as follows:

Network	Number of Networks	Hosts Per Network
10.0.0.0/8	1	16777214
172.16.0.0/16 through 172.31.0.0/16	16	65534
192.168.0.0/24 through 192.168.255.0/24	256	254

We chose the 192.168.x.y networks for Chicago and Atlanta because they are small and only need to support about 20 hosts each, easily fitting within the 254 maximum allowed. We could have used subnets of the 10 or 172 networks instead, but we are lazy and would rather use networks that do not require custom subnetting.

Unless you have large blocks of IP addresses allocated to you—which is very rare these days—you should consider using RFC 1918 networks that are dedicated for internal use while using network address translation (NAT) on your gateway to the Internet. It is customary to use similar network numbers for all your internal networks, as we have in our sample network. You might even want to use conventions for your networks—for example, using 10.x.y.z for standard internal networks, 192.168.x.y for VPN links and dedicated lines, and so on.

The important thing is to make sure you pick networks that do not conflict with each other and to use the smallest subnetworks possible such that you do not run out of IP ranges.

Netmasks

If you are new to networking, you are probably wondering what all these /24 and /8 things are. These are called Classless Interdomain Routing (CIDR) blocks, and the network 192.168.1.0/24 is written in CIDR notation.

To understand this, let's start with a history lesson. In the beginning (we love saying that), the IP space was broken into the following blocks:

[0-127].x.y.z	Class A
	16777214 hosts per network
[128-191].x.y.z	Class B
	65534 hosts per network
[192-223].x.y.z	Class C
	254 hosts per network
[224-239].x.y.z	Class D
	Available for multicast network protocols only
[240-255].x.y.z	Class E
	Reserved for future use

There were 128 Class A blocks, each capable of supporting 16777214 hosts. There's no way a single network with 16777214 hosts could have any hope of good performance. Thus, networks were broken up into subnets. Hosts were put onto different subnets based on function or location, and routers connected the various subnets.

Let's say we take the Class A network 10.x.y.z and break it up into 256 Class B networks of the form 10.[0-255].y.z. Each network now has 65534 possible hosts (still a relatively unreasonable number from a management perspective).

By default, a host that saw that its IP address was 10.1.1.1 assumed it was on a full Class A and assumed that if it wanted to communicate with 10.2.2.2, they were on the same physical wire. To be able to correctly understand that 10.2.2.2 was on a different network, the concept of subnet masks was formed.

A *subnet mask* is simply a dotted quad (like an IP address) that signifies how much of an IP address is the network portion and how much is the host portion. The Class A networks have a default subnet mask of 255.0.0.0, the Class B networks have a default subnet mask of 255.255.0.0, and the Class C networks have a default subnet mask of 255.255.255.0.

To determine the network portion of an IP address, you can perform a bitwise (or Boolean) AND of the IP and netmask. To break our huge Class A network into 256 smaller networks, the administrators use a netmask of 255.255.0.0 instead of the default. Thus, the host 10.2.2.2 is on the 10.2.x.y network, and the host 10.1.1.1 is on the 10.1.x.y network.

A different way of viewing the subnet mask is to represent it in binary form. The common netmasks would be represented as follows:

Subnet Mask	Binary Form	CIDR Notation
255.0.0.0	11111111.00000000.00000000.00000000	/8
255.255.0.0	11111111.11111111.00000000.00000000	/16
255.255.255.0	11111111.11111111.11111111.00000000	/24

The CIDR notation at the end is simply a shortcut you can use to specify an IP address and its netmask in one quick form.

Thus, our machine 10.1.1.1 with a netmask 255.255.0.0 could be written as 10.1.1.1/16. The number after the slash is simply the number of 1s in the binary form of the subnet mask.

You can pick any subnet that is more restrictive than the default (that is, you could not pick a subnet of 255.0.0.0 for 172.x.y.z) when designing your networks. Most people find it easiest to use one of the standard subnets /8, /16, or /24.

This makes recognizing the network portion easier because the network portion always falls at a byte boundary.

For example, 192.168.5.0/24 is clearly on a different network than 192.168.10.0/24 simply by reading the first three numbers.

Addresses and Subnets That Are Unavailable

Under ordinary circumstances, the first and last IP addresses of any subnet are not available for use by an actual host. The first is reserved to identify the network itself, and the last is used for the broadcast address of the subnet. Thus, on the 172.20.5.0/24 network, you can neither use 172.20.5.0 (this network) nor 172.20.5.255 (all hosts on this network).

Additionally, some network equipment might not let you use the first subnet at all, because it could cause confusion associated with having network and subnet addresses that are indistinguishable. If your hardware does not support using the first subnet, the entire 172.20.0.0/24 network is also off limits.

The most notable instances of this router behavior are older versions of Cisco's IOS. Unless you configured your router with the `ip subnet-zero` option, the first subnet was off limits. Cisco IOS >= 12.0 includes `ip subnet-zero` by default. If you are using IOS prior to 8.3, the configuration option is named `service subnet-zero`.

In general, you should pick the smallest subnet possible that enables you to host your current and expected hosts. Usually, this means using a /24 subnet.

There are two special cases in which you might use subnets that are even more restrictive. If you are creating a network with only two hosts, such as a dedicated line between two hosts, you might want to use a /30:

IP address	Netmask	CIDR Notation
192.168.254.253	255.255.255.252	/30
192.168.254.254	255.255.255.252	/30

Here we have a network with only two hosts and no IPs left unused. Don't forget that the first and last are reserved for network and broadcast.

The other special case is a point-to-point link. In this case, you do not create a specific network at all; instead, you use a /32 (host) subnet. Take the following `ifconfig` output, for example:

```
$ ifconfig ppp0
ppp0      Link encap:Point-to-Point Protocol
          inet addr:192.168.254.254  P-t-P:192.168.254.253  Mask:255.255.255.255
```

Here we have a local address 192.168.254.254/32 that is connected via a point-to-point link to 192.168.254.253/32. This is commonly used for dial-up connections, but some of our VPNs will use this style of networking as well.

Network Conflicts

Sometimes you will find yourself in a position in which you have networks to connect that overlap. If this is because you planned poorly, you are now feeling the pain.

More commonly, this is caused by two companies merging. They both might have correctly picked networks from those available per RFC 1918, but they happened to pick the same ones. Ugh.

What do you do in this situation? Well, it's a nasty one. Changing all the IP addresses on one of the offending networks is certainly the cleanest option, though it might be time consuming. If you already allocate IP addresses with DHCP, you will be patting yourself on the back. You can simply change the DHCP server to use the new network and have machines reboot; they'll automatically be reconfigured. You must then only visit hard-coded machines and change them manually.

If changing IP addresses automatically is not an option, you can try to use network address translation (NAT) or port address translation (PAT) on your VPN servers to rewrite the outbound address. Let's say Atlanta and Chicago both use the same network addresses, 192.168.2.0/24.

If you configure Bears to rewrite all the Chicago addresses as if it came from itself, using a nonconflicting address (say, 192.168.3.1), Chicago machines will be able to access Atlanta machines even though they actually have the same network IP address conflicts. You'll need to perform some DNS trickery to supply Chicago hosts with fictitious IP addresses for the Atlanta hosts.

In short, it is possible, but you're going to need a network guru, some heavy planning, and many aspirin. In the end, you might just decide it's better to renumber one of the networks and save yourself the maintenance headaches of this horrible hack.

DNS for VPN

One often-overlooked requirement of a functioning VPN is DNS. For any host-network or network-network VPN, you will be enabling access to machines that are not available on the Internet at large. Unless you want to access machines only by their IP address, you want to have DNS work cleanly.

The easiest way to accomplish this is to create a new domain name for your internal networks. Let's say our company owns example.com, which we use for our external systems. We could create chicago.example.com and atlanta.example.com as internal domain names. We then would run a DNS server internally to support those domains.

Let's assume we install a DNS server on the internal machines Cubs and Braves. We can make Cubs authoritative for the chicago.example.com domain and Braves authoritative for the atlanta.example.com domain. We set up each machine to be secondary for the internal domains it does not serve, which will enable them to send updates cleanly between them.

You then configure Cubs and Braves to relay all other queries to an external DNS server (say, one at your ISP), making sure you have recursive queries allowed from internal addresses. You configure all your internal machines to use Cubs and Braves as their DNS servers, preferring whichever is on the local network to avoid sending DNS traffic across the VPN.

Let's say a user on Bulls wants the IP address for thrashers.atlanta.example.com. Cubs already knows the answer because it is a secondary DNS server for the domain. Should Bulls request the IP for `www.buildinglinuxvpns.net`, Cubs will forward the query to an external DNS server and return the answer to Bulls when it is received.

This situation works seamlessly for all hosts on networks that are connected via dedicated VPNs. The only tricky situation is supporting roaming users. Because those VPNs are created only periodically and the users might want to be connected to the Internet without using the VPN, you cannot hard-code their DNS setting to use the internal DNS servers.

If possible, configure their machines to use the internal DNS servers only when the VPN is active. This can be done by munging the `ip-up` script when using a PPP-related VPN, for example, or by any other method you desire to rewrite `/etc/resolv.conf` when the VPN is established.

The worst-case scenario (next to remembering IP addresses, that is) is to simply point first to an internal DNS server and then to an external server, as seen here:

```
$ cat /etc/resolv.conf
search chicago.example.com example.com
nameserver 192.168.1.10          # cubs
nameserver 345.6.7.8             # My ISP
```

The internal DNS server Cubs (192.168.1.10) is first in the list. If the VPN is available, Cubs will handle your DNS requests for both internal and external domains. If the VPN is not up, the DNS request to Cubs will fail, and your machine will then query 345.6.7.8. This machine will be able to respond for all Internet addresses but not the internal chicago.example.com addresses. This is not a problem, however, because the internal addresses aren't available except when the VPN is running anyway.

You will experience some name-resolution lag when using such a setup when the VPN is not established. DNS queries contact hosts in the order specified in `/etc/resolv.conf`, only moving onto the next in the list after determining that the first server isn't responding. Some resolver libraries try to consider this and will stop asking a nonresponding server for a while.

Routing

As has been alluded to in the previous sections, we must make sure our hosts send their traffic to the correct hosts.

In the case in which you have a simple network connected to the Internet, from the viewpoint of one of the machines on the network, you usually have only two classes of hosts that are accessible.

The first class comprises those on the internal network, which can be contacted directly. The second class comprises all other hosts on the Internet, which you contact via your Internet firewall or gateway/router.

To set up routing for the hosts on our Chicago network, you need to do two things. First, you must assign IP addresses to their network interfaces. Second, you must add a default route to the gateway/router using the following command:

```
cubs# route add default gw 192.168.1.1
```

The preceding command shows how you can manually add routes. How you permanently set up a default route depends on your Linux distribution.

For example, Red Hat machines use the file /etc/sysconf/network, Debian uses /etc/network/interfaces, and so on. You can view your routing table with the netstat command. For example, the routing table on Cubs might look like the following:

```
cubs# netstat -rn
Destination Gateway      Genmask        Flags  MSS Window  irtt Iface
default     192.168.1.1  255.255.255.0  UG     0   0       0    eth0
192.168.1.0 0.0.0.0      255.255.255.0  U      0   0       0    eth0
127.0.0.0   0.0.0.0      255.0.0.0      U      0   0       0    lo
```

Based on this routing table, all traffic originating from Cubs destined for 192.168.1.0/24 (the internal network) is sent directly to the eth0 interface. All other traffic originating from Cubs is sent using the default route to the gateway, 192.168.1.1. The gateway then performs NAT, if necessary, and forwards the traffic to its destination on the Internet.

Explicit VPN Routing Configuration

We've discussed three potential VPN and firewall topologies. In the case in which your VPN and firewall are the same machine, it should be obvious that your default route should point to the firewall, which is also conveniently the VPN server. This machine should be smart enough to know where packets should go, and thus the client should need no configuration changes.

So, what do you need to do when the firewall/gateway and VPN server are separate machines? You could configure the client machines to explicitly route VPN packets to the VPN server. If our remote VPN network were 192.168.2.0/24 and our VPN server were 192.168.1.13, we would run the following:

```
cubs# route add -net 192.168.2.0/24 192.168.1.13

cubs# netstat -rn

Destination Gateway      Genmask        Flags  MSS Window  irtt Iface
default     192.168.1.1  255.255.255.0  UG     0   0       0    eth0
192.168.1.0 0.0.0.0      255.255.255.0  U      0   0       0    eth0
```

```
192.168.2.0 192.168.1.13 255.255.255.0      UG    0   0   0   eth0
127.0.0.0   0.0.0.0       255.0.0.0          U    0   0   0   lo
```

Creating these VPN-related routes explicitly means you can clearly see exactly where your packets should go. It is a burden to set these up on each client, however.

The plain fact is that if you set up your firewall/gateway correctly, you have absolutely no need to explicitly define VPN-related routes on your client. We will see how this works in the next section.

Although explicitly defined VPN-related routes are not needed when you have a functioning VPN, they can be very helpful when setting up your VPN for the first time or when you need to debug problems.

If you are setting up a new VPN to connect to a remote network that is already available by other means (an existing VPN, a leased line, and so on), the only way to test the new VPN is by configuring static routes on one or more machines to test.

In the general case, however, you should avoid these static routes because they can only cause you headaches later should you change your network topology and find yourself fixing the routes on each and every client.

Centralized VPN Routing Configuration

If you prefer to configure your clients with a default route only rather than explicitly hard-coding each and every VPN-related route, we have good news for you: It's a cinch. Leave your client with the default gateway route and teach your default gateway the actual routes that should be used.

Let's say our firewall, 192.168.1.1, has the following routing table:

```
firewall# netstat -rn
```

```
Destination Gateway       Genmask           Flags   MSS Window   irtt Iface
default      280.8.8.7     255.255.255.0      UG     0    0       0    eth0
280.8.8.0    0.0.0.0       255.255.255.248    U      0    0       0    eth0
192.168.1.0  0.0.0.0       255.255.255.0      U      0    0       0    eth1
127.0.0.0    0.0.0.0       255.0.0.0          U      0    0       0    lo
192.168.2.0 192.168.1.13 255.255.255.255     UG     0    0       0    eth1
```

Our firewall machine has local interfaces eth0 (the Internet segment) and eth1 (the internal segment). It has a default route to the Internet via 280.8.8.6 (the router to the ISP) and a route for our Atlanta network, 192.168.2.0/24, through 192.168.1.13, our internal VPN server.

The clients all point to our firewall as the default gateway, so when Cubs wants to establish a TCP connection to braves.atlanta.example.com (192.168.2.15) through the VPN, the following packets will be sent:

```
Packet #   source   dest        tcpdump info

1          cubs     firewall    04:43:55.731166 < cubs.1600 > braves.www: S
➥669411963:669411963(0) win 32120 <mss 1460,sackOK,timestamp 79542679
➥0,nop,wscale 0> (DF)
```

```
2          firewall cubs        04:43:55.912572 > firewall > cubs: icmp: redirect
           braves to host bears [tos 0xc0]
3          cubs     bears       04:43:55.931166 < cubs.1600 > braves.www: S
           669411963:669411963(0) win 32120 <mss 1460,sackOK,timestamp 79542679
           0,nop,wscale 0> (DF)
4          bears    cubs        04:43:56.104105 > braves.www > cubs.1600: S
           1678687708:1678687708(0) ack 669411964 win 1460 <mss 1460> (DF)
5          cubs     bears       04:43:56.106602 < cubs.1600 > braves.www: .
           1:1(0) ack 1 win 32120 (DF)
6          cubs     bears       04:43:56.120659 < cubs.1600 > braves.www: P
           1:8(7) ack 1 win 32120 (DF)
7          bears    cubs        04:43:57.373603 > braves.www > cubs.1600: P
           1:200(199) ack 8 win 2920 (DF)
```

The preceding list is the output of `tcpdump` (a packet sniffer) watching the packets. Here's an explanation of each packet:

- Packet 1: Cubs sends a TCP packet to the firewall (its default gateway) with the final destination of Braves (192.168.2.15).

- Packet 2: The firewall, which knows that the 192.168.2.0/24 network is served by a different machine (Bears) tells Cubs "Hey, send data destined for braves to the machine bears instead." This is called an ICMP REDIRECT.

- Packet 3: Cubs resends the TCP packet to Bears with the final destination Braves (192.168.2.15).

- Subsequent packets: Cubs will talk to Bears directly for all communication to Braves. Bears handles sending this through the VPN.

Note

For your Linux VPN hosts to support ICMP REDIRECT messages arriving from a firewall, use the following:

```
root@fox # echo "1" > /proc/sys/net/ipv4/conf/all/accept_redirects
```

You can enable ICMP Redirects on the firewall as follows:

```
root@fox # echo "1" > /proc/sys/net/ipv4/conf/all/send_redirects
```

The ICMP REDIRECT is only needed for the first packet you want to send to a machine over the VPN. For the life of that connection, the client will automatically send the packets through the VPN server. There is no performance overhead to this configuration, save the one single ICMP REDIRECT at the beginning of each connection. As you can see from the timestamps in the `tcpdump` output earlier, this lag is hardly even worth mentioning.

We suggest that you configure all hosts to have a single default gateway and teach that gateway the VPN-related routes. This makes client configuration much easier because they need only the default route set up. It also means you have only one place you need to set up this route. If your firewall or gateway can exchange routing information with other routing hardware (via protocols such as RIP, OSPF, and so on), this makes the single point of configuration even more appealing.

VPN Server Behind a Firewall and NAT Traversal

If you use a routable IP address for the external interface (the one that is not on 192.168.1.0/24) of the Chicago VPN server, you can use the explicit or centralized routing configurations described earlier.

If you can't use a routable IP for the Chicago VPN server outside interface, you'll most likely need to get your VPN server to work over a NAT. Getting VPN solutions to work over NAT can be tricky.

For instance, for an IPSec-based solution, the easiest way is to have it work in tunnel mode. This is because one-to-one NAT mapping can be established (that is, the private IP address of the VPN server will be mapped to the routable IP address of the firewall). In transport mode, one-to-one mapping is a problem because packets can be coming from different IP addresses. Although a number of techniques have been proposed to deal with the problem, as of now, IPSec still does not have an official standard defining IPSec interoperation with NAT. (Check `www.ietf.org/html.charters/ipsec-charter.html` for more up-to-date information.)

Overall, NAT traversal is very implementation dependent and can be affected by a number of factors such as the transport protocols your VPN solution uses and so on. Your best bet is probably to consult the documentation and mailing lists for your particular VPN solution.

Trust Level

Trust is important in an environment in which security is a concern. (In a paranoid world, this would mean *every* environment.) Which systems you trust should be considered carefully, and even if you do trust a system, be sure to trust it as minimally as possible.

The principle of least privilege should be used on any system that is providing a service out to the Internet. This means don't give people outside of your network access to servers or services they do not need. In regard to VPNs, this means don't run any services that aren't absolutely necessary. Ideally, your machine that provided VPN access should be running only the VPN-related services, thus limiting the services that attackers could try to exploit.

Realistically, you will probably have to be running a service or two for management access to the box. To maintain security, these services should be of the encrypted variety: SSH instead of Telnet, SCP instead of FTP, and so on.

Further, access to these services should be limited to a small range of IPs, at least limited only to your local LAN. This could be done through TCP wrappers or your firewall but preferably should be done on both. A little bit of redundancy can buy you some additional time for damage control if someone manages to break in.

This section so far has discussed trust as it applies to outsiders trying to get in. We will next discuss trust as it applies to site-to-site and end-user VPN connections. You need to apply the principle of least privilege to these connections as well. The intent is not to mistrust the users on your VPN (although you might) but to minimize the possible business impact should one of the users' machines be compromised.

Limiting access to users can be done with the firewall of your choice on the VPN machine. There are two basic ways to limit access: by IP or by the inbound interface on the VPN server. The latter solution is a little more basic and does not provide as much control over the traffic. Most VPNs provide a local interface that is a logical entryway to the VPN. A firewall rule can be placed on this interface, limiting destination traffic. If you choose to limit by IP, you can restrict entire networks. This is useful if you have provisioned a certain range of IPs for a specific group of users.

For example, if you have given your sales team the IP network of 192.168.6.0/24 and it needs access to only one server, 192.168.1.100, you could use `ipchains`/`iptables` on your VPN server or firewall to restrict the sales network to access only that server. If you are concerned about security, you could further limit the access by application type. If in this example the sales team only uses that server for POP and SMTP connections, you could limit the access to port 110 and port 25.

Again, you will need to decide how much trust you will need for both your users and your Internet-facing servers. Hopefully, this section has imparted to the reader the importance of limiting trust as much as possible.

Logging

Logging is one of the most powerful techniques you can use to keep a constant eye on your system. In addition to system logs, we recommend that you set up your VPN server to log all connections to your VPN, whether successful or not.

Usually, you can specify different debugging levels to your VPN software when starting it or put them into configuration files. For example, if you use FreeS/WAN, you can use the following options in its `ipsec.conf` to determine the amount of debugging info that is written:

[...]
```
# Debug-logging
# See ipsec_klipsdebug(8), ipsec_pluto(8) for details
klipsdebug=esp
plutodebug=all
```

We suggest that you replicate your logs on a machine removed from VPN activity. Having the logs from your VPN server stored on a different machine ensures that if the VPN server is compromised, the attackers will not be able to cover their tracks easily by modifying log files.

For example, on our system, we use the following lines in `/etc/syslog.conf` to log all authentication events, including successes and failures. The events are logged both locally and to a dedicated logger machine, Blackhawks (192.168.1.30):

```
auth.debug              /var/log/messages
auth.debug              @192.168.1.30
authpriv.debug          /var/log/secure
authpriv.debug          @192.68.1.30
```

The `auth` facility is used for authentication events viewable by everyone. `Authpriv` is used for private authentication events, meaning authentication events that might have privileged or sensitive information in them. That is why `authpriv` events are sent to `/var/log/secure`, which is usually set so that only root can view it. The facilities you need to log depend on your VPN software. See `syslogd(1)` man page for more details.

> **Note**
>
> Although this is a good practice to keep your logs safe, all the remote messages will be stored in a single file on the logging machine. To make things a little easier, you can look into `syslog-ng`. This new implementation of `syslogd` enables you to log to a destination based on pattern matching. Thus, all logs from a specific remote machine can be kept in a separate file. More info can be found at `www.balabit.hu/en/products/syslog-ng/`.

Performance

VPN performance depends on many factors, including the type of VPN package you are using, the operating system you are using, the hardware it runs on, and so forth. This section will discuss techniques you can use to measure server and network performance of your VPN components.

Server Performance

Server performance should be periodically reviewed to make sure the machine is not throttling under the load of the VPN. The easiest way to gather information on how your server is performing is to use tools like `top` and `vmstat`.

The `top` command can be used to give you a real-time estimate of what each process on your system is doing. The following is part of a listing from the output of `top`:

```
  PID USER    PRI  NI  SIZE  RSS SHARE STAT %CPU %MEM  TIME COMMAND
  485 root      9   0  3096 2500  2436 S     5.0  4.0  0:00 VPN-PROC
23713 root     18   0  1016 1016   812 R     0.9  1.6  0:00 top
23699 root     10   0  1068 1052   884 S     0.1  1.6  0:00 sshd
    1 root      8   0   160  128   108 S     0.0  0.2  0:04 init
    2 root      9   0     0    0     0 SW    0.0  0.0  0:00 keventd
    3 root      9   0     0    0     0 SW    0.0  0.0  0:55 kswapd
    4 root      9   0     0    0     0 SW    0.0  0.0  0:00 kreclaimd
    5 root      9   0     0    0     0 SW    0.0  0.0  0:09 bdflush
    6 root      9   0     0    0     0 SW    0.0  0.0  0:03 kupdated
```

Here we can see that the system is relatively idle. The process `VPN-PROC` represents a VPN process; watching it as clients begin connecting to your machine can give you an idea of how many clients your server can handle.

To collect utilization statistics, you can use `cron` to schedule the `vmstat` command to run at regular intervals during the day.

Network Performance

In most cases, VPNs will perform worse than an identical network without a VPN because VPNs must encrypt and decrypt the data. (The decrease in performance can potentially be mitigated if your VPN solution compresses traffic—for example, the IPCOMP protocol in IPSec.) When testing your VPN solution, it is a good idea to see how it performs over time.

Some VPN technologies give you different choices that might affect performance. You might find that one encryption cipher outperforms others on your hardware. In general, the weaker the encryption, the faster it is. However, you might find that some strong ciphers outperform weaker ciphers. (We discuss cipher-related issues in Appendix B, "Selecting a Cipher.")

Over time, your VPN performance will change, perhaps because new users are added, network needs are different, or your hardware starts failing. It would behoove you to have an idea of how your VPN performs now and has performed in the past, before your users start complaining.

To view your current network usage, you can use a number of tools. Our favorite is the Multi Router Traffic Grapher (MRTG). We will also describe how you can use ttcp to gather some simple network performance measurements.

MRTG

Before you bring your VPN into production, you should first understand the amount of bandwidth currently in use for user traffic. An excellent lower-level tool for monitoring bandwidth is MRTG.

MRTG is a free tool that produces graphs on your current network traffic in addition to weekly, monthly, and yearly graphs. It uses SNMP to gather utilization statistics from interfaces on servers and routers. MRTG shows only bandwidth utilization; it does not show a breakdown of utilization by traffic type, such as SMTP traffic or web traffic.

Tightening up SNMP Security

Although SNMP on a gateway device can be considered a security risk, it can be useful to have it enabled for monitoring certain types of events. To tighten the security on SNMP, you can take the following steps:

1. Make your community string read-only. This prevents outsiders from making changes to devices even if they have the community string.

2. Create a firewall (or access list) entry, preventing SNMP traffic from entering from the Internet.

3. Make sure to change the default community strings. They are often "public" for the read-only string and "private" for the read-write strings. In SNMP, these strings are treated as passwords and should be changed regularly, just like any other password.

After you have gotten an idea of your normal bandwidth utilization, you should try connecting to your Linux server with a single VPN client. Just as you did when measuring the server performance, you will use this client connection as your baseline bandwidth requirement.

Again, as with server performance, make sure you do this for each type of connection that your server will be initiating. Once the server is in production, MRTG can be used to monitor your VPN interfaces, such as an ipsec, tun, or ppp. This will give you a good idea of your current utilization trends.

ttcp

To get a rough estimate of what kind of overhead the VPN will have on your traffic, you can use the `ttcp` command and compare throughput.

Using VTun as an example, we first measure the normal throughput. We will send some data (in this case, the Linux kernel sources) over and measure its performance. First, we test the connection between the two VPN machines, Bears and Falcons, using their public IP addresses. This tests the actual connection of the machines without any of the VPN overhead. The non-VPN IP addresses we are using are 280.8.8.8 and 270.7.7.7.

```
bears# ./ttcp -t 270.7.7.7 < ../linux-2.4.12.tar.bz2
ttcp-t: buflen=8192, nbuf=2048, align=16384/0, port=5001  tcp  -> 192.168.1.2
ttcp-t: socket
ttcp-t: connect
ttcp-t: 21508430 bytes in 26.00 real seconds = 807.94 KB/sec +++
```

The last line of the output gives us a throughput of 807.94 KB/s. Next, we run the same tests but use the VPN IP addresses this time, 192.168.1.1 and 192.168.2.1. By using these addresses, we will be sending data over the VPN.

```
bears# ./ttcp -t 192.168.2.1 < ../linux-2.4.12.tar.bz2
ttcp-t: buflen=8192, nbuf=2048, align=16384/0, port=5001  tcp  -> 10.0.0.2
ttcp-t: socket
ttcp-t: connect
ttcp-t: 21508430 bytes in 29.59 real seconds = 709.78 KB/sec +++
```

As you can see, the throughput this time is 709.78 KB/s. There is a throughput loss of almost 100 KB/s due to VPN overhead. The numbers you receive in your testing will vary, but you get the idea. You can get `ttcp` from `www.mentortech.com/learn/tools/tools.shtml`.

Summary

One of the essential things we wanted to convey in this chapter is the importance of planning for your VPNs. When building VPNs, we recommend that you always keep in mind fundamental considerations, particularly scalability, interoperability, and key distribution. You also need to have a clear understanding of what topology is the best for your scenario, how packets are going to be routed, what parts of your network are protected, what are the possible points of failure, and so forth.

Once your VPN has been deployed, it is important to know how to maintain it. In this chapter, we described two common maintenance tasks: performance measurements and logging. In addition, you might want to consider other areas related to maintenance, including upgrades, adding new users, and defining security policies. The rest of this book will focus on the details of various VPN solutions and protocols. Use the knowledge from this chapter with the VPN solutions we describe to effectively deploy and maintain your VPN.

II

Implementing Standard
VPN Protocols

3

Building a VPN with SSH and PPP

ONE OF THE FIRST ROLL-YOUR-OWN VPN solutions was to connect two networks with PPP over an SSH session. This method is an established practice, but it might feel a bit clunky to someone who is new to the protocols involved. When you finish this chapter, you'll be able to create an SSH/PPP VPN either by hand or by using a set of scripts we provide.

PPP-over-SSH Overview

To better understand the PPP-over-SSH implementation, let's discuss the two protocols involved.

PPP

PPP stands for the Point-to-Point Protocol. PPP is a derivation of the popular High Level Data Link Control (HDLC) (another layer 2 point-to-point protocol, commonly used on T1 lines) used to accomplish line control activities and encapsulate user data. PPP is most commonly used to establish a connection between modems over phone lines, such as when dialing up an ISP. Most Linux distributions come with tools such as `wvdial` or `xisp` that let you establish modem connections without fiddling with the underlying PPP commands and configurations. PPP, however, is not restricted to physical connections only; PPP connections can be established between any hosts that have network connectivity. Our goal will be to establish a PPP connection between different machines on the Internet, which we will use to establish a VPN.

To run pppd, the PPP protocol daemon, you must have a kernel that supports it. PPP is often compiled as a module that you can query with the command lsmod. If so, it should load automatically when needed. Most Linux distributions build their kernels with PPP support, so this should not be an issue.

Most Linux distributions also come with precompiled versions of PPP that you can install. Thus, you likely will not need to compile and install pppd yourself. However, for reasons that are discussed later, we suggest pppd version 2.3.7 or better.

The focus of PPP has never been on the privacy of the transmitted data, and as a direct result, it relies on external encryption methods to address this need. The risks of PPP data interception on phone lines are limited to line taps or a physical presence at either end of the PPP link. However, because we want to use PPP to establish a network connection by sending the traffic over the Internet, we must tunnel this PPP connection inside an encryption layer.

SSH

The Secure Shell (SSH) protocol is most frequently used to provide secure shell access and file transfer with other hosts over the network, secure authentication, and data privacy. It was developed as a secure drop-in replacement for Telnet and the Berkeley r-commands rlogin, rsh, and rcp.

SSH supports strong encryption and advanced user authentication methods that have stood the test of time. OpenSSH, an implementation of the SSH protocol written by folks at OpenBSD and ported to Linux by the OpenSSH portability team, is now included with many Linux distributions by default. SSH is the de facto secure login and file-transfer method for UNIX-like systems.

There is SSH software from other vendors such as ssh.com. We prefer OpenSSH, however, because it comes with most Linux distributions, is easier to configure, is more consistent between versions, and supports both version 1 and 2 of the SSH protocol. The setup in this chapter assumes you are using OpenSSH.

Issues of Protocol

The SSH protocol has gone through several different versions since it was created in 1995, the major ones being version 1.5 (referred to here as SSH1) and version 2 (SSH2). OpenSSH 2.0, which was released in June of 2000, supports both protocols natively. (Commercial SSH also can support both protocols but only by fork/execing the version 1 sshd binary when needed, creating a large performance hit.)

The two SSH protocols are not compatible, and you should determine which one you prefer to use. The SSH1 protocol has had security problems at times. Even now, there remains a theoretical insertion attack against the SSH1 protocol, but this is mitigated with the deattack patch supplied by CORE-SDI back in 1998. SSH1 has been around the longest and has a broader support base. SSH1 only supports RSA asymmetric cryptography, which was patented until September of 2000 in the USA. Because this patent has now expired, however, the RSA requirement is no longer an issue.

SSH2 is a newer, more feature-rich protocol and has stood up relatively well to the level of scrutiny applied thus far. Although SSH2 connections take much longer to establish, recent OpenSSH versions have greatly sped up this handshake. SSH2 supports both RSA and DSA asymmetric algorithms.

Regardless of which SSH protocol you choose, make sure you are using a recent version of OpenSSH. Historically, there have been vulnerabilities from time to time in OpenSSH, such as two separate 'UseLogin' holes, or the integer overflow in the original deattack patch which could lead to root compromise. OpenSSH has been doing much better than its SSH peers, however, with respect to security. It even includes countermeasures to esoteric attacks such as keystroke timing, in which an attacker uses the time between packets to determine how close together the keys you typed are and can use this to infer what you have typed.

We will be using SSH identities (asymmetric cryptographic keys used for authentication, described in detail later) to allow our VPN client to log in to the VPN server. Unfortunately, the identity format for SSH1 is different than for SSH2. Thus, although OpenSSH supports versions of the SSH protocol, we will need to decide which version we want to use for our VPN. If you have a recent version of OpenSSH (which you should), we suggest you use SSH2. We provide details for creating your SSH identities for both SSH1 and SSH2, so the choice is yours.

Our Sample Network

The theory is simple: Establish an SSH connection from the VPN client to the VPN server and have PPP daemons run on both ends that talk to each other to create our VPN. We will create a VPN between the hosts Bears (the VPN server) and Falcons (the VPN client), as seen in Figure 3.1.

Both Bears and Falcons have networks behind them that are to be connected securely. The dotted line designates the virtual network created between the two hosts.

What About the VPN-HOWTO?

The definitive reference for establishing a PPP-over-SSH VPN is the Linux VPN-HOWTO, written in 1997 and available at `www.linuxdoc.org/HOWTO/mini/VPN.html`. Unfortunately, this document is rather dated at this point, and it assumes you already know the protocols and theories well.

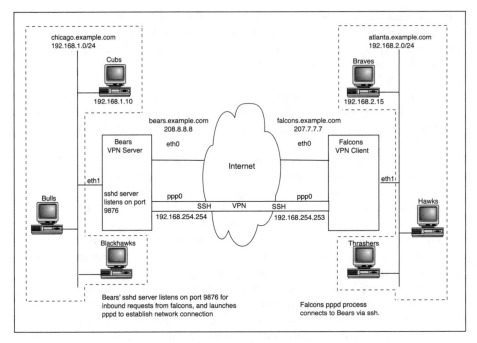

Figure 3.1   Our VPN network.

We will show you how to create a VPN using the same protocols but in greater detail and with some features not available or discussed in the HOWTO, as follows:

- Both client and server run their software as a dummy user, not root. The best security practice is to run as little as root as possible.
- Restrictions placed on the server to prevent the dummy user from logging in, which could be used to gain additional privileges.
- The server controls almost all aspects of the connection, providing a single point of configuration.
- The pty-redir hack from the VPN-HOWTO is no longer needed.
- Dedicated SSH server with restrictive configuration such that we do not interfere or rely on the actual SSH server used for normal users.
- SSH1 and SSH2 protocols and identities are described.
- SSH host key verification is discussed to avoid man-in-the-middle attacks.
- PPP authentication (PAP/CHAP, an additional password requirement) to provide another layer of VPN authentication.
- New VPN-dependent routes will be added automatically after the VPN connection is established by utilizing the `ip-up` script.

The biggest problem with the VPN-HOWTO is that it was written for an older version of pppd. As we describe later, pppd requires a tty over which it communicates. The pty-redir hack was used to supply a tty over which the SSH connection could be established. Now this can be done more cleanly with the pty argument to pppd. Also, by using the ip-up script, which is called by pppd after a connection is established, we can have our routes added immediately. Most other PPP-related VPN methods rely on a sleep 10 command to wait until the PPP connection is done before adding routes, which might delay the VPN completion if PPP is established quickly or might prevent correct routing if PPP takes a while to finish its handshake.

Setting up PPP over SSH Manually

To begin, we will show you the various pieces involved by creating a VPN between two hosts manually. This will lay the groundwork for what we do in our later scripts and will help teach you what is going on. This will aid in debugging the connection if necessary.

Installing and Verifying PPP

First, determine that PPP is installed on both your VPN client and VPN server. On a Debian or other dpkg-based system, you would type the following:

```
root@debian$ dpkg -l ppp ¦grep ppp
ii  ppp            2.3.11-1.4     Point-to-Point Protocol (PPP) daemon.
```

On a Red Hat or other rpm-based system, you would type the following:

```
root@redhat# rpm -q ppp
ppp-2.3.11-4
```

Make sure that the version of ppp you have installed is 2.3.7 or greater because that is the first version that supports the pty argument necessary for setting up a pty automatically.

Enabling IP Forwarding

Most Linux distributions do not allow IP packet forwarding by default, but we must enable this to route VPN packets through the PPP interface. You can change the status of IP forwarding by modifying the appropriate kernel parameter. Though it is possible to recompile your kernel to change the default settings, the easiest way is to use the /proc file system. Files in /proc are not actually files but ways of accessing and/or modifying kernel parameters, and you must be root to change these. Thus, the simplest way to turn on port forwarding is to run the following command:

```
root# echo 1 > /proc/sys/net/ipv4/ip_forward
```

This automatically turns on IP packet forwarding on all interfaces by default. If you are making a host-host VPN, this is sufficient. If you want to create a network-network or host-network VPN, you might want to turn on IP forwarding for only those interfaces that you explicitly want to forward. For example, on a large VPN server, you might want to forward via all the ppp interfaces (the VPN links) and via eth1 (an internal interface) but not via all the ethernet interfaces. To do so, you could use the following shell script:

```
#!/bin/sh

echo "Setting up IP forwarding rules"
echo 1 > /proc/sys/net/ipv4/ip_forward
echo -n "/proc/sys/net/ipv4/ip_forward: "
cat /proc/sys/net/ipv4/ip_forward

for forwarding in /proc/sys/net/ipv4/conf/*/forwarding
do
      echo -n "$forwarding: ";

      interface=`dirname $forwarding`
      interface=`basename $interface`

      case "$interface" in
            ppp*|eth1)   # list of interfaces through which
                         # forwarding should be enabled
                         echo 1 > $forwarding
                         ;;

                  *)     # Turn off forwarding for all other interfaces
                         echo 0 > $forwarding
                         ;;
      esac

      cat $forwarding
done
```

Make sure you tweak the preceding case statement to fit your IP forwarding policy. In this case, eth1 and all ppp interfaces (ppp0, ppp1, ...) will be allowed to forward packets, and all other interfaces will drop packets not destined for that interface.

Creating the VPN Users

Next, you must create the user that will be running the VPN commands on both ends. We will assume that you use the username sshvpn on both ends, though you can use any username you want. Although the usernames don't have to be the same on both machines, it does make things easier. For example, you might create the user as follows:

```
root# groupadd sshvpn
root# useradd -m -d /opt/ssh-vpn -c "SSH VPN User" -g sshvpn sshvpn
```

The `useradd` program creates users with a locked password by default, ensuring that no one can log in to this account. The only way in which these accounts can be accessed for now is by using `/bin/su` as root. Later, we will set up special SSH access to these user IDs. The home directory we use for this user is traditionally `/opt/ssh-vpn`. Although we could have created the home directory in `/home`, this user is going to be used more like a software product. Thus, installing in `/opt` (or `/usr` and so on) seems more in line with its function. So, hereafter we will use `/opt/ssh-vpn`, though you can use anything you want.

Naming Conventions

To keep our two hosts straight, we will call the machine that starts the process the VPN client and call the other machine the VPN server. The VPN client will use SSH to connect to the VPN server.

We must also come up with a name for our VPN. For our examples, we will use `vpn1`. Our scripts can establish more than one VPN at a time, and this name helps differentiate them.

Establishing Passwordless SSH Login

Our VPN user on the VPN client must be able to log in to the VPN server without a password. We can do this in several different ways with SSH. The two standard methods are host-based authentication and SSH identity authentication. Other methods, such as kerberos, generally involve too much maintenance and hassle to use in situations such as ours.

Host-based authentication involves establishing a trust relationship between hosts; in this relationship, any user on one host (client) can log in to the other host (server) without a password. Without going into too much detail, this involves installing a copy of the client's SSH host public key onto the server in `/etc/ssh/ssh_known_hosts` and putting the client machine name into `/etc/shosts.equiv`. When the client connects, the host key it presents is checked against the host key stored in that file. If they match, the server knows the client is authentic, and the user is allowed in without a password. We will see later how SSH host keys work when we establish our actual connection. If you want to use host-based authentication for other projects, consult the `sshd` manual page for details.

The problem with host-based authentication is that it allows all users on the client to log in to their accounts on the server without restrictions. In our situation, we want only one specific user to be able to log in, and we will be placing restrictions on the command that that user can run and will be denying interactive logins alltogether. Thus, host-based authentication is overly permissive for our needs.

An SSH identity is simply a public/private key pair that is housed on the SSH client. By placing the public key of this identity in the `$HOME/.ssh/authorized_keys` file on the SSH server, any user that has the correct identity can log in to the server. Normally, these identities are created such that they require a passphrase to be used.

Thus, a trust model using an SSH identity will allow the VPN user on the client to connect without a password to the server, without allowing any other server logins. We will see that an SSH identity can be restricted in other beneficial ways later.

Setting Up the SSH Identity

First, we must create our SSH identity on the VPN client. Become the sshvpn user and create the .ssh directory:

```
root@falcons-client# su - sshvpn
sshvpn@falcons-client$ pwd
/opt/ssh-vpn
sshvpn@client$ mkdir .ssh
sshvpn@client$ chmod 700 .ssh
```

If you want to use the SSH1 protocol, run the following commands to create a non-password-protected SSH identity in ~/.ssh/identity:

```
sshvpn@falcons-client$ ssh-keygen -t rsa1 -N ''
Generating public/private rsa1 key pair.
Enter file in which to save the key (/opt/ssh-vpn/.ssh/identity):
Your identification has been saved in /opt/ssh-vpn/.ssh/identity.
Your public key has been saved in /opt/ssh-vpn/.ssh/identity.pub.
The key fingerprint is:
a8:28:08:2b:3c:b3:52:13:26:f0:ac:5e:43:df:20:fb sshvpn@client
```

If you want to use the SSH2 protocol, run the following commands to create a non-password-protected SSH DSA identity in ~/.ssh/id_dsa:

```
sshvpn@falcons-client$ ssh-keygen -t dsa -N ''
Generating public/private dsa key pair.
Enter file in which to save the key (/opt/ssh-vpn/.ssh/id_dsa):
Your identification has been saved in /opt/ssh-vpn/.ssh/id_dsa.
Your public key has been saved in /opt/ssh-vpn/.ssh/id_dsa.pub.
The key fingerprint is:
6c:e7:e7:bb:71:da:68:8c:d8:5f:ae:e0:90:e6:c8:d2 sshvpn@client
```

If you prefer, you could create an RSA identity for SSH2 by using -t rsa instead. For our purposes, it does not matter which you use, so we will assume that you are using a DSA identity.

Making Identities for Multiple VPNs

If you plan to have more than one VPN, you might want to create different SSH identities for each VPN. Simply specify a filename with the -f filename argument to ssh-keygen.

Now your identity has been created. You can view the public part of the identity by viewing the .pub version of your key:

```
sshvpn@falcons-client$ cat .ssh/identity.pub     # for SSH1
or
sshvpn@falcons-client$ cat .ssh/id_dsa.pub       # for SSH2
```

On the server, create `sshvpn`'s `.ssh` directory as follows:

```
root@bears-server# su - sshvpn
sshvpn@bears-server$ mkdir .ssh
sshvpn@bears-server$ chmod 700 .ssh
```

You must now copy this public key to the server. You can use any method you prefer:
`scp`, `sftp`, or even cut and paste. If you are using SSH1, copy this file into
`~sshvpn/.ssh/authorized_keys` on the VPN server. If you are using SSH2, then copy
this file into `~sshvpn/.ssh/authorized_keys2` on the VPN server. When you are done
you, will have the following files if you are using SSH1:

```
sshvpn@bears-server$ ls -l /opt/ssh-vpn/.ssh
-rw-------   1 sshvpn    sshvpn         330 Apr 19 04:43 authorized_keys
sshvpn@bears-server$ cat /opt/ssh-vpn/.ssh/authorized_keys
1024 35 12849455402044458154167142590652980977941666182144....
```

That ugly string of numbers is the identity public key. SSH2 pub keys look similar:

```
sshvpn@bears-server$ ls -l /opt/ssh-vpn/.ssh
-rw-------   1 sshvpn    sshvpn         600 Apr 19 04:43 authorized_keys2
sshvpn@bears-server$ cat /opt/ssh-vpn/.ssh/authorized_keys2
ssh-dss AAAAB3NzaC1kc3MAAACBAM228h8QJ+QPkauTanmmhMwKykctqLh....
```

Accept and Verify the SSH Host Key of the Server

We must now connect to the server for the first time. When we do so, we will be
asked to accept the server's key:

```
sshvpn@falcons-client$ ssh server.example.com
The authenticity of host 'server.example.com' can't be established.
RSA1 key fingerprint is 57:9d:59:1e:75:58:61:5b:ca:3f:e1:5c:96:59:e9:1a.
Are you sure you want to continue connecting (yes/no)? yes
```

At this prompt, type `yes` (the whole word, not just y). You should now be logged in to
the server without having typed a password and have saved a copy of the SSH server's
host key on the client.

Using Additional SSH Arguments

If you have any other arguments that you must supply for your SSH connection, such as `-p portnum` or
`-l remoteusername`, make sure you supply them on the `ssh` command line. We assume that you don't
require any other arguments at this point. Later in this chapter, we will show you how you can hard-code
these extra arguments into `.ssh/config` so that you don't need to type them every time.

You now must verify that the server's host key that you just blindly accepted is, in fact,
the key for the server and that you have not been the subject of a man-in-the-middle
attack. If you do not do this, you are not able to verify that the remote end of the
SSH connection is authentic. `Dsniff` by Dug Song, for example, is easily able to
perform such a man-in-the-middle attack. This risk is real.

When you typed yes, the server's host key was saved in $HOME/.ssh/known_hosts. The entries in this file are strings of numbers and/or letters that look similar to identity public keys. For example, look at this RSA1 host key:

```
sshvpn@falcons-client$ head -1 $HOME/.ssh/known_hosts
server.example.com 1024 35
156449784716965160094593358239694655813315060606031.....
```

You must verify that this key matches the public key of the server. The server's public key is usually located in one of the following files:

```
/etc/ssh/ssh_host_key.pub
/etc/ssh/ssh_host_rsa_key.pub
/etc/ssh/ssh_host_dsa_key.pub
```

These files might be in /etc instead of /etc/ssh, depending on how your SSH server software was compiled by your Linux distribution. Find the key that matches the key in your $HOME/.ssh/known_hosts file and verify that they are the exact same string. If they differ, something fishy is going on and your VPN is not secure.

Verify Passwordless Login

Now try to log from the client to the server once again. If all is set up correctly, you should be able to do this without a password and without any host key questions:

```
sshvpn@falcons-client$ ssh server 'echo `hostname`'
server.example.com
sshvpn@falcons-client$
```

If you are not able to log in without a password, check the following:

- **Permissions.** OpenSSH is very restrictive as to what file permissions it finds acceptable. Make sure that ~sshvpn and ~sshvpn/.ssh are mode 700 and that the authorized_keys{2} file is mode 600.

- **Protocol incompatibilities.** Make sure that both your client and your server support the SSH protocol you've picked. Also, OpenSSH might be attempting to use the wrong protocol by default. You can force a given protocol to be used by specifying ssh -1 ... or ssh -2 ... on the command line.

If neither of these is the cause, check the syslog information on the server (traditionally /var/log/messages) and give ssh the -v option on the command line to give enhanced debugging. If you are still having trouble, check the ssh(1) man page, look up the SSH FAQ at http://www.employees.org/~satch/ssh/faq, or ask for help on the SSH mailing list. Mailing list information is available on the SSH FAQ.

Set Up *Sudo*

The pppd program, which is used to establish the network link between our VPN hosts, can only be run by the root user. Because we want to run our VPN scripts on both ends as a dummy user, we will need a way to gain root privileges to run this program.

Sudo is a versatile program that enables users to run a restricted set of commands as root. We will be creating a very simple set of rules that will enable us to run the pppd command.

Sudo can be found at www.courtesan.com/sudo/. It is included with many Linux distributions as well, so you might not need to compile it yourself.

After *Sudo* is installed, run the visudo command to edit the /etc/sudoers file. Do not edit this file manually (without using visudo) or you run the risk of corrupting it! Add the following lines to the end of the file:

```
Cmnd_Alias VPN=/usr/sbin/pppd
sshvpn     ALL=NOPASSWD: VPN
```

Replace the path for /usr/sbin/pppd if it is in a different location for your system. Also, replace sshvpn in the second line with the dummy user you have created for the SSH VPN if you picked something different. When finished, simply write your changes and exit your editor.

The preceding lines will allow the sshvpn user to run the command /usr/sbin/pppd with any arguments desired. Because of the NOPASSWD entry, the user will not be required to enter his or her password before being granted access to these programs. Because we need these commands to be executed automatically from our scripts, it would be impossible to enter a password.

To test this briefly, simply type the following on both the client and server machines:

```
root@machine# su - sshvpn
sshvpn@machine$ sudo /usr/sbin/pppd noauth
~ÿ}#À!}!}!} }4}"}&} } } } }%} (more gobeldygook continues....)
```

The funny characters are the result of pppd attempting to handshake with your terminal. Jump to another window and killall -HUP pppd to stop the pppd process.

If you have not set up the sudoers file correctly, you will be asked to enter your password. Verify your syntax in the sudoers file. Again, make sure you are using the visudo program and not editing /etc/sudoers manually.

Set Up PPP

We will need to run pppd on both hosts. Table 3.1 provides a list of useful pppd arguments.

Table 3.1 *pppd* **Arguments**

Argument	Purpose
updetach	Once the connection is established, have pppd detach from its tty and become a daemon (child of init).
nodetach	Don't detach from our tty. Useful during debugging.

continues

Table 3.1   **Continued**

Argument	Purpose
proxyarp	Add an entry to the ARP table (lookup of IP to ethernet address) with the address of the peer. Can be used to make the other end appear to be on the local network to other machines. Optional.
debug	Optionally used to allow increased debugging information.
linkname *name*	The name of this PPP link. Useful for differentiating this PPP connection from others. Also used by pppd to create /var/run/ppp-*name*.pid in addition to the standard /var/run/ppp-device.pid.
noauth	Do not require any PPP peer authentication. This is a perfectly acceptable level of security because we have SSH handling validation of both endpoints. Incompatible with require-pap and require-chap.
require-pap	Require PAP authentication of the PPP peer. Optional.
papcrypt	If using PAP authentication, this option says that all PAP secrets are encrypted in the /etc/ppp/pap-secrets file.
require-chap	Require CHAP authentication of the PPP peer. Optional.
name *name*	The name of the local system for PPP authentication purposes. Optional but helpful when authentication is used.
remotename *name*	The name of the remote system for PPP authentication purposes. Optional but helpful when authentication is used.
user username	The username used for PPP authentication. Defaults to the local system name if not supplied.
show-password	Show the password used for authentication in the logs. This is useful only during the debugging phase and should be turned off once PPP is working properly between hosts.
connect-delay #	The number of seconds to wait for a valid PPP packet from the peer. We set this to 10000 (10 seconds) to make sure SSH has time to establish its connection. This command is only used on the client end.
pty *command*	Instead of using a terminal/serial device, run the command listed on its own pseudo tty. This will be our ssh command that connects to the remote end. This command is only used on the client end.

Argument	Purpose
usepeerdns	Set up the local machine to use DNS servers on the remote end for name lookups. Good for allowing the roaming client to access internal DNS servers to reach internal machines, for example. It's only logical to use this on one of the two ends, not both.

Bypassing PPP Authentication

PPP is usually used for creating a network connection between hosts over a modem and almost always requires user authentication to the server before establishing the connection. We will discuss how you can enable PPP peer authentication later in this chapter when we present our ready-to-go VPN scripts. For now, however, we will want to eliminate that variable and allow SSH to do all our authentication for us. Thus, for now, we will not be using any of the `require-pap`, `require-chap`, `name`, `remotename`, or `user` arguments.

Establishing a Manual PPP Connection

We now have all the pieces we need to connect our two networks:

- The capability to log in from the client to the server without a password using SSH identities

- The capability to run `pppd` as root through `sudo`

So let's run `pppd` on the client, connecting to the remote end and running `pppd` there:

```
sshvpn@falcons-client$ sudo /usr/sbin/pppd updetach noauth \
                       pty "sudo -u sshvpn ssh -t -t server.example.com \
                       sudo pppd noauth 192.168.254.254:192.168.254.253"
Using interface ppp0
Connect: ppp0 <--> /dev/pts/2
Deflate (15) compression enabled
local  IP address 192.168.254.253
remote IP address 192.168.254.254
```

Let's examine that awful command line in detail:

```
sudo /usr/sbin/pppd updetach noauth
```

Run `pppd` as root via `sudo`. Don't detach from our `tty`, which will let us see the IP address information before `pppd` detaches. Don't require authentication.

```
pty "sudo -u sshvpn ssh -t -t server.example.com \
```

The `pty` argument specifies a command to run that will connect it to the remote PPP service. Because PPP is running as `root` (via `sudo`) the `ssh` command will run as root. This is a bad idea because then we are at the mercy of `root`'s `/root/.ssh` directory contents. Thus, we want to run `ssh` as `sshvpn`, using `sudo -u sshvpn ssh ...`. The `-t` `-t` arguments force `pty` allocation on the server for this connection, which is required for `pppd`. `Server.example.com` is, obviously, the name of the server.

```
sudo pppd noauth 192.168.254.254:192.168.254.253"
```

Because we are logged in to the VPN server as the `sshvpn` user, we must use `sudo` to run `pppd` as root. The `noauth` argument again enables us to use PPP without any user/password authentication. The two IP addresses specify the local and remote IP addresses of this PPP connection. Make sure you choose networks that are not in use on either machine. The netmask on this link is 255.255.255.255, meaning you could create as many IP address pairs as you want on separate PPP links as long as you don't duplicate IP addresses already in use.

> ### Interference by Other SSH Output
> If your VPN server automatically outputs anything when you log in (such as the contents of /etc/motd), your PPP process might see this and get terribly confused. Try setting the `PrintMotd` variable in /etc/{ssh}/sshd_config to no.

Test the Connection

At this point, you should be able to ping 192.168.254.254 and 192.168.254.253 from both the client and server:

```
machine$ ping 192.168.254.253
PING 192.168.254.253 (192.168.254.253): 56 data bytes
64 bytes from 192.168.254.253: icmp_seq=0 ttl=255 time=10.7 ms
64 bytes from 192.168.254.253: icmp_seq=1 ttl=255 time=11.7 ms
...
```

You should also be able to look at the interface information:

```
bears-server$ ifconfig ppp0
ppp0  Link encap:Point-to-Point Protocol
      inet addr:192.168.254.254  P-t-P:192.168.254.253  Mask:255.255.255.255
      UP POINTOPOINT RUNNING NOARP MULTICAST  MTU:1500  Metric:1
      RX packets:33 errors:0 dropped:0 overruns:0 frame:0
      TX packets:36 errors:0 dropped:0 overruns:0 carrier:0
      collisions:0 txqueuelen:10
```

Note that the IP addresses listed match those we specified in the `pppd` command line.

Adjust Your Routing Table

The last step is to set up the routing tables on both client and server to tunnel the appropriate data over the PPP link:

```
sshvpn@falcons-client$ sudo route add -net 192.168.1.0/24 gw 192.168.254.254
sshvpn@bears-server$ sudo route add -net 192.168.2.0/24 gw 192.168.254.253
```

At this point, you should be able to ping from one network to the other at will. Here
we show an example of a machine, cubs, behind the VPN server bears:

```
user@cubs-192.168.1.10$ ping braves.atlanta.example.com
PING braves.atlanta.example.com (192.168.2.15) 56 data bytes
64 bytes from 192.168.2.15 icmp_seq=0 ttl=255 time=13.4 ms
64 bytes from 192.168.2.15 icmp_seq=1 ttl=255 time=12.5 ms
...
```

Note that for this to work, all the machines behind the VPN machines must have their
VPN machine as their default gateway, as seen here:

```
user@cubs-192.168.1.10$ netstat -rn
Kernel IP routing table
Destination     Gateway         Genmask         Flags  MSS Window  irtt Iface
192.168.1.0     0.0.0.0         255.255.255.0   U        0 0          0 eth0
127.0.0.0       0.0.0.0         255.0.0.0       U        0 0          0 lo
0.0.0.0         192.168.1.1     0.0.0.0         UG       0 0          0 eth0

user@braves-192.168.2.15$ netstat -rn
Kernel IP routing table
Destination     Gateway         Genmask         Flags  MSS Window  irtt Iface
192.168.2.0     0.0.0.0         255.255.255.0   U        0 0          0 eth0
127.0.0.0       0.0.0.0         255.0.0.0       U        0 0          0 lo
0.0.0.0         192.168.2.1     0.0.0.0         UG       0 0          0 eth0
```

Increasing the Security of Your VPN

You can do several things to enhance the security of your VPN connection, particularly in the area of authentication. If you have followed the appropriate procedures,
particularly the secure generation and installation of the SSH identity on the client
and the verification of the SSH server's host key, these enhancements are not necessary
for a secure VPN. However, adding more granular controls can't hurt. We suggest the
following restrictions for the paranoid.

Requiring PPP Authentication

Now that we have proven that we can create a VPN, we can start adding more security by requiring peer authentication. The PPP protocol includes methods of authentication via the Password Authentication Protocol (PAP) and the Challenge Handshake
Authentication Protocol (CHAP).

PAP authentication sends the secret (password) over the connection in the clear,
whereas CHAP authentication does not. Instead, it sends a hash of the secret and the
challenge supplied by the peer. Because our PPP connection will be established over
an encrypted SSH link, there is no compelling reason to prefer CHAP over PAP in
this case.

You can have the PPP daemon on both ends require authentication to be absolutely sure that you have connected to the correct endpoint. This might be overkill, however, because we will be verifying the authenticity of both endpoints automatically via SSH: the client by the SSH identity and the server by its SSH host key.

Regardless, if you want to establish PAP or CHAP authentication for your PPP connection, you will need to edit the /etc/ppp/pap-secrets or /etc/ppp/chap-secrets files, respectively. By careful choice of the name, remotename, and user arguments supplied to pppd, we can make our /etc/ppp/{pap,chap}-secrets files easy to read.

For example, on the client, we will use the following pppd arguments:

```
debug require-pap show-password name vpn1-client \
    user vpn1-client remotename vpn1-server
```

On the server, we will use the following arguments:

```
debug require-pap show-password name vpn1-server \
    user vpn1-server remotename vpn1-client
```

The following in /etc/ppp/pap-secrets will be on both hosts:

```
# Username      Server          Password        ip_addrs
vpn1-server     vpn1-client     "somepw"        *
vpn1-client     vpn1-server     "otherpw"       *
```

For extra security, you can encrypt the password with crypt() on the machine requiring the authentication. In other words, the vpn1-client does not need to know the password for the vpn1-server and could have an encrypted form in the password field. Thus, the client /etc/ppp/pap-secrets file could read as follows:

```
# User/client   server          password                ip_addrs
vpn1-server     vpn1-client     "8x5X.K/YftXJQ"         *
vpn1-client     vpn1-server     "someotherpassword"     *
```

A quick way to generate a crypt() version of a password would be to use the following one-line Perl script:

```
machine$ perl -e 'print( "Encrypted Password: ", crypt("somepw", "8x"), "\n")'
```

The output from the script would look like the following:

```
Encrypted Password: 8x5X.K/YftXJQ
```

To use CHAP instead of PAP, follow the preceding procedures but use the /etc/ppp/chap-secrets file instead, specify require-chap on the pppd command line, and do not encrypt the password using crypt(). CHAP authentication cannot handle encrypted passwords due to its design.

In the preceding example, we required authentication of both the client and the server. You could require it for only one of the endpoints if desired simply by replacing require-{pap,chap} with noauth on the endpoint that does not need to perform peer authentication.

Putting Restrictions on SSH Identities

You can place restrictions on the SSH identities you accept by modifying the
.ssh/authorized_keys{2} file. Simply prepend the line containing the public key you
want to affect with a list of restrictions. The restrictions most useful include those
shown in Table 3.2.

Table 3.2   **Useful SSH Identity Restrictions**

Restriction	Description
from="pattern-list"	A comma-separated list of hostnames for which this identity will be honored. If the identity comes from a different machine, the connection will not be granted. The wildcards ★ and ? are allowed, as is ! for negation. Used for restricting which machines can connect with that identity.
command="command"	Regardless what command (if any) the client attempts to run, instead run the command specified. This will be the shell script that launches pppd with the appropriate arguments later in this chapter.
environment="VARIABLE=value"	Create an environment variable VARIABLE with the value value. We'll use this later to specify which VPN name is associated with this connection.
no-port-forwarding	Disable SSH's port forwarding. Port forwarding is not needed for our VPN.
no-X11-forwarding	Disable SSH's X11 forwarding. X11 is not needed for our VPN.
no-agent-forwarding	Disable SSH's agent forwarding. SSH agent forwarding is not needed for our VPN.

These options must be joined with commas and placed as the first argument on the
authorized_keys{2} line with the SSH identity. Thus, an example might be as follows:

```
from="client.example.com",command="/usr/bin/sudo /usr/sbin/pppd noauth
➥192.168.254.254:192.168.254.253",environment="vpn_network=vpn1",
➥no-port-forwarding,no-X11-forwarding,no-agent-forwarding 1024 35
➥12849455402044458154167142590652980977941666182446...
```

In the preceding example, we will allow this identity to come from client.example.
com only, an appropriate sudo pppd command will be forced, all unnecessary forward-
ings in SSH will be turned off, and the vpn_network environment variable will be set
to vpn1 for use later.

Adding these options can lead to very, very long lines. Make sure you're using an
editor that can handle long lines properly. Old versions of vi, for example, might not
be able to edit or show them properly. We suggest using vim or emacs.

Use the Most Recent OpenSSH

This is just another reminder that you should make sure you're using the most recent version of OpenSSH. For example, versions of OpenSSH before 2.9.9p2 have a bug in which a user with a valid SSH identity can establish an SFTP session to the server and bypass the identity restrictions. (This is only possible with the SSH2 protocol). If an attacker had this identity, he or she could remove the command restriction simply by replacing the authorized_keys2 file with a new one that didn't have the command option. If you cannot upgrade your OpenSSH server, at least comment out the Subsystem sftp line in /etc/ssh/sshd_config.

Running a Custom *ssh* Daemon on the VPN Server

You can use your existing ssh daemon on the VPN server for the VPN's SSH logins. However, if you want to be more restrictive—the defaults for SSH are overly permissive for our purposes, and healthy paranoia is always a good thing—you can run a separate ssh daemon on the VPN client.

All we need to do is create a second sshd_config file that specifies a different port number than the default (22) and our restrictive options. The sshvpn user on the client then connects to this ssh daemon instead. Here is our new sshd_config, which we place in /opt/ssh-vpn/etc:

```
Port 9876
PidFile /var/run/sshd_vpn.pid

HostKey /etc/ssh/ssh_host_key
HostKey /etc/ssh/ssh_host_rsa_key
HostKey /etc/ssh/ssh_host_dsa_key

ServerKeyBits 768
LoginGraceTime 600
KeyRegenerationInterval 3600

SyslogFacility AUTH
LogLevel INFO

RSAAuthentication yes
AllowUsers sshvpn

# Restrictive settings
#
IgnoreRhosts yes
IgnoreUserKnownHosts yes
PermitRootLogin no
StrictModes yes

PasswordAuthentication no
PermitEmptyPasswords no
ChallengeResponseAuthentication no
RhostsAuthentication no
```

```
RhostsRSAAuthentication no
X11Forwarding no
PrintMotd no
KeepAlive yes
```

The preceding configuration allows only the `sshvpn` user to log in, no authentication methods except SSH identities are allowed, and the port is set to 9876. You can use kernel ACLs with `ipchains`/`iptables` to restrict access to this port if desired. By using a different port, you can apply different ACLs to the `ssh` daemon used for VPN access than you do for standard SSH logins on port 22.

You then start this daemon simply by running `/usr/sbin/sshd -f /opt/ssh-vpn/etc/sshd_config`. You might want to modify the existing `sshd` startup script in `/etc/init.d` to start this daemon as well. Any VPN clients that want to connect to this SSH daemon need to specify the new port using the `-p portnum` command-line arguments to `ssh`.

Placing SSH Options in *.ssh/config*

`ssh` reads the file `$HOME/.ssh/config` before making an outbound connection. This file contains arguments for `ssh` that will be used for the connection, saving you the trouble of typing in the arguments manually. We will use this to create an "alias" of sorts for our SSH connection.

Say we want to name our VPN vpn1. The remote server is called `server.example.com`, and the remote server is running `ssh` on port 9876, as seen in the previous section. Let's assume that, for some reason, the `sshvpn` user on the server is actually called pppme. Create the following entries in `~sshvpn/.ssh/config`:

```
Host vpn1
Hostname server.example.com
Port 9876
User pppme
```

These arguments will automatically be applied when we `ssh` to the vpn1 alias, as follows:

```
sshvpn@falcons-client$ ssh -v vpn1
debug: Reading configuration data /opt/ssh-vpn/.ssh/config
debug: Applying options for vpn1
debug: Connecting to server.example.com [XXX.XXX.XXX.XXX] port 9876.
....
```

Thus, we will create `.ssh/config` options for each VPN connection we need, allowing us to simply use `ssh vpnname` and have the options handled by `ssh` for us automatically.

VPN Scripts

Now that you know how to create a VPN manually, it's time to show you our scripts that will do most of the work for you. Here is a quick look at the necessary steps:

1. Install PPP.

2. Set up IP forwarding.

3. Set up the `sshvpn` users on both systems, including home directories.

4. Pick a VPN name (we'll use `vpn1`).

5. Pick an SSH protocol version, create your SSH identity on the client, and copy it to the server's `authorized_keys{2}`.

6. Set up `sudo` on both machines.

7. Set up `/etc/ppp/{pap,chap}-secrets` if desired.

8. Create an `sshd_config` for VPN purposes and start the `ssh` daemon if desired.

9. Establish passwordless login and verify the server's host key.

10. Set up an `ssh` host alias for `vpn1` via `~sshvpn/.ssh/config` on the client, such that `ssh vpn1` connects you to the remote system automatically.

11. Install the scripts `vpn-server` and `vpn-client` in `/opt/ssh-vpn/bin`.

12. Create a `symlink` to `vpn-server` or `vpn-client` in `/etc/init.d`.

13. Configure `pppd` to run our VPN scripts via `ip-up`.

14. Modify the `authorized_keys{2}` on the server file to force the `vpn-server` command.

15. Create our VPN configuration files.

16. Start the VPN.

We already discussed items 1 through 10 in this chapter. We will now look at the new configuration items.

Installing *vpn-server* and *vpn-client*

Two programs are needed for our VPN connection: `vpn-client` establishes the PPP connection to the server over SSH, and `vpn-server` accepts the connection. You can download these files from our web page at `www.buildinglinuxvpns.net/`. We'll install these in sshvpn's home directory as follows on both the client and the server:

```
falcons-client# mkdir /opt/ssh-vpn/bin;  chmod 755 /opt/ssh-vpn/bin
falcons-client# cp vpn-client /opt/ssh-vpn/bin; chmod 755 /opt/ssh-vpn/bin/*


bears-server# mkdir /opt/ssh-vpn/bin;  chmod 755 /opt/ssh-vpn/bin
bears-server# cp vpn-server /opt/ssh-vpn/bin; chmod 755 /opt/ssh-vpn/bin/*
```

We install these programs as root so that a compromise of the sshvpn account would not allow the files to be changed.

The `vpn-client` and `vpn-server` programs are seen here in Listings 3.1 and 3.2, respectively. Rather than typing them in, you should grab them from our web page because we will maintain the latest versions of these programs online.

Listing 3.1   **The *vpn-client* program.**

```sh
#!/bin/sh

# Change me to the appropriate location of
# your SSH VPN installation directory
SSH_VPN_DIR=/opt/ssh-vpn


# No changes should be necessary from here down.


vpn_config () {
        vpn_network=$1

     # Grab global variables
     . $SSH_VPN_DIR/etc/ssh-vpn.conf || exit 0

     # Grab vpn-specific variables
     VPN_CONFIG=$SSH_VPN_DIR/etc/$vpn_network
     . $VPN_CONFIG || exit 0

     if [ "$client_debug" = "yes" ] ; then
           set -x
           client_pppd_args="$client_pppd_args debug"
     fi
}

run_as_sshvpn () {
        whoami=`$WHOAMI`
        pwd=`pwd`
        case "$whoami" in
                root)           exec $SU - $SSH_VPN_USER "-ccd $pwd;$0 $*";
                                exit 0; ;;
                $SSH_VPN_USER)  ;;
                *)              echo "$0 Must be run as $SSH_VPN_USER" >&2;
                                exit 1; ;;
        esac
}

# Determine how we should behave:

if [ ! -z "$LINKNAME" ] ; then
        # We were called as the ip-up script from pppd

        vpn_config $LINKNAME

        # Configure our new route
        # sudo not needed -- we were run from pppd as root
```

continues

Listing 3.1   **Continued**

```
            # $IPREMOTE is set by pppd for us
            [ "$server_network" ] && $ROUTE add -net $server_network gw $IPREMOTE

            exit 0;

elif [ "$1" = "stop" ] ; then
            # We were invoked init.d style, as one of the following:
            # /etc/init.d/vpn-client stop vpn1
            # /etc/init.d/vpn1 stop
            # /etc/rcX.d/S##vpnname stop

            [ "$2" ]    && vpn_config "$2" \
                       || vpn_config `basename $0 ¦ sed -e 's/^[SK][0-9][0-9]//'`

            # Kill off the pppd and stunnel processes
            kill `head -1 $PIDDIR/ppp-$vpn_network.pid` 2>/dev/null
            exit 0;

elif [ "$1" = "start" ] ; then
        # started init.d style, similar to above.

            [ "$2" ]    && vpn_config "$2" \
                       || vpn_config `basename $0 | sed -e 's/^[SK][0-9][0-9]//'`

            run_as_sshvpn "$@"              # Make sure we're not root, etc.

            # Fall through to actual startup stuff.

elif [ $# -eq 1 ] ; then
            vpn_config $1
            run_as_sshvpn "$@"              # Make sure we're not root, etc.

        # Fall through to actual startup stuff.

else
            echo "Usage: $0 destination start¦stop" >&2
            echo "Usage: $0 start¦stop" >&2
            echo "Usage:      (if $0 is a vpn name)" >&2
            exit 1
fi


# Universal ssh arguments
#   (yes, that's two '-t' entries here)
SSH_ARGS="-oBatchMode=yes -enone -t -t"

# Universal pppd arguments
PPPD_ARGS="updetach lock connect-delay 10000 name $vpn_network-client \
      user $vpn_network-client linkname $vpn_network \
      remotename $vpn_network-server $client_pppd_args pty"
```

```
# Munge PPPD_ARGS for desired auth level
if [ "$client_require_pap" = "yes" ] ; then
        PPPD_ARGS="require-pap $PPPD_ARGS"
elif [ "$client_require_chap" = "yes" ] ; then
        PPPD_ARGS="require-chap $PPPD_ARGS"
else
        PPPD_ARGS="noauth $PPPD_ARGS"
fi


# Start our pppd/ssh processes
$SUDO $PPPD $PPPD_ARGS \
        "$SUDO -u $SSH_VPN_USER $SSH $SSH_ARGS $client_ssh_args $vpn_network"
```

Listing 3.2   **The *vpn-server* program.**

```
#!/bin/sh

# Change me to the appropriate location of
# your SSH VPN installation directory
SSH_VPN_DIR=/opt/ssh-vpn

# No changes should be necessary from here down.


vpn_config () {

        # Configure our VPN variables
        vpn_network=$1

        # Grab global variables
        . $SSH_VPN_DIR/etc/ssh-vpn.conf


        # Grab vpn-specific variables
        VPN_CONFIG=$SSH_VPN_DIR/etc/$vpn_network
        . $VPN_CONFIG || exit 0    # Make sure we're configured.  It could
                                   # be we were called from an ip-up
                                   # script when a different VPN was
                                   # created.  If so, simply exit.

        if [ "$server_debug" = "yes" ] ; then
                set -x
                server_pppd_args="$server_pppd_args debug"
        fi
}
```

continues

Listing 3.2 **Continued**

```
run_as_sshvpn () {
        whoami=`$WHOAMI`
        pwd=`pwd`
        case "$whoami" in
                root)           exec $SU - $SSH_VPN_USER "-ccd $pwd;$0 $*";
                                exit 0; ;;
                $SSH_VPN_USER)  ;;
                *)              echo "$0 Must be run as $SSH_VPN_USER" >&2;
                                exit 1; ;;
        esac
}

if [ "$LINKNAME" ] ; then
        # We were called as the ip-up script from pppd

        vpn_config $LINKNAME

        # Configure our new route
        # sudo not needed -- we were run from pppd as root
        # IPREMOTE set by pppd for us
        [ "$client_network" ] && $ROUTE add -net $client_network gw $IPREMOTE

        exit 0

elif [ "$1" = "pppd" ] ; then
        # We were called from the authorized_keys{2} file
        #    ala 'vpn-server pppd vpn1' as SSH_VPN_USER

        vpn_config $2

        # Universal pppd arguments
        PPPD_ARGS="updetach linkname $vpn_network \
                remotename $vpn_network-client user $vpn_network-server \
                name $vpn_network-server $server_pppd_args"

        if [ "$server_require_pap" = "yes" ] ; then
                PPPD_ARGS="require-pap $PPPD_ARGS"
        elif [ "$server_require_chap" = "yes" ] ; then
                PPPD_ARGS="require-chap $PPPD_ARGS"
        else
                PPPD_ARGS="noauth $PPPD_ARGS"
        fi

        # Launch pppd
        $SUDO $PPPD $PPPD_ARGS $server_ppp_ip:$client_ppp_ip

elif [ "$1" = "stop" ] ; then
        # We were invoked init.d style
```

```
            [ "$2" ]   && vpn_config "$2" \
                 || vpn_config `basename $0 | sed -e 's/^[SK][0-9][0-9]//'`


            # Kill off the pppd process
            kill `head -1 $PIDDIR/ppp-$vpn_network.pid` 2>/dev/null
        exit 0;

    elif [ "$1" = "start" ] ; then
            # We were invoked init.d style

            echo "You can't start an SSH-VPN connection from the server." >&2
            exit 1;

    else
            echo "Usage: $0 stop" >&2
            echo "" >&2
            echo "This program is meant to be called by sshd or to stop " >&2
            echo "an existing VPN.  It cannot be called manually." >&2
            exit 1
    fi
```

Linking to *vpn-{server,client}* in */etc/init.d*

Scripts used to start and stop system services are located in the /etc/init.d directory.
(On some Linux distributions, notably earlier Red Hat systems, they are kept in
/etc/rc.d/init.d instead). These scripts are usually linked from one of the
/etc/rcX.d directories to determine in which runlevel the service should be active.

Our scripts are designed to be able to run directly as one of these start/stop scripts,
so all we need to do is link to them. Let's say we want to have our VPN named vpn1
start in runlevel 2. We'd create the following symlink:

```
bears-server# ln -s /opt/ssh-vpn/bin/vpn-server /etc/rc2.d/S99vpn1
bears-server# ln -s /opt/ssh-vpn/bin/vpn-server /etc/init.d/vpn1

falcons-client# ln -s /opt/ssh-vpn/bin/vpn-client /etc/rc2.d/S99vpn1
falcons-client# ln -s /opt/ssh-vpn/bin/vpn-client /etc/init.d/vpn1
```

These commands set up our VPN to be started as the last program as runlevel 2 is
begun. You can change the 99 to be appropriate for your system. We'd also create a
generic init.d entry for ease of use.

Configuring *ip-up* to Run Our VPN Scripts

Immediately after a PPP connection is established, pppd will run the script
/etc/ppp/ip-up. We can use this fact to set up our routes automatically instead of
resorting to "sleep hacks" (in which you run a sleep 10 command after starting pppd

and before adding your routes, with the hope that everything completes in a timely manner) that are used in many publicly available VPN creation methods. pppd sets up various environment variables, such as `LINKNAME` and `IPREMOTE`, that make it easy for our VPN scripts to determine which VPN has just been established and to learn the necessary network parameters. Thus, we will have ip-up launch our vpn-server or vpn-client program automatically to set up the new routes.

pppd always calls /etc/ppp/ip-up, but the way this file works is radically different between Linux distributions. For some, it is not provided at all. Thus, we will cover a few methods you can use to point ip-up to our VPN scripts.

> **PPP Customizations**
>
> In the following examples, we assume that you have a default pppd installation. If you have created the PPP-related files that we assume are not around, our symlink solution will not work for you. Instead, append a line to your ip-up-related script that launches vpn-client or vpn-server manually.

Slackware: No *ip-up* Script

Slackware doesn't provide an ip-up script at all. Thus, we need to create one to point to our VPN scripts. The easiest way to do this is by using a symlink:

```
falcons-client# ln -s /opt/ssh-vpn/bin/vpn-client /etc/ppp/ip-up
```

or

```
bears-server# ln -s /opt/ssh-vpn/bin/vpn-server /etc/ppp/ip-up
```

Debian: */etc/ppp/ip-up.d*

The Debian ip-up script will automatically launch any scripts contained in the /etc/ppp/ip-up.d directory. Thus, we need only create a link to our VPN scripts in this directory, as follows:

```
falcons-client# ln -s /opt/ssh-vpn/bin/vpn-client /etc/ppp/ip-up.d/vpn-client
```

or

```
bears-server# ln -s /opt/ssh-vpn/bin/vpn-server /etc/ppp/ip-up.d/vpn-server
```

Red Hat: */etc/ppp/ip-up.local*

The ip-up script for Red Hat and other Red Hat–based distributions automatically launches /etc/ppp/ip-up.local after performing its own processing. All we need to do is create a symlink pointing to our VPN scripts named ip-up.local.

```
falcons-client# ln -s /opt/ssh-vpn/bin/vpn-client /etc/ppp/ip-up.local
```

or

```
bears-server# ln -s /opt/ssh-vpn/bin/vpn-server /etc/ppp/ip-up.local
```

Modifying *authorized_keys{2}*

We will place some restrictions on the use of the SSH identity supplied by the client by adding an initial options field to the `~sshvpn/.ssh/authorized_keys{2}` file. To simplify our programs, we will force the VPN server to automatically launch our `vpn-server` script. This also increases the security of the server because if the identity is somehow stolen, an attacker cannot log in to the server; he or she can only attempt to establish a VPN.

We will also set the environment variable `vpn_network` to the name (`vpn1`) that we have associated with this VPN. This variable will control several things:

- The local machine name and username used for (optional) PPP authentication, in this case `vpn1-server`
- The configuration file sourced by the `vpn-server` script, in this case `/opt/ssh-vpn/etc/vpn1`

You can include a `from` argument to restrict what machine(s) can try to establish this VPN. We'll also include all the restrictive `no-*-forwarding` options because these aren't necessary for our VPN, they add overhead, and they could be used potentially to circumvent security policies. So our example becomes the following:

```
from="client.example.com",command="/opt/ssh-vpn/bin/vpn-server pppd vpn1",no-port-
➥forwarding,no-X11-forwarding,no-agent-forwarding " 1024 35
➥12849455402044458154167142590652980977941666182144...
```

The only required pieces for our purposes are the command and option. Note that we are launching `vpn-server` with two arguments, `pppd` and the vpn name (`vpn1`). It will use these arguments to determine how it behaves. Without these, our SSH VPN scripts will not function.

Creating our Global VPN Configuration File

Both the `vpn-client` and `vpn-server` scripts will read the file `/opt/ssh-vpn/etc/ssh-vpn.conf`. This file is also located on our web page for easy download. Install it for both the client and server, as follows:

```
root# mkdir /opt/ssh-vpn/etc; chmod 755 /opt/ssh-vpn/etc
root# cp ssh-vpn.conf /opt/ssh-vpn/etc
root# chmod 644 /opt/ssh-vpn/etc/ssh-vpn.conf
```

This file contains the pathnames of external commands that might be needed:

```
# Location of programs.  These are probably fine
# for your system, but you should verify.
SU=/bin/su
```

```
SUDO=/usr/bin/sudo
PPPD=/usr/sbin/pppd
ROUTE=/sbin/route
SSH=/usr/bin/ssh
WHOAMI=/usr/bin/whoami

PIDDIR=/var/run
```

It also includes the variable SSH_VPN_USER. Set this to the name of the user who runs the vpn-client script on the client, sshvpn in our examples:

```
SSH_VPN_USER=sshvpn
```

The vpn-client program will initially verify that it is running as the correct user and will later use this value in the pty argument, as follows:

```
pty "$SUDO -u $SSH_VPN_USER $SSH ..."
```

Again, this is required because pppd is running as root via sudo, but we want the ssh connection in the pty command to run as the SSH_VPN_USER. Gosh, that's a mouthful.

Creating a VPN-Specific Configuration File

Our vpn-server and vpn-client programs are written to be able to establish any number of arbitrary VPN connections. These commands determine which VPN they should be creating by checking the program name and arguments. If two arguments are specified as in vpn-server start vpn1, the second argument is the VPN name. If invoked via a symlink such as /etc/init.d/vpn1 or /etc/rc2.d/S99vpn1, it will use the program name, stripping away any leading S## (or K##), again yielding the VPN name vpn1. In other words, the script tries to figure out what you want as intuitively as possible. On the server, it determines the VPN name via the command-line arguments we set via the command option in the authorized_keys{2} file.

Once the VPN name is determined, it will get its configuration variables from the file /opt/ssh-vpn/etc/*vpn_name*. Thus, for our VPN named vpn1, we would create the file /opt/ssh-vpn/etc/vpn1. Each variable in the configuration file begins with server_ or client_, meaning you can create one file with all the necessary values and share it between the systems, if you desire, without worry about conflicts. The variables shown in Table 3.3 are required.

Table 3.3   **Configuration File Variables**

Variable	Used By	Example	Explanation
client_network	server	192.168.1.0/24	The network on the VPN client. This is used by the VPN server to establish the route to the remote network via the route add command.
server_network	client	192.168.2.0/24	The network on the VPN server. This is used by the VPN client to establish the route to the remote network via the route add command.
server_ppp_ip	server	192.168.254.254	The IP address of the VPN server end of the PPP link. Make sure this address is not on a network available to either machine.
client_ppp_ip	server	192.168.254.253	The IP address of the VPN client end of the PPP link. Make sure this address is not on a network available to either machine.

The variables shown in Table 3.4 are optional.

Table 3.4   **Configuration File Optional Variables**

Variable	Used By	Example	Explanation
client_debug	client	yes	Add the debug option to pppd arguments and enable set -x for command-by-command output of the vpn-client script.
server_debug	server	yes	Add the debug option to pppd for more verbose logging.
client_ssh_args	client	-c 3des	Additional ssh arguments specific to this VPN.
client_pppd_args	client	usepeerdns	Additional command-line arguments for pppd that are specific to this VPN.
server_pppd_args	server	proxyarp	Additional command-line arguments for pppd that are specific to this VPN.

continues

Table 3.4 **Continued**

Variable	Used By	Example	Explanation
client_require_pap	client	yes	The VPN client will require PAP authentication of the server. Any value other than yes is equivalent to no.
server_require_pap	server	yes	The VPN server will require PAP authentication of the client. Any value other than yes is equivalent to no.
client_require_chap	client	yes	Same as client_require_pap but for the CHAP protocol.
server_require_chap	server	yes	Same as server_require_pap but for the CHAP protocol.

A sample configuration might look like the following:

```
# VPN1 Configuration File
# /opt/ssh-vpn/etc/vpn1

# The networks being connected on both sides, suitable for
# the 'route' command
client_network=192.168.2.0/24
server_network=192.168.1.0/24

# Do we need debugging information?
client_debug="no"
server_debug="yes"

# Pick different IPs for each VPN you need.
server_ppp_ip=192.168.254.254
client_ppp_ip=192.168.254.253

# Should we require PPP authentication?
client_require_pap="yes"
server_require_pap="yes"
client_require_chap="no"
server_require_chap="no"

# Need any non-standard pppd arguments?  Put them here.
#client_pppd_args="usepeerdns"
#server_pppd_args="proxyarp"

# Need any extra ssh arguments?  Put them here
#client_ssh_args="-C"
#server_ssh_args=""
```

You have two main methods of controlling your `ssh` command. The first is by creating entries in `~/.ssh/config`, as shown earlier in this chapter. You can alternatively (or additionally) place them in the `client_ssh_args` variable. This variable is a simple string placed immediately after the `$SSH` command is specified in the `pty` argument to `pppd`.

You can include options like `-l remoteusername` or `-p 9876`. You can also place any arbitrary option available in `~/.ssh/config`, but you must rewrite them slightly. For example, the command-line variant of the `~/.ssh/config` option `Hostname client.example.org` would be `-ohostname=client.example.org` when used on the command line.

We generally prefer to put all our `ssh` options in one location, either in `~/.ssh/config` or in the `/opt/ssh-vpn/etc/vpn_name` configuration files. This makes it much easier to see all the options at once.

Starting and Stopping the VPN

To start your VPN manually, you can simply run the following on the client:

```
falcons-client# /etc/init.d/vpn1 start
```

You can only start the VPN on the client because it is the machine that begins the SSH connection. To stop the VPN, you can run the following:

```
root# /etc/init.d/vpn1 stop
```

You can stop the VPN from the client or the server because all it does is kill the relevant `pppd` command. You can also start or stop the VPN by specifying the VPN name manually to the `vpn-server` or `vpn-client` program, for example:

```
bears-server# /opt/ssh-vpn/bin/vpn-server stop vpn1
falcons-client# /opt/ssh-vpn/bin/vpn-client start vpn1
```

Supporting Multiple VPNs

Our scripts are designed to support any number of VPN connections, and the number you initiate or sustain is limited only by the resources available (memory, processing power, number of processes, and so on) on the machines involved.

Each VPN must use its own distinct SSH identity. This is required because the server uses the client's SSH identity to set the VPN network name in the `authorized_keys{2}` file via the command option.

Let's say we want to create a second VPN connection named vpn2. In the identity creation phase, we would create a new SSH identity with `ssh-keygen` but include a filename argument, as follows:

```
sshvpn@falcons-client$ ssh-keygen -f /opt/ssh-vpn/.ssh/identity.vpn2 -t rsa1 -N ''
```

(Replace `-t rsa1` with `-t dsa` or `-t rsa` to create SSH2 keys.)

To force our `vpn-client` script to use this key instead of the default, add the following to `/opt/ssh-vpn/.ssh/config`:

```
Host vpn2
Identity /opt/ssh-vpn/.ssh/identity.vpn2
```

You could also add the following to the `vpn2` configuration file, `/opt/ssh-vpn/etc/vpn2`:

```
client_ssh_args="-i /opt/ssh-vpn/.ssh/identity.vpn2"
```

Troubleshooting

PPP over SSH is a tricky beast. The following sections discuss several helpful troubleshooting measures you might need when trying to get it working.

PPP Failures

If `pppd` is failing to properly set up a PPP connection, use the `debug` option on both ends to see why `pppd` is failing and then review your system logs.

If you're having trouble seeing debugging information, make sure you have `syslogd` configured to report all debugging messages. `pppd` is typically compiled to use the daemon facility, so make sure your `/etc/syslog.conf` has a line similar to `daemon.debug /var/log/messages`. You might instead want to use the logfile option to `pppd`.
If you're having PAP or CHAP authentication problems, consider using the `show-password` argument to `pppd` for additional debugging. You might want to turn off PAP or CHAP requirements until you verify that they are the source of the problem.

If your PPP connection is being established correctly but you're not getting routes added, make sure the scripts are being called from `ip-up` in an appropriate way for your Linux distribution. Also make sure you have values set for `client_network` and `server_network` in the VPN configuration file. To verify your syntax, you might want to try adding the route manually using the value you specified in those variables.

SSH Failures

Try to `ssh` manually from the client to the server (using the same arguments you intend to use for the VPN) and see if you can get in without a password. If set up properly, the remote end should automatically start `pppd`, and you should see the PPP handshake junk on your screen.

If you get the error `Aborted by user`, make sure you do not have `BatchMode` set for your SSH login until you have accepted and verified the server's host key.

Make sure you have placed the client pub key in the correct file: `~/.ssh/authorized_keys` for SSH1, `~/.ssh/authorized_keys2` for SSH2.

On the client, use the `-v` option to `ssh` to get verbose debugging information. On the server, check your system logs. Make sure you are logging all debugging messages via `syslogd`. OpenSSH typically uses the auth facility, so make sure your `/etc/syslog.conf` has a line similar to `auth.debug /var/log/messages`. Alternatively, you might try running `sshd` manually with the `-d` option to run in the foreground with debugging messages to your terminal.

If the SSH connection is not allowed, try specifying which SSH protocol version you want explicitly in the `~sshvpn/.ssh/config` or the `client_ssh_args` environment variable. Also make sure you're using an identity that is compatible with your protocol. It is a good idea to run the same version of OpenSSH on both machines because you will face fewer interoperability issues.

Networking Issues

If your PPP connection is established but you find that some or all IP packets aren't making it through, recheck for appropriate IP forwarding values in `/proc/sys/net/ipv4/ip_forward` and friends. Also check to see if you have any `ipchains` or `iptables` rules that could be blocking the packets. Use the `-l` option to the `ipchains`/`iptables` command to log denied packets and watch your system logs.

If you are having trouble looking up hostnames on the remote network, consider using the `usepeerdns` option to PPP, typically on the client.

Limitations

The VPN we created runs over SSH, which is a TCP protocol. TCP, the Transmission Control Protocol, is an IP protocol that automatically handles retransmission of any packets that were not received by the remote end. Thus TCP is a reliable protocol: Either a packet has made it to the other end and is acknowledged in a timely manner, or the connection is terminated after an arbitrary timeout period.

The use of TCP for our VPN has a drawback. We are encapsulating different IP protocols (TCP, UDP, ICMP) over this SSH connection. In particular, UDP (the User Datagram Protocol) is used for situations in which guaranteed delivery is not required, such as streaming protocols in which loss of a packet or two is not traumatic. However, when these UDP packets are sent over our TCP connection, their transmission is guaranteed, and a packet that normally might have been lost with no ill effect will instead be retransmitted. This can cause our VPN to be slower than necessary.

PPP was originally built only to handle IP protocols such as TCP, UDP, and ICMP. Thus, any non-IP protocol traffic would not be able to traverse the VPN. `pppd` does have support for IPX (Internet Packet eXchange, the protocol used by Novell NetWare), however. There are several IPX-related options to `pppd` that you might need to tweak to get it working correctly. Consult the `pppd(8)` manual page.

Summary

In this chapter, we have discussed all the pieces needed to successfully create a secure VPN using PPP and SSH. We have provided you with ready-to-use scripts that are both extensible and easy to use. However, even with these in hand, setting up a PPP/SSH VPN is a headache the first several times. You might find yourself suddenly troubleshooting the connection even though it had been working properly for months.

However, a VPN created by PPP over SSH is a tried-and-true method. The protocols are solid, are well defined, and—most importantly—are not in the state of flux that many other VPN technologies are in.

4

Building a VPN with SSL/TLS and PPP

MOST PEOPLE WHO HAVE WANTED TO USE PPP to establish a VPN have used SSH. This was partly due to the easy availability of SSH when VPNs were beginning to be created. PPP can be encapsulated in any secure protocol, and SSL certainly fits the bill. However, few people have tried this method.

When you finish this chapter, you'll be able to create a VPN using SSL/TLS and PPP either by hand or by using a set of scripts provided. We think you'll find it similar enough to PPP over SSH to be familiar and perhaps even less bulky and cleaner than using SSH.

PPP-over-SSL Overview

To understand the PPP-over-SSL/TLS implementation, we must first describe the two protocols involved.

PPP

PPP stands for the Point-to-Point Protocol. PPP is a derivation of the popular High Level Data Link Control (HDLC) (another layer 2 point-to-point protocol, commonly used on T1 lines) used to accomplish line control activities and encapsulate user data. PPP is most commonly used to establish a connection between modems over phone lines, such as when dialing up an ISP. Most Linux distributions come with tools such as `wvdial` or `xisp` that let you establish modem connections without fiddling with the underlying PPP commands and configurations. PPP, however, is not restricted to physical connections only; PPP connections can be established between any hosts that have network connectivity. Our goal will be to establish a PPP connection between different machines on the Internet, which we will use to establish a VPN.

To run `pppd`, the PPP protocol daemon, you must have a kernel that supports it. PPP is often compiled as a module that you can query with the command `lsmod`. If so, it should load automatically when needed. Most Linux distributions build their kernels with PPP support, so this should not be an issue.

Most Linux distributions also come with precompiled versions of PPP that you can install. Thus, you likely will not need to compile and install `pppd` yourself. However, for reasons that are discussed later, we suggest `pppd` version 2.3.7 or later.

The focus of PPP has never been on the privacy of the transmitted data, and as a direct result, it relies on external encryption methods to address this need. The risks of PPP data interception on phone lines are limited to line taps or a physical presence at either end of the PPP link. However, because we want to use PPP to establish a network connection by sending the traffic over the Internet, we must tunnel this PPP connection inside an encryption layer.

SSL/TLS

The secure sockets layer (SSL) protocol was created to allow secure network communications. SSL uses strong encryption to protect clear-text protocols by encapsulating them—literally wrapping them inside a secure crypto layer. The encapsulated protocol, such as HTTP, POP, or NNTP, doesn't need to know anything about cryptography. In fact, it doesn't even need to know that it's being securely transmitted via SSL. All of the encryption and decryption is done transparently by the SSL layer.

SSL provides more than just an encryption layer to plain text transmissions. It also can provide authentication of the endpoints involved in the communication. It does this by checking certificates, which will be discussed later.

SSL is most commonly used to protect HTTP (Hypertext Transfer Protocol) transmissions, and this is the purpose for which it was originally created. However, SSL is also commonly used to protect mail protocols such as POP and IMAP. Versions of the SSL-protected protocols usually take on a new name and port number. When encrypted with SSL, HTTP became HTTPS on port 443, POP3 became POP3S on port 995, and IMAP became IMAPS on port 993, for example. There are SSL versions of many other protocols such as TELNET, FTP, IRC, LDAP, and more.

When Not to Use SSL

If you want to have a secure login or file transfer method, we strongly suggest using SSH, the Secure Shell protocol. OpenSSH, an implementation of the SSH protocol by the OpenBSD development team, is available on most UNIX-like operating systems and comes with most Linux distributions now. Though you can tunnel TELNET, FTP, RCP, and friends through SSL, using OpenSSH will save you the headache of reinventing the wheel—and for this purpose, OpenSSH is a very stable wheel.

SSL/TLS History

SSL was created by Netscape Communications. The initial protocol design, SSL version 1.0, was completed in July of 1994 but was not released. SSL version 2.0 was released in December of 1994 and was included in the Netscape Navigator browser. SSLv2 was found to have some flaws, the most notable of which was the capability for an attacker to trick the endpoints into using weak encryption even when higher grade ciphers were supported.

Netscape released SSL version 3.0, which corrected these flaws, in November of 1995. It also included a number of enhancements such as supporting additional cipher algorithms, decoupling the authentication and encryption keys, allowing cipher renegotiation, and increasing the speed of the protocol.

In January of 1999, SSLv3 was used as the basis of the Transport Layer Security (TLS) protocol, a specification defined in RFC-2246. TLS includes all the functionality of SSLv3, but it does so in a way that is redefined enough to not be compatible with the older SSLv3 protocol. However, the TLS specification defines how software can transparently fall back to SSLv3 when the remote end does not speak TLS. Thus, when we refer to SSL/TLS, we mean the TLS protocol and its automatic capability to fall back to SSLv3 when needed.

SSL/TLS Authentication

SSL/TLS has built in support for host authentication. This authentication is done in a way that ensures that an attacker cannot read or manipulate the data being transmitted and that the endpoints are the ones you expect. This authentication is not mandatory but obviously is a good idea.

For a server or client to be authenticated, it must have two things. The first is a public/private-key pair, which is an RSA or DSA key. The second is a certificate, which is a signed version of the public RSA or DSA key. This certificate is essentially a piece of data that says "I, the signer, promise that this key pair belongs to the owner." The certificates used in SSL/TLS are X509 structures, and for our purposes, you don't need to know what that actually means.

In a standard SSL/TLS transaction, the client will always authenticate the server's certificate; however, the converse might not be true. HTTPS transactions, for example, seldom require the client (the web browser) to have a certificate for authentication. To make sure that we are requiring the highest level of security, we will require certificate validation of both the server and the client. Certificates can be signed in a variety of ways, however, and it is up to us to determine what sort of certificate we will choose to use. There are two main certificate signing methods: third-party certificates and self-signed certificates.

Third-Party Certificates

The most widely used type of certificate is one in which the administrator has its public key signed by a trusted third party. These third parties are called Certificate Authorities (CAs.)

Your web browser contains a long list of public CAs. When connecting to a web site, the certificate presented by the server is checked; if the public key of the server is signed by one of these trusted Cas, the connection is allowed. If the certificate is not correctly signed by one of the acceptable CAs, a warning dialog box is usually presented, and you are asked if you want to continue anyway.

These CAs are usually large companies (such as Thawte or Equifax) that verify that the company requesting a certificate has a right to the certificate requested. This is accomplished out-of-band through various means such as verifying your company information in databases or verifying your phone numbers and addresses, the ownership of your domain name, and other things for which they charge you a lot of money. After they have determined that you are legitimate, they will sign your public key and return this certificate to you.

Public CAs Aren't Perfect

Even given this level of paranoia, public CAs don't always get it right. For example, Verisign issued two Microsoft certificates in January of 2001 to someone not affiliated with Microsoft at all and didn't notice until six weeks later. During that time, the person who received the certificate could have used it to pose as Microsoft when serving web pages or signing software, for example.

Getting a third-party certificate requires time (generally a week or two) and the hassle of filling out information. It also requires money. A standard web site certificate costs about $350.

For our purposes, there's no reason why we can't simply use self-signed certificates and save ourselves the trouble and cost of third-party certificates.

Self-Signed Certificates

Any public/private key can create a certificate. There isn't anything special about the CA keys except for the fact that they are preinstalled in your web browser.

A common method to avoid getting an "official" certificate from one of the CAs is to have your key signed by itself. This is called a self-signed certificate.

In our VPN setup, we will be creating a public/private-key pair for our client and server and will generate self-signed certificates for each. The client will authenticate the server by checking a local copy of the server's certificate and vice versa.

If we were to use a third-party signed certificate, we would install a local copy of the CA key on each host instead of a copy of the self-signed certificate. As long as you verify the integrity of the self-signed certificates when you install them, there is really no security difference between using a self-signed certificate and a third-party certificate in this instance, and we'll choose the faster and cheaper route.

What If You Already Have Your Own CA?

If you have your own CA in house, you might want to sign all the VPN keys with this CA instead of using self-signed certificates. If this is the case, you already have the knowledge that will let you create and manage the certificates, and we're surprised you're reading this section at all.

Establishing an SSL/TLS Connection

All SSL/TLS connections begin with a handshake that allows the two machines to communicate securely. In a nutshell, the SSL/TLS handshake looks like this:

The client initiates the connection request with a "client hello" packet. The server then responds with a "server hello." These hello messages establish the SSL/TLS protocol version, the cipher suites they support, and a bit of random data. The server then sends the client its certificate, and the client verifies it. If desired, the server will request a certificate from the client and verify it as well.

The two machines then use the *changecipher spec* (an SSL component process independent of the Handshake Protocol) to finalize the ciphers to be used for this session and to agree on a key to use. This key is protected from prying eyes by encrypting it with the peer's public key.

Having verified the authenticity of the remote end, agreed on an encryption cipher, and securely communicated the key to be used, the SSL/TLS negotiation is complete, and each end indicates success. At this point, the actual application data is sent encapsulated in the SSL/TLS connection.

This was a brief overview of the SSL/TLS setup. If you want the nitty-gritty of SSL/TLS, read RFC-2246 and the SSL specification located at `http://home.netscape.com/eng/ssl3/`. Believe it or not, the entire handshake can take place in only four packets.

So, when encapsulating a protocol (for example HTTP) inside SSL/TLS, the connection looks like this:

1. The client connects to the server on port 443 (HTTPS).

2. The client and server negotiate and enable SSL/TLS.

3. HTTP begins over the encrypted connection.

Our Sample Network

The theory is simple: Establish an SSL/TLS connection from the VPN client to the VPN server and have PPP daemons run on both ends that talk to each other to create our VPN. We will create a VPN between the hosts Bears (the VPN server) and Falcons (the VPN client), as seen in Figure 4.1.

Both Bears and Falcons have networks behind them that are to be connected securely. The dotted line designates the virtual network created between the two hosts.

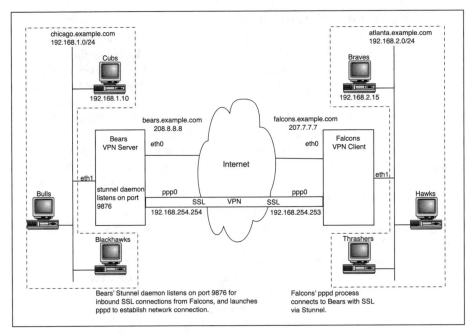

Figure 4.1 Our VPN network.

Setting up PPP over SSL/TLS Manually

To begin, we will show you the various pieces involved by creating a VPN between two hosts manually. This will lay the groundwork for what we do in our later scripts and will help teach you what is going on. This will aid in debugging the connection if necessary.

Installing and Verifying PPP

First, determine that ppp is installed on both your VPN client and VPN server. On a Debian or other dpkg-based system, you would type the following:

```
root@debian# dpkg -l ppp |grep ppp
ii  ppp         2.3.11-1.4    Point-to-Point Protocol (PPP) daemon.
```

On a Red Hat or other rpm-based system, you would type the following:

```
root@redhat# rpm -q ppp
ppp-2.3.11-4
```

Make sure that the version of ppp you have installed is 2.3.7 or greater because that is the first version that supports the pty argument necessary for setting up a pty automatically.

Enabling IP Forwarding

Most Linux distributions do not allow IP packet forwarding by default, but we must enable this to route VPN packets through the PPP interface. You can change the status of IP forwarding by modifying the appropriate kernel parameter. Though it is possible to recompile your kernel to change the default settings, the easiest way is to use the /proc file system. Files in /proc are not actually files but ways of accessing and/or modifying kernel parameters, and you must be root to change these. Thus, the simplest way to turn on port forwarding is to run the following command:

```
root# echo 1 > /proc/sys/net/ipv4/ip_forward
```

This automatically turns on IP packet forwarding on all interfaces by default. If you are making a host-host VPN, this is sufficient. If you want to create a network-network or host-network VPN, you might want to turn on IP forwarding for only those interfaces that you explicitly want to forward. For an example of how you can do this, see the section "Enabling IP Forwarding" in Chapter 3, "Building a VPN with SSH and PPP."

Creating the VPN Users

Next, you must create the user that will be running the VPN commands on both ends. We will assume you use the username sslvpn on both ends, though you can use any username you want. Although the usernames don't have to be the same on both machines, it does make things easier. For example, you might create the user as follows:

```
root# groupadd sslvpn
root# useradd -m -d /opt/ssl-vpn -c "SSL VPN User" -g sslvpn sslvpn
```

A sample /etc/shadow entry might look like this:

```
sslvpn:!:11429:0:99999:7:::
```

The useradd program creates users with a locked password by default, ensuring that no one can log in to this account. The only way in which these accounts can be accessed for now is by using /bin/su as root. The home directory we use for this user is traditionally /opt/ssl-vpn.

Although we could have created the home directory in /home, this user is going to be used more like a software product. Thus, installing in /opt (or /usr and so on) seems more in line with its function. So, hereafter we will use /opt/ssl-vpn, though you can use anything you want.

Naming Conventions

To keep our two hosts straight, we will call the machine that establishes the VPN the VPN client and call the other machine the VPN server. The VPN client will establish an SSL connection to the VPN server.

We must also come up with a name for our VPN. For our examples, we will use vpn1. Our scripts can establish more than one VPN at a time, and this name helps differentiate them.

Creating Your Keys and Certificates

We want to have our SSL connection authenticated at both ends, thus ensuring that the endpoints are legitimate. To do so, we must create keys and certificates for both our client and server. We will have our VPN server require peer certificate authentication on both ends, which is not the default for SSL connections.

Because we are striving for laziness, we will create keys that are self-signed. To generate our keys, we must create an OpenSSL configuration file. One is already provided for you in the Stunnel distribution, called stunnel.cnf. You can either use this file or create one of your own. The following is the configuration file we normally use:

```
[ req ]
default_bits = 1024
encrypt_key = yes
distinguished_name = req_dn
x509_extensions = cert_type

[ req_dn ]
countryName                       = Country Name (2 letter code)
countryName_default               = US

stateOrProvinceName               = State or Province Name (full name)
stateOrProvinceName_default       = IL

localityName                      = Locality Name (eg, city)
localityName_default              = Chicago

0.organizationName                = Organization Name (eg, company)
0.organizationName_default        = Building Linux VPNs

0.commonName                      = Common Name (FQDN of your server)
0.commonName_default              = fictitious.example.com

[ cert_type ]
nsCertType = server
```

We will need to put our keys and certificates in specific directories for Stunnel to find them. To make it possible to have multiple VPNs with different keys and certificates available, we will create a directory named /opt/ssl-vpn/etc/*vpnname*/ (replacing *vpnname* with your actual VPN name), where we will store these files. Because the OpenSSL configuration file is the same regardless of the VPN we are using, save the file previously shown as /opt/ssl-vpn/etc/sslvpn.cnf.

To create our key and sign it in one simple command, we will run the following:

```
bears-server$ cd /opt/ssl-vpn/etc/vpn1
bears-server$ openssl req -new -x509 -days 365 -nodes \
         -config /opt/ssl-vpn/etc/sslvpn.cnf \
         -out server.pem -keyout server.pem
```

On the client, we will run:

```
falcons-client$ cd /opt/ssl-vpn/etc/vpn1
falcons-client$ openssl req -new -x509 -days 365 -nodes \
         -config /opt/ssl-vpn/etc/sslvpn.cnf \
         -out client.pem -keyout client.pem
```

The openssl arguments used mean the following:

req -new -x509	Generate a new SSL private key and self-signed certificate.
-days 365	This certificate is good for one year. Change this value as desired.
-nodes	Do not encrypt the private key with a pass phrase.
-config ...	The path to the OpenSSL configuration file.
-out ...	The file in which to save the certificate.
-keyout ...	The file in which to save the private key.

Generating Keys Without a Pass Phrase

We would like our VPN to be able to connect without the need for administrator assistance, such as from a start script at bootup, a cron job, and so on. To do so, our SSL private might not be protected by a pass phrase, so we use the -nodes option when creating the key. If you prefer to have this extra level of security and don't mind manually starting the connection, leave this option out. You will need to specify a pass phrase when generating your key and when starting your VPN.

The openssl program will take some time to generate the private key and will then ask you to fill in the certificate information such as your location and organization. To pick something other than the default, type in the value you want. To accept a default, just press Enter.

Is All That Info Relevant?

Stunnel doesn't care about the actual data you specify. Thus, you could just use the same data on both ends. We will see later, however, that this information is used by Stunnel to look up the certificate, so you should ensure that both client and server certificates are generated with unique information. It doesn't need to be accurate information, but it does need to be different for each certificate.

```
Using configuration from ./stunnel.cnf
Generating a 1024 bit RSA private key
............++++++
```

```
.........++++++
writing new private key to 'stunnel.pem'
. . . . .
```

You are about to be asked to enter information that will be incorporated
into your certificate request.
What you are about to enter is what is called a Distinguisted Name or a DN.
There are quite a few fields but you can leave some blank.
For some fields there will be a default value,
If you enter '.', the field will be left blank.
```
. . . . .
```
```
Country Name (2 letter code) [US]:
State or Province Name (full name) [IL]:
Locality Name (eg, city) [Chicago]:
Organization Name (eg, company) [Building Linux VPNs]:
Common Name (FQDN of your server) [fictitious.example.com]:
```

The Common Name Field

SSL browsers require the Common Name (CN) field of the certificate to match the fully qualified domain
of the server. Thus, if a machine connects to www.example.com, the CN must have www.example.com
as well. Stunnel does not have this requirement and will simply check the certificate presented by the
peer against a list of valid certificates locally installed.

Our key and certificate have now been created as `server.pem` or `client.pem` as appropriate. This is saved in Privacy Enhanced Mail (PEM) format, a pure text representa-
tion (base64 encoded) of the numeric data. There are other formats you can generate
with OpenSSL, but `stunnel` only supports PEM format. The file itself will look something like this:

```
-----BEGIN RSA PRIVATE KEY-----
MIICXQIBAAKBgQClhlHLkMcLKcUG10CZFNF6X7kBc2GJWU7IoVaG2/ptNAfAYjZ7
....
xIwjVVHLFTqBhtRHbt1gijQ+CfJpJ+Al1ZKpnKrz+LCE
-----END RSA PRIVATE KEY-----
-----BEGIN CERTIFICATE-----
MIICYTCCAcqgAwIBAgIBADANBgkqhkiG9w0BAQQFADBrMQswCQYDVQQGEwJVUzEL
....
B0BctMgv4T1/82uVUsdwzjNmJHoWiDkXD4JR+EoI1joBvLBVYA==
-----END CERTIFICATE-----
```

The first section is the private key, and the second section is the certificate. Stunnel
requires that these be in the same file. To see the information associated with the certificate, run the following command:

```
bears-server$ openssl x509 -subject -issuer -dates -fingerprint
              -noout -in server.pem
subject=/C=US/ST=IL/L=Chicago/O=Building Linux VPNs/CN=fictitious.example.com
issuer= /C=US/ST=IL/L=Chicago/O=Building Linux VPNs/CN=fictitious.example.com
notBefore=Sep 17 00:00:00 2001 GMT
notAfter=Sep 17 00:00:00 2002 GMT
MD5 Fingerprint=74:8C:A2:B8:63:A6:FB:BA:7B:24:33:CD:9F:A0:19:C5
```

Using Third-Party Certificates

If you prefer to use third-party certificates, you should instead generate your keys using the following command:

```
bears-server$ openssl req -newkey -x509 -days 365 -nodes \
    -config /opt/ssl-vpn/etc/sslvpn.cnf \
    -keyout server.pem
```

Only a private key will be saved in `server.pem`. A certificate request will be output to the screen, and you should have this signed by your Certificate Authority. Usually this involves pasting a copy of the certificate request into the CA's order form. When you receive their certificate, append it to the `server.pem` file and you're ready to go. Use the same method to generate the client.pem file as we proceed.

The last thing to do is to make a copy of our certificate without the private key. Though you can simply cut and paste the certificate from the `{server,client}.pem` file, it's quicker to use `openssl` to do this for you:

```
bears-server$ openssl x509 -in server.pem -out server.cert
falcons-client$ openssl x509 -in client.pem -out client.cert
```

These files now contain only the certificate and do not contain the private key information. Because we created our private keys without any pass phrase, it is imperative to keep them on the local machine only.

Installing the Certificates

We must now copy the certificate of the server to the client for use in verification and vice versa. Our directories currently look like this:

```
bears-server$ ls /opt/ssl-vpn/etc/vpn1
server.cert server.pem

falcons-client$ ls /opt/ssl-vpn/etc/vpn1
client.cert client.pem
```

Copy the `cert` files to the other machine in whatever method you prefer—be it `scp`, `sftp`, cut and paste, or `ftp` if you're feeling lucky. This makes our directories look as follows:

```
bears-server$ ls /opt/ssl-vpn/etc/vpn1
client.cert server.cert server.pem

falcons-client$ ls /opt/ssl-vpn/etc/vpn1
client.cert client.pem server.cert
```

Because the security of our VPN is based on the verification of these certificates, you should check and make sure they were transferred correctly. You can visually compare them if you are extremely paranoid. However, it's probably easiest to just do a quick comparison of checksums:

```
bears-server$ md5sum /opt/ssl-vpn/etc/vpn1/client.cert
      3c97f5840b4a0068fe3a03ca5c7a5d56
falcons-client$ md5sum /opt/ssl-vpn/etc/vpn1/client.cert
      3c97f5840b4a0068fe3a03ca5c7a5d56
```

The md5sum generates a checksum of the contents of the file. If the files are identical, the result (the number that begins with 3c97f58 ...) will be the same. Make sure to verify both the client and server cert on both machines.

When Stunnel gets the certificate from the remote end during its SSL handshake, it will attempt to verify it by looking in this directory for a local copy of the certificate. It will take a hash of the certificate, which generates a hexadecimal eight-character string such as 1c40c052. Stunnel will then open a file named *hash*.0 in this directory and compare its contents to the certificate presented by the peer. If they match, the remote end has been authenticated. If not, the connection will be dropped.

To determine the hash value of a certificate, we again turn to the openssl binary:

```
falcons-client$ openssl x509 -hash -noout -in server.cert
1c40c052
```

So, with the preceding example, the client needs to have a file named 1c40c052.0 that contains the server certificate. We find that it's easiest to create symlinks for the hash filenames, making it easier to see exactly which files are which. Thus, we can run the following to generate the links for us automatically:

```
falcons-client$ ln -s server.cert `openssl x509 -hash -noout -in server.cert`.0
bears-server$ ln -s client.cert `openssl x509 -hash -noout -in client.cert`.0
```

As our last step, let's make sure everything is readable only by sslvpn by running the following commands on both hosts:

```
$ chmod 400 *
```

At this point, our directories now look as follows:

```
bears-server$ ls /opt/ssl-vpn/etc/vpn1
-r--------  1 sslvpn   sslvpn     1762 Jul  3 10:43 client.pem
lrwxrwxrwx  1 sslvpn   sslvpn       11 Jul  3 10:45 de40764b.0 ->
client.cert
-r--------  1 sslvpn   sslvpn      887 Jul  3 10:44 server.cert
-r--------  1 sslvpn   sslvpn     1774 Jul  3 10:42 server.pem

falcons-client$ ls /opt/ssl-vpn/etc/vpn1
lrwxrwxrwx  1 sslvpn   sslvpn       11 Jul  3 10:45 1c40c052.0 ->
server.cert
-r--------  1 sslvpn   sslvpn      887 Jul  3 10:44 client.cert
-r--------  1 sslvpn   sslvpn     1762 Jul  3 10:43 client.pem
-r--------  1 sslvpn   sslvpn     1774 Jul  3 10:42 server.cert
```

Testing our Certificate Verification

Before we proceed to make a PPP connection between the two hosts, we'll first verify that our certificates were properly installed and that the two hosts are communicating properly. We'll run an `Stunnel` server on the server that simply prints out the /etc/passwd file by running the following command:

```
bears-server$ stunnel -D7 -f -a /opt/ssl-vpn/etc/vpn1 -v3 -S0
              -p /opt/ssl-vpn/etc/vpn1/server.pem \-d 9871
              -L /bin/cat cat /etc/passwd
falcons-client$ stunnel -D7 -f -a /opt/ssl-vpn/etc/vpn1 -v3 -S0
              -p /opt/ssl-vpn/etc/vpn1/client.pem \-c
              -r server:9871
```

The arguments used are described in Table 4.1. Not all of the arguments in the table were used in the preceding example.

Table 4.1   **Common Options**

Argument	Description
ARGUMENTS FOR EITHER CLIENT OR SERVER	
-D7	Show all debugging information.
-f	Stay in the foreground. This makes sure logging info goes to our terminal instead of `syslog` and keeps the server from forking off and going into the background.
-a dir	The directory in which certificates can be found.
-v3	Require a certificate of the peer and match it against certificates in the `-a` directory.
-p file	Location of the PEM (private key and certificate) file.
-S0	Verify certificates using the sources (`-a dir`) specified only. `Stunnel` will also check various OpenSSL default certificate verification sources unless this option is specified. This can make troubleshooting more difficult and might lead to successful authentication when the connection is not actually legitimate.
-P *file*	Write the PID of the `Stunnel` process into the specified file.
-N *name*	Use *name* as the TCP wrapper service name when checking /etc/hosts.{allow,deny}.
ARGUMENTS SPECIFIC TO THE SERVER	
-d *portnum*	Listen on this port for incoming connections.
-L *prag arg [arg...]*	Run the program listed. Note that the first argument should (usually) be the same as the program name itself. Thus, if calling /usr/bin/perl, the first argument should be `perl`.
ARGUMENTS SPECIFIC TO THE CLIENT	
-c	Run `Stunnel` in client mode.
-r *machine:port*	Connect to the machine on the port specified.

If your connection is successful, you will see a great deal of debugging info in both the client and server windows. In the client window, you will also see a copy of the server's /etc/passwd file in the middle of the Stunnel debug messages.

In both the server and client output, you should see lines similar to the following:

```
LOG5[19001:1024]: VERIFY OK: depth=0: /C=US/ST=IL/L=Chicago/O=Building Linux
    VPNs/CN=fictitious.example.com
```

This line indicates that the peer's certificate was verified successfully. If you have set up your certificates incorrectly, you will instead see an error like the following:

```
LOG4[19006:1024]: VERIFY ERROR: depth=0 error=self signed certificate:
    /C=US/ST=IL/L=Chicago/O=Building Linux VPNs/CN=fictitious.example.com
    LOG3[19006:1024]: SSL_connect: error:14090086:SSL
    routines:SSL3_GET_SERVER_CERTIFICATE:certificate verify failed
```

If you get either of the following two errors, make sure you have specified the correct server hostname and port number on the client.

```
SSL_connect: error:1408F10B:SSL routines:SSL3_GET_RECORD:wrong version number:

remote connect: Connection refused (111)
```

You can always verify that the server is listening and reachable on the desired port by telneting manually:

```
falcons-client$ telnet server 9871
Trying XXX.YYY.XXX.YYY...
Connected to server.example.com
Escape character is '^]'.
```

If you are not connected, either you have specified the wrong host and port, or you have other elements preventing the communication, such as a firewall access restriction or a routing problem.

Setting Up *Sudo*

The pppd program, which is used to establish the network link between our VPN hosts, can only be run by the root user. Because we want to run our VPN scripts on both ends as a dummy user, we will need a way to gain root privileges to run this program.

Sudo is a versatile program that allows users to run a restricted set of commands as root. We will be creating a very simple set of rules that will enable us to run the pppd command.

Sudo can be found at www.courtesan.com/sudo/. It is included with many Linux distributions as well, so you might not need to compile it yourself.

After Sudo is installed, run the visudo command to edit the /etc/sudoers file. Do not edit this file manually (without using visudo) or you run the risk of corrupting it! Add the following lines to the end of the file:

```
Cmnd_Alias SSLVPN=/usr/sbin/pppd
sshlvpn     ALL=NOPASSWD: SSLVPN
```

Replace the path for /usr/sbin/pppd if it is in a different location for your system. Also replace sslvpn in the second line with the dummy user you have created for the VPN if you picked something different. When finished, simply write your changes and exit your editor.

The preceding lines will allow the sslvpn user to run the command /usr/sbin/pppd with any arguments desired. Because of the NOPASSWD entry, the user will not be required to enter his or her password before being granted access to these programs.

Because we need these commands to be executed automatically from our scripts, it would be impossible to enter a password. To test this briefly, simply type the following on both the client and server machine:

```
root@machine# su - sslvpn
sslvpn@machine$ sudo /usr/sbin/pppd noauth
~ÿ}#À!}!}!} }4}"}&} } } } }%} (more gobeldygook continues....)
```

The funny characters are the result of pppd attempting to handshake with your terminal. Jump to another window and run killall -HUP pppd to stop the pppd process.

If you have not set up the sudoers file correctly, you will be asked to enter your password. Verify your syntax in the sudoers file. Again, make sure you are using the visudo program and not editing /etc/sudoers manually.

Setting Up PPP

We will need to run pppd on both the server and the client. pppd accepts a very long list of options. We will only need a small subset of them to create our VPN. Refer to Table 3.1 in the preceding chapter for the list of commands we will be using to control how our PPP connections are established.

Not Requiring PPP Authentication

PPP is usually used for creating a network connection between hosts over a modem and almost always requires user authentication to the server before establishing the connection. We will discuss how you can enable PPP peer authentication later in this chapter when we present our ready-to-go VPN scripts. For now, however, we will want to eliminate that variable and allow SSL to do all our authentication for us. Thus, for now, we will not be using any of the require-pap, require-chap, name, remotename, or user arguments.

Establishing a Manual PPP Connection

We now have all the pieces we need to establish a PPP connection over SSL:

- Stunnels on both sides that can perform certificate authentication.
- Sudo is set up to enable us to run pppd as root.

So let's start up the `Stunnel` process on the server, as follows:

```
bears-server$ stunnel -v3 -a /opt/ssl-vpn/etc/vpn1 -v3 \
    -p /opt/ssl-vpn/etc/vpn1/server.pem -f -D7 \
    -d 9871 -L sudo pppd pppd debug noauth 192.168.254.254:192.168.254.253
```

This starts up an `Stunnel` process with the appropriate certificate authentication options, which will listen on port 9871. We start it in the foreground to make it easier to see what's going on and to enable lots of debugging info. When the client connects, the process will open a `tty` and launch `pppd`.

On the client, we will run `pppd` as follows:

```
falcons-client$ sudo pppd updetach debug noauth pty \
   "sudo -u sslvpn stunnel -v3 -a/opt/ssl-vpn/etc/vpn1 -S0 \
    -f -D7 -p/opt/ssl-vpn/etc/vpn1/client.pem \
    -c -r server:9871 "
```

This command starts up `pppd` as root, which will launch the command specified after the `pty` argument. This command will run `Stunnel` as `sslvpn` (there's no reason to run it as root) with the appropriate certificate verification options and connect to the server on port 9871.

If all goes well, when you run `pppd` on the client, it will communicate with the server via `Stunnel`. The server will automatically run `pppd` from its `Stunnel` daemon, and the two `pppd` processes will talk happily.

On the client, you will see a good deal of `Stunnel` debug output followed by `pppd` debug output, ending finally with the listing of the two IP addresses of this connection:

```
LOG7[16830:1024]: SSL negotiation finished successfully
LOG6[16830:1024]: server.9871 opened with SSLv3, cipher DES-CBC3-SHA (168 bits)
sent [IPCP ConfReq id=0x2 <addr 192.168.254.253> <compress VJ 0f 01>]
rcvd [CCP ConfAck id=0x1 <deflate 15> <deflate(old#) 15> <bsd v1 15>]
Deflate (15) compression enabled
rcvd [IPCP ConfAck id=0x2 <addr 192.168.254.253> <compress VJ 0f 01>]
local  IP address 192.168.254.253
remote IP address 192.168.254.254
```

Testing the Connection

At this point, you should be able to ping 192.168.254.254 and 192.168.254.253 from both the client and server:

```
machine$ ping 192.168.254.253
PING 192.168.254.253 (192.168.254.253): 56 data bytes
64 bytes from 192.168.254.253: icmp_seq=0 ttl=255 time=10.7 ms
64 bytes from 192.168.254.253: icmp_seq=1 ttl=255 time=11.7 ms
...
```

You should also be able to look at the interface information:

```
bears-server$ ifconfig ppp0
ppp0      Link encap:Point-to-Point Protocol
          192.168.254.254  P-t-P:192.168.254.253  Mask:255.255.255.255
```

```
UP POINTOPOINT RUNNING NOARP MULTICAST  MTU:1500  Metric:1
RX packets:33 errors:0 dropped:0 overruns:0 frame:0
TX packets:36 errors:0 dropped:0 overruns:0 carrier:0
collisions:0 txqueuelen:10
```

Note that the IP addresses listed match those we specified in the pppd command line.

Adjusting Your Routing Table

The last step is to set up the route tables on both client and server to tunnel the appropriate data over the PPP link:

```
sslvpn@falcons-client$ sudo route add -net 192.168.1.0/24 gw 192.168.254.254
```

```
sslvpn@bears-server$ sudo route add -net 192.168.2.0/24 gw 192.168.254.253
```

At this point, you should be able to ping from one network to the other at will. Here we show an example of a machine, cubs, behind the VPN server bears:

```
user@cubs-192.168.1.10$ ping braves.atlanta.example.com
PING braves.atlanta.example.com (192.168.2.15) 56 data bytes
64 bytes from 192.168.2.15 icmp_seq=0 ttl=255 time=13.4 ms
64 bytes from 192.168.2.15 icmp_seq=1 ttl=255 time=12.5 ms
...
```

Note that for this to work, all the machines behind the VPN machines must have their VPN machine as their default gateway, as seen here:

```
user@cubs-192.168.1.10$ netstat -rn
Kernel IP routing table
Destination     Gateway          Genmask          Flags   MSS Window  irtt Iface
192.168.1.0     0.0.0.0          255.255.255.0    U         0 0          0 eth0
127.0.0.0       0.0.0.0          255.0.0.0        U         0 0          0 lo
0.0.0.0         192.168.1.1      0.0.0.0          UG        0 0          0 eth0

user@braves-192.168.2.15$ netstat -rn
Kernel IP routing table
Destination     Gateway          Genmask          Flags   MSS Window  irtt Iface
192.168.2.0     0.0.0.0          255.255.255.0    U         0 0          0 eth0
127.0.0.0       0.0.0.0          255.0.0.0        U         0 0          0 lo
0.0.0.0         192.168.2.1      0.0.0.0          UG        0 0          0 eth0
```

Increasing the Security of Your VPN

You can do several things to enhance the security of your VPN connection, particularly in the area of authentication. If you have followed the procedures previously outlined, these enhancements are not necessary for a secure VPN. However, adding additional requirements can't hurt.

Requiring PPP Authentication

Now that we have verified that we can create a VPN between our hosts, you can beef up the security of your VPN by requiring that the two pppd processes authenticate each other. You would normally use this option if you were not already requiring authentication of the endpoints using SSL certificates because it's a bit redundant. However, it does add one additional layer of authentication, which can be helpful should an SSL private key be discovered by an attacker. (And if the attacker somehow snagged your SSL private key, you would likely have other security concerns to address.) We showed you how to implement PPP authentication in Chapter 3, and you can gauge your own circumstances for applicability. We tend to use it as part of a defense-in-depth approach.

Specifying Cipher Suites

SSL/TLS supports many different encryption ciphers. The server and client will negotiate the strongest cipher they have in common automatically. OpenSSL creates a default list of ciphers in the preferred order when it is installed. To see this list, use the `openssl` command as follows:

```
$ openssl ciphers
EDH-RSA-DES-CBC3-SHA:EDH-DSS-DES-CBC3-SHA:DES-CBC3-SHA:DES-CBC3-MD5:DHE-DSS-RC4-
SHA:IDEA-CBC-SHA:RC4-SHA:RC4-MD5:IDEA-CBC-MD5:RC2-CBC-MD5:RC4-MD5:RC4-64-
MD5:EXP1024-DHE-DSS-RC4-SHA:EXP1024-RC4-SHA:EXP1024-DHE-DSS-DES-CBC-SHA:EXP1024-DE
S-CBC-SHA:EXP1024-RC2-CBC-MD5:EXP1024-RC4-MD5:EDH-RSA-DES-CBC-SHA:EDH-DSS-DES-CBC-
SHA:DES-CBC-SHA:DES-CBC-MD5:EXP-EDH-RSA-DES-CBC-SHA:EXP-EDH-DSS-DES-CBC-SHA:EXP-
DES-CBC-SHA:EXP-RC2-CBC-MD5:EXP-RC4-MD5:EXP-RC2-CBC-MD5:EXP-RC4-MD5
```

As you can see, the list of ciphers is extremely long and somewhat cryptic. However, for the security of your VPN, you might want to limit the ciphers you support by selecting only the strongest ciphers. This list can be created easily by running `openssl` as follows:

```
$ openssl ciphers HIGH
EDH-RSA-DES-CBC3-SHA:EDH-DSS-DES-CBC3-SHA:DES-CBC3-SHA:DES-CBC3-MD5
```

If you want more verbose output about each cipher, you can supply `-v` as well:

```
$ openssl ciphers -v HIGH
EDH-RSA-DES-CBC3-SHA    SSLv3 Kx=DH      Au=RSA   Enc=3DES(168) Mac=SHA1
EDH-DSS-DES-CBC3-SHA    SSLv3 Kx=DH      Au=DSS   Enc=3DES(168) Mac=SHA1
DES-CBC3-SHA            SSLv3 Kx=RSA     Au=RSA   Enc=3DES(168) Mac=SHA1
DES-CBC3-MD5            SSLv2 Kx=RSA     Au=RSA   Enc=3DES(168) Mac=MD5
```

To require a particular set of ciphers, use the `-C` *cipherlist* argument to `Stunnel`, as follows:

```
stunnel ... -C EDH-DSS-DES-CBC3-SHA:DES-CBC3-SHA ...
```

This will instruct `Stunnel` to only allow one of the specified ciphers to be negotiated. You only need to specify this option on one of the two ends of the SSL connection.

Because cryptographic strength usage is federally regulated and is prone to change depending on the political situation of the day, you will want to check into the current U.S. export law before choosing your ciphers. Depending on the vertical industry your company is in and whether or not you are connecting to branch offices or subsidiaries, U.S. laws might restrict you to using an "exportable" cipher (read: easy to crack) on your international links. See the `ciphers(1)` OpenSSL man page for a list of different cipher strengths (such as 'HIGH' and 'EXPORT') that can be listed.

IDENT Checking

`Stunnel` has the capability to query the user on the remote end of the connection. This is handled by using the IDENT protocol, which is described in RFC 1413.

For this to work, the other end of the connection must be running the `identd` daemon, which is often off by default. By querying the `identd` daemon, we can verify that the remote end running `Stunnel` is running with the username we expect. To enforce this requirement, simply add -u *username* to the `stunnel` arguments (for example, -u sslvpn).

One problem is that the `identd` server might not respond with the actual username. For privacy reasons, it might respond with a user ID or other unique but cryptic piece of information. Thus, the easiest way to determine what you should put in the *username* field is to establish a connection and query `identd` manually.

Start up your sslvpn without any -u *username* (option). Once connected, determine which ports are in use for the connection. We assume you're using port 9871 as in the
example.

```
falcons-client$ netstat -nat |grep 9871
tcp  0  0 client:4725   server:9871   ESTABLISHED
```

This shows that the VPN client has established its connection from port 4725 to the server on port 9871. We then query the IDENT daemon on the server as follows:

```
falcons-client$ telnet server ident
Trying server...
Connected to server.
Escape character is '^]'.
9871,4725
9871, 4725 : USERID : OTHER :sslvpn
quit
```

IDENT vs AUTH

If your machine does not recognize ident as a port name, try using auth, which is the older name for this protocol. You alternatively use the port number, 113, explicitly.

The server indicates that the user associated with this port is sslvpn. The output might be different for you depending on how your `identd` daemon is configured. To require `identd` restrictions, add -u sslvpn to the `Stunnel` arguments on the client.

`identd` verification can be enabled on the server as well. Follow the same logic as before, but switch the order of the ports when connecting to the `identd` server with `telnet`.

identd verification is not a terribly important requirement for VPN security—an attacker could supply any IDENTD results desired—but it is an extra precaution you can enable for paranoid environments.

VPN Scripts

As you can see, setting up a secure VPN with Stunnel and PPP involves many steps. In an effort to make it simpler, we now present the scripts we use to create such tunnels easily. First, here is the complete checklist you will need to follow to get your Stunnel/PPP VPN up and running:

1. Install PPP.
2. Set up IP forwarding.
3. Set up the sslvpn users on both systems, including home directories.
4. Pick a VPN name (we'll use vpn1).
5. Create your SSL keys and certificate on the client and server.
6. Distribute the certificates to both hosts and create the *hash*.0 symlink.
7. Set up sudo on both machines.
8. Set up PPP authentication via /etc/ppp/{pap,chap}-secrets, if desired.
9. Install the scripts vpn-server and vpn-client in /opt/ssl-vpn/bin.
10. Create a symlink to vpn-client or vpn-server in /etc/init.d.
11. Configure pppd to run our VPN scripts via ip-up.
12. Create our VPN configuration files.
13. Start the VPN.

We already discussed items 1 through 8 in this chapter, so refer to the appropriate sections to set them up.

Installing *vpn-server* and *vpn-client*

Two programs are needed for our VPN connection: vpn-client establishes the PPP connection to the server over Stunnel, and vpn-server launches an Stunnel daemon ready to run its own copy of pppd. You can download these files from our web page at http://www.buildinglinuxvpns.net/. We'll install these in sslvpn's home directory as follows on both the client and the server:

```
falcons-client# mkdir /opt/ssl-vpn/bin; chmod 755 /opt/ssl-vpn/bin
falcons-client# cp vpn-client /opt/ssl-vpn/bin; chmod 755 /opt/ssl-vpn/bin/*

bears-server# mkdir /opt/ssl-vpn/bin; chmod 755 /opt/ssl-vpn/bin
bears-server# cp vpn-server /opt/ssl-vpn/bin; chmod 755 /opt/ssl-vpn/bin/*
```

We install these programs as root so that a compromise of the sslvpn account would not allow the files to be changed.

The vpn-client and vpn-server programs are seen here in Listings 4.1 and 4.2, respectively. Rather than typing them in, you should grab them from our web page because we will maintain the latest versions of these programs online.

Listing 4.1   **The *vpn-client* program.**

```
#!/bin/sh -x

# Change me to the appropriate location of
# your SSL VPN installation directory
SSL_VPN_DIR=/opt/ssl-vpn

# No changes should be necessary from here down.

vpn_config () {
        vpn_network=$1

        # Grab global variables
        . $SSL_VPN_DIR/etc/ssl-vpn.conf || exit 0

        # Grab vpn-specific variables
        VPN_ETC=$SSL_VPN_DIR/etc/$vpn_network
        . $VPN_ETC/config || exit 0
}

run_as_sslvpn () {
        whoami=`$WHOAMI`
        case "$whoami" in
                root)       exec su - $SSL_VPN_USER "-c$0 $*"; exit 0; ;;
                $SSL_VPN_USER)   ;;
                *)          echo "$0 Must be run as $SSL_VPN_USER" >&2;
                            exit 1; ;;
        esac
}

if [ ! -z "$LINKNAME" -a $# -eq 0 ] ; then
        # We were called as the ip-up script from pppd

        vpn_config $LINKNAME

        # Configure our new route
        # sudo not needed -- we were run from pppd as root
        # $IPREMOTE is set by pppd for us
        [ "$server_network" ] && $ROUTE add -net $server_network gw $IPREMOTE

        exit 0;

elif [ "$1" = "stop" ] ; then
        # We were invoked init.d style, as one of the following:
        # /etc/init.d/vpn-client stop vpn1
```

continues

Listing 4.1 **Continued**

```
            # /etc/init.d/vpn1 stop
            # /etc/rcX.d/S##vpnname stop


            [ "$2" ]   && vpn_config "$2" \
                    || vpn_config `basename $0 | sed -e 's/^[SK][0-9][0-9]//'`

            echo "$$: Stopped from init.d" >>/tmp/debug

            # Kill off the pppd and stunnel processes
            kill `head -1 $PIDDIR/ppp-$vpn_network.pid` 2>/dev/null
            kill `$PIDDIR/stunnel.$vpn_network.pid` 2>/dev/null
            exit 0;

elif [ "$1" = "start" ] ; then
            # started init.d style, similar to above.

            [ "$2" ]   && vpn_config "$2" \
                    || vpn_config `basename $0 | sed -e 's/^[SK][0-9][0-9]//'`

            run_as_sslvpn "$@"              # Make sure we're not root, etc.

            # Fall through to actual startup

elif [ $# -eq 1 ] ; then
            echo "$$: Being pppd " >>/tmp/debug

            vpn_config $1
            run_as_sslvpn "$@"                 # Make sure we're not root, etc.
else
            echo "Usage: $0 destination start|stop" >&2
            echo "Usage: $0 start|stop" >&2
            echo "Usage:      (if $0 is a vpn name)" >&2
            exit 1
fi


if [ "$client_debug" = "yes" ] ; then
            set -x
            client_pppd_args="$client_pppd_args debug"
            stunnel_debug="-D7"
fi


# Universal Stunnel args
STUNNEL_ARGS="$stunnel_debug -P $PIDDIR/stunnel.$vpn_network.pid \
            -N $vpn_network \ -p $VPN_ETC/client.pem -a $VPN_ETC \
            -v 3 -S 0 -f -c $client_stunnel_args \
            -r $server:$server_stunnel_port"
```

```
# Universal pppd arguments
PPPD_ARGS="updetach lock connect-delay 10000 name $vpn_network-client \
      user $vpn_network-client linkname $vpn_network \
      remotename $vpn_network-server $client_pppd_args pty"

# Munge PPPD_ARGS for desired auth level
if [ "$client_require_pap" = "yes" ] ; then
      PPPD_ARGS="require-pap $PPPD_ARGS"
elif [ "$client_require_chap" = "yes" ] ; then
      PPPD_ARGS="require-chap $PPPD_ARGS"
else
      PPPD_ARGS="noauth $PPPD_ARGS"
fi

# Start our Pppd/Stunnel processes
$SUDO $PPPD $PPPD_ARGS \
      "$SUDO -u $SSL_VPN_USER $STUNNEL $STUNNEL_ARGS"
```

Listing 4.2   **The *vpn-server* program.**

```
#!/bin/sh -x


# Change this to wherever you've installed this software
SSL_VPN_DIR=/opt/ssl-vpn

# Ok, no more changes needed from here down.


vpn_config () {
      # Configure our VPN variables
      vpn_network=$1

      # Grab global variables
      . $SSL_VPN_DIR/etc/ssl-vpn.conf

      # Grab vpn-specific variables
      VPN_ETC=$SSL_VPN_DIR/etc/$vpn_network
      . $VPN_ETC/config || exit 0      # Make sure we're configured.  It could
                                       # be we were called from an ip-up
                                       # script when a different VPN was
                                       # created.  If so, simply exit.

      if [ "$server_debug" = "yes" ] ; then
            set -x
            server_pppd_args="$server_pppd_args debug"
```

continues

Listing 4.2 **Continued**

```
                stunnel_debug="-D7"
        fi
}


run_as_sslvpn () {
        whoami=`$WHOAMI`
        pwd=`pwd`
        case "$whoami" in
                root)       exec su - $SSL_VPN_USER "-ccd $pwd;$0 $*";
                            exit 0; ;;
                $SSL_VPN_USER)     ;;
                *)          echo "$0 Must be run as $SSL_VPN_USER" >&2;
                            exit 1; ;;
        esac
}


# Determine how we should behave:

if [ "$LINKNAME" ] ; then
        # We were called as the ip-up script from pppd

        vpn_config $LINKNAME

        # Configure our new route
        # sudo not needed -- we were run from pppd as root
        # IPREMOTE set by pppd for us
        [ "$client_network" ] && $ROUTE add -net $client_network gw $IPREMOTE

        exit 0

elif [ "$1" = "pppd" ] ; then
        # We were called from Stunnel ala 'vpn-server pppd vpn1' as SSL_VPN_USER

        vpn_config $2

        # Universal pppd arguments
        PPPD_ARGS="updetach linkname $vpn_network \
            remotename $vpn_network-client user $vpn_network-server \
            name $vpn_network-server $server_pppd_args"

        if [ "$server_require_pap" = "yes" ] ; then
            PPPD_ARGS="require-pap $PPPD_ARGS"
        elif [ "$server_require_chap" = "yes" ] ; then
            PPPD_ARGS="require-chap $PPPD_ARGS"
        else
            PPPD_ARGS="noauth $PPPD_ARGS"
        fi
```

```
        # We've been called from Stunnel -- launch pppd
        $SUDO $PPPD $PPPD_ARGS $server_ppp_ip:$client_ppp_ip
        exit 0

elif [ "$1" = "stop" ] ; then
        # We were invoked init.d style

        [ "$2" ]    && vpn_config "$2" \
                    || vpn_config `basename $0 | sed -e 's/^[SK][0-9][0-9]//'`


        # Kill off the pppd and stunnel processes
        kill `head -1 $PIDDIR/pppd-$vpn_network.pid` 2>/dev/null
        kill `cat $PIDDIR/stunnel.$vpn_network.pid` 2>/dev/null
        exit 0;

elif [ "$1" = "start" ] ; then
        # We were invoked init.d style


        [ "$2" ]    && vpn_config "$2" \
                || vpn_config `basename $0 | sed -e 's/^[SK][0-9][0-9]//'`


        run_as_sslvpn "$@"      # Make sure we're not root, etc.

elif [ $# -eq 1 ] ; then
        # argument is the vpn name - start it

        vpn_config $1
        run_as_sslvpn "$@"

else
        echo "Usage: $0 {vpn_name|start|stop}" >&2
        exit 1
fi



# Ok, we've got our variables set up, time to do the
# real work, depending on how we were called.

$STUNNEL -p $VPN_ETC/server.pem -N $vpn_network \
     -P $PIDDIR/stunnel.$vpn_network.pid \
     -d $server_stunnel_port $stunnel_debug $server_stunnel_args \
     -L $0 $vpn_network pppd $vpn_network

exit 0;
```

Linking to *vpn-{server,client}* in */etc/init.d*

Scripts used to start and stop system services are located in the /etc/init.d directory. (On some Linux distributions, notably earlier Red Hat systems, they are kept in /etc/rc.d/init.d instead). These scripts are usually linked from one of the /etc/rcX.d directories to determine in which runlevel the service should be active.

Our scripts are designed to be able to run directly as one of these start/stop scripts, so all we need to do is link to them. Let's say we want to have our VPN named vpn1 start in runlevel 2. We'd create the following symlink:

```
bears-server# ln -s /opt/ssl-vpn/bin/vpn-server /etc/rc2.d/S99vpn1
bears-server# ln -s /opt/ssl-vpn/bin/vpn-server /etc/init.d/vpn1

falcons-client# ln -s /opt/ssl-vpn/bin/vpn-client /etc/rc2.d/S99vpn1
falcons-client# ln -s /opt/ssl-vpn/bin/vpn-client /etc/init.d/vpn1
```

These commands set up our VPN to be started as the last program as runlevel 2 is begun. You can change the 99 to be appropriate for your system. We'd also create a generic init.d entry for ease of use.

Configuring *ip-up* to Run Our VPN Scripts

When a PPP connection is established, pppd will run the script /etc/ppp/ip-up. In the preceding chapter, we showed you how to create symlinks that ip-up will use to call our vpn-server or vpn-client program to set up routes.

See the section "Configuring ip-up to Run Our VPN Scripts" in Chapter 3 for details of how this works. If you just want to cut to the chase, here are the appropriate commands for some popular distributions:

Slackware:

```
falcons-client# ln -s /opt/ssl-vpn/bin/vpn-client /etc/ppp/ip-up
bears-server# ln -s /opt/ssl-vpn/bin/vpn-server /etc/ppp/ip-up
```

Debian:

```
falcons-client# ln -s /opt/ssl-vpn/bin/vpn-client /etc/ppp/ip-up.d/vpn-client
bears-server# ln -s /opt/ssl-vpn/bin/vpn-server /etc/ppp/ip-up.d/vpn-server
```

Red Hat:

```
falcons-client# ln -s /opt/ssl-vpn/bin/vpn-client /etc/ppp/ip-up.local
bears-server# ln -s /opt/ssl-vpn/bin/vpn-server /etc/ppp/ip-up.local
```

Creating Our Global VPN Configuration File

Both the vpn-client and vpn-server scripts will read the file /opt/ssl-vpn/etc/ssl-vpn.conf. This file is also located on our web page for easy download. Install it for both the client and server, as follows:

```
root# mkdir /opt/ssl-vpn/etc; chmod 755 /opt/ssl-vpn/etc
root# cp ssl-vpn.conf /opt/ssl-vpn/etc
root# chmod 644 /opt/ssl-vpn/etc/ssl-vpn.conf
```

This file contains the path names of external programs that might be needed:

```
# Location of programs.  These are probably fine
# for your system, but you should verify.
SU=/bin/su
SUDO=/usr/bin/sudo
PPPD=/usr/sbin/pppd
ROUTE=/sbin/route
STUNNEL=/usr/bin/stunnel
WHOAMI=//bin/whoami

PIDDIR=/var/run
```

It also includes the variable SSL_VPN_USER. Set this to the name of the user who runs the vpn-client script on the client, sslvpn in our examples:

```
SSL_VPN_USER=sslvpn
```

The vpn-client program will initially verify that it is running as the correct user and will later use this value in the pty argument, as follows:

```
pty "$SUDO -u $SSL_VPN_USER $STUNNEL ..."
```

Again, this is required because pppd is running as root via sudo, but we want the SSL connection in the pty command to run as the SSL_VPN_USER. Got it? Whew!

Creating a VPN–Specific Configuration File

Our vpn-server and vpn-client programs are written to be able to establish any number of arbitrary VPN connections. These commands determine which VPN they should be creating by checking the program name and arguments. If two arguments are specified as in vpn-server start vpn1, the second argument is the VPN name. If invoked via a symlink such as /etc/init.d/vpn1 or /etc/rcX.d/S99vpn1, it will use the program name, stripping away any leading S## (or K##), again yielding the VPN name vpn1. In other words, the script tries to figure out what you want as intuitively as possible.

Once the VPN name is determined, it will get its configuration variables from the file /opt/ssl-vpn/etc/*vpn_name*/config.

Thus, for our VPN named vpn1, we would create the file /opt/ssl-vpn/etc/vpn1/config. Each variable in the configuration file begins with server_ or client_, meaning you can create one file with all the necessary values and share it between the systems, if you desire, without worry about conflicts. The variables shown in Table 4.2 are the most important.

Table 4.2 **Configuration File Variables**

Variable	Used By	Example	Explanation
client_network	server	192.168.1.0/24	The network on the VPN client. This is used by the VPN server to establish the route to the remote network via the `route add` command. If not set, the client is assumed to be a host, not a gateway, and no route is added.
server_network	client	192.168.2.0/24	The network on the VPN server. This is used by the VPN client to establish the route to the remote network via the `route add` command. If not set, the server is assumed to be a host, not a gateway, and no route is added.
server_ppp_ip	server	192.168.254.254	The IP address of the VPN server end of the PPP link. Make sure this address is not on a network available to either machine.
client_ppp_ip	server	192.168.254.253	The IP address of the VPN client end of the PPP link. Make sure this address is not on a network available to either machine.
server_stunnel port	both	9871	The port `Stunnel` should bind on the server and to which the client should connect.
OPTIONAL VARIABLES			
client_debug	client	yes	Add the `debug` option to `pppd` arguments, add `-D7` to `stunnel` arguments, and enable `set -x` for command-by-command output of the `vpn-client` script.
server_debug	server	yes	Same as `client_debug` on the server side.
client_stunnel_args	client	-u sslvpn	Additional `Stunnel` arguments for the client.

Variable	Used By	Example	Explanation
server_stunnel_args	client	-C DES-CBC3-SHA	Additional Stunnel arguments for the server.
client_pppd_args	client	usepeerdns	Additional command-line arguments for pppd that are specific to this VPN.
server_pppd_args	server	proxyarp	Additional command-line arguments for pppd that are specific to this VPN.
client_require_pap	client	yes	The VPN client will require PAP authentication of the server. Any value other than yes is equivalent to no.
server_require_pap	server	yes	The VPN server will require PAP authentication of the client. Any value other than yes is equivalent to no.
client_require_chap	client	yes	Same as client_require_pap but for the CHAP protocol.
server_require_chap	server	yes	Same as server_require_pap but for the CHAP protocol.

A sample configuration might look like the following:

```
# VPN1 Configuration File
# /opt/ssl-vpn/etc/vpn1

# The networks being connected on both sides, suitable for
# the 'route' command
client_network=192.168.2.0/24
server_network=192.168.1.0/24

# Do we need debugging information?
client_debug="yes"
server_debug="yes"

# Pick different IPs for each VPN you need.
server_ppp_ip=192.168.254.254
client_ppp_ip=192.168.254.253

# Should we require PPP authentication?
client_require_pap="no"
server_require_pap="no"
client_require_chap="yes"
server_require_chap="yes"
```

```
# Need any non-standard pppd arguments?  Put them here.
#client_pppd_args="usepeerdns"
#server_pppd_args="proxyarp"

# Need any extra stunnel arguments?  Put them here
#client_stunnel_args="-C HIGH"
#server_stunnel_args=""
```

Starting and Stopping the VPN

To start your VPN manually, you can simply run the following commands:

```
bears-server# /etc/init.d/vpn1 start
falcons-client# /etc/init.d/vpn1 start
```

You must run the start command on the server first so that the Stunnel daemon is ready to accept the connection from the client. To stop the VPN, you can use the stop argument on either host:

```
root# /etc/init.d/vpn1 stop
```

This will kill the VPN connection. If you terminate the VPN on the client, the Stunnel process will still be running on the server, waiting for new VPN connections, and you can reestablish a VPN at any time. If you terminate the VPN on the server, the Stunnel process will also be killed, and you must start it again if you want to accept new connections.

You can also start or stop the VPN by specifying the VPN name to the vpn-server or vpn-client program manually, as follows:

```
bears-server# /opt/ssl-vpn/bin/vpn-server start vpn1
falcons-client# /opt/ssl-vpn/bin/vpn-client start vpn1
```

Supporting Multiple VPNs

Our scripts make it easy to support more than one VPN on your machines. You are only limited by the resources available (memory, processing power, number of processes, and so on) on the machines involved. Each VPN must have its own VPN name associated with it, such as vpn1, chicago_office, or reegen_laptop. You must then create the same /etc/init.d or /etc/rcX.d/ links to the vpn-server or vpn-client scripts as appropriate and create the configuration files (/opt/ssl-vpn/etc/*vpn_name*/config) for each VPN. These files will likely be the same except for the network information and Stunnel port.

Current versions of Stunnel do not export any information about the certificate presented by the peer. Contrast this with our SSH VPN in the preceding chapter, where we were able to call vpn-server with different arguments using identity entries in authorized_keys{2}. Because we cannot have an Stunnel daemon distinguish one incoming connection from another, we must run one Stunnel daemon per VPN we want to support. So when creating your VPN configuration files, make sure you have separate `server_stunnel_port` values for each VPN.

Troubleshooting

As with PPP over SSH, PPP over SSL/TLS can require some troubleshooting. The following sections cover the common issues you might run into.

PPP and Networking Problems

Creating a PPP connection is troublesome to set up in the best of cases. See the sections "PPP Failures" and "Networking Issues" in Chapter 3 for a list of common PPP and networking problems and solutions.

Stunnel Issues

Getting your `Stunnel` processes to communicate should be a straightforward process, but several common problems can keep you from properly establishing an TLS/SSL connection.

Certificate Verification Errors

If `Stunnel` is unable to verify the peer certificate, it will log entries such as the following:

```
VERIFY ERROR: depth=0 error=self signed certificate:
  /C=US/ST=IL/CN=server.example.com
  SSL_connect: error:14090086:SSL      routines:SSL3_GET_SERVER_CERTIFICATE:
  certificate verify failed
```

You should first verify that you copied the certificate correctly to the other machine and that you created the *hash.0* file correctly. Aside from checking the certificate file visually—a thorough but boring approach to the task—you could check the information and fingerprint by comparing output of the following commands:

```
bears-server$ openssl x509 -hash -fingerprint -subject -noout -in certfile

falcons-client$ openssl x509 -hash -fingerprint -subject -noout -in certfile
```

Verify that the hash file has been correctly created:

```
falcons-client$ ls /opt/ssl-vpn/etc/vpn1/hash.0
```

where *hash* is the value from `openssl x509 -hash -noout -in certfile`.

If you get a `VERIFY ERROR` that is not followed by a `certificate verify failed` error, such as the following:

```
VERIFY ERROR: depth=0 error=self signed certificate:
  /C=US/ST=IL/CN=server.example.com
  SSL_connect: error:0D08707B:asn1 encoding routines:d2i_ASN1_UTCTIME:invalid
  time format
```

Your certificate is properly linked via *hash*.0, but the certificate is not properly formed. This usually indicates that the file was corrupted in transport somehow, and you should reupload the certificate.

No Shared Ciphers

Unless your server and client both can agree on a cipher to use, you will not be able to establish an SSL connection. This is logged with a message like the following:

```
SSL_accept: error:1408A0C1:SSL routines:SSL3_GET_CLIENT_HELLO:no shared cipher
```

This is most common if you have manually specified a list of ciphers on both machines that is not compatible. Try removing any `-C ciphers` arguments and testing the connection again. If it works, make sure you pick your ciphers more carefully. If it doesn't work, either `Stunnel` or OpenSSL was not compiled correctly. Recompile and install OpenSSL and `Stunnel` from scratch, making sure you use the same version of each package on both machines.

Limitations

Our PPP-over-SSL/TLS VPN suffers from the same problems as our PPP-over-SSH VPN in the preceding chapter. Briefly, SSL/TLS is a TCP protocol, which is a reliable protocol (lost packets are retransmitted until received.) The problem occurs when we want to send UDP or other nonreliable packets across the VPN. Whereas normally we accept that some packets will be lost and design our applications around that fact (for example, streaming media), when tunneled over a reliable transport mechanism like TCP, we needlessly guarantee that all these packets will be transmitted and received.

For more details about this problem, see the "Limitations" section in Chapter 3.

Summary

This chapter discussed all the pieces you need to successfully create a secure VPN using PPP and `Stunnel`. We have provided you with ready-to-use scripts that are both extensible and easy to use.

If you have attempted a PPP-over-SSH VPN in the past, you might find that a PPP-over-SSL/TLS connection is easier to set up and maintain. Because we have custom daemons on both ends, it is a relatively clean solution: We do not rely on an existing SSH daemon, our host authentication with certificates is more straightforward than the combination of SSH identities and host keys, and there is less "manual editing" of files all around.

If you want to implement a "PPP-over-crypto" VPN, we would suggest you try a PPP-over-`Stunnel` VPN because of its more straightforward setup.

5

IPSec

IPSEC IS AN IETF CONCEPT ENCOMPASSING a set of protocols designed to protect IP traffic. IPSec has become a de facto standard for the majority of commercial VPN solutions as well as many open-source ones. If your VPN solution uses IPSec, it is important for you to understand how it works.

This chapter is not intended to be yet another summary of IPSec RFCs. Instead, it will focus on helping you understand how IPSec works. It will also explain important data structures, but only to the extent necessary for you to better understand IPSec. If you need more information, see RFCs 2401–2412.

IPSec Architecture, Components, and Concepts

IPSec stands for *IP security*. It adds protection to IP packets. Both IPv4 and IPv6 are supported. (For IPv6, IPSec is mandatory.) As of today, IPSec functionality is deployed on a number of operating systems. For instance, FreeS/WAN is an open-source IPSec implementation for Linux (see Chapter 6, "FreeS/WAN"); KAME is a free IPSec implementation for ⋆BSD (FreeBSD, BSDI, NetBSD, and OpenBSD). The following sections will describe the basic concepts, components, and functioning of IPSec.

How IPSec Works

We will introduce you to IPSec using two examples that show IPSec in action. The examples are somewhat generalized, but they should at least give you the basic ideas needed to understand IPSec.

The first example shows how an *outbound* IP packet is processed. The second example explains how an *inbound* IP packet is processed. If you see terms you are not familiar with, just try to understand the main idea. We will provide additional details following this section.

Outbound Traffic

When your system (say, 192.168.1.1) needs to send an IP packet out to the network and you have IPSec turned on, the IPSec kernel module will see the packet and will need to decide what to do with it. It can drop the packet, let it go through without applying IPSec protection, or protect the packet using IPSec.

To determine exactly what to do with the outbound packet, IPSec checks its Security Policy Database (SPD) defined by a system administrator. The database contains rules that tell IPSec what to do with packets. Table 5.1 shows an example of an SPD containing three rules:

Table 5.1   **An Example of an SPD**

Rule #	Src IP	Dst IP	Src Port	Dst Port	Action	IPSec Protocol*	Mode*	Outbound SA Index
1	192.168.1.1	192.168.2.1	Any	80	IPSec	AH	Tunnel	400
2	192.168.1.23	192.168.2.5	Any	22	Accept	——	——	8500
3	192.168.1.99	192.168.2.1	Any	Any	IPSec	ESP	Transport	6025

These two fields can be omitted because they are present in the Security Association (SA) to which this SPD refers.

According to the preceding SPD, if you are sending a packet to 192.168.2.1 with any source port and a destination port of 80, rule 1 will be applied. The rule says that the matching packet should be protected using the Authentication Header (AH) IPSec protocol that adds authentication, integrity protection, and replay protection but does not provide confidentiality (which is to say that it does not encrypt the data).

Then next thing the IPSec module needs to do is determine what specific parameters should be used to protect the packet (keys, sequence numbers for replay protection, and so on). These parameters are defined in the Security Association(s) (SA[s]) that points to a matching SPD entry. In our example, the SA number 400 will be used.

You can set SAs up *manually* on all peers. However, if you have a large network, manual setups can be a problem. SAs can also be negotiated *automatically* between your computer and the IPSec hosts with which it interacts. For instance, in our case, the SA for 192.168.2.1 was automatically negotiated by the IPSec IKE daemon by talking to 192.168.2.1.

Inbound Traffic

To illustrate, let's assume that an IPSec-protected packet has just arrived from 192.168.1.23. The IPSec module will not check the SPD immediately because the inbound traffic processing is different. Instead, the first thing the IPSec module will try to do is determine the inbound Security Association for the packet.

The SA is found in the SA database on the receiving host using the following triple:

1. Security Parameters Index (SPI)

2. Destination IP address

3. IPSec Data Manipulation Protocol (AH or ESP)

The three pieces of information shown here are obtained from the header of the received packet. The Security Parameters Index is just a 32-bit number serving as an index into the receiver's Security Associations Database.

After the appropriate SA has been determined, the next step is to perform the necessary authentication/decryption, such as verifying the identity of the sender using that Security Association, extracting the data for the encapsulated packet if necessary.

One of the reasons the data extraction is done before checking the SPD is because the packet can, for example, contain an encrypted TCP header. The information contained in the header (such as port numbers, for instance) might be needed when going through the SPD rules, so the packet has to be decrypted/decapsulated first.

Having finished with the authentication and decryption, the IPSec module turns to the SPD. The appropriate SPD entry is found using the reference contained in the SA determined earlier. The SPD entry is checked to decide what to do next. If necessary, the packet is forwarded, dropped, or handed over to the Transport layer for further processing.

At this point, you should have the basic idea of how IPSec works. Again, if you are confused, don't worry about it. You'll begin to understand more about each of the components used in our examples in the following sections.

IPSec Components

The current version of IPSec is based on several protocols. These protocols can be classified into two groups: those related to *key management* and those related to *packet data manipulation*, such as adding authentication or encryption, compressing data, and so on. The key management category comprises the following:

- Internet Key Exchange Protocol (IKE). It is *based on* the following protocols:

    A. Internet Security Association and Key Management Protocol (ISAKMP)

    B. Oakley Key Determination Protocol

The packet manipulation, authentication, encryption, and compression category comprises the following:

- Authentication Header (AH)
- Encapsulating Security Payload (ESP)
- IP Compression (IPCOMP)

The key management protocols are responsible for negotiating and storing keys. They help establish the IPSec SAs mentioned earlier. The packet manipulation protocols use the SAs to add security features to packets. See RFC 2401 for more details on the IPSec architecture.

> **Note**
>
> You might have noticed certain ambiguity in the AH, ESP, and IPCOMP definitions. Are these protocols or data formats? The RFCs sometimes refer to AH, ESP, and IPCOMP as *protocols* and sometimes as *data formats*. To avoid confusion, in the rest of this chapter, we regard AH, ESP, or IPCOMP as *protocols* by default. When a different interpretation applies, it will be explicitly noted.

Where IPSec Can Be Implemented

IPSec functionality can be either integrated into your OS (native implementation) or implemented as an additional component, package, or hardware device. The following three cases represent various ways of adding IPSec if your system does not support it natively.

Hooks into IP Stack

This requires changes to the IP stack on a target system. IPSec functionality is usually added as a patch to the target system's kernel source. What you need to do in most cases is patch, recompile, and reload your kernel. Currently, this is how FreeS/WAN is installed on Linux distributions that do not support IPSec natively (see FreeS/WAN documentation for the details).

Proxy Between IP Stack and Device Drivers (BITS)

The IPSec RFCs call this approach bump-in-the-stack (BITS). It does not require changes to the existing IP stack because the IPSec module is inserted *between* the IP stack and network device drivers. This approach is particularly useful when adding IPSec support to legacy systems; it might also refer to external software-based solutions.

External Piece of Hardware (BITW)

This approach is sometimes called bump-in-the-wire (BITW). In BITW, IPSec is usually implemented as an external device connected to a router. The device's function is to secure IP packets. It is also possible to have a security gateway—a system running IPSec to which unprotected traffic is diverted to add protection. This term can also be used to refer to a hardware add-on card for an existing platform. Simply put, when you hear BITS, think software; when you hear BITW, think hardware.

Security Features

The following are the four main classes of security features that IPSec offers to IPv4 and IPv6 traffic:

- **Authentication.** Verifies the identity of the sender of a packet.
- **Integrity protection.** Ensures that data has not been changed while in transit.
- **Replay protection.** Prevents an attacker from saving encrypted packets and replaying them later without being detected.
- **Confidentiality.** Conceals traffic being transmitted by encrypting it using a key shared by the sender and the receiver.

The particular set of security features that will be used to protect IP traffic on your system depends on the chosen protocol (AH, ESP, or both). For instance, AH provides the first three features mentioned here but does not provide confidentiality. ESP, in contrast, can provide all four.

Note

With ESP, it is possible to use encryption (confidentiality protection) without authentication. Failing to provide authentication, however, might leave your system vulnerable to an attack. See Steve Bellovin's paper at www.research.att.com/~smb/papers/badesp.ps.

Basic Concepts

This section provides the definitions of various important IPSec concepts.

IPSec Modes

Currently, IPSec can create packets in the two formats corresponding to the two supported modes: *Transport* and *Tunnel*.

In the *Transport* mode, IPSec takes a packet to be protected, preserves the packet's IP header, and modifies only the upper layers portion by adding IPSec headers and the requested kinds of protection between the upper layers and the original IP header. This mode was designed to be used mainly by hosts that want to protect IP traffic between each other. The Transport mode packet format is depicted in Figure 5.1.

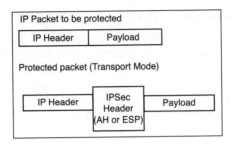

Figure 5.1   IPSec Transport mode.

In the *Tunnel* mode, IPSec treats the entire packet as a block of data, adds a new header, and protects the data (the original packet) by making it part of the encrypted payload of the new packet. This mode is typically used to *tunnel* traffic between gateways. The Tunnel mode packet format is shown in Figure 5.2.

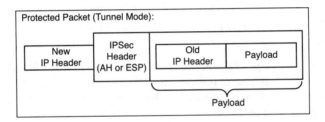

Figure 5.2   IPSec Tunnel mode.

It is common to use gateways to transparently tunnel all traffic that hosts send. It is important to note, however, that using this method might also imply that the local/proximal network(s) will be "trusted" to carry the unencrypted traffic to the aforementioned gateways.

Security Associations (SA)

When you want to protect traffic between hosts or gateways, you need to specify which cryptographic algorithms, keys, and so on will be used. Such information is stored in *Security Associations (SAs)*.

SAs (we will also refer to them as IPSec SAs) are kept in a repository called the Security Associations Database (SAD). Because SAD contains sensitive information such as keys, sequence numbers and so on, it must be stored in a secure place to which access is restricted.

SA Parameters

Each SA can contain a number of parameters. Some of these parameters can be used as *selectors* to choose what types of inbound and outbound packets should be protected using the SA. For example, source and destination IP addresses, port numbers, and protocol types can be used as selectors.

Generally, SA parameters include names of algorithms to be used to protect packets, keys, sequence numbers, and so on. The following is a list of possible SA parameters:

- Security Parameters Index (SPI). SPI is one of the three parameters that uniquely identify an SA. The other two parameters are destination IP address and a security protocol name.

- Source and destination IP address.

- Source and destination port number.

   The last two parameters can be used as selectors along with the transport protocol name.

- Name—either a user ID or a system name. The user ID allows for differentiation between traffic from specific users. If a system name is used, it can be either a fully qualified DNS host name, an X.500 Distinguished Name, or an X.500 general name, similar to the subject name in the X.509v3 digital certificates.

- Security Protocol—currently either AH or ESP.

- Authentication parameters (for example, signature or cryptographic hashing algorithm, keys, and so on).

- Replay protection parameters (for example, the sequence number counter and sequence number counter overflow flag for outbound SAs, or the replay protection window and replay protection counter for inbound Sas).

- Mode (Transport or Tunnel).

- SA lifetime—specified as time or as a number of bytes processed (for example, 45 seconds, 1,024 KB of data, and so on). Often, a combination of time and bytes processed is used to determine SA lifetime.

   When an SA expires, the associated packets that arrive are usually being dropped until a new SA is negotiated. Therefore, some IPSec implementations start renegotiating a new SA shortly before it is due to expire (for example, the IPSec implementation in Cisco routers; also see the *rekeymargin* parameter to Pluto – IKE daemon in FreeS/WAN).

   Make sure, however, that if you set up your system to renegotiate SAs before they expire, you also stagger the renegotiation times. If IKE starts renegotiating all SAs at the same time, it will require your system to support a high peak load (CPU usage, bandwidth, and so on).

- Fragmentation parameters (Path MTU).

The largest MTU on the path between two IPSec peers. The PMTU is usually discovered by probing. The probing begins by sending the largest packet allowed by the maximum transfer unit (MTU) on the first link with the DF (do not fragment) bit set.

The first router on the path that needs to fragment the packet will send an ICMP destination unreachable with option code 4 (fragmentation needed and DF bit set) response back so that in the next probe the length of the packet is decreased. The process continues until all the routers on the path between the two IPSec peers can forward packets without the need to fragment them and the length of the last probe becomes the PMTU. PMTU discovery is not without its problems, and some of them might affect you from time to time. These issues and their possible fixes are discussed in greater detail in RFC 2923. For a more detailed discussion on how PMTU discovery works in general, see RFCs 792 and 1191.

SA Bundles

Each SA can offer only the protection of one IPSec security protocol (that is, AH or ESP). Sometimes you might need to use several kinds of protection on the same traffic flow.

To solve this problem, IPSec defines a mechanism for combining SAs. The mechanism is called *SA bundles*. Two methods can be used to combine SAs into bundles: transport adjacency and iterated tunneling. The names look fancy, but the concepts are actually quite simple.

The *transport adjacency* method enables you to apply both AH and ESP to packets. The protection is added in Transport mode, and only one ordering is possible—the first header is IP, then AH, and then ESP. An example of a SAD with two SAs bundled together is shown in Table 5.2.

Table 5.2   **A SAD With Two SAs**

SPI	SA Bundle	Src IP	Dst IP	IPSec Protocol	Mode	Type	SPD Entry
280	1	192.168.1.5	192.168.2.1	AH	Transport	Outbound	1
300	1	192.168.1.5	192.168.2.1	ESP	Transport	Outbound	1

As you can see from the table, the SAs have different SPIs, but they both have the same source and destination addresses as well as the same SA bundle number.

The exact method for informing your IPSec implementation of your desire to bundle the two SAs shown here is implementation specific. For example, if you use FreeS/WAN, you can use the `ipsec spigrp` command to bundle or unbundle SAs.

The *iterated tunneling* method enables you to nest as many AH or ESP headers as necessary. It can also bundle SAs that overlap but have different source or destination addresses. The idea is shown in Figure 5.3.

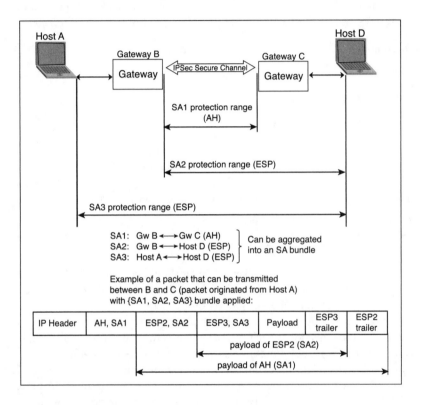

Figure 5.3 SA bundles using iterated tunneling.

Three cases are possible if you use iterated tunneling. The three cases are based on the source and destination IP addresses of the SAs that are bundled.

The first case is when all SAs have the same source and destination IP addresses. The second case is when either the source or destination IP is the same for all SAs in a bundle. The third case is when both source and destination IPs are different for all SAs. According to the IPSec specs, the last two cases are mandatory to implement.

Here is one of the ways to bundle several SAs together using iterated tunneling in FreeS/WAN:

```
root@fox # ipsec spigrp inet 192.168.2.1 0x6310 tun  inet 192.168.2.1 0x7800 esp
➥inet 192.168.2.1 0x7900 ah
```

The preceding command combines three SAs in a bundle. All of the SAs are destined for 192.168.2.1. Notice that the command does not show which of the three cases previously described applies. Because the destination address is the same, it can be either the first or the second case.

Now let's turn to the details of the command itself. The first SA used in the command is a tunnel that has an SPI of 0x6310. The second SA adds ESP protection, and its SPI is 0x7800. The third SA adds AH protection, and has an SPI of 0x7900.

SAD Example

Consider the following example of a SAD (see Table 5.3):

Table 5.3 **A Sample SAD**

SPI	Src IP	Dst IP	Src Port	Dst Port	Various Parameters (AH/ESP, Mode, SA Lifetime, Keys, etc.)	Type	Pointer to SPD Entry
580	192.168.2.1	192.168.1.1	Any	Any	...	Inbound	4
974	192.168.1.1	192.168.2.1	Any	80	...	Outbound	7

If an incoming IPSec-protected packet arrives, it should contain an SPI. The SPI, the destination IP, and the security protocol of the packet header will be used to refer to the entry in the SAD to be used to process the packet.

Note that SAs can be defined for each simplex (one-way) connection. That is, if you have a TCP connection, which is usually two-way, a pair of SAs will need be negotiated—one for inbound traffic and the other for outbound traffic.

Additionally, SAs might have different levels of granularity. For example, you can have a fine-grained SA for a specific HTTP session or a coarse-grained SA protecting all HTTP traffic between your network and a web-hosting provider hops away.

Security Policy Database (SPD)

The Security Policy Database (SPD) consists of an ordered set of policy rules. Each rule consists of a number of *selectors*. SPD selectors carry information similar to that of the selectors in the Security Associations previously described.

SPD has a different purpose, however, namely to make a high-level decision on what to do with specific IP packets (discard, pass on, or apply IPSec). Thus, in contrast to SAD, SPD enforces protection policy, whereas SAD supplies the necessary parameters and makes it possible.

An SPD Example

A simple SPD can have the information shown in Table 5.4. (Note that the exact structure of the table depends on your IPSec implementation.)

Table 5.4 **A Simple SPD**

Rule #	Src IP	Dst IP	Src Port	Dst Port	Action	IPSec Protocol	Mode	Outbound SA Index
1	192.168.1.1	192.168.2.1	Any	23	IPSec	ESP	Tunnel	400
2	192.168.1.23	192.168.2.5	Any	443	IPSec	AH	Tunnel	1

The first entry of the preceding SPD protects all Telnet traffic from 192.168.1.1 to 192.168.2.1 by tunneling it using the IPSec ESP protocol. The second entry ensures that SSL traffic is not encrypted because SSL encrypts traffic itself. However, authentication, integrity, and replay protection are still added by specifying that the IPSec AH Protocol be used to tunnel packets.

SPD rules might overlap, particularly when wildcards are used as selectors. This makes rule selection and evaluation complicated. It might also create problems when merging several policy repositories. Thus, a "decorrelation technique" is used to make sure two rules do not apply to the same packet. For example, consider the SPD shown in Table 5.5.

Table 5.5 **An SPD**

Rule #	Src IP	Dst IP	Src Port	Dst Port	Action	IPSec Protocol	Mode	Outbound SA Index
1	192.168.1.1	192.168.2.1	Any	Any	IPSec	AH	Tunnel	1
2	192.168.1.23	192.168.2.5	Any	80	IPSec	AH	Tunnel	2

After the decorrelation, the modified SPD will look as shown in Table 5.6

Table 5.6 **The Modified SPD After Decorrelation**

Rule #	Src IP	Dst IP	Src Port	Dst Port	Action	IPSec Protocol	Mode	Outbound SA Index
1	192.168.1.1	192.168.2.1	Any	Not 80	IPSec	AH	Tunnel	1
2	192.168.1.23	192.168.2.5	Any	80	IPSec	AH	Tunnel	2

Finally, it is important to remember that SPD is used in a different way for inbound versus outbound traffic. For outbound traffic, SPD is used first to determine what to do with a packet. Then, depending on a specific policy, the IPSec module *might* need to look through SAD.

For inbound traffic, however, the IPSec module considers SAD first. The appropriate SA is then selected to verify the identity of the sender. Normally, only after the identity has been verified, the IPSec module proceeds to SPD.

Security Parameters Index (SPI)

The SPI is a 32-bit index into the Security Association Database. When an IPSec packet comes in, the SPI contained in the header of the packet, in combination with the packet's destination IP and the security protocol (AH, ESP), uniquely identifies the SA to be used with that packet. The SPI can reside in both AH and ESP protocol headers of IPSec-protected packets.

The set of SPI values 1 through 255 is reserved by IANA for future use. The SPI of 0 is reserved for local use and must not be used in the packets that are sent out.

IPSec Key Exchange and Management Protocols

The preceding sections described Security Associations and Security Policy Databases. These databases can be set up either manually or automatically. If you want it to be done automatically, you will need to use key exchange and management protocols embedded in your IPSec solution. This section will describe such protocols.

IKE, Photuris, and SKIP

IKE is the protocol that combines elements, definitions, and functionalities from such protocols as ISAKMP, SKEME, and Oakley to exchange and manage keys as well as SAs.

The Internet Security Association and Key Management Protocol (ISAKMP, RFC2408) defines a general framework for establishing and managing Security Associations between peers that want to communicate securely. ISAKMP is quite abstract, so to use it with IPSec, a domain of interpretation (DOI) had to be defined (see RFC 2407).

The Internet Key Exchange Protocol (IKE) uses the ISAKMP framework to exchange keys and to establish SAs among peers. As previously mentioned, in addition to using ISAKMP, IKE takes advantage of other concepts and protocols as well. For instance, IKE uses the Oakley key determination protocol (see RFC 2412) as well as SKEME for key exchange.

IKE, ISAKMP, SKEME, and Oakley tuples have their alternatives. One of them is Photuris. It is has been used in the OpenBSD IPSec implementation in addition to IKE. SKIP is another alternative, but it has not been widely implemented.

In this section, we will focus on IKE and its fundamental principles.

> **Note**
>
> The IKE module in one of the Linux IPSec implementations—FreeS/WAN—is called Pluto. The Pluto dae-
> mon works in user space, negotiating and renegotiating keys and SAs when necessary.

Overview of IKE

IKE enables you to automatically negotiate SAs. IKE works over UDP, port 500. Thus, you'll need to enable UDP traffic from/to that port to use IKE. If you use `ipchains` on Linux, you can enable IKE traffic as follows:

```
root@fox # /sbin/ipchains -A input -p UDP -d
<your_ipsec/ike_peer's_ip>/32 500 -j ACCEPT
```

IKE was designed to address a number of security concerns. It provides protection from an attacker replaying, removing, or changing messages. IKE can also support Perfect Forward Secrecy (PFS).

> **Note**
>
> PFS is usually implemented as an option you can turn on when configuring IKE. With PFS, if a key is
> compromised, only the data encrypted by that key is compromised. Without PFS, the other keys/SAs can
> also be affected. We recommend that you enable this option.

The protocol consists of the two phases described in the next two sections.

Phase I

The purpose of this phase is to establish a secure channel used to protect subsequent Phase II negotiations. To establish the channel, both peers need to share a secret key and other parameters.

The secure channel is created by negotiating an ISAKMP SA between the peers. It is important to note that Phase I negotiations typically take place less frequently (once an hour or perhaps once a day) than Phase II negotiations (say, once every minute or every 1024K of encrypted data).

Phase II

The purpose of this phase is to negotiate the IPSec SAs used to protect IP traffic. All messages exchanged during Phase II are protected using the secure channel established during Phase I.

To demonstrate, if hosts A and B want to protect traffic between each other using IPSec, they need to share a SA. If a packet is to be sent from A to B and there is no applicable SA in A's SAD, IKE can be asked to negotiate a new IPSec SA with B.

When asked to negotiate a new SA, IKE first checks whether there is an ISAKMP SA to B; if there is not, a new ISAKMP SA is negotiated (Phase I). The ISAKMP SA is then used to securely negotiate the requested IPSec SA to protect traffic between A and B (Phase II). Next, the IPSec SA is saved in both A's and B's SAD.

Authentication Methods

It is crucial for peers participating in IKE negotiations to authenticate each other; otherwise, the security of the key exchange is questionable. To authenticate peers, IKE can utilize the methods discussed in the following sections.

Pre-shared Key (PSK)

The authentication is performed by means of proof-of-possession of the shared key because only the participating peers are supposed to know the key. The problem is to distribute the key(s) in a secure and scalable manner.

Public Key Algorithms

The authentication uses public key algorithms to encrypt data using a public key and decrypt it with private key. The method relies on two facts, namely:

A. The public key received is indeed the peer's public key. The problem is reliable distribution of the public keys.

B. If A is true, then possession of the private key associated with the public key previously mentioned may serve as a proof of identity.

Digital Signatures (DSS or RSA Signature)

The peer to be authenticated electronically signs data with his or her private key. If the signature is verified using the public key of that peer, the peer's identity is also verified.

To deal with the problem of distributing public keys, the digital signatures method can use digital certificates and rely on a trusted third party to bind the identity of the peer to be authenticated to its public key. In general, this method is considered better than exchanging public keys directly.

Under certain circumstances, however, it can still be exploited. See www.cc. gatech.edu/~ok/mitm for more information.

> **Note**
>
> In addition to the three generic authentication methods previously mentioned, the IPSec RFCs state that IPSec implementations *may* use Kerberos for authentication. One of the implementations that actually does so is Windows 2000's IPSec.

IKE Phase I Essentials

During Phase I, IKE has to carry out several important operations. One is to negotiate cryptographic protocols and parameters that will be used for authentication and encryption. The other is to authenticate peers using the negotiated algorithms. Finally, a shared secret needs to be established based on the exchanged information.

The outcome of Phase I is a secure channel that can be used between peers to perform Phase II negotiations of IPSec SAs.

There are three possible Phase I modes:

- Main mode
- Aggressive mode
- Base mode

Main Mode

In the *Main mode*, six UDP datagrams are exchanged. If hosts A and B are the peers, the first Main mode message *makes a proposal*—offers a list of alternative protocols for B to choose from. In the second message, B returns the protocols it wants to use along with other information.

Here is a simplified example of the protocols that A could send in a proposal:

From A to B:

{3DES, MD5}, {BLF, SHA-1, DH-G1}, {CAST, MD5, DH-G1}, {3DES, SHA-1, DH-G2}

From B to A:
{3DES, SHA-1, DH-G2}

As you can see, A offers four choices in its proposal. Each choice includes one cipher, one cryptographic hash, and one key exchange algorithm (unless Preshared Key (PSK) is used). The DH-G★ codes specify different groups of the Diffie-Hellman key exchange algorithm.

> **Note**
>
> The difference between various DH groups previously mentioned is either in the length of the prime modulus (MODP) applied when performing DH calculations or in the basis of the DH algorithm. DH Groups 1, 2, and 5 use 768-, 1024-, and 1536-bit primes as modula; DH groups 3 and 4 are based on elliptic curves.
>
> The bottom line is that, generally, the bigger the DH prime is, the better. Using Group 1 is not a good idea, though, so if you are to choose, go with Group 5 or bigger primes. FreeS/WAN, the Linux IPSec implementation, supports DH Groups 2 and 5 as of version 1.91.

In the next messages, peers exchange key material and establish shared keys. (Diffie-Hellman is typically used to perform the key exchange.) Finally, the peers authenticate each other using the authentication method selected in the first messages. (Currently, it can be one of the three methods described earlier: PSK, public key algorithms, or digital signatures/certificates.)

> **Note**
>
> In the Main mode, peers verify each other's identities *after* the protocols and parameters have been negotiated. At the time of negotiation, the only identity information available to peers is their IP addresses. Thus, it is not possible to reliably attach a specific set of keys and security parameters to an identity before negotiating the protocols.

Aggressive Mode

In the *Aggressive mode*, three UDP datagrams are transmitted. This mode is a compressed version of the Main mode. Therefore, fewer packets are necessary to establish a Phase I ISAKMP SA.

Among the advantages of this mode are not only the decreased number of messages but also the possibility of associating the identity of the peer (not just the IP address, as in Main mode) with a specific preshared key or a security policy. This is possible because the identity information is exchanged *before* a shared key has been established.

The major drawback of this mode is that resource-consuming calculations are performed immediately in response to the first (proposal) message. This means that an attacker can potentially send a number of proposals with spoofed source IP addresses, which might affect the receiver's performance and lead to the denial of service.

To conclude, we'd like to note that the IPSec working group is currently considering the removal of the Aggressive mode altogether. Therefore, it might be a good idea to stick with the Main mode for now.

Base Mode

The *Base mode* was devised to capitalize on the Aggressive mode's advantages and deal with its disadvantages. Four UDP datagrams are sent in the Base mode. The mode defers the computationally intensive key establishment part until a response has been received from the initiating party to confirm its existence.

The Base mode does not address all the problems of the Aggressive mode, though. For instance, unless public key encryption is used, the identity of the communicating parties is not protected. This is because the shared keys are calculated after the peers have exchanged and verified each other's identity information.

Overall, the Base mode has its pluses and minuses. However, it has not been as widely implemented as the Main and Aggressive modes.

Phase II Essentials

After Phase I negotiations have been completed, both peers should share a new ISAKMP SA. The new ISAKMP SA will be used to protect the subsequent Phase II negotiations.

The protocol for Phase II negotiations is called *Quick mode (QM)*. The Quick mode consists of three messages and allows for negotiation of one or more IPSec SAs. Either peer can initiate the negotiations. Each negotiated IPSec SA will then be shared by peers and stored in their SADs.

In QM, both parties need to negotiate an IPSec protocol or a combination of protocols to be used with each IPSec SA. As in Phase I, the parties exchange proposals. A proposal includes a list of protection suites for each proposed IPSec SA. For instance, a proposal might include the following:

```
ESP-3DES
ESP-3DES-SHA
ESP-3DES-MD5
ESP-3DES-SHA-PFS

AH-3DES-MD5
AH-3DES-SHA
AH-3DES-MD5-PFS
AH-3DES-SHA-PFS
```

With each proposal, additional information is also sent, in particular:

- Proposed IPSec SA lifetime
- DH Group
- Transport or Tunnel mode indicator
- Key information

You are probably wondering: If more than one IPSec SA is negotiated, should they all be protected with the same ISAKMP SA? Obviously, if the ISAKMP SA is compromised, all the IPSec SAs protected with that ISAKMP SA can be compromised. This is where Perfect Forward Secrecy can help.

If you enable PFS, a separate Diffie-Hellman exchange will be performed for each IPSec SA (that is, an ISAKMP SA will only be used to protect *one* IPSec SA). This will make IPSec SAs/keys independent from each other, and if the ISAKMP key is compromised, only one IPSec SA/key is compromised. The downside of PFS is that the additional DH exchanges required for each IPSec SA will affect performance.

IPSec Packet Manipulation Protocols

As discussed earlier, the IPSec protocol suite consists of three main elements that manipulate IP packet data:

- Authentication Header (AH)
- Encapsulating Security Payload (ESP)
- IP Compression (IPCOMP)

If you use AH to protect IP traffic, you get authentication, integrity protection, and replay protection. However, your data will be transmitted in cleartext. Choose ESP if you want to add encryption to make your data confidential. Furthermore, with ESP, you also get the three kinds of protection that AH offers.

At this point, you might wonder why you should use AH at all. There are two arguments substantial enough to consider.

First, AH provides slightly more authentication and integrity protection than ESP. AH covers both the outer IP header and the packet's payload, whereas ESP only covers the payload.

Second, encrypting data in addition to authenticating it and protecting its integrity requires additional processing time.

Unless you want to transmit packets in cleartext, we recommend that you combine AH and ESP or use ESP by itself. Typically, you have the following options:

- AH only: Advanced authentication, integrity, and antireplay
- ESP only: Authentication (optional), integrity, antireplay, and encryption
- ESP and AH: Advanced authentication, integrity, antireplay, and encryption
- ESP and IPCOMP: Authentication, integrity, antireplay, encryption, and compression.
- ESP, AH, and IPCOMP: Advanced authentication, integrity, antireplay, encryption, and compression

You can also combine multiple protocols by using several SAs for the same packet. In the example shown in Table 5.7, both AH and ESP will be applied to packets going to 192.168.2.1, port 53.

Table 5.7 **Application of AH and ESP**

SPI	Src IP	Dst IP	Src Port	Dst Port	Params (Keys, Ciphers, etc.)	IPSec Proto	Type	Pointer to SPD Entry
280	192.168.1.8	192.168.2.1	Any	53	[...]	AH	Outbound	5
386	192.168.1.8	192.168.2.1	Any	53	[...]	ESP	Outbound	5

We will now describe AH, ESP, and IPCOMP in more detail.

Note

In contrast to IKE, the three IPSec packet manipulation protocols work at the IP level, so there are no ports associated with them. However, ESP and AH both have protocol numbers associated with them (50 and 51).

Because there is no guarantee that your firewall will like packets with unknown protocol numbers, you might want to add specific firewall rules to let these protocols go through. If you use `ipchains`, you can enable AH and ESP traffic as follows:

```
root@fox # ipchains -A input -p 50 -s <your_ip> -j ACCEPT
root@fox # ipchains -A output -p 50 -d <your_peer's_ip> -j ACCEPT
root@fox # ipchains -A input -p 51 -s <your_ip> -j ACCEPT
root@fox # ipchains -A output -p 51 -d <your_peer's_ip> -j ACCEPT
```

Authentication Header (AH)

As previously mentioned, the Authentication Header (AH) protocol provides authentication, integrity, and replay protection. For authentication and integrity protection, AH relies on keyed cryptographic hash algorithms.

The keyed algorithms are used because they make it impossible for attackers to modify and generate valid cryptographic hashes for intercepted AH-protected packets without knowing the keys shared by AH peers.

Adding AH Protection

When AH protection is added to an IP packet, a new AH is inserted immediately after the IP header of the packet. (IPv6 will have extension headers before the new AH.) Figure 5.4 shows how AH protection is added to an IP packet.

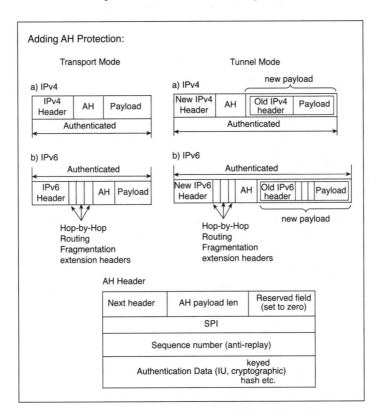

Figure 5.4 Adding AH protection.

The added AH is typically 24 bytes long, consisting of six fields. The fields are as follows:

- Next header (1 byte index, 50 for ESP, 51 for AH and others).

  For IPv4, it contains the protocol index of one of the following protocols: ESP, IPCOMP, TCP, or UDP. For IPv6, it contains the next extension header.

- AH length in 4-byte dwords (1 byte).
- Reserved field (2 bytes).
- SPI (4 bytes).
- Antireplay sequence number (4 bytes).

  Sender's and receiver's counters are reset to 0 when SA is established. This number must not be allowed to cycle, so it is reset by establishing a new SA after 2^{32} AH packets protected using the SA are transmitted.

- Authentication data (variable length, multiple of 4).

  Usually consists of a 12-byte stripped-down version of a 128-bit or 160-bit cryptographic hash output.

Two keyed algorithms must be present in all AH implementations: HMAC-MD5 and HMAC-SHA1. The output of the keyed hash algorithm to be used by IPSec peers is stored in the Authentication Data field of the added AH as previously mentioned.

AH Step by Step

The basic steps AH has to perform to add protection are as follows:

1. Insert the AH header into the IP packet being processed.
2. Update the sequence number in the associated SA and store it in the new AH header. When a new SA is negotiated, its sequence number is reset to zero. The counter is incremented each time AH protection is added to a packet.
3. Add HMAC authentication data. The algorithm defined in the SA (for example, HMAC-MD5 or HMAC-SHA1) is used to generate a new message authentication code based on the contents of the IP packet. The authentication algorithm output is then cut down to 96 bits and stored in the AH header.
4. Fragment the new AH-protected packet if necessary.

End-to-End Protection

You need to understand that unless AH covers the complete path of an IP packet from one end to the other, the security of your AH-protected channel can be breached.

For example, if hosts send traffic to a gateway that then protects the traffic using AH, an intruder can change the traffic before it gets to the gateway. In this case, the change will not be detected, and AH protection is useless.

To deal with such problems, use end-to-end protection. In other words, start protecting traffic right where it originates and continue that protection all the way to its destination. The idea is illustrated in Figure 5.5.

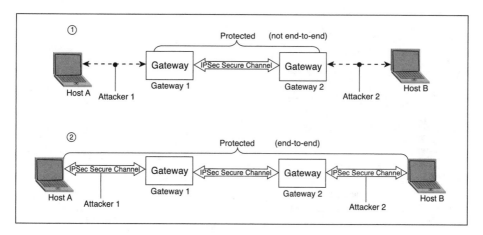

Figure 5.5 End-to-end protection.

Here is how you can better protect your network. First, set up all the hosts on your local network to protect their traffic using Transport mode AH or ESP. Next, set up your gateways to protect all traffic originating from the hosts using IPSec ESP in Tunnel mode. As a result, even if attackers gain access to your network, they still will not be able to alter or read your traffic.

Encapsulating Security Payload (ESP)

As you've already learned, you can use the Encapsulating Security Payload (ESP) protocol to add the three types of protection offered by AH (authentication, integrity, and replay protection) plus confidentiality.

As previously noted, ESP enables you to select just confidentiality (data encryption). Again, before implementing this protection alone, review the findings of Steve Bellovin (see `www.research.att.com/~smb/papers/badesp.ps`) to understand the implications of such a decision. We highly recommend using authentication and integrity protection whether you enable confidentiality or not.

Adding ESP Protection

When ESP protection is added to an IPv4 packet, a new ESP header will be inserted either immediately after the AH header or after the IP header of the packet (if there is no AH header). For IPv6, the new ESP header becomes one of the extension headers. The ESP processing is depicted in Figure 5.6.

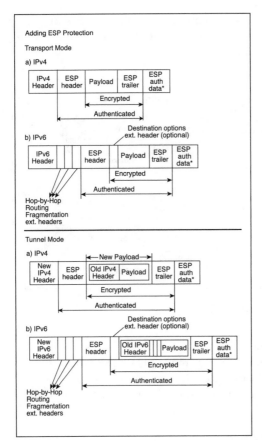

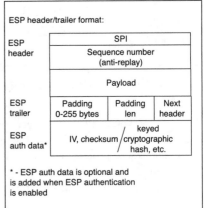

Figure 5.6 Adding ESP protection.

The added ESP header consists of seven fields, two of which are optional. The fields include:

- SPI (4 bytes)
- Antireplay sequence number (4 bytes)
- Payload data (for instance, encrypted IP packet when ESP is used in Tunnel mode)
- Padding (optional, 0–255 bytes)
- Padding length in bytes (1 byte)
- Authentication data (if required, variable length; similar to the AH's Authentication Data field)

Before adding the ESP header, the ESP protocol performs encryption of the payload data and padding, if necessary. The data to be encrypted is divided into blocks and then is encrypted block by block. The block length and the type of chaining applied to the blocks are specified in the associated SA.

Currently, the ESP specs list 56-bit DES-CBC as the minimum mandatory block cipher to be implemented. However, the 56-bit DES does not provide adequate protection, so many implementations (for example, FreeS/WAN) dropped 56-bit DES in favor of 168-bit 3DES, which is more secure.

After the ESP protocol is done processing the data, the ESP header is added. Next, authentication and integrity-protection values are calculated either by ESP itself or by AH.

ESP Step by Step

Summarizing the information in the previous section, here are the basic steps performed when adding ESP protection to an IP packet:

1. Insert the ESP fields into the packet being processed. Pad the packet if necessary, filling out the Pad Length and Padding fields.

2. Encrypt the ESP payload with the algorithm and parameters specified in the associated SA. A special type of encryption algorithm—NULL—disables encryption.

3. Update the sequence number. This is done the same way as in AH.

4. Calculate authentication data if it is required. The data is calculated on the ESP packet, with the last field where the authentication data will be stored reset to all zeros. Skip this step if no authentication is required.

5. Fragment the new ESP-protected packet, if necessary.

ESP Interoperability and End-to-End Protection

If interoperability is a concern, at this time, your best bet is HMAC-MD5 or HMAC-SHA-1 as a cryptographic hash algorithm and 3DES-CBC as a block cipher.

AES Rijndael might also be a viable choice because it has been selected as the DES replacement. However, AES has not yet been implemented as widely as 3DES. See the following sections for more information on interoperability.

Another important thing to consider is end-to-end protection. The problem is similar to the one described for AH earlier. In the case of ESP, however, the outer header is not authenticated. Hence, an attacker might be able to modify the IP headers of the packets on the local network even if ESP is used between a host and a gateway. You can solve this problem by protecting traffic end to end (as with AH) by using both AH and ESP at the same time.

IPCOMP

The IPCOMP compression must be completed before authentication or encryption takes place. The IPCOMP header contains, among other elements, a Compression Parameters Index (CPI) that defines a well-known compression algorithm to be used.

One important thing you should know about IPCOMP is that if you are already using it at the IP level, (corresponding to the Network Layer of the OSI model), turning the compression on at lower layers, such as the Data-Link Layer or the Physical Layer, will not do you much good.

The lower layers will try to compress data that has already been compressed. It will make your system slower without providing much compression in most cases. For example, if you have IPSec with IPCOMP turned on and it works over PPP or CSLIP, make sure you have PPP or CSLIP compression turned off.

Creating a VPN with IPSec

We recommend that you take all VPNs, including IPSec based, one point-to-point link at a time. Creating an IPSec point-to-point VPN link will usually require you to do the following:

1. Identify the endpoints of your VPN link and make sure they support IPSec.

    For example, if you want to use FreeS/WAN on Linux, you will need to add IPSec support to the kernel (KLIPS) as well as compile and install IKE binaries (PLUTO).

2. Configure IPSec on both peers: generate keys, define security policy, enable IPSec/IKE traffic, and determine the IP addresses of the tunneled networks and peers' interfaces.

3. Choose a way to authenticate peers: preshared key (PSK), public key algorithms, or digital signatures.

    In the case of PSK, you will need to manually set up Security Associations on both peers specifying the same key.

    For public-key algorithms and digital signatures, you will need to distribute public keys so that each peer knows the public RSA/DSA key(s) of the other peer(s).

3. Bring the IPSec interface up and run the IKE daemon, if necessary.

4. Test your new IPSec VPN link.

IPSec Road Warriors

In a road warrior scenario, we assume that one of the IPSec peers has a dynamic IP address. For example, you might have an employee who travels and who needs to securely connect to your company's internal network while on the road using a laptop.

Another example is when one of your IPSec peers obtains its IP address from a DHCP server and the IP address changes from time to time. This concept is depicted in Figure 5.7.

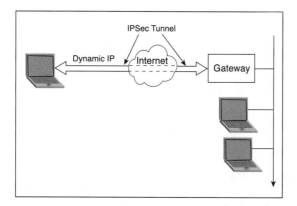

Figure 5.7   The road warrior scenario.

Because the IP address of one of your IPSec peers is dynamic, your IPSec server can't use it to verify the identity of the connecting peer. Therefore, if you want to support the road warrior scenario, you have to be able to authenticate incoming IPSec messages regardless of their source IP. To do that, you can use one of the three authentication methods described earlier (PSK, public keys, or digital signatures).

Interoperability of IPSec Implementations

IPSec RFCs are known to leave a number of details at the implementers' discretion. This is why making sure IPSec implementations interoperate is crucial (unless you are able to restrict all your VPN components to the same vendor). Remember that if you see a vendor offering an IPSec implementation, it does not necessarily mean the implementation will interoperate with other IPSec implementations. To get a list of some common reasons for interoperability faults, go to www.icsalabs.com/html/ communities/ipsec/lab/testing/CommonFaults.shtml.

FreeS/WAN

For many IPSec implementations, you can find a list of the implementations with which they have been successfully tested. To illustrate, we have compiled a list of IPSec implementations that have a basic level of compatibility (the explanation for this is given after the list) with FreeS/WAN v1.91:

- KAME: FreeBSD, NetBSD, OpenBSD, BSDI
- PGPnet
- Windows 2000
- F-Secure VPN
- IRE Safenet/SoftPK
- SSH IPSec Express
- Gauntlet GVPN
- Xedia's AccessPoint QVPN
- Checkpoint SecuRemote VPN-1/Firewall-1
- Raptor Firewall, Raptor MobileNT 5

By a basic level of compatibility between FreeS/WAN and another IPSec implementation, we mean that somebody was able to get FreeS/WAN to work with that implementation in one way or another. Note that, in many cases, testing was not comprehensive, so you might need to take a closer look on a case-by-case basis.

Web-Based Interoperability Testing

Several organizations created web-based interoperability testing pages that you can use to test how your IPSec implementation interoperates with theirs. For example, NIST offers an interoperability page based on its reference implementation of IPSec called Cerberus. The IKE part of Cerberus is called PlutoPlus. You can test how your IPSec implementation interoperates with both at `http://ipsec-wit.antd.nist.gov`.

The NIST testing system supports both manual (PSK) and automatic (IKE) key negotiation. For PSK-based testing, Security Associations are established manually. For IKE-based testing, a Security Association is automatically negotiated between your implementation and Cerberus.

Both the manual key test system and the IKE test system then use the negotiated Security Association to ping your system. The test results can be viewed on your browser or be sent to you via email.

Another web-based interoperability testing system is offered by SSH. It offers to test your system with the SSH IPSec Express implementation. Go to `http://isakmp-test.ssh.fi` for more information.

Conformance Testing

The VPN Consortium came up with an IPSec conformance-testing page for its members. The idea is to define tests for various parts of the IPSec standards. If an IPSec implementation passes a conformance test, it gets a logo that constitutes VPNC's belief that the implementation conforms to the appropriate set of the IPSec standards. The VPNC initiative is well on its way with its first logos issued in July 2000.

Currently, three conformance tests are available from VPNC—Basic, Rekeying, and Certificates. A short description of each test and a list of the IPSec products that passed are given below. See `www.vpnc.org/conformance.html` for more details. Note that the list of conforming products is limited. In particular, it does not include free IPSec implementations.

Basic Test

The Basic test requires an IPSec product to be able to initiate an IPsec ESP tunnel to each of the two test gateways. The tunnel requires 3DES for encryption, SHA-1 for cryptographic hash, Diffie-Hellman Group 5 (1,024-bit MODP) for key exchange, and preshared key for authentication. As the term "Basic" implies, every IPsec implementation shipped today should have these features.

Currently, this is the list of commercial IPSec implementations that have passed the Basic test:

- ADTRAN, NetVanta
- Alcatel (Timestep), Secure VPN Gateway 7130 series
- Ashley Laurent, BroadWay SDS
- Avaya, VSU Series of VPN Gateways
- Cisco, IOS IPsec
- Cisco, VPN 3000 Concentrator
- CoSine Communications, IPSX 9000
- CyberGuard, Premium Appliance Firewall Family
- Cylink, NetHawk
- DigiSAFE, BigBouncer
- DigiSAFE, NetProtect
- Enterasys Networks, Aurorean Virtual Network
- eSoft, InstaGate EX
- Hi/fn, IPSECure
- Microsoft, Windows 2000 SP1
- NetScreen, NetScreen
- Nokia, Nokia VPN

- RapidStream, RapidStream
- RedCreek Communications, Ravlin
- SafeNet, SafeNet
- SSH Communications Security, IPSEC Express
- Spring Tide Networks, IP Service Switch 5000
- WindRiver, WindNet

Rekeying Test

The Rekeying test requires the same kind of tunnel as in the Basic test. However, the tested IPSec implementation should be able to automatically rekey the Phase 2 SA when it is needed. The Phase 2 SAs must also use perfect forward secrecy.

Currently, this is the list of commercial IPSec implementations that have passed the Rekeying test:

- Alcatel (Timestep), Secure VPN Gateway 7130 series
- Ashley Laurent, BroadWay SDS
- Avaya, VSU Series of VPN Gateways
- Cisco, IOS IPSec
- Cisco, VPN 3000 Concentrator
- CyberGuard, Premium Appliance Firewall Family
- DigiSAFE, BigBouncer
- DigiSAFE, NetProtect
- Enterasys Networks, Aurorean Virtual Network
- eSoft, InstaGate EX
- Microsoft, Windows 2000 SP1
- NetScreen, NetScreen
- RapidStream, RapidStream
- SSH Communications Security, IPSEC Express
- WindRiver, WindNet

Certificates Test

The Certificates test requires the setting up of the same type of IPsec tunnel as in the Basic test. However, X.509v3 certificates should be used instead of PSK.

This is the list of commercial IPSec implementations that have passed the Rekeying test to date:

- Cisco, VPN 3000 Concentrator
- DigiSAFE, BigBouncer

- NetScreen, NetScreen
- RapidStream, RapidStream
- SSH Communications Security, IPSEC Express

Conformance vs. Interoperability

Beware that conformance does not mean interoperability. Conformance means that an implementation passed a set of predefined tests. Although the fact that IPSec implementations passed the same conformance tests means increased probability of them being interoperable, it does *not* guarantee their interoperation.

So what should you do? From our experience, the best way to determine what IPSec implementations your implementation can interoperate with is to search for relevant details through mailing lists or using Internet search engines. In addition, you can always try establishing an IPSec link and see if it actually works.

Opportunistic Encryption

As you might have noticed, your IPSec implementation needs to have information about the hosts to which it can send protected traffic. What if you want to protect traffic to a random IP address of which you have no prior knowledge?

Opportunistic encryption (OE) aims at adding secure connectivity between any two hosts that support IPSec. OE will try to protect packets destined not only for the IP addresses of hosts your system knows but also for other hosts without the need to prearrange the connection. In other words, OE negotiates secure tunnels with strangers.

To demonstrate how OE works, assume that a packet destined for www.yahoo.com arrives at your IPSec gateway. The IPSec module on the gateway picks up the packet, looks at the destination address, and checks the local SPD and SAD.

If no matching Security Association is found and there is no knowledge about the destination of the packet, a regular IPSec module would either drop the packet or send it unprotected. However, with OE enabled, the IPSec module might decide to establish a secure channel to www.yahoo.com.

To do that, your IPSec module turns to DNS where the public key for www.yahoo.com can be stored. First, the IP address of www.yahoo.com (obtained from the header of the received packet) is used to find a reverse DNS record. The reverse DNS record will contain the public key for www.yahoo.com.

To illustrate, we will assume that www.yahoo.com does not support IPSec, so the record will refer us to an IPSec gateway that does. The IPSec gateway will be responsible for tunneling traffic to www.yahoo.com.

The information retrieved from the reverse DNS record can be as follows:

```
223.76.58.64.in-addr.arpa. IN PTR www.yahoo.com.
                           IN TXT "X-IPsec-Server(10)=64.58.76.250
                           AEfjDFfjfkKKr...5gjjGKKGJ"
```

In the preceding example, 64.58.76.223 is the IP address of www.yahoo.com, and 64.58.76.250 is the IP address of an IPSec gateway that will be tunneling traffic to www.yahoo.com.

In the next step, the IP address contained in the "X-IPsec-Server" of the IN TXT field will be used to get the key of the IPSec server to contact (also from a reverse DNS map). The key of the IPSec server found in the DNS will read as follows:

```
Ipsec-gw.yahoo.com.    IN A 250.76.58.64
Ipsec-gw.yahoo.com.    IN KEY 0x4200 4 1 AQNJjkKlIk9...nYyUkKK8
```

After the key has been retrieved, it will be used to negotiate an SA with ipsec-gw.yahoo.com using IKE/ISAKMP. The SA will then be utilized to protect traffic to www.yahoo.com.

Note

The main problem with this approach is getting the right public key for www.yahoo.com. As you know, regular DNS is not authenticated and can be spoofed. Thus, to ensure the authenticity of public keys, OE has to rely on DNSSEC, which is still somewhat a work in progress.

OE functionality has been added to FreeS/WAN v1.91. For more information on FreeS/WAN support for OE, see www.freeswan.org/freeswan_trees/freeswan-1.91/doc/HowTo.html.

If you want to find out more about OE as a concept, go to www.freeswan.org/freeswan_trees/freeswan-1.91/doc/opportunism.spec.

Limitations and Conclusions

Beware of the following things if you are going to use IPSec to build your VPN:

- IPSec cannot make up for poor design choices or insecure end systems.

  You need to understand that IPSec is not a silver bullet that makes your system secure. Obviously, if your system has already been compromised, adding IPSec will not help you much. This is true for the majority of security concepts and packages, so we recommend that you take protecting your system against intrusions very seriously.

- IPSec only provides mechanisms to secure your system; *you* provide the policy.

  Be careful when choosing a policy to be used on your IPSec systems. Remember the importance of the end-to-end protection described earlier and make sure your policy protects traffic all the way from its source to its destination. Combine ESP and AH for better security.

- IPSEC does not protect against denial-of-service attacks.

  The fact that IPSec protects IP traffic does not mean it will protect you from someone flooding your routers with packets. If you are careful with the types of traffic you allow to go through your firewall, you can mitigate the effect of a DoS attack, but you can't stop it from using IPSec.

Overall, the biggest limitation of the current version of IPSec is probably its complexity. As many cryptographers argue, complexity is the enemy of security. To address this concern, a number of improvements are being considered. In particular, complete removal of such parts of IPSec as Transport mode, Aggressive mode, and even the AH protocol has been proposed. Also see `www.ietf.org/internet-drafts/draft-ietf-ipsec-improveike-00.txt`.

In conclusion, despite IPSec's complexity and imperfections, it is probably your best bet at this time if you want a widely supported and implemented industry–level solution.

Summary

In this chapter, we described functioning and key elements of IPSec protocol suite. We focused on explaining IPSec from a practical perspective, covering the essential things a system or security administrator would need to know in order to successfully configure, monitor, and maintain an IPSec-based VPN.

6

FreeS/WAN

I N THIS CHAPTER, WE WILL DESCRIBE how to set up an IPSec VPN using the freely available FreeS/WAN (www.freeswan.org). We will provide an overview of the internals of the FreeS/WAN code and how it operates and will provide some concrete examples of how to plan, configure, and troubleshoot a FreeS/WAN implementation.

The intent of this chapter is to enable you to pick up the book, read through this chapter, and be 95% prepared to implement a FreeS/WAN VPN. There's a lot of information here, and if you follow the text step by step, you should be able get this VPN working.

Be aware (read: forewarned) that we're dealing with more than just the FreeS/WAN software here. You'll also need to work with the Linux kernel and possibly some supporting software. As formidable a task as that might seem, it's actually quite simple.

Throughout this chapter, unless explicitly stated, we'll assume that static IP addresses are used.

Overview

This section will present the different parts of FreeS/WAN from a high-level perspective. It's good to understand the constituent parts before attempting to set up a FreeS/WAN VPN.

Background

FreeS/WAN is an open-source package that provides RFC-compliant IPSec capabilities. The FreeS/WAN project was founded in 1996 by John Gilmore with the intent of providing a free mechanism to begin the overwhelming process of securing the Internet; this is a task in which any single component could be formidable by itself.

Quite a bit of history and politics surround the FreeS/WAN project and cryptography in general. (For an in-depth presentation of this, refer to the FreeS/WAN documentation.) To some degree, this has influenced the project's progress and direction; for the most part, however, it has been more of an inconvenience than a significant impediment.

FreeS/WAN is composed of two primary pieces: KLIPS and Pluto.

KLIPS

KLIPS (kernel IP security) is source code that is integrated into the Linux kernel. KLIPS provides low-level drivers that allow IPSec functionality to be independent of communication interfaces and higher-level user-space code. KLIPS can be compiled either into the kernel or as a module for runtime insertion or removal.

Pluto

Pluto is a daemon that performs IPSec IKE key exchanges and manages the IPSec keyring. It interfaces with kernel-level KLIPS when necessary. Pluto is started automatically by the included FreeS/WAN initialization scripts.

Opportunistic Encryption

One of the goals of the FreeS/WAN project is to influence the IPSec community to incorporate Opportunistic Encryption into the IPSec standard. Opportunistic Encryption allows for a more dynamic security environment, providing fallback mechanisms if an IPSec connection fails. It also provides easier keyring management because encryption key information can be stored in DNS for automatic retrieval and revocation. This greatly simplifies the administration and maintenance of IPSec.

Unfortunately, Opportunistic Encryption is still in an experimental stage and therefore is not recommended for a production environment. Because of this, we will not be discussing Opportunistic Encryption in any detail. If you're interested, refer to the copious amounts of information found in the FreeS/WAN documentation.

Keep in mind that Opportunistic Encryption is experimental, which means that experimenting with it is a *good thing*. It definitely works as it should more often than not, and if you're the heir apparent to the VPN administrator's job, it could make your life a lot easier. If, when you complete this chapter, you're sold on planning a large VPN implementation using FreeS/WAN, be sure to read all of the available documentation on Opportunistic Encryption.

Planning Your VPN

One of the biggest roadblocks in a VPN implementation is the lack of planning. Oftentimes, there's more than one person involved in the setup of a VPN, and there's a great deal of information to track and understand. Proper planning is crucial to the success of a VPN.

Mapping It Out

The first thing to do is to make a visual map of your intended solution. This is helpful for a variety of reasons, many of which we'll discuss throughout this chapter. A map could look very much like the network-network configuration shown in Figure 6.1.

As you can see, the two VPN gateways have a spatial affinity to either the left or right side of the diagram. FreeS/WAN configuration files refer to these gateways as either "left" or "right," so we've already intuitively identified which is which. Whether a VPN device is "left" or "right" is completely arbitrary. Also notice that first consecutive routers are identified.

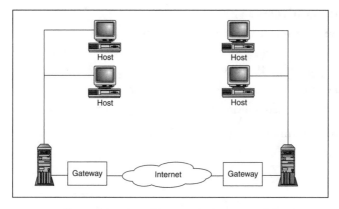

Figure 6.1 A vanilla map of VPN networks.

Naming Conventions

We now need to prescribe an index (or name) to each of our gateways. This can be done in a variety of ways, but it is suggested that you use fully qualified domain names (FQDNs) preceded with an "at" symbol (@). The @ symbol tells FreeS/WAN not to resolve the name; this is useful if DNS or another nameservice is not available. It also enables you to name your VPN connections meaningfully without relying on another service to regulate the names.

For the purposes of this example, we're going to name the "left" gateway @cn.exemplify.com and the "right" gateway @de.exemplify.com (see Figure 6.2).

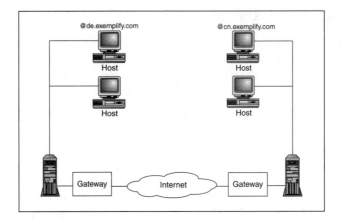

Figure 6.2   The VPN map with indices.

Collecting Addresses

Now that we've identified and named our gateways, we need to collect IP addresses and add them to our map. The following information is needed from each side:

- Gateway interface IP addresses
- Private subnet network number and netmask
- Routing information from each gateway to the Internet

You can make a form similar to the following to keep track of information:

index: _____

eth0: _____

eth1: _____

default route: _____

eth1 subnet/netmask: _____

eth0 subnet/netmask: _____

Complete the form for each VPN gateway. For example, for @de.exemplify.com, it would look like this:

index:	@de.exemplify.com
eth0:	10.1.10.50
eth1:	192.168.10.1
default route:	10.1.10.1
eth1 subnet/netmask:	255.255.255.0
eth0 subnet/netmask:	255.255.255.0

For @cn.exemplify.com, it would look like this:

index:	@cn.exemplify.com
eth0:	10.126.5.241
eth1:	192.168.20.1
default route:	10.125.5.1
eth1 subnet/netmask:	255.255.255.0
eth0 subnet/netmask:	255.255.255.0

Now that we have the IP address information, we can update our map. It might look like the map shown in Figure 6.3.

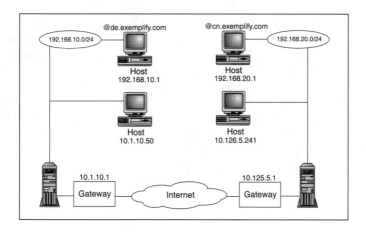

Figure 6.3 The VPN map with IP addresses.

FreeS/WAN Compilation

There's a lot of source code to compile, so let's begin the process. We'll assume you're using an x86-compatible system, and our instructions will be centered on that assumption. Also, in some instances, you might be able to find a precompiled package for your distribution. Be aware that the only precompiled packages you'll be able to use are those for the GMP library and modutils.

GMP

Grab a copy of the GMP (GNU Multiple Precision) library. This can be obtained at Ibiblio's FTP archive (`ftp://ftp.ibiblio.com/pub/gnu/gmp/`). Grab the latest version of the library. As of this writing, the current version is 3.1.1, and that version works well with FreeS/WAN.

If you prefer, you can find a precompiled package (RPM, DEB, or whatever you prefer) from your Linux distribution vendor. However, be sure you get both the libraries and the headers. These are sometimes two separate packages, and both are needed to successfully compile FreeS/WAN.

If you get the source code, you'll need to compile it. Here's a brief synopsis of how to do this using GMP 3.1.1. Run the following commands:

```
# tar zxvf gmp-3.1.1.tar.gz
# cd gmp-3.1.1
# ./configure --prefix=/usr/local
# make
# make install
```

You can put the GMP package wherever you like, as specified in the `--prefix` option. Be aware that, if you do this, you might need to explicitly state the path to the libraries and header files (by modifying Makefiles or defining certain environment variables) for subsequent compilations. It is suggested that you put the GMP files in either `/usr` or `/usr/local` because these are standard locations.

One last thing: Because you've just compiled some shared libraries, you need to make sure the Linux dynamic linker knows that the libraries are there. Edit the file `/etc/ld.so.conf` and add the library path to the file. For instance, because we installed GMP in `/usr/local`, we add the following line to `/etc/ld.so.conf`:

```
/usr/local/lib
```

Now, as root, type the following command to update the dynamic linker database:

```
# ldconfig
```

modutils

`modutils` is a set of utilities that load, unload, and find dependencies between kernel modules. If you're upgrading from a 2.2 kernel to a 2.4 kernel or if you're using an older 2.4.x version of `modutils`, you'll probably want to upgrade to the latest version. As of this writing, the current version of `modutils` is 2.4.8. It can be downloaded from `www.kernel.org` or one of its mirrors.

Compilation of `modutils` is exceedingly simple. Grab the tarball, save it in the `/usr/src` directory, and perform the following commands:

```
# cd /usr/src
# tar zxvf modutils-2.4.8.tar.gz
# cd modutils-2.4.8
# ./configure --prefix=/
# make
```

Everything should have completed successfully. If not, try to find out why it's not compiling correctly and remedy the situation. *Do not* proceed to the next step until `modutils` has compiled successfully!

Your Linux distribution already installed a version of `modutils`, so you should remove that first. On a RedHat Linux system:

```
# rpm -e --nodeps modutils
```

The `--nodeps` option is necessary because the whole system depends on this package. You won't be able to remove the package without specifying this option. Keep in mind that, in general, it's not a good idea to use the `--nodeps` option frivolously. This case is an exception to the rule, but you could seriously damage your system by removing packages that other packages require.

Now that the package is removed, we can install the `modutils` package as follows:

```
# cd /usr/src/modutils-2.4.8 && make install
```

Be sure you have completed all the steps listed before restarting your system. Your system requires the `modutils` software to function.

Kernel Compilation

Now you need to get some kernel source. It is up to you to decide which kernel to use, but it is recommended that you use kernel 2.2.19 or above for the 2.2 kernels, or kernel 2.4.5 or 2.4.6. Much of the work done for this chapter used kernel 2.4.6 on i386 platforms and 2.2.19 on Sparc platforms. If you run into problems compiling the kernel on your system, try using a different kernel.

Note
There are rumors about FreeS/WAN being compatible with kernels 2.4.10 and above. Feel free to try it.

Kernel source can be obtained from www.kernel.org or one of its mirrors. Be sure to get the kernel source, not just a patch! Kernel source files follow the naming convention `linux-<version>.tar.gz` or `linux-<version>.tar.bz2`. The `.gz` signifies `gzip` compression, and the `.bz2` extension signifies `bzip2` compression.

Save the kernel source to the directory /usr/src and decompress it with the appropriate command as shown. For `gzip` compression, use the following:

```
# tar zxvf linux-<version>.tar.gz
```

For `bzip2` compression, use the following:

```
# tar Ixvf linux-<version>.tar.bz2
```

For newer versions of GNU Tar (such as the one packaged with RedHat 7.1), use the j flag instead of the I flag for `bzip2` decompression. Both will work, but use of the I flag is deprecated.

The kernel source will be untarred into the directory /usr/src/linux. At this point, you'll probably want to do some symlinking to keep track of kernel versions. Move the `linux` directory to `linux-<version>` and then symlink the new directory to the symlink "linux". This can be done as follows:

```
# cd /usr/src
# mv linux linux-<version>
# ln -s linux-<version> linux
```

By doing this, you will have a much easier time maintaining different kernel versions. Also, the next kernel you untar will overwrite the /usr/src/linux directory, although not completely. That's a really easy way to mess up your kernel source! So you will need to keep things separate. Just be sure to remove the "linux" symlink before unpacking your next kernel!

Now we have to make more symlinks. Some Linux distributions do not come ready to work with kernel source because they assume that you will be using the package management that comes with the distribution or that you might opt not to install kernel source. The following commands configure your file system properly:

```
# cd /usr/include
# mv linux linux.old
# mv asm asm.old
# ln -s ../src/linux/include/linux linux
# ln -s ../src/linux/include/asm asm
```

The preceding commands ensure that subsequent compilations use the proper kernel include files, which can vary from one kernel version to another. Many failures in compilations are a result of misdefined data types and function prototypes in old header files.

Now that we've unpacked the kernel source and made the appropriate modifications to our file system, we can proceed to configure our new kernel. Type the following:

```
# cd /usr/src/linux
# make menuconfig
```

Note

menuconfig is a curses-based kernel configuration utility. To use this, you need the curses library installed on your system. Most distributions install this package automatically.

If you are using X-Windows, you can type this instead:

```
# cd /usr/src/linux
# make xconfig
```

Note

If make xconfig fails, it might be because you don't have Tcl/Tk installed. If that's the case, just use menuconfig.

Either way, you'll be provided with an interface in which you can select kernel configuration parameters. If you've compiled a kernel before, you probably know what to do. If not, refer to the Kernel-HOWTO (www.linuxdoc.org/HOWTO/Kernel-HOWTO. html) for additional details. Select the options particular to your system and then save

and quit the interface. This will save your configuration to a file named /usr/src/
linux/.config. Go ahead and make a backup copy of this file somewhere else on your
file system.

> **Note**
>
> If you're setting up a VPN gateway, be sure to enable the option Networking Options -> Forwarding.
> This will enable forwarding between interfaces on that host.

At this point, issue the following commands:

```
# make dep
# make bzImage
```

> **Note**
>
> Alternatively, you could issue the following command:
>
> ```
> # make zImage
> ```
>
> However, this results in a bigger kernel because gzip compression is not as efficient as bzip2
> compression. Either way works.

If you run into any problems, refer to the Kernel-HOWTO.

FreeS/WAN Compilation

If everything is successful, grab the FreeS/WAN tarball from www.freeswan.org. As of
this writing, the current version is 1.91, and that version was used for the writing of
this chapter. Save the tarball in the /usr/src directory.

Untar the source in the /usr/src directory:

```
# cd /usr/src
# tar zxvf freeswan-1.91.tar.gz
```

This will create the directory /usr/src/freeswan-1.91. At this point, all the defaults
for compilation are set appropriately, so we can dive right into FreeS/WAN compilation. Type the following:

```
# cd /usr/src/freeswan-1.91
# make menugo
```

Or, if you used the X-Windows interface during kernel compilation, type this instead:

```
# cd /usr/src/freeswan-1.91
# make xgo
```

You'll be presented with the same kernel configuration interface as before, and the
kernel configuration you previously performed will be saved, so you don't have to go
through and make all the selections you did before.

However, you need to make one modification: Under the Networking Options
menu, scroll down to the bottom. There you'll find a new menu option called IP

Security Protocol (FreeS/WAN IPSec). You can either compile this into the kernel or make it a module. It is suggested that you make it a module because you can completely reset the state of the IPSec kernel information during runtime simply by removing the module and inserting it again. Otherwise, "left-over" configuration parameters might continue to reside in the memory address space and could make troubleshooting difficult. If you'd like a monolithic kernel or if you want to compile the FreeS/WAN modules directly into the kernel, it's best to initially set up and troubleshoot the IPSec tunnel as a module and then recompile your kernel with the FreeS/WAN code.

So, initially, select to compile the IPSec code as a module and select all the suboptions to the FreeS/WAN module. Your screen should look something like Figure 6.4 (in menugo mode).

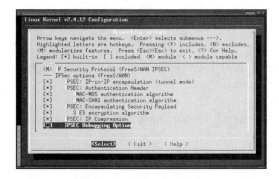

Figure 6.4 The menugo screenshot.

Or, in xgo mode, it should look like Figure 6.5.

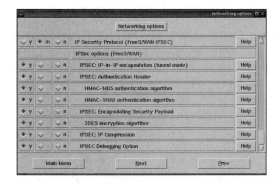

Figure 6.5 The xgo screenshot.

For future reference, let's take a look at what each of these options means.

IP Security Protocol (FreeS/WAN IPSec)

This is the main body of the KLIPS code. The options available signify to include the KLIPS code directly into the kernel (y), to compile the code as a module (m), or not to include it at all (n). If you want IPSec functionality, select y or m here (preferably m).

IPSec: IP-in-IP Encapsulation (Tunnel Mode)

IPSec can operate in one of two modes: Tunnel or Transport. The difference between these two modes is described in Chapter 5, "IPSec." You probably want to use Tunnel mode.

IPSec: Authentication Header

IPSec can provide two different types of service: AH and ESP. AH mode only provides authentication, so you'll probably not want to use AH without ESP. Using ESP mode without AH mode is perfectly acceptable because ESP provides authentication and encryption. The decision to use AH should be based on your requirements. If you want to use IPSec in AH mode, select y here. Otherwise, select n.

HMAC-MD5 Authentication Algorithm

One of the hashing functions available to IPSec AH mode is HMAC-MD5. Your choice to use this mode is dependent on whether the other endpoint in the IPSec connection requires the HMAC-MD5 algorithm.

HMAC-SHA1 Authentication Algorithm

The other hashing algorithm included in FreeS/WAN is HMAC-SHA1. HMAC-SHA1 has been shown to be cryptographically stronger than HMAC-MD5, and it should be noted that this increased level of security comes at a moderate performance cost. Regardless, your decision to use this protocol should be based on the requirements of your VPN.

IPSec: Encapsulating Security Payload

By selecting y here, you signify that you want to use IPSec in ESP mode. This is the mode you want to use because it provides mathematically sound confidentiality and authentication services.

3DES Encryption Algorithm

If you want to use IPSec in ESP mode, definitely select y here. Otherwise, it won't work. It's the only algorithm available at this time.

IPSec: IP Compression

This option will compress IP packets in Tunnel mode. Because encryption of data can sometimes result in larger data, it's good to compress that data as it passes through the

VPN device. However, this requires more computation time. If you're using a slow box for your VPN solution and the performance isn't that great, try disabling this option.

IPSec Debugging Option

This tells KLIPS to output debugging information. It's a good idea to select y here.

Go ahead and select everything (you can worry about optimization later) and then save and exit the configuration interface. The kernel and modules will now be recompiled. Even though the exit screen of the kernel configuration says you should do a make dep, don't do it. The FreeS/WAN Makefile will do it for you.

You shouldn't see any fatal errors, although some warnings will probably pop up. When it completes, the kernel and FreeS/WAN utilities have been compiled, but modules have not been installed. To install the modules, type the following:

```
# cd /usr/src/linux
# make modules_install
```

This will install the kernel modules. Of all the points in this process that could fail, module compilation and installation have the highest probability. The compilation could bomb during make modules, and you'll need to track down the source of the problem. If it bombs, you'll see a whole bunch of error messages. Open the file /usr/src/freeswan-1.91/out.kbuild and try to trace the problem back to the module creating the error. If you start from the end of the error messages, go back until you see a line that says something like make -C <something or other>. That will give you some information as to what module or what type of module is creating the problem.

The other place in which the process could bomb is the last step in the module installation process, when an external program is executed to find dependencies between modules. You'll know it has failed if you see some messages like the following:

```
depmod: *** Unresolved symbols in
       /lib/modules/2.4.6/kernel/drivers/net/tokenring/ibmtr.o
depmod: *** Unresolved symbols in
       /lib/modules/2.4.6/kernel/drivers/net/tokenring/lanstreamer.o
depmod: *** Unresolved symbols in
       /lib/modules/2.4.6/kernel/drivers/net/tokenring/olympic.o
```

There are a few reasons why this could be happening. One, you didn't include a kernel configuration that these modules depend on. If that's the case, go back and read the "help" associated with the module to see if you need to include something else in the configuration. Two, the source code could have a problem. Unless you're a really good coder and you're very familiar with the kernel source, you probably can't do much about this. If you absolutely need this module, try a different kernel version. Otherwise, remove the module from the kernel configuration. Three, you didn't install a new version of modutils. Go back to section "modutils" and install the latest version.

If the module's compilation and installation go well, you'll now need to install the kernel. Type the following:

```
# cd /usr/src/linux/arch/i386/boot
# cp bzImage /boot/vmlinuz-<linux version>
```

This will copy the kernel to the /boot directory. It's important to keep track of your kernel versions, hence the `<linux version>` appended to the kernel.

Next, you need to edit the /etc/lilo.conf file to make LILO aware of the new kernel. Open the file and add the following lines:

```
image=/boot/vmlinuz-<linux version>
        label=linux-vpn
        read-only
        root=<insert from other entries>
```

The `root=` parameter tells LILO which device contains the root file system. This field should be the same as any of the other `root=` fields in the other entries. If it doesn't appear in any of the other entries, don't include it in the new entry.

The one other line you should change is the one that reads `default=<kernel label>`. Change this to read `default=linux-vpn`. This will make the new kernel boot by default.

The final step is to execute the following command:

```
# /sbin/lilo
```

The output of this step should list the different kernels listed in the /etc/lilo.conf file. The `linux-vpn` should have a following asterisk, signifying the default kernel to boot.

Rebooting

Close all your programs, reboot, and cross your fingers. Look for a line during bootup that mentions IPSec, and you should be in pretty good shape. Unfortunately, it's impossible to accurately predict all of the problems that might occur during a new kernel installation, so we leave the rest of the troubleshooting up to you.

Where Things Are

It's helpful to know where things have been placed on your file system, so here's a brief list of files and directories:

```
/etc/ipsec.conf
/etc/ipsec.secrets
/usr/local/sbin/ipsec
/usr/local/lib/ipsec/*
/etc/rc.d/init.d/ipsec
```

During runtime operation, the following files are created:

```
/var/run/pluto.pid
/var/run/pluto.ctl
```

File System Security

Immediately after installation, you should check the permissions of certain files and directories and change them if needed. Even though most of the permissions listed are set during the installation, it's good practice to periodically verify that the permissions on these files and directories have not changed.

The following commands will change the permissions of these files and directories so that they are secure:

```
# chown -R root.root /usr/local/lib/ipsec
# chown root.root /etc/ipsec.conf
# chown root.root /etc/ipsec.secrets
# chown root.root /usr/local/sbin/ipsec
# chmod -R 755 /usr/local/lib/ipsec
# chmod 644 /etc/ipsec.conf
# chmod 600 /etc/ipsec.secrets
# chmod 755 /usr/local/bin/ipsec
# chmod 755 /var/run
```

Configuring FreeS/WAN

In this section, we'll configure a few different types of VPN tunnels with FreeS/WAN. Based on what is available to you, pick a basic tunnel type and set that up first. Proceed through the troubleshooting steps until your first tunnel is configured and working properly. Everything from that point on should come somewhat easily.

Cryptographic Keys

In this section, we'll create the cryptographic keys for FreeS/WAN. After you generate a key and add the appropriate information, copy the file to /etc/ipsec.secrets. After you copy it, be sure the permissions on the file are set to 600 (rw-------). Otherwise, your cryptographic key could be compromised.

There are two types of cryptographic keys: RSA public keys and PSK shared keys. You can mix and match these however you like, but each set of keys between two hosts or gateways must use the same type of key. For instance, gateway A and gateway B can both use RSA keys, and gateway A and mobile host C can both use PSK keys, but gateway A and gateway B cannot use both RSA and PSK keys between each other.

RSA Key Generation

Even though an RSA key was generated for you during installation, let's go through the process of generating one anyway. It's good practice to change keys periodically, and this is how you do it.

In a secure working directory (that is, a directory with permission **700** (rwx- - - - - -)), type the following:

```
# ipsec rsasigkey --verbose 2048 > rsakey.tmp
```

You'll see some output that states that the program is looking for a large prime number. This could take a while no matter what kind of system you have, so be patient.

After the command completes, you'll have to add some information to the rsakey.tmp file to make this understandable to FreeS/WAN. The format for this file is as follows:

```
: RSA        {
       <TAB> output of rsakeygen
       <TAB>
       <TAB>}
```

The indentation of this file is crucial. Do not forget to begin every line after the first line with a <TAB>. In addition, lines can be very long and might not fit on a single line in your terminal window. This is okay as long as the whole line is technically on a single line (that is, no new lines within the data).

The following is a sample configuration file. An ellipsis (...) is used when lines are too long to show, and the sample data is unnecessary to convey meaning.

```
: RSA    {
       # RSA 2048 bits    p0pp3r    Tue Sep 18 23:40:28 2001
       # for signatures only, UNSAFE FOR ENCRYPTION
       #pubkey=0sAQNv7EnikLXTlFvXPP+H...
       #IN KEY 0x4200 4 1 AQNv7EnikL8...
       # (0x4200 = auth-only host-level, 4 = IPSec, 1 = RSA)
       Modulus: 0x6fec49e290b5d3945df...
       PublicExponent: 0x03
       # everything after this point is secret
```

```
        PrivateExponent: 0x12a761a544c...
        Prime1: 0xca559da58af7bfeccab6...
        Prime2: 0x8d9bcab6aceddf1cab6a...
        Exponent1: 0x86e3be6e5cacab6a7...
        Exponent2: 0x5e67dc79c81cd35ae...
        Coefficient: 0x58e114c8834bff4...
    }
```

Like most shell–oriented *NIX things, a hash (#) denotes comments that are to be
ignored. However, the text following the `pubkey=` keyword is your public key. This is
the string of text that must be sent to the other host(s) participating in the VPN.
Because it's a public key, this text can safely be posted to web sites for easier
distribution.

It is possible to have multiple keys in the `ipsec.secrets` file, but each key must
have an index associated with it. The following example shows two keys with the
indices @ex1.exemplify.com and @ex2.exemplify.com:

```
@ns1.exemplify.com: RSA    {
        # RSA 2048 bits     ex1    Tue Sep 18 23:40:28 2001
        # for signatures only, UNSAFE FOR ENCRYPTION
        #pubkey=0sLXTlFvXPP+H...
        #IN KEY 0x4200 4 1 ikL8...
        # (0x4200 = auth-only host-level, 4 = IPSec, 1 = RSA)
        Modulus: 0x0b5d3945df...
        PublicExponent: 0x05
        # everything after this point is secret
        PrivateExponent: 0x1a544c...
        Prime1: 0x8af7bfeccab6...
        Prime2: 0xceddf1cab6a...
        Exponent1: 0x5cacab6a7...
        Exponent2: 0xc81cd35ae...
        Coefficient: 0x8834bff4...
    }


@ns1.exemplify.com: RSA    {
        # RSA 2048 bits     ex2    Tue Sep 18 23:40:28 2001
        # for signatures only, UNSAFE FOR ENCRYPTION
        #pubkey=0sAQNv7Enik\...
        #IN KEY 0x4200 4 1 AQNv7E...
        # (0x4200 = auth-only host-level, 4 = IPSec, 1 = RSA)
        Modulus: 0x6fec49e29...
        PublicExponent: 0x03
        # everything after this point is secret
        PrivateExponent: 0x12a76...
        Prime1: 0xca559da5...
        Prime2: 0x8d9bcab6...
        Exponent1: 0x86e3be6...
        Exponent2: 0x5e67dc79...
        Coefficient: 0x58e114...
    }
```

After you have generated your keys and arranged the file in the proper format, copy it to /etc/ipsec.secrets. The file already exists, but you can simply write over it:

```
# cp -f rsakey.tmp /etc/ipsec.secrets
```

Symmetric Key Generation

Using a symmetric cipher for IKE initialization encryption is slightly simpler than using the RSA cipher. Performance is a little better because public-key ciphers are more computationally intensive, but that shouldn't be an issue. Be aware, however, of the pitfalls when using a symmetric cipher.

To generate a symmetric key, enter the following command:

```
# ipsec ranbits --continuous 128 > secretkey.tmp
```

This will place a pseudo-randomly generated number into the file secretkey.tmp. You then need to add some configuration text to this file to make sure FreeS/WAN can understand it. Also, where we previously used the "RSA" identifier to signify an RSA key, we will now use the "PSK" (private shared key) identifier to denote a secret key. The resulting file looks like this:

```
@ex1.exemplify.com
        @ex2.exemplify.com:
        PSK "<randomly generated number in hexidecimal>"
```

If we generated the secret key as follows:

```
0x4e4cfabea0714f72d582892cd08078a6
```

Our /etc/ipsec.secrets file would look like this:

```
@ex1.exemplify.com
        @ex2.exemplify.com:
        PSK "0x4e4cfabea0714f72d582892cd08078a6"
```

Notice that there are two indices for this key because this tells FreeS/WAN which key to use for which hosts. Also note that the entry is split across multiple lines and that every line following the first line is indented with a <TAB>. This is absolutely necessary. Otherwise, FreeS/WAN will interpret the unindented lines as separate entries.

More than two indices can share the same PSK key, but this use is not recommended. Although it could make key management easier, it introduces too many points of failure within your VPN. It's best to only use PSK keys between two hosts.

Connecting to the Network

In this section, we will cover configuration and testing of your network connection.

Configuration

If you haven't already done so, you'll need to set up networking on your system. You should already have a map with the necessary information, so let's go ahead and get the network running. We'll assume that you'll only be using a single network interface at first, and we'll deal with dual-homed hosts when needed.

> **Note**
> If you know that your network is working properly, you can skip this section.

Using the information from our map in the section "Mapping It Out," let's set up the external interface (`eth0`) for @de.exemplify.com.

```
# ifconfig eth0 <ipaddr> netmask <nm>
# route add default gw <defroute>
```

That's it! Of course, if you want your system to boot and initialize these values automatically, you'll need to modify your configuration files. For instance, you can place the necessary commands in the `/etc/rc.d/rc.local` script, or on a RedHat system, you can modify the `/etc/sysconfig/network` file and the `/etc/sysconfig/network-scripts/ifcfg-eth*` files. For more information, refer to the Net-HOWTO (`www.linuxdoc.org/HOWTO/Net-HOWTO/index.html`), Olaf Kirch's Linux Network Administration Guide (`www.linuxdoc.org/LDP/nag2/index.html`), Frisch's book on UNIX system administration (`www.oreilly.com/catalog/esa2/`), or your Linux vendor's documentation. These resources should help you configure your system for automatic initialization.

Testing Your Network

To ensure that your network is operating properly, you should try a variety of methods to test the network. First, `ping` the default gateway:

```
# ping <gateip>
```

You should see some output that looks like the following:

```
64 bytes from <gateip>: icmp_seq=0 ttl=255 time=0.0 ms
64 bytes from <gateip>: icmp_seq=1 ttl=255 time=0.0 ms
64 bytes from <gateip>: icmp_seq=2 ttl=255 time=0.0 ms
64 bytes from <gateip>: icmp_seq=3 ttl=255 time=0.0 ms

--- <gateip> ping statistics ---
4 packets transmitted, 4 packets received, 0% packet loss
round-trip min/avg/max = 0.0/0.0/0.0 ms
```

You should see 0% packet loss; otherwise, you're dropping packets, and there are other problems with your network. Contact your network administrator to resolve these problems.

Next, try pinging the other end of the VPN connection. A small percentage of packet loss is acceptable, but anything more might make setting up the VPN difficult.

Lastly, perform a `traceroute` to the other VPN gateway:

```
# traceroute <ipaddr of @cn.exemplify.com>
```

You should see some output that looks like this:

```
traceroute to 10.56.133.41, 30 hops max, 38 byte packets
 1  10.80.241.254      1.234 ms  0.050 ms  0.035 ms
 1  10.10.5.1          1.846 ms  0.080 ms  0.090 ms
 1  172.25.99.86       2.154 ms  0.110 ms  0.098 ms
 1  192.168.55.12      2.551 ms  0.151 ms  0.115 ms
 1  10.56.133.41       3.005 ms  0.189 ms  0.139 ms
```

The first line of the output will be your default gateway, and the last line should be the other VPN gateway. If this process terminates abnormally or you see repeated lines with three asterisks (★) per line, a router or host might be down at some point in the path. If you can `ping` the other end of the VPN connection without much packet loss, someone along the line is filtering traceroutes or possibly all UDP traffic. If this is the case, contact your network administrator and your ISP to resolve these questions. If UDP traffic is filtered, your IPSec VPN isn't going to work because Pluto operates on UDP port 500.

Fields in *ipsec.conf*

Here's a general `ipsec.conf` file:

```
config setup
        interfaces="ipsec0=eth0 ipsec1=eth1"
        klipsdebug=none
        plutodebug=none
        plutoload=%search
        plutostart=%search
        uniqueids=yes

conn %default
        keyingtries=0
        authby=rsasig

conn denet-cnnet
        left=10.1.10.50
        leftsubnet=192.168.10.0/24
        leftnexthop=10.1.10.1
        leftid=@de.exemplify.com
        leftrsasigkey=0sAQNv7EnikLXT1...
        right=10.126.5.241
        rightsubnet=192.168.20.0/24
        rightnexthop=10.126.5.1
        rightid=@cn.exemplify.com
        rightrsasigkey=0sAQN9oqZTrwju...
        auto=add
```

Let's deconstruct this file so that you understand what each field does. Table 6.1 provides a description of each field.

Table 6.1 *ipsec.conf* **File Settings**

Setting	Description
config setup	These are general settings that specify default, connection-independent parameters.
interfaces="..."	Specifies to which physical interfaces the IPSec virtual interfaces should be bound. Multiple bindings can be specified with a <SPACE> delimiter. This field must be surrounded by double quotes (unless using the %defaultroute directive).
klipsdebug=	Specifies the KLIPS debugging level.
plutodebug=	Specifies the Pluto debugging level.
plutoload=	Specifies whether Pluto should load IPSec connections into its database upon startup. The %search directive enables you to set values for each connection through the auto= field.
plutostart=	Specifies whether Pluto should attempt to negotiate IPSec connections upon startup. The %search directive enables you to set values for each connection through the auto= field.
uniqueids=	Tells Pluto that only one ID can be used simultaneously for a connection.
conn %default	This section enables you to set default values for every subsequent conn section.
keyingtries=	Specifies the number of keying attempts to make before failing. The value of "0" denotes an infinite number of attempts.
authby=	Specifies how connections should be authenticated.
conn <name>	This is a specific connection definition.
left -or- right	These parameters denote the IP address of the left and right VPN devices, respectively.
*subnet	Specifies the subnet residing behind the specified VPN gateway. For a single host (nongateway), this parameter is not needed.
*id	Denotes the index of the specified VPN device. This index should take the form of @something.
*nexthop	Specifies the next hop, or the default route, of the respective VPN device. This is needed except when using the %defaultroute directive.
*rsasigkey	Specifies the respective RSA public key for authentication purposes.
auto=	Specifies how Pluto should handle this connection. Only useful when plutostart=%search.

Host-Host Configuration

We'll begin with a simple host-host IPSec tunnel. This is the easiest tunnel to set up, and the configuration files stay relatively lean.

Using the information from our VPN map, we create the following file:

```
config setup
        interfaces="ipsec0=eth0"
        klipsdebug=none
        plutodebug=none
        plutoload=%search
        plutostart=%search
        uniqueids=yes

conn %default
        keyingtries=0
        authby=rsasig

conn de-cn
        left=10.1.10.50
        leftnexthop=10.1.10.1
        leftid=@de.exemplify.com
        leftrsasigkey=0sAQNv7EnikLXTl...
        right=10.126.5.241
        rightnexthop=10.126.5.1
        rightid=@cn.exemplify.com
        rightrsasigkey=0sAQN9oqZTrwju...
        auto=add
```

This file should be copied to /etc/ipsec.conf on both hosts. This should already exist because it was placed there during FreeS/WAN installation. However, the existing file does not contain your configuration information and is therefore relatively worthless.

One field that might not be intuitive is the *rsasigkey field. This field is the RSA public key for each index (or host). This key comes from the /etc/ipsec.secrets file under the field labeled pubkey.

Another field that is not straightforward is the interfaces field. This parameter tells KLIPS to which interface it should bind. You should only have a single interface on this host, but if you have more than one, be sure you specify the proper interface (that is, the interface closest to the other host in the VPN tunnel).

We can simplify our configuration by using the %defaultroute parameter. The %defaultroute parameter does some of the configuration work for us because it automatically detects IP address information and fills in the host's IP address and the nexthop parameter.

The resulting files look like this for @de.exemplify.com and @cn.exemplify.com, respectively:

```
config setup
        interfaces=%defaultroute
        klipsdebug=none
        plutodebug=none
```

```
        plutoload=%search
        plutostart=%search
        uniqueids=yes

conn %default
        keyingtries=0
        authby=rsasig

conn de-cn
        left=%defaultroute
        leftid=@de.exemplify.com
        leftrsasigkey=0sAQNv7EnikLXT1...
        right=10.126.5.241
        rightnexthop=10.126.5.1
        rightid=@cn.exemplify.com
        rightrsasigkey=0sAQN9oqZTrwju...
        auto=add

config setup
        interfaces=%defaultroute
        klipsdebug=none
        plutodebug=none
        plutoload=%search
        plutostart=%search
        uniqueids=yes

conn %default
        keyingtries=0
        authby=rsasig

conn de-cn
        left=10.1.10.50
        leftnexthop=10.1.10.1
        leftid=@de.exemplify.com
        leftrsasigkey=0sAQNv7EnikLXT1...
        right=%defaultroute
        rightid=@cn.exemplify.com
        rightrsasigkey=0sAQN9oqZTrwju...
        auto=add
```

As you can see, the /etc/ipsec.conf file now differs between the two hosts. This should be expected because each host can only automatically determine information about itself.

At this point, you'll want to double-check that all the data in the /etc/ipsec.conf files are correct. Talk to the administrator on the other end of the connection to validate the information.

Now we're ready to start the connection. Enter the following, as root, on the command lines of both hosts:

```
# /etc/rc.d/init.d/ipsec restart
```

This will reinitialize the Pluto daemon with the new configuration values. Once this completes, type the following on one host:

```
# ipsec auto --up <connection name>
```

In our example, we would type the following:

```
# ipsec auto --up de-cn
```

Some output will appear that looks like the following:

```
104 "de-cn" #9: STATE_MAIN_I1: initiate
106 "de-cn" #9: STATE_MAIN_I2: from STATE_MAIN_I1; sent MI2, expecting MR2
108 "de-cn" #9: STATE_MAIN_I3: from STATE_MAIN_I2; sent MI3, expecting MR3
004 "de-cn" #9: STATE_MAIN_I4: ISAKMP SA established
112 "de-cn" #10: STATE_QUICK_I1: initiate
004 "de-cn" #10: STATE_QUICK_I2: sent QI2, IPsec SA established
```

If the ISAKMP key exchange times out repeatedly and never connects, you'll need to troubleshoot the connection. Refer to the section "Running and Troubleshooting FreeS/WAN" for more troubleshooting details. Try to ping the host on the other end to validate the tunnel. If it works, congratulations! You've successfully set up the VPN!

Host-Network Configuration

Let's now try setting up a host-network IPSec tunnel. Using our example, we'll treat @de.exemplify.com as a VPN gateway and @cn.exemplify.com as a VPN host. We'll call this connection "denet-cn".

First, we need to enable routing on @de.exemplify.com. Set up both interfaces to operate on their respective network and validate that they're working. Next, you'll need to tell the kernel to forward packets between interfaces. To do this, type the following:

```
# echo 1 > /proc/sys/net/ipv4/ip_forward
```

You should have already traded public keys, and you don't need different keys for the different VPN connections, so we'll show sample /etc/ipsec.conf files for each host. Notice that we're explicitly setting the IP addresses and *nexthop parameters rather than using the %defaultroute directive.

For @de.exemplify.com, you would have the following:

```
config setup
        interfaces="ipsec0=eth0 ipsec1=eth1"
        klipsdebug=none
        plutodebug=none
        plutoload=%search
        plutostart=%search
        uniqueids=yes

conn %default
        keyingtries=0
        authby=rsasig
```

```
conn denet-cn
        left=10.1.10.50
        leftsubnet=192.168.10.0/24
        leftnexthop=10.1.10.1
        leftid=@de.exemplify.com
        leftrsasigkey=0sAQNv7EnikLXT1...
        right=10.126.5.241
        rightnexthop=10.126.5.1
        rightid=@cn.exemplify.com
        rightrsasigkey=0sAQN9oqZTrwju...
        auto=add
```

For @cn.exemplify.com, you would have the following:

```
config setup
        interfaces="ipsec0=eth0"
        klipsdebug=none
        plutodebug=none
        plutoload=%search
        plutostart=%search
        uniqueids=yes

conn %default
        keyingtries=0
        authby=rsasig

conn denet-cn
        left=10.1.10.50
        leftnexthop=10.1.10.1
        leftsubnet=192.168.10.0/24
        leftid=@de.exemplify.com
        leftrsasigkey=0sAQNv7EnikLXT1...
        right=10.126.5.241
        rightnexthop=10.126.5.1
        rightid=@cn.exemplify.com
        rightrsasigkey=0sAQN9oqZTrwju...
        auto=add
```

As you can see, we've added some information to the `interfaces` line of the `/etc/ipsec.conf` file on @de.exemplify.com. This is necessary because there is more than one interface on the host.

Another field we've added in the `/etc/ipsec.conf` file on both hosts is the `leftsubnet` parameter. This specifies the internal network of the VPN gateway, and it tells FreeS/WAN how to adjust the routing tables on each host to provide connectivity to the "hidden" subnet.

Once you've validated the configuration information with the administrator on the other end, restart the `ipsec` service on both hosts and issue the following command on one host:

```
# ipsec auto --up denet-cn
```

You should see the same ISAKMP key exchange as you saw in the host-host configuration. If it fails, continue on to the section "Running and Troubleshooting FreeS/WAN" later in this chapter for troubleshooting. Otherwise, try pinging a host on the internal subnet (192.168.10.0/24) from @cn.exemplify.com. Also, try pinging @cn.exemplify.com from a host on the internal subnet. An attempt to `ping` @cn.exemplify.com from @de.exemplify.com should fail because @de.exemplify.com tries to route send the packet directly instead of throughout the VPN connection. Lastly, `ping` a non-VPN host from the internal subnet (such as `www.freeswan.org`) to ensure that non-VPN traffic is being forwarded properly.

Network-Network Configuration

As in the host-network configuration, we need to enable routing on the VPN gateways. On each gateway, type the following command:

```
# echo 1 > /proc/sys/net/ipv4/ip_forward
```

Now we will set up a network-network VPN. At this point, the same `/etc/ipsec.conf` file can be used on both hosts because the information contained within should be the same.

```
config setup
        interfaces="ipsec0=eth0 ipsec1=eth1"
        klipsdebug=none
        plutodebug=none
        plutoload=%search
        plutostart=%search
        uniqueids=yes

conn %default
        keyingtries=0
        authby=rsasig

conn denet-cnnet
        left=10.1.10.50
        leftsubnet=192.168.10.0/24
        leftnexthop=10.1.10.1
        leftid=@de.exemplify.com
        leftrsasigkey=0sAQNv7EnikLXTl...
        right=10.126.5.241
        rightsubnet=192.168.20.0/24
        rightnexthop=10.126.5.1
        rightid=@cn.exemplify.com
        rightrsasigkey=0sAQN9oqZTrwju...
        auto=add
```

In this configuration, both gateways have the `*subnet` parameter, and both gateways explicitly state the interface bindings in the `interfaces` parameter.

To start the VPN tunnel, both hosts need to restart the `ipsec` services and then start the VPN tunnel:

```
# ipsec auto --up denet-cnnet
```

If everything is configured correctly, the VPN tunnel should initialize successfully and become operational. Try pinging from a host on one internal subnet to a host on the other internal subnet to validate that the tunnel is operating.

Road Warrior Configuration

The "road warrior configuration" is simply a VPN in which one of the hosts is mobile and therefore has a dynamic IP address. It's impossible to predict from which IP address a mobile host will be coming, so we must allow all authenticated IP addresses to connect. Keep in mind that the VPN administrator probably won't have access to the mobile client once it's out in the field. If you're trying to set up a road warrior VPN, it's best to do it in a controlled environment at first and then deploy the config-uration to the needed mobile hosts.

> **Note**
>
> A VPN host is authenticated by the Pluto initialization process through verification of the preconfigured cryptographic key.

For the purposes of description, we'll use @de.exemplify.com as the VPN gateway and @alice.exemplify.com as the mobile user's index. The VPN gateway must be able to forward packets between its network interfaces, and the mobile host must be able to connect to an ISP and obtain IP address information.

The `/etc/ipsec.conf` configuration file is fairly straightforward for @de. exemplify.com:

```
config setup
        interfaces="ipsec0=eth0 ipsec1=eth1"
        klipsdebug=none
        plutodebug=none
        plutoload=%search
        plutostart=%search
        uniqueids=yes

conn %default
        keyingtries=0
        authby=rsasig

conn denet-alice
        left=10.1.10.50
        leftsubnet=192.168.10.0/24
        leftnexthop=10.1.10.1
        leftid=@de.exemplify.com
        leftrsasigkey=0sAQNv7EnikLXTl...
```

```
        right=%any
        rightid=@alice.exemplify.com
        rightrsasigkey=0sR7gh8Gdr337...
        auto=add
```

The main difference in this configuration file is that there is no defined `right` IP address: The parameter is simply set to the `%any` directive, and there is no `rightnexthop` parameter. This tells FreeS/WAN to accept VPN connections from any host as long as the RSA key matches the defined key.

The configuration file is different on @alice.exemplify.com:

```
config setup
        interfaces=%defaultroute
        klipsdebug=none
        plutodebug=none
        plutoload=%search
        plutostart=%search
        uniqueids=yes
conn %default
        keyingtries=0
        authby=rsasig

conn denet-alice
        left=10.1.10.50
        leftsubnet=192.168.10.0/24
        leftnexthop=10.1.10.1
        leftid=@de.exemplify.com
        leftrsasigkey=0sAQNv7EnikLXT1...
        right=%defaultroute
        rightid=@alice.exemplify.com
        rightrsasigkey=0sR7gh8Gdr337...
        auto=add
```

This is the basic host-network VPN configuration file, with the `%defaultroute` directive replacing explicit IP address information.

As always, restart the `ipsec` service. Then start the VPN on the mobile host:

```
# ipsec auto --up denet-alice
```

Note

You can't start the VPN from the VPN gateway because the gateway doesn't know the IP address of the mobile client. However, the VPN gateway can be prepared to accept VPN connections from the mobile clients.

The VPN should initialize successfully. If not, there's another problem somewhere. The section "Running and Troubleshooting FreeS/WAN" later in this chapter contains some helpful troubleshooting procedures to remedy the situation.

Shutting Down the VPN

When you want to shut down the IPSec connection, issue the following command on both hosts:

```
# ipsec auto --down <connection name>
```

You might notice that, if there is a significant amount of time between executing this command on the hosts, the connection is reestablished. This is because the other VPN device renegotiates the connection. It can do this because the connection is still in the Pluto database on both hosts. To delete the connection from the Pluto database, type the following on both hosts:

```
# ipsec auto --delete <connection name>
```

If at any point you want to reestablish the connection after deleting it from Pluto's database, execute the following commands on both hosts:

```
# ipsec auto --add <connection name>
```

Then execute the following on one host:

```
# ipsec auto --up <connection name>
```

The IPSec connection should renegotiate.

Firewalls

If your VPN sits behind a firewall, you'll need to adjust your firewall ruleset. Based on your configuration, you'll need to add two out of three possible rules:

- In any case, you need to allow traffic on UDP port 500 (ISAKMP) to and from the VPN device. This enables the Pluto daemon to exchange keys with other VPN devices.

- If you're using IPSec ESP mode, you'll need to allow IP protocol 50 (ipv6-crypt) to and from the VPN device.

- If you're using IPSec in AH mode, you'll need to allow IP protocol 51 (ipv6-auth) to and from the VPN device.

NAT and IP Masquerading

Unfortunately, dealing with situations in which a VPN device sits behind a router performing NAT or IP masquerading is beyond the scope of this text. If this situation applies to you, visit Jean-Francois Nadeau's FreeS/WAN page (`http://jixen.tripod.com/`) for more information.

Synopsis of IPSec Commands

Table 6.2 presents the different FreeS/WAN `ipsec` commands and descriptions of each one.

Table 6.2   FreeS/WAN *ipsec* commands

Command Name	Description
auto	Controls automatically keyed VPN connections
barf	Shows all FreeS/WAN debugging information
eroute	Shows/modifies the extended routing table
klipsdebug	Configures KLIPS debugging features
look	Shows condensed debugging information
manual	Controls manually keyed VPN connections
pluto	Manipulates the IKE keying daemon directly
ranbits	Generates and prints random bits in hexadecimal
rsasigkey	Generates RSA keys for Pluto authentication
setup	Controls the interface to FreeS/WAN operation
showdefaults	Prints default routing and interface information
showhostkey	Shows the hostkey in a format suitable for use in DNS
spi	Manipulates SA parameters
spigrp	Manages SPI groups
tncfg	Associates virtual IPSec interfaces with real network interfaces
whack	Controls the interface to Pluto

For More Information

Many more options give you more granular control over the Security Associations (SA), key lifetimes, and automatic initialization of VPN tunnels. If we were to cover all that here, we'd basically be rewriting all the documentation that already exists on FreeS/WAN. So please refer to FreeS/WAN documentation for clarification or further understanding.

Running and Troubleshooting FreeS/WAN

In this section, we'll discuss different ways to gather information about your running FreeS/WAN configuration. This step is crucial to any VPN implementation because you have to ensure that it's actually encrypting and authenticating traffic.

Packet Sniffing

One of the most useful tools in any network administrator's toolkit is a packet sniffer. Most current Linux distributions come with at least one packet sniffer such as tcpdump.

> **Note**
>
> If you don't have `tcpdump` on your system, it can be obtained from `www.tcpdump.org` or from your Linux vendor.

Before starting the FreeS/WAN VPN tunnel, run the sniffer on the command line and save the output. Set it to listen on your external network interface and filter out all traffic except that going to/from the other end of the VPN. From @de.exemplify.com, this would look like the following:

```
# tcpdump -vvv -x -s 0 -X -i eth0 host 10.126.5.241
```

> **Note**
>
> For details about `tcpdump` command-line options, refer to the `tcpdump` manpage. In addition, the `-X` flag only seems to work on newer versions of `tcpdump`.

On a different command line, `ping` the remote host. You should see some output from `tcpdump` that looks like this:

```
01:01:14.904597 10.1.10.50 > 10.126.5.241: icmp: echo reply (ttl 255, id 19428,
len 84)
0x0000   4500 0054 4be4 0000 ff01 65f3 ac18 00fb    E..TK.....e.....
0x0010   1825 4499 0000 9535 880d 0400 9ab2 b23b    .%D....5.......;
0x0020   99cb 0d00 0809 0a0b 0c0d 0e0f 1011 1213    ................
0x0030   1415 1617 1819 1a1b 1c1d 1e1f 2021 2223    .............!"#
0x0040   2425 2627 2829 2a2b 2c2d 2e2f 3031 3233    $%&'()*+,-./0123
0x0050   3435 3637                                  4567
```

As you can see in the first line of the packet dump, this is an ICMP echo reply. It is unencrypted and easily readable. Now initialize the VPN tunnel and sniff the connection the same way as before. This time, the output should look similar to the following:

```
01:02:41.175674 10.1.10.50 > 10.126.5.241: ESP(spi=0xed1815da,seq=0x4) (ttl 64, id
➥19436, len 136)
0x0000   4500 0088 4bec 0000 4032 d52b ac18 00fb    E...K...@2.+....
0x0010   ac18 0001 ed18 15da 0000 0004 f5e7 0964    ...............d
0x0020   cdf4 b37b e3ce bdee e73a a897 215c f9d4    ...{.....:..!\..
0x0030   c3aa 9ab4 c9d5 cf79 5eed e1c2 70f4 891b    .......y^...p...
0x0040   52d6 565f c7b5 e0f1 98b4 4b2a 2419 38c2    R.V_......K*$.8.
0x0050   c280 3078 3522 4422 8a5f c410 d15f 965d    ..0x5"D"._..._.]
0x0060   a02a a151 1cae 0b1d 586c 8bcd 32c0 be49    .*.Q....Xl..2..I
0x0070   9a42 b793 364a 1100 7b93 1572 8337 dff4    .B..6J..{..r.7..
0x0080   b9bc c7cc ab2a e7a0                        .....*..
```

Notice that the packet is labeled as an ESP packet and that the contents are gibberish. If the `ping` was successful, your IPSec tunnel is working.

ping, traceroute, Telnet

The same tools that you use to test normal network connectivity can be used to test your VPN as well. We've already used `ping` quite a bit, so we'll not reiterate.

`traceroute` output can be very interesting because the results should be drastically different. Without the VPN, your `traceroute` output would presumably show a number of hops (usually greater than five) between the endpoints of your VPN. However, for a host-host VPN, there should only be one hop: the other end of the VPN. For a network-network VPN, the only hops should be the hosts on the internal networks and the VPN gateways. This quickly shows you the drastic, logical simplification of your network when using a VPN.

Another very useful troubleshooting tool is plain-old `Telnet`. Because `telnet` is an unencrypted protocol (also known as unencrypted SSH), you can watch usernames and passwords and all keystrokes between one host and another in cleartext.

> **Note**
>
> Although you now have this information at your disposal, we urge you to use the information ethically and not for malicious purposes such as forgery of identification or compromising private information.

In the same way that we sniffed the pings between hosts, sniff a `Telnet` session both without and with the VPN. Without the VPN, you should be able to pick out a username and password in the data portion of the packet. With the VPN, you shouldn't be able to decipher anything. If this is the case, your VPN is doing its job.

Other IPSec Commands

Thus far, we've only used a few of the interactive commands that are part of FreeS/WAN. Most of the other commands are useful in checking the running state of FreeS/WAN. Of particular interest are the following commands:

```
# ipsec spi
```

```
# ipsec tncfg
```

```
# ipsec eroute
```

```
# ipsec look
```

`spi` is the interface for viewing and setting IPSec SA parameters. Get familiar with the (somewhat cryptic) output so that you know what the different fields mean. The man page `ipsec_spi.8` details the information presented.

`tncfg` is the interface for viewing and configuring running ipsecN -> ethN interface bindings. This can be helpful if your key exchange is successful but your VPN tunnel is failing. If this is the case, it's probably due to the virtual `ipsec` interface being bound to the wrong physical network interface.

`eroute` is the interface for viewing and setting the FreeS/WAN extended routing tables. FreeS/WAN must maintain its own routing table because it operates at a deeper kernel level than the TCP/IP stack and thus cannot fully depend on the TCP/IP configuration.

look merely outputs the information from each of the preceding commands. It only makes your life a little easier.

Get to know these commands and how they affect the running configuration, although it is suggested that you make configuration changes through the /etc/ipsec.conf file. An IPSec VPN can be a complicated beast, and unless you keep copiously detailed notes, it's best to keep track of your configuration changes so that you know when you've gotten something right.

"Gotchas"

Several problems are frequently experienced when setting up a FreeS/WAN VPN, and we will go thorough a couple of them in this section. The first one you might encounter looks like this:

```
no default route, %defaultroute cannot cope!!!
```

This occurs when the /etc/rc.d/init.d/ipsec initialization script is executed before your network interfaces are initialized. This is usually the case with road warriors because they usually initialize their PPP connection after their system is booted.

The best solution is to remove the FreeS/WAN code from startup upon bootup. You can do this in a variety of ways, but the easiest way is to issue the following command as root:

```
# chkconfig --del ipsec
```

Then, after your PPP connection is set up and you have Internet connectivity, issue the following command as root and proceed to initialize your VPN tunnel:

```
# /etc/rc.d/init.d/ipsec start
```

Another error you might run into is the following:

```
Error parsing ipsec.conf file
```

Unless you're masochistic, you probably cut-and-pasted the RSA public keys into your /etc/ipsec.conf file. Unfortunately, new-line characters can sometimes be automatically inserted into really long lines when cutting and pasting. Make sure each key exists on a single line. Also make sure you've indented properly.

You might run into this one as well:

```
modprobe: Can't locate module ipsec
```

Did you install your modules after you compiled your kernel? If you're unsure, do this:

```
# cd /usr/src/linux
# make modules_install
```

If FreeS/WAN startup still doesn't work, are you using the appropriate version of the modutils package? If you're using an old version, upgrade to the latest version of modutils and try again.

Summary

There's much more to FreeS/WAN than can be expressed in this chapter. For instance, Opportunistic Encryption is an interesting concept and can make configuration and maintenance of FreeS/WAN VPNs much easier. Also, you might consider adjusting encryption parameters to boost performance. We didn't even discuss the use of IPSec AH mode in this chapter, and your application might require it.

You can also set up multiple tunnels between many different networks, set up VPN "hubs" to which mobile users can connect and access resources anywhere on the company intranet, and even set up tunnels within tunnels (very useful for a cryptographically separate administration network). After you're comfortable setting up simple FreeS/WAN VPNs, try redesigning your networks using VPNs.

For more information on some of the topics discussed in this chapter, see the following:

- Kernel-HOWTO: www.linuxdoc.org/HOWTO/Kernel-HOWTO.html
- Net-HOWTO: www.linuxdoc.org/HOWTO/Net-HOWTO/index.html
- Kirch-NAG: www.linuxdoc.org/LDP/nag2/index.html
- Frisch1995: www.oreilly.com/catalog/esa2/
- Nadeau2001: http://jixen.tripod.com/

7

PPTP

THIS BOOK IS DEDICATED TO BUILDING VPNs on the Linux operating system. Sometimes, however, we Linux bigots find ourselves in the unfortunate position where we must support non-UNIX-like systems directly. One of the worst-case scenarios is when you need Linux-to-Windows VPN interoperability.

PPTP, the Point-to-Point Tunneling Protocol, is an enhancement to PPP developed by Microsoft. PPTP is used almost exclusively to create VPN sessions for roaming users in host-network or host-host configurations. PPTP is fairly well integrated into Windows, making it an appealing solution for the unfortunate soul with a Windows desktop.

You are likely to need to use PPTP on Linux for one of the following two reasons:

- You need to support VPNs for remote Windows desktops.
- You need to establish a VPN from your Linux machine to your office, which only allows PPTP connections.

You will seldom (we'd almost say never) see PPTP used to connect two Linux machines. The other solutions we describe in this book already handle this situation more than adequately. And due to some problems with the PPTP protocol in the past—and the fact that it was developed by Microsoft—you'll find that most Linux folks try to steer clear of PPTP whenever possible.

The PPTP Protocol

PPTP is a generic framework you can use to establish secure VPN connections. Data packets that traverse the VPN are first encapsulated inside PPP packets. (We discussed PPP, the Point-to-Point Protocol, in Chapter 3, "Building a VPN with SSH and PPP," and Chapter 4, "Building a VPN with SSL/TLS and PPP.") These packets are then encapsulated into Generic Routing Encapsulation (GRE) packets and are sent to the other end of the link. GRE is its own IP protocol, just as ICMP, TCP, and UDP are protocols. The protocol number for GRE is 47. (/etc/protocols contains a list of commonly used IP protocols, if you're curious.)

In addition to the GRE packets, which comprise the actual PPTP data, a second control channel is used for the PPTP connection. This is a simple TCP connection from the PPTP client to port 1723 on the PPTP server. It is used to send signaling information and to check the status of the PPTP connection.

PPTP itself does not specify what authentication or encryption algorithms should be used. Instead, the algorithms are negotiated by the underlying PPP session.

Microsoft's PPTP Implementation

For authentication and encryption to be enabled for the PPTP session, Microsoft needed to add a few algorithms to PPP. For authentication, a variant of the Challenge/Reply Handshake Protocol (CHAP), named MS-CHAP, was added. This method is based on two other Microsoft methods used for file sharing and authentication, the LAN Manager hash (based on DES encryption) and the Windows NT hash (based on the MD4 hash function). The LAN Manager hash is known to be a weak algorithm, easily crackable by software such as L0phtcrack.

The second extension to PPP is MPPE, the Microsoft Point-to-Point Encryption protocol. This protocol handles the actual encryption of the packets. It uses the RC4 stream cipher to encrypt the data with a 40- or 128-bit key. The encryption key used by the cipher is derived partially from the user's password via the LAN Manager hash or NT hash. The session keys used for encryption are changed periodically, typically after every 256 packets.

Problems with Microsoft's Implementation of PPTP

The first version of PPTP released by Microsoft faced some strict cryptographic scrutiny by the online community. In 1998, two leading crypto and security experts, Bruce Schneier of Counterpane Systems and Mudge of L0pht Heavy Industries, analyzed the protocol and found numerous show-stopping problems with it.

Among the problems with Microsoft's PPTPv1 were the following:

- MS-CHAPv1 sends the client password in two forms, a LAN Manager hash and an NT hash. The former is a very weak hash algorithm. The tool L0phtcrack could be used to break the LAN Manager hash and use it to attack the stronger NT hash, leading to the recovery of the user's password.

- The encryption keys are derived from the user's password. Thus, passwords with low entropy lead to low-level encryption, even when 128-bit encryption is used.

- MPPE used the same encryption key for both directions of the communication. This meant that the same key was used to encrypt two different cleartext streams. This is a big crypto no-no, allowing cryptographic analysis to derive the key or plaintext much more quickly.

- The key used for MPPE is changed every 256 packets. However, an attacker can spoof resynchronize keys packets before the rekeying phase, which can be used to ensure that the key is never changed.

- There was no method for a client to authenticate the server, allowing an attacker to impersonate the server.

These vulnerabilities were addressed in the next version of Microsoft PPTP, dubbed PPTPv2. It included a new version of the authentication protocol, MS-CHAPv2. MS-CHAPv2 is incompatible with the original. It increases the randomness of the keys, eliminates sending the weaker LAN Manager password hash, and allows MPPE to use different encryption keys for each direction of VPN traffic.

Microsoft PPTP still suffers from a few problems. First, the protocol is built to support older software by falling back to the insecure MS-CHAPv1 authentication if both endpoints do not support MS-CHAPv2. Such backward compatibility is good from a user-friendliness standpoint, but it's a detriment to security in this context.

The biggest problem, however, is that PPTPv2 still derives the encryption keys from the user's password. Most user passwords do not contain 40 bits of entropy, even on a good day. Thus, regardless of how many bits the cipher might be using, your effective encryption is only as strong as your password.

How Strong Is Your Password?

T.M. Cover and R.C. King conducted experiments to determine how much entropy is contained in standard English ("A Convergent Gambling Estimate of the Entropy of English." *IEEE Transactions on Information Theory*, July, 1978). They gave subjects strings of letters and had them bet on what the next letters would be. By comparing the actual results with the bets placed, they determined the entropy of English strings to be about 1.3 bits per letter.

Thus, this sentence has about 64 bits of entropy.

That's obviously not enough for a strong 128-bit key, and you can bet that most folks don't normally use passwords as long as the preceding sentence. (NT only allows 14 characters, for example.) Use of numbers, punctuation, other characters, and variation of case can be used to create stronger keys.

Experiments performed by other scientists range in their entropy estimation from 0.6 to 1.6 bits per character.

Just to stress this again, the problems described in this section are not with PPTP itself—which does not specify which authentication or encryption algorithms are used—but with the Microsoft implementation of PPTP. Unfortunately, Microsoft's implementation is the only one you're likely to use because it's the only one supported by Windows machines.

The complete analysis of PPTPv1 and PPTPv2 by Schneier and Mudge can be found at www.counterpane.com/pptp.html. Before deciding to use PPTP, we suggest that you read their results and decide whether PPTP fits your security requirements.

Though most of Schneier and Mudge's security concerns with Microsoft's PPTP have been addressed in PPTPv2, they still sum up their opinion of the protocol succinctly: "At this point we still do not recommend Microsoft PPTP for applications where security is a factor."

PPTP on Linux

Though PPTP was a creation of Microsoft, the company has released the specifications in various documents and RFCs. Thus, it is possible for others to write software that supports Microsoft PPTP.

Both server and client PPTP implementations have been created for Linux. Both require a version of pppd that supports the Microsoft encryption (MPPE) and authentication (MS-CHAPv2) extensions. A patched version of pppd was developed that supports these algorithms, and it is necessary regardless of whether you are supporting PPTP on a Linux client or server. The client has a program, pptp, that is used to set up outbound calls, as well as a menu-driven Perl script that can help you with configuration. The server has a program, pptpd, that accepts inbound PPTP connections.

PPTP, Packet Filters, and Firewalls

Getting PPTP to work well with Linux firewalls or packet filters takes planning, care, and a healthy dose of debugging. This is mainly because you have two connections at work: the TCP control channel and the GRE data channel.

PPTP and Packet Filters

Many folks, ourselves included, like to restrict the packets that are able to pass through our Linux servers by implementing kernel packet filters. These are configured using the ipchains command for 2.2 kernels and the iptables command for 2.4 kernels. (If you're using a 2.0 or older kernel, you really should upgrade.)

In general, we like to explicitly list which packets our machine can accept and deny all others. If you do this, your PPTP sessions will probably not work because the packets are being dropped. You will need to add rules such as the following:

```
# For 2.2 kernels
root@firewall# ipchains -A input -p 47 -j ACCEPT
root@firewall# ipchains -A output -p 47 -j ACCEPT

  # PPTP Servers
  root@firewall# ipchains -A input -p TCP -d 0.0.0.0/0 1723 -j ACCEPT
  root@firewall# ipchains -A output -p TCP -s 0.0.0.0/0 1723 -j ACCEPT
```

```
# PPTP Clients
root@firewall# ipchains -A input -p TCP -s 0.0.0.0/0 1723 -j ACCEPT
root@firewall# ipchains -A output -p TCP -d 0.0.0.0/0 1723 -j ACCEPT


# For 2.4 kernels

root@firewall# iptables -A INPUT -p 47 -j ACCEPT
root@firewall# iptables -A OUTPUT -p 47 -j ACCEPT

  # PPTP Servers
  root@firewall# iptables -A INPUT -p TCP -d 0.0.0.0/0
--destination-port 1723 -j ACCEPT
  root@firewall# iptables -A OUTPUT -p TCP -s 0.0.0.0/0
--source-port 1723 -j ACCEPT

  # PPTP Clients
  root@firewall# iptables -A INPUT -p TCP -s 0.0.0.0/0
--source-port 1723 -j ACCEPT
  root@firewall# iptables -A OUTPUT -p TCP -d 0.0.0.0/0
--destination-port 1723 -j ACCEPT
```

These rules simply say to allow both inbound and outbound packets that match the two connections used by PPTP. Make sure to apply the server or client rules as appropriate. (You could apply all rules and things will still work; you'll just have some extraneous ACCEPT rules.)

PPTP and Firewalls

PPTP does not play well with firewalls that perform IP masquerading. Masquerading is the method that a Linux firewall can use to allow multiple inside machines to access the Internet. All the packets to and from the Internet appear to come from the firewall itself, which handles rewriting the packets and sending them back into the machines that established the connections.

An ipchains/iptables masquerading firewall works great for TCP and UDP protocols. There are some annoying protocols, such as FTP, that are difficult to support because they use multiple ports at a time. These are handled by modules such as ip_masq_ftp. Unfortunately, there is no standard module to support GRE and PPTP packets, and the kernel does not support this functionality.

Thus, the only method available is to patch the kernel itself to understand how to deal with the special GRE packets. Because its substantial, we do not have the space here to describe the installation and configuration that's needed to get this to work. Instead, we'll simply refer you to a few sources:

- http://www.linuxdoc.org/HOWTO/VPN-Masquerade-HOWTO.html

  Start here, at the Linux VPN masquerade how-to. It discusses supporting PPTP, IPSec, and others.

- `http://www.impsec.org/linux/masquerade/ip_masq_vpn.html`

  The Linux VPN masquerade home page.

- `http://bmrc.berkeley.edu/people/chaffee/linux_pptp.html`

  A kernel patch to support PPTP only. If you don't need to support IPSec as well, this might be simpler to use. It creates a module `ip_masq_pptp` that does the work for you.

- `http://cag.lcs.mit.edu/~cananian/Projects/IPfwd/`

  Ipfwd is an IP protocol redirection tool. It's another way to tunnel GRE packets through your firewall, simply by listening for them and sending them through. It runs in userspace, not in the kernel.

If you have a masquerading firewall and do not want to trudge through all this documentation to get your PPTP connection working, we suggest you consider an alternative: Have your firewall make the PPTP connection. If the PPTP connection starts at the firewall, no GRE patches are needed because the firewall will receive them directly. You then need only add routes to the firewall, allowing the packets to be forwarded from your internal machines over the VPN, as well as `ipchains`/`iptables` rules similar to the following to allow them to forward the packets:

```
# 2.2 kernels
root@firewall# ipchains -A forward -s INTERNAL_NET -d REMOTE_NET_1 -j ACCEPT
root@firewall# ipchains -A forward -d INTERNAL_NET -s REMOTE_NET_1 -j ACCEPT
root@firewall# ipchains -A forward -s INTERNAL_NET -d REMOTE_NET_2 -j ACCEPT
root@firewall# ipchains -A forward -d INTERNAL_NET -s REMOTE_NET_2 -j ACCEPT
...

# 2.4 kernels
root@firewall# iptables -A FORWARD -s INTERNAL_NET -d REMOTE_NET_1 -j ACCEPT
root@firewall# iptables -A FORWARD -d INTERNAL_NET -s REMOTE_NET_1 -j ACCEPT
root@firewall# iptables -A FORWARD -s INTERNAL_NET -d REMOTE_NET_2 -j ACCEPT
root@firewall# iptables -A FORWARD -d INTERNAL_NET -s REMOTE_NET_2 -j ACCEPT
...
```

Replace *INTERNAL_NET* with your internal network (192.168.1.0/24, for example) and *REMOTE_NET_X* with your remote VPN networks (10.1.0.0/24, ...) You will need to coordinate with the administrator on the other end to ensure that the networks do not conflict and that routing is set up properly on both sides.

The preceding `ipchains`/`iptables` rules must be before your normal masquerading rules (for example, `ipchains -A forward -i eth1 -j MASQ`); otherwise, the packets will get masqueraded instead of forwarded properly.

Installing *ppp-mppe*

Both our PPTP server and PPTP client require a version of `pppd` that supports the Microsoft extensions MPPE (Microsoft Point-to-Point Encryption) and MS-

CHAP/MS-CHAPv2 (Microsoft's enhanced CHAP authentication.) The software package ppp-mppe is a special version of the standard Linux ppp package that includes these extensions.

The code for ppp-mppe is available from the PPTP page at http://pptpclient. sourceforge.net/ in several different forms:

```
ppp-mppe-VERSION.alpha.rpm # Precompiled binaries for Alpha
ppp-mppe-VERSION.i386.rpm  # Precompiled binaries for Intel
ppp-mppe-VERSION.src.rpm   # The source as an RPM
ppp-mppe-VERSION.tar.gz.   # The source as a tar archive
```

If you want to install the binary rpms, simply download the one appropriate to your architecture and run the following:

```
$ rpm -i filename.rpm
```

We will describe the method of installing ppp-mppe from the source using the tar archive.

Installing *ppp-mppe* from the Source

First, download the tar archive from http://pptpclient.sourceforge.net/ and extract these files:

```
$ tar xzvf ppp-mppe-VERSION.tar.gz

$ cd ppp-mppe-VERSION

$ sh unpack.sh
```

The unpack.sh script does the following automatically for you:

- Creates the ppp-**VERSION** build directory.
- Unpacks and patches the OpenSSL sources. Only the parts of OpenSSL needed for ppp-mppe are included.
- Rewrites the OpenSSL Makefiles to only build the functions necessary for ppp-mppe.
- Patches OpenSSL source files to include a new get_key() function, required by the Microsoft algorithms.
- Patches the pppd source to support the PPTP-related extensions, such as the MS-CHAP authentication methods, and so on.
- Unpacks kernel modules and module sources into the build directory.

Patching *ppp-mppe* Sources

If you want to apply any pppd patches, this is the time. There are currently two patches available at http://themm.net/ that might be useful depending on your environment.

The first (`strip-MSdomain-patch.diff`) is a patch that configures MS–CHAP to ignore any NT domain supplied as part of the username. In other words, `DOMAIN\\` `user` will become simply `user` for authentication purposes, making your `/etc/ppp/chap-secrets` file less cluttered.

You can turn this option on by adding `chapms-strip-domain` to your `/etc/ppp/` `options` file.

The second patch (`require-mppe.diff`) is one we strongly suggest for VPN users. It is a patch that can be used to force MPPE encryption, which is triggered when the directive `require-mppe` is added to `/etc/ppp/options`. If you do not apply this patch, your PPTP connection might be established correctly but not use any encryption at all, meaning your VPN is not secure. Another option available if you use this patch is `require-mppe-stateless`. This requires that stateless MPPE be negotiated, which in turn provides a higher degree of security because keys are renegotiated for each packet rather than every 256.

To apply these patches, go into the `ppp` source directory and run the `patch` command as follows:

```
$ cd ppp-VERSION
$ patch -p1 < /path/to/patch.diff
```

Then add the options you desire to `/etc/ppp/options`:

```
# Require encryption
require-mppe
require-mppe-stateless

# Strip NT domain cruft
chapms-strip-domain
```

Again, we strongly suggest that you apply the `require-mppe.diff` patch. It is the only way you can be sure your VPN is using encryption. If you don't mind having user-names in `/etc/ppp/chap-secrets` that contain the NT domain, the other patch isn't necessary.

Building *pppd*

You then go into the new build directory and compile the software:

```
$ cd ppp-VERSION          # if you haven't already
$ ./configure
Creating links to Makefiles.
  Makefile -> linux/Makefile.top
  pppd/Makefile -> Makefile.linux
  pppstats/Makefile -> Makefile.linux
  chat/Makefile -> Makefile.linux
  pppdump/Makefile -> Makefile.linux
$ make
```

This will compile the MPPE-enhanced PPP software. It shouldn't take long, perhaps a few minutes on a slow processor. Once done, you must make a decision about where to install the software.

Installing *ppp-mppe* in the Default Location

By default, ppp-mppe wants to be installed into the normal system directories such as /etc, /usr/sbin, and /usr/man. This will likely conflict with the default installation of your Linux distribution's PPP installation. This means it would overwrite your existing binaries, such as /usr/sbin/pppd, and could cause problems with your package manager (RPM, DPKG, and so on). If you do not use PPP on your machine at all, we suggest that you deinstall your current PPP package so that you do not have this conflict:

```
root@redhat# rpm -e ppp
root@debian# dpkg -r ppp
etc...
```

Once you've removed your existing ppp installation, run make to install the ppp-mppe software:

```
root@machine# make
```

Installing *ppp-mppe* in a Different Location

The ppp-mppe software should be compatible with your existing ppp software so that you can simply overwrite your current binaries with the new versions. This angers package managers, however, and could cause problems when your Linux distribution has updates to its ppp software—updates that could overwrite your ppp-mppe versions. Thus, you might want to install the ppp-mppe software in a different location.

We like to install our software into /opt/pkgs, so we would run the following commands to install ppp-mppe there:

```
# DESTDIR=/opt/pkgs/ppp-mppe
# export DESTDIR
# make install
```

This creates the following directory structure:

```
/opt/pkgs/ppp-mppe/etc        # This directory is not actually
                              # used.  /etc/ppp is used when
                              # the ppp programs are called.
                              # You can ignore the files
                              # herein.

/opt/pkgs/ppp-mppe/usr/sbin   # location of the binaries
                              # chat, pppd, pppdump, and
                              # pppstats

/opt/pkgs/ppp-mppe/usr/man    # manual pages
```

Because we used a nonstandard spot for our MPPE-enhanced PPP, we will need to change pathnames later when we establish connections. We'll point out these occurrences.

PPP Kernel Modules

Using PPP requires that the kernel be built with PPP support, either in the kernel itself or in kernel modules. The ppp-mppe tarball comes with some precompiled kernel modules that you can install if needed, as well as instructions on how you can recompile your kernel with PPP support if necessary.

Most Linux distributions already come with PPP support in their kernels. Thus, the chance that you will need to recompile your kernel is very small, and we won't take the time to cover it here. The ppp-mppe software works with your existing PPP support, so you do not need to "upgrade" your kernel or kernel modules for it to work.

You can quickly check whether you have PPP support in modules (the way most Linux distributions choose) by running the following commands:

```
# insmod slhc
# insmod ppp
# lsmod | egrep 'slhc|ppp|Module'
Module                Size  Used by
ppp                  21036  0  (unused)
slhc                  4440  0  [ppp]
```

The slhc module contains routines used by the PPP module, thus the order in which we loaded them. The pppd program we will run automatically handles loading these modules if needed, so you should never need to load these manually anyway.

If the preceding commands fail, you either have PPP support compiled directly into your kernel (not as a module), or you do not have PPP support at all and should recompile your kernel. Again, if you have an off-the-shelf Linux installation, you probably have PPP support compiled as a kernel module already and need do nothing.

Installing the *mppe* Kernel Module

If you want to have encryption available for your PPTP connection (which is the whole point if you want to use it for a VPN), you need to compile the mppe kernel module. The source is part of the tarball you've already unpacked. Run the kmod-build.sh script to compile the kernel module:

```
# cd ppp-VERSION/linux-kernel
# sh kmodbuild.sh
```

After a flash of compilation messages, you'll be greeted with instructions for how to install your newly created modules:

```
Your kernel modules are in kernel-modules/new-VERSION
In order to use the new kernel modules, you need to install them in
/lib/modules/VERSION
```

There is a second script you can use to install the modules automatically. Simply run the following:

```
# kernel-modules/kmodinst.sh kernel-modules/new-VERSION
```

Replace *VERSION* with your actual kernel version number. If you'd rather do things manually, here are the steps you need to take:

1. Remove the `mppe` and `ppp` modules from the running kernel as follows:

    ```
    # rmmod mppe; rmmod ppp
    ```

2. Copy the file `kernel-modules/new-VERSION/mppe.oto`
    `/lib/modules/VERSION/misc/mppe.o`.

3. Copy the file `kernel-modules/new-VERSION/ppp.oto`
    `/lib/modules/VERSION/net/ppp.oto`

4. Edit `/etc/modules.conf`. Make sure the following lines are present, adding any that are missing:

    ```
    alias ppp-compress-18 mppe
    alias ppp-compress-21 bsd_comp
    alias ppp-compress-24 ppp_deflate
    alias ppp-compress-26 ppp_deflate
    alias char-major-108  ppp
    ```

    These lines define loadable module associations, used by `kerneld` and `modprobe` to load them when needed by `pppd`.

5. Run `depmod -a` to rebuild the module dependency database.

All of these actions are performed safely by the `kmodinst.sh` script, so you can bypass manual installation by using the shell script if you prefer.

Building a PPTP VPN Client

A Linux machine can connect to a PPTP VPN server by using the software named `pptp-linux`. (It can also be compiled for some other UNIX-like operating systems such as *BSD and Solaris, though Linux is its primary system.) It's been around a few years and works well with PPTP servers run on Windows (NT and so on) as well as the server PPTP package discussed later in this chapter.

`pptp-linux` consists of several pieces. The first is the `pptp` program, which handles making an outbound connection to the server, establishing the PPTP control and GRE channels. It calls a modified version of the PPP daemon, called `ppp-mppe`, to handle the network connection and calls Microsoft extensions for authentication and encryption.

`pptp-linux` also includes a Perl script named `pptp-command`, which can greatly simplify the configuration of PPTP VPNs through a simple menu interface. You do not need to use this program if you don't want to—we will show you the files it modifies so that you can do the complete configuration on your own if you prefer.

Figure 7.1 shows you our sample VPN network. The client, wildcat, is a Linux machine connected to the Internet by a dial-up PPP connection. Any network connection would apply, but this seems to be the most common and what you would experience with a roaming user on a laptop, for example.

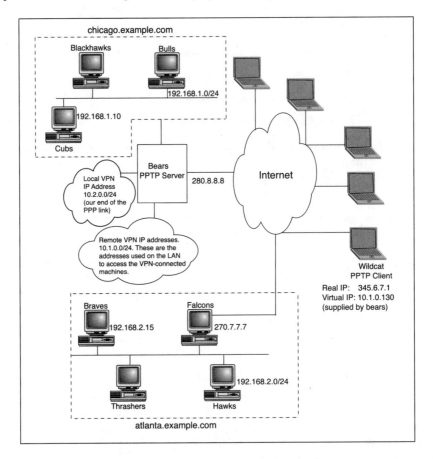

Figure 7.1   Our sample PPTP VPN network.

We'll assume that the PPTP server is the machine bears.example.com (280.8.8.8), which, for some unfortunate reason, is a Windows NT machine in the CHICAGO domain. (If it were a Linux machine, we'd be able to use something other than PPTP for our VPN.) The PPTP client is a Linux machine named wildcat, dialed up to the Internet with a modem. Thus ppp0 will be our Internet interface, and we'll assume that the IP address from our ISP is 345.6.7.1 and that the ISP's DNS server is 345.6.7.8.

We'll assume that Bears and Falcons already have a VPN established between them so that we have secure traffic between Chicago and Atlanta. Dial-in users will be able to connect to the Chicago PPTP server and have access to both networks.

Client PPTP Software Installation

The software consists of two main pieces:

- pptp   A program to start the PPTP connection
- pptp-command   A Perl script that helps you configure your VPN

You must have already installed the modified pppd software (ppp-mppe) as described earlier because this is used by the pptp program. The pptp-linux code is available from the PPTP page at http://pptpclient.sourceforge.net in binary, source RPM, and tarball formats. The precompiled versions are available for x86 and alpha. In general, we prefer to install software from the tarball and will show you how to do so. This is also important in case your machines are of a different architecture such as Sun Sparc, which we use for some of our test machines.

Installing *pptp-linux*

After downloading the tarball, extract the files:

```
$ tar xzvf pptp-linux-VERSION.tar.gz
$ cd pptp-linux-VERSION
```

This directory contains the options.pptp file we will use later, the pptp-command we can use to easily set up our PPTP tunnel, and the actual source tarball. Unpack the actual pptp source:

```
$ tar xvzf pptp-linux-VERSION.tar.gz
$ cd pptp-linux-VERSION
```

If you installed the ppp-mppe software into a nonstandard location, you will need to edit the Makefile manually before compiling. Locate the following section of the Makefile:

```
################################################################
# CHANGE THIS LINE to point to the location of your pppd binary.
CFLAGS += '-DPPPD_BINARY="/usr/sbin/pppd"'
################################################################
```

Change the path /usr/sbin/pppd to the actual location of the pppd program you installed. In our example, we installed ppp-mppe into /opt/pkgs/ppp-mppe, so we'd use /opt/pkgs/ppp-mppe/usr/sbin/pppd here. When done, simply run make:

```
$ make
```

The PPTP source does not have a simple make install command, so you'll need to copy the resulting programs manually as root:

```
# cp pptp /usr/sbin
# cp pptp_callmgr /usr/sbin
# chmod 700 /usr/sbin/pptp*
# chown root:root /usr/sbin/pptp*
```

Installing pptp Elsewhere

If you prefer to install the pptp program in a different location, that is fine. You will need to modify the pptp-command, as described in the next section.

Installing the *pptp-command* Script

The pptp-linux source comes with a Perl script named pptp-command. This script provides a quick and easy way to configure, start, or stop a PPTP connection. You can do all these things manually if you prefer—we will show you the actions the script actually takes so that you understand them—but even we use the script because it's so easy to use.

To install the script, simply copy it to your favorite system directory:

```
# cp pptp-command /usr/sbin
# chmod 700 /usr/sbin/pptp-command
```

If you installed pptp to somewhere other than /usr/sbin, you will need to locate the following section of code in pptp-command, found in the start subroutine:

```
if ($child == 0) {
    exec "/usr/sbin/pptp $server call $tunnel";
    die "exec of pptp failed.";
}
```

Replace /usr/sbin/pptp with the correct pathname to your pptp program. Some versions of the pptp-command were written with Perl's Taint Mode turned on. This is a good security measure that forces programmers to write clean and paranoid code. Unfortunately, if not all the data was "untainted" properly, you could get an error like the following:

```
Insecure dependency in BLAH while running with -T switch ...
```

If you are a Perl guru, you can fix the code to properly untaint the data being used. If not, the easiest way to bypass this problem is to turn off Taint Mode in the pptp-command by changing the first line of the script from

```
#!/usr/bin/perl -wT
```

to

```
#!/usr/bin/perl -w
```

Setting Up Your PPTP Tunnel Client

We'll show you how to set up your PPTP tunnel by showing you the pptp-command in action. The pptp-command is simply a menu-driven interface that enables you to configure various ppp-related files. At each step, we'll also show you what changes the pptp-command program performs so that you can make these modifications manually if you prefer.

Start off by running the pptp-command script and selecting setup:

```
wildcat# pptp-command
1.) start
2.) stop
3.) setup
4.) quit
What task would you like to do?: 3
1.) List CHAP secrets
2.) Add a New CHAP secret
3.) Delete a CHAP secret
4.) List PPTP Tunnels
5.) Add a NEW PPTP Tunnel
6.) Delete a PPTP Tunnel
7.) Configure resolv.conf
8.) Select a default tunnel
9.) Quit
```

Configuring CHAP Secrets

The first thing you need to do is store the passwords that will be used for the PPTP connection. There are two usernames and passwords in question. The pptp-command script calls them the local name and remote name. Not obviously, the local name is the username used for authentication on the PPTP server, which you learn from your administrator. The remote name is usually PPTP unless configured differently by the server administrator.

If you are connecting to an NT PPTP server and that machine is part of an NT domain, you must include the domain name as part of your local name argument, separated by double backslashes from your username. So, if your username was REEGEN and the NT domain was CHICAGO, you would use CHICAGO\\REEGEN for the local name.

Select the Add a new CHAP secret option from the setup menu:

```
1.) List CHAP secrets
2.) Add a New CHAP secret
3.) Delete a CHAP secret
4.) List PPTP Tunnels
5.) Add a NEW PPTP Tunnel
6.) Delete a PPTP Tunnel
7.) Configure resolv.conf
8.) Select a default tunnel
9.) Quit
?: 2
```

```
Add a NEW CHAP secret.
NOTE: Any backslashes (\) must be doubled (\\).
Local Name: CHICAGO\\REEGEN
Remote Name [PPTP]: PPTP
Password: sup3r$secretP&ssw0rd
```

All the `pptp-command` script actually does is create new entries in the `/etc/ppp/chap-secrets` file. If you prefer to do this manually, you would add the following lines to `/etc/ppp/chap-secrets`:

```
# Client           Server           Secret
CHICAGO\\REEGEN    PPTP             sup3r$secretP&ssw0rd
PPTP               CHICAGO\\REEGEN  sup3r$secretP&ssw0rd
```

The remote name should be set to PPTP (yes, all caps) because this is the name the `pptp` program uses when launching `pppd`.

Configuring PPTP VPN Parameters

The `pptp-command` script will help you set up your PPTP tunnel parameters easily. Select the `Add a NEW PPTP Tunnel` option from the menu and answer the questions by selecting a name for the tunnel and the IP address or hostname of the server:

```
Add a NEW PPTP Tunnel.
1.) Other
Which configuration would you like to use?: 1
Tunnel Name: Chicago
Server IP: bears.example.com
```

At this point, you are able to define which routes should be created when the PPTP connection is established. Two special strings are available to you. `TUNNEL_DEV` will be replaced by the device of the tunnel interface (for example, ppp1), and `DEF_GW` will be replaced by the default gateway. You specify a route command exactly as you would from the command line, leaving off the `route` command name itself from the beginning.

```
What route(s) would you like to add when the tunnel comes up?
          The syntax to use is the same as the route(8) command.
          Enter a blank line to stop.
          route: add -net 192.168.1.0/24 TUNNEL_DEV
          route: add -net 192.168.2.0/24 TUNNEL_DEV
          route: <enter>
```

You then must specify which name to use for authentication. This is the `local name` you created in the previous section, in the example CHICAGO\\REEGEN:

```
Local Name and Remote Name should match a configured CHAP secret.
Local Name: CHICAGO\\REEGEN
Remote Name [PPTP]:
Adding Chicago - 280.8.8.8 - CHICAGO\\REEGEN - PPTP
Added tunnel Chicago
```

The pptp-command script simply takes the information you provide and creates a file called /etc/ppp/peers/NAME, where NAME is the tunnel name you specified. This file is used by pppd to set the options name and remote name. However, it also has comment lines that are ignored by pppd but that are used by the pptp-command to determine IP address and route information used to establish the tunnel:

```
# PPTP Tunnel configuration for tunnel Chicago
# Server IP: 280.8.8.8
# Route: add -net 192.168.1.0/24 TUNNEL_DEV
# Route: add -net 192.168.2.0/24 TUNNEL_DEV

# Tags for CHAP secret selection
#
name CHICAGO\\REEGEN
remotename PPTP
```

Configuring /etc/resolv.conf

The file /etc/resolv.conf dictates how your machine should perform DNS lookups. For example, the following /etc/resolv.conf file says to query the name servers on 127.0.0.1 and 345.6.7.8 (the DNS server at our ISP) for DNS responses, and that when a nonfully qualified hostname such as test is requested, to first try test.example.com and then test.example.org:

```
search example.com example.org
nameserver 127.0.0.1
nameserver 345.6.7.8
```

The resolv.conf file that works for you when connected to the Internet in general might not be suitable when you are using your VPN. In our network diagram, we have DNS servers (Cubs and Braves) inside the Chicago office that can provide lookups for the internal machines such as blackhawks.chicago.example.com; however, these machines are only available when using the VPN.

pptp-command enables you to rotate your /etc/resolv.conf file easily when a VPN is created or destroyed. To set up your separate resolv.conf files, select the Configure resolv.conf option:

```
Use a PPTP-specific resolv.conf during tunnel connections? [Y/n]:y
1.) Other
Which configuration do you want to use?: 1
What domain names do you want to search for partially specified names?
Enter all of them on one line, seperated by spaces.
Domain Names: chicago.example.org example.org
Enter the IP addresses of your nameservers
Enter a blank IP address to stop.
Nameserver IP Address: 192.168.1.10
Nameserver IP Address: 192.168.2.15
Nameserver IP Address: 345.6.7.8
Nameserver IP Address:
```

```
Copying /etc/resolv.conf to /etc/resolv.conf.real...
Creating link from /etc/resolv.conf.real to /etc/resolv.conf
```

pptp-command uses this information to create the following files:

/etc/resolv.conf.real	Your current resolv.conf file
/etc/resolv.conf.pptp	The VPN–specific resolv.conf file
/etc/resolv.conf	A symlink

When you establish your PPTP tunnel, pptp-command will change the symbolic link /etc/resolv.conf to point to whichever of the two actual resolv.conf.{real,pptp} files is appropriate. This is an easy way to have access to your internal name servers without the rigmarole of modifying or rotating your resolv.conf file manually.

Starting the PPTP VPN

The pptp-command script will let you easily start and stop the PPTP VPN from the main menu:

```
wildcat# pptp-command
1.) start
2.) stop
3.) setup
4.) quit
What task would you like to do?: 1
1.) Chicago
Start a tunnel to which server?: 1
Route: add -net 192.168.1.0/24 dev ppp1 added
Route: add -net 192.168.2.0/24 dev ppp1 added
All routes added.
Tunnel Chicago is active on ppp1.
```

You can see that the connection was successful by looking at your routing table and device (ppp1) interface statistics:

```
wildcat# netstat -rn
Kernel IP routing table
Destination     Gateway         Genmask          Flags  MSS Window  irtt Iface
10.1.0.130      0.0.0.0         255.255.255.255  UH      0 0        0 ppp1
192.168.1.0     192.168.1.1     255.255.255.0    U       0 0        0 ppp1
192.168.2.0     192.168.1.1     255.255.255.0    U       0 0        0 ppp1
127.0.0.0       0.0.0.0         255.0.0.0        U       0 0        0 lo
345.6.7.1       0.0.0.0         255.255.255.255  U       0 0        0 ppp0
0.0.0.0         345.6.7.9       0.0.0.0          UG      0 0        0 ppp0

wildcat# ifconfig ppp1
ppp1      Link encap:Point-to-Point Protocol
          inet addr:10.1.0.130  P-t-P:10.2.0.102 Mask:255.255.255.255
          UP POINTOPOINT RUNNING NOARP MULTICAST  MTU:1500  Metric:1
          RX packets:13 errors:0 dropped:0 overruns:0 frame:0
          TX packets:143524 errors:0 dropped:0 overruns:0 carrier:0
          collisions:0 txqueuelen:10
```

The `ppp0` lines in `netstat` output are those of the machine's normal dial–up modem connection. The `ppp1` entries are the PPTP VPN tunnel and related routes. Note that both IP addresses of the `ppp1` link are supplied by the VPN server, in this case 10.1.0.130 for our end and 10.2.0.102 for its end. Assuming that the PPTP VPN server is set up properly, the values it supplies should work.

For each established outbound PPTP connection, you will actually have three processes: a call manager, a GRE/PPP encapsulator/decapsulator, and the `pppd` process to handle the encryption and network connectivity. These processes are easily visible via the `ps` command:

```
wildcat$ ps -ef | egrep 'pptp|pppd'
root      5755     1  0 04:43 pts/1     00:00:00 /usr/bin/pptp pptp:
   call manager for xxx.xxx.xxx.xxx
root      5757     1  0 04:43 pts/1     00:00:00 /usr/bin/pptp pptp: GRE-to-PPP
   gateway on /dev/pts/5
root      5762     1  0 04:43 pts/5     00:00:00 /opt/pkgs/ppp-mppe/usr/sbin/pppd
   /dev/pts/5 38400 call Chicago
```

You can stop the PPTP VPN tunnel simply by killing the `pppd` process:

```
wildcat# kill 5762
```

If you started the VPN with the `pptp-command` script, you can kill it using the script as well:

```
wildcat# /opt/bin/pptp-command
1.) start
2.) stop
3.) setup
4.) quit
What task would you like to do?: 2
Sending HUP signal to PPTP processes...
```

Starting the PPTP VPN Manually

If you prefer doing things manually rather than using `pptp-command`, it's easy enough from the command line. You must have already configured your CHAP secret, either using `pptp-command` or the manual method we described.

To start a session, you need the external IP address of the PPTP server and the name of your PPTP VPN (that is, the filename in `/etc/ppp/peers`.) Then call `pptp` as follows:

```
wildcat# pptp bears.example.com call Chicago
```

You must manually add your network routes and modify `/etc/resolv.conf` if needed because these are normally handled by the `pptp-command` program for you.

To stop the VPN, assuming it is using device `ppp1`, you could kill the `pppd` process as follows:

```
wildcat# kill `cat /var/run/ppp1.pid`
```

Advanced *pptp-command* Options

The `pptp-command` script has some additional brains that can make your life easier by freeing you of the menuing interface.

Selecting a Default PPTP Tunnel

If you want to be lazy (and all good Linux administrators should), you can set a default PPTP connection. This will enable you to start and stop your default PPTP connection without entering the `pptp-command` menuing system.

Start up the `pptp-command` and go to the `Select a default tunnel` menu:

```
1.) Chicago
2.) Atlanta
3.) cancel
Which tunnel do you want to be the default?: 1
```

You can then start the tunnel from the command line as follows:

```
wildcat# pptp-command start
```

Or you can stop it similarly:

```
wildcat# pptp-command stop
```

Creating a Generic */etc/pptp.d config* File

If you are the PPTP server administrator and have many users who want to connect, you can make it easier for them to configure their PPTP settings by supplying them with a `pptp-command` configuration file. This file, when placed in `/etc/pptp.d`, will preload configurations for user. For example, if we had PPTP servers in both Atlanta and Chicago, we could create the following `pptp-command` configuration file:

```
# PPTP Connection definitions.  Format:
#
# PPTP_tunnel_name    IP_ADDRESS
#      route command
#      route command
#      ....
#
Chicago    280.8.8.8
     add -net 192.168.1.0/24 TUNNEL_DEV
     add -net 192.168.2.0/24 TUNNEL_DEV

Atlanta    270.7.7.7
     add -net 192.168.1.0/24 TUNNEL_DEV
     add -net 192.168.2.0/24 TUNNEL_DEV

# You need this line to say we're doing nameserver
# definitions now.
nameservers
# Nameserver definitions go here.  Format:
```

```
# PPTP_tunnel_name:search_domain search_domain ...:DNS_server DNS_server ...
#
Chicago:chicago.example.com example.com:192.168.1.10 192.168.2.15
Atlanta:atlanta.example.com example.com:192.168.2.15 192.168.1.10
```

If the user installs this file as /etc/pptp.d/my_company, then when adding a new PPTP tunnel for the first time, most of the questions will be answered for him:

```
Add a NEW PPTP Tunnel.

1.) my_company-chicago
2.) my_company-atlanta
3.) Other
Which configuration would you like to use?: 1
Local Name: CHICAGO\\REEGEN
Remote Name [PPTP]:
Adding my_company-chicago - 280.8.8.8 - CHICAGO\\REEGEN - PPTP
```

The IP addresses and routing information will automatically be set up from the configuration. Similarly, the configuration file will make configuring the resolv.conf a breeze:

```
Use a PPTP-specific resolv.conf during tunnel connections? [Y/n]:y
1.) my_company-chicago
2.) my_company-atlanta
3.) Other
Which configuration do you want to use?: 1
Copying /etc/resolv.conf to /etc/resolv.conf.real...
Creating link from /etc/resolv.conf.real to /etc/resolv.conf
```

By distributing the my_company PPTP configuration file, users need only set up their CHAP secrets and pick which city they want to connect to for PPTP and resolv.conf setup.

Building a PPTP VPN Server

A Linux machine can function as a PPTP VPN server, allowing incoming connections from Windows machines or any other software supporting Microsoft's PPTP implementation. As seen previously in Figure 7.1, our sample network includes our Chicago network, with bears.example.com as our PPTP server.

We can support many remote clients with this one PPTP server. We provide each of them with an address in the network range 10.1.0.0/24 on the Chicago LAN. Additionally, the actual PPTP connection will have an IP address associated with both endpoints because it is essentially an enhanced PPP link. We chose 10.2.0.0/24 as the range of client-side PPP IP addresses, pretty much out of thin air. All of the network configuration is handled by the PPTP server, and we'll see how you set these values later in this chapter.

Installing *pptpd*

The PPTP server software is called PoPToP, a clever pun we heartily admire. It was built for Linux but can work on some other UNIX-like operating systems such as Solaris. It is simply a daemon that accepts inbound PPTP connections and forks copies of itself to handle the TCP control channel and GRE packets, shuttling data to PPP to handle the actual point-to-point link, authentication, and encryption.

To install PoPToP, snag a copy of the source from `http://poptop.lineo.com` and extract it:

```
root# tar xzvf pptpd-VERSION.tar.gz
root# cd pptpd-VERSION
```

Pptpd comes with a configure script to choose compile time settings. Some of the more useful command-line options are as follows:

`--prefix=DIR`	Install the software into `DIR` instead of `/usr/local`
`--with-libwrap`	Include TCP Wrapper support
`--with-pppd-ip-alloc`	Allow `pppd` to allocate fixed IP addresses
`--with-slirp`	Use SLiRP instead of `pppd` (more on this later)

We generally configure `pptpd` as follows:

```
root# ./configure --prefix=/opt/pkgs/pptpd --with-libwrap \
    --with-pppd-ip-alloc
```

This puts the `pptpd` programs in `/opt/pkgs/pptpd` and uses TCP Wrappers. Unfortunately, there is no configuration option you can use to change the default location in which `pptpd` looks for your `pppd` binary. If you installed it in a nonstandard location earlier, you will need to modify the following lines in the `config.h` file (which was generated from your `./configure` command) to reflect the correct location:

```
/* Where is my pppd? */
#define PPP_BINARY "/usr/sbin/pppd"
```

In our installation example earlier in the chapter, we installed `pppd` in the `/opt/pkgs/ppp-mppe` directory hierarchy, which means we'll need to change the preceding line as follows:

```
#define PPP_BINARY "/opt/pkgs/ppp-mppe/usr/sbin/pppd"
```

Once done with any customizations, simply compile and install the software:

```
root# make
root# make install
```

What are TCP Wrappers?

TCP Wrappers enable you to control which machines are allowed to connect to your PPTP server based on the rules defined in `/etc/hosts.deny` and `/etc/hosts.allow`. TCP Wrappers are an option for most server software. See the `hosts.allow` man page for more information.

Install *ppp-mppe* for PoPToP

PoPToP hands off the GRE-encapsulated PPP data to your local `pppd` command. This program must support the Microsoft extensions for authentication and encryption.

The software of choice to handle this is `ppp-mppe`. It is a patched version of the standard PPP Linux software that incorporates the additional bits, interfacing with OpenSSL for the cryptographic algorithms. We covered the installation of `ppp-mppe` earlier in this chapter when we discussed Linux PPTP clients. Install `ppp-mppe` as we described there.

PPTPD and SLiRP

One of the `pptpd` configuration options we mentioned was `--with-slirp`. SLiRP is a TCP/IP emulator that essentially enables you to take a normal shell account and turn it into a full-blown SLIP/PPP account. (SLIP was the protocol of choice for modem dial-in before PPP became common.)

You could use SLiRP instead of using the `pppd` program from the `ppp-mppe` package. `ppp-mppe` requires a Linux kernel module, making it very Linux specific, whereas SLiRP is more cross-platform. So if you wanted to run a PPTP server on Solaris, for example, SLiRP would be something to look into.

We suggest, however, that you stick with `ppp-mppe` for the following reasons:

- SLiRP is no longer maintained.
- The version of SLiRP that supports the Microsoft PPTP Extensions, 1.3b, is a beta.
- SLiRP was written to work with SSLeay 0.9.0b. SSLeay was the predecessor to OpenSSL, which is now at 0.9.6c as of this writing. Many flaws have been found and fixed since the SSLeay days.
- SLiRP is based on the PPP 2.2 code base. Version 2.3 currently is standard, and 2.4 is also widely deployed.
- The PPTP-Linux client software requires `ppp-mppe`, so if you need to support both client and server, you are already familiar with `ppp-mppe` anyway.

SLiRP is available from `http://blitzen.ise.canberra.edu.au/slirp` (official home page) and `http://www.serc.nl/people/vogt/vpn` (the beta versions with PPTP support.) The SLiRP tarball contains some good information about how you integrate it with PPTPD, and the two do actually work well together.

If you want to use SLiRP, we suggest you compile it to interface with OpenSSL instead of SSLeay so that you get the benefit of the bug fixes that have been made in the last few years. Getting SLiRP to compile with recent OpenSSL versions is not trivial, unfortunately, due to changes in the OpenSSL interfaces.

Creating the PPTPD Configuration Files

The pptpd daemon looks in the file /etc/pptpd.conf for configuration options that are similar to those used by pppd in /etc/ppp/options. The PoPToP tarball includes a sample pptpd.conf file in the samples directory. We use the following:

```
# Speed used by pppd.  (Often ignored or irrelevant anyway)
speed 115200


# Option file for pppd, passed on the command line by pptpd.
# We use a different one than the default here
# s.t. you can include different requirements here, such
# as +chapms, without interfering with normal PPP connections.
option /etc/ppp/pptp-options


# Set debug mode for pptpd?
# (This does not apply to pppd, however.)
debug


# Local IP Address List
# This is a list of IP addresses for our side of the PPTP
# (ppp0, ppp1, etc) link.
localip 10.1.0.1-254


# Remote IP Address List
# This is a list of IP addresses that will be given to
# the remote end of the link (ie the ppp# interface on
# the PPTP client.)
remoteip 10.2.0.0.1-254


# The address on which pptpd should listen.  Useful
# if you have multiple interfaces (which is likely)
# and you don't want to listen on all of them.
# We use the external interface here.
listen 280.8.8.8


# Pid file, if you don't want the default of /var/run/pptpd.pid
#pidfile /path/to/pid/file.pid
```

The local and remote IP address lists are used to set the IPs of the VPN links that are created. They can take a list of addresses by separating addresses with a ',', or a range of addresses using '-', such as:

10.1.0.1,10.1.0.2,10.1.0.5	The three IP addresses .1, .2, and .5.
10.1.0.1-200	All IP addresses from 10.1.0.1 to 10.1.0.200
10.1.0.1-5,10.1.0.50-100	All IP addresses from 10.1.0.1 to 10.1.0.5 and 10.1.0.50 to 10.1.0.100

No spaces are permitted in the IP address list. The range operator only works on the final byte of the IP address.

You only need to have one local IP address available because multiple point-to-point links can have the same source address. We tend to prefer using separate local IP addresses just because it makes debugging a bit easier.

The remote address must be different for each incoming connection. Thus, you must have as many remote addresses available as the number of concurrent PPTP VPN connections you expect to support.

If you compiled pptpd with the `--with-pppd-ip-alloc` option at configure time, the actual remote IP addresses that are given are not defined in this file. If you want to give out static IP addresses, you need not consider them when determining the IP ranges used here. (You do need to make sure they do not conflict, however.)

The local and remote IP address ranges used must not conflict with any existing IP address space. The remote IP addresses will be the ones seen on your local LAN, being tunneled in via the VPN. The local IP addresses need only be visible to the VPN server. We used the 10.x.y.z network because it clearly differentiated the VPN networks from the actual internal 192.168.x.y networks.

Creating the *pppd* Options File

If you configured a nondefault options file for pppd in the `/etc/pptpd.conf` file (which we strongly suggested), you will need to create this file with appropriate configuration options. We use the following:

```
# File: /etc/ppp/pptp-options
# Used by pppd when accepting incoming PPTP VPN sessions

# Debug?  Heck yeah.
debug

# Server Name, used with the /etc/ppp/chap-secrets file
# We like the server name 'pptpd' since it makes it
# easier to see how folks are logging in.
name pptpd

# Domain name
domain chicago.example.org

# Some authentication settings
auth
+chapms-v2
mppe-128
mppe-stateless

# Insecure options we'd prefer to keep off
#+chapms
#mppe-40
```

```
# These available only if you applied the
# optional pppd-mppe patches
require-mppe
require-mppe-stateless
#chapms-strip-domain

# Some options to help out Windows clients find their
# network settings.  Replace IPs as appropriate.
ms-dns IP.AD.DR.ES
ms-wins IP.AD.DR.ES

# Standard options necessary to support the
# inbound connection.  See our ppp options
# discussion in Chapter 3
proxyarp
lock
...
```

Setting Up the *chap-secrets* File

PPTP VPN remote users must have their passwords stored on the server in
/etc/ppp/chap-secrets. This file simply contains the client name (username), server
name, secret (the password), and optionally an IP address. The pptp program calls pppd
with the argument name pptp, so the second field in /etc/ppp/chap-secrets must be
pptp. A sample file might look like this:

```
# Client     Server     Secret                     IP Address
reegen       pptp       l!ttleW!ldc&7
bree         pptp       d&mNc\/t3                   10.1.0.201
```

In this example, Reegen will get an IP address from the range set in /etc/pptpd.conf.
If you compiled pptpd with the --with-pppd-ip-alloc option, Bree will always get
the static address 10.1.0.201; otherwise, she also will get a random IP address from the
range in /etc/pptpd.conf.

Don't Forget the NT Domain Names

If you didn't apply the strip-MSdomain-patch, you will need to supply the NT domain name as part of the
username. Assuming your domain is CHICAGO and Reegen is using a Windows machine that sends the
domain name, the first line should instead read as follows:

```
CHICAGO\\reegen          pptp          l!ttleW!ldc&7
```

Starting *pptpd*

Starting pptpd is as simple as running the following:

```
bears-pptpserver# pptpd
```

pptpd runs as a daemon, meaning it is available to handle multiple incoming connections. For each successful connection, there are two processes to handle the VPN:

```
bears$ ps -ef | egrep 'pptpd|pppd'
root     23201    1  0 04:43 ?       00:00:00 /usr/sbin/pptpd
root      2024 23201  0 04:43 ?       00:00:00 pptpd [IP.AD.DR.ES]
root      2025  2024  0 04:43 ?       00:00:00 /usr/sbin/pppd local file
/etc/ppp/pptpd-options ....
```

The first process is simply the pptpd daemon, which listens for additional connections. The second pptpd process is the GRE/PPP encapsulator/deencapsulator. Lastly, the pppd handles the encryption and network layer of the VPN. If you want to kill a particular VPN connection, simply kill the associated pppd process.

You can create a start/stop script in /etc/init.d easily by copying templates from your Linux distribution. If you want an extremely generic one, simply save the following as /etc/init.d/pptpd:

```
#!/bin/sh

# Replace with the actual path to your pptpd program
PPTPD=/opt/pkgs/pptpd/sbin/pptpd

case "$1" in
    start)
            echo "Starting PPTPD Daemon"
            $PPTPD
            echo "pptpd."
            ;;
    stop)
            echo "Stopping PPTPD Daemon"
            kill `cat /var/run/pptpd.pid`
            ;;
    restart)
            echo "Restarting PPTPD Daemon"
            sh $0 stop; sh $0 start
            ;;
    *)
            echo "Usage: /etc/init.d/pptpd {start|stop|restart}"
            exit 1;
            ;;
esac
exit 0
```

Then simply link it to be run at bootup. If you boot into init state 2, for example, you might want to do the following:

```
bears-pptpserver# ln -s ../init.d/pptpd /etc/rc2.d/S99pptpd
```

Thereafter, the pptpd server will always start on bootup and stop before rebooting. You can start or stop the server manually with the following two commands:

```
bears-pptpserver# /etc/init.d/pptpd start
bears-pptpserver# /etc/init.d/pptpd stop
```

This script will stop all existing PPTP VPN connections when it stops the pptpd daemon itself. If you want to only stop a specific VPN, kill the pppd process that is associated with it.

Troubleshooting

Because there are many pieces to the PPTP VPN puzzle, you might find yourself in a number of sticky situations.

PPTP Modules Not Loaded

Several kernel modules must be loaded for PPP and PPTP to work. Attempt to establish a PPTP connection and check the list of loaded modules:

```
# lsmod
Module            Size  Used by
mppe             22240  0  (unused)
ppp_deflate      40188  2  (autoclean)
bsd_comp          3852  0  (autoclean)
ppp              21036  2  (autoclean) [mppe ppp_deflate bsd_comp]
slhc              4440  1  (autoclean) [ppp]
```

There will likely be other modules loaded as well, but these are the ones that are necessary for PPTP to function as a VPN. The mppe module is not supplied by your Linux distribution but was compiled earlier in this chapter. The rest most likely come preinstalled. If your kernel is compiled with PPP support in the kernel rather than as a loadable module (which is unlikely), you will not see the last four modules in lsmod output.

Refer to the section "PPP Kernel Modules" earlier in this chapter to make sure you've properly installed the modules necessary. If you failed to update /etc/modules.conf or to run depmod -a, you might experience problems loading the new modules.

Enabling Debugging

You can force additional debugging info by adding debug to the list of options for the PPTP programs. The files you want to modify are as follows:

```
/etc/ppp/options       For pppd (client and/or server)
/etc/ppp/options.pptp  For pptp (client)
/etc/ppp/pptpd-options For pptpd (server)
```

Other options that might be helpful include show-password, which will let you see the username/password being used for authentication. You should turn this option off when you are done debugging the connection, of course.

Incompatible Encryption Options

You can tailor the methods of authentication and the ciphers used for your connection in the various ppp/pptp options files. The relevant options are as follows:

```
+chapms
+chapms-v2
mppe-40
mppe-128
mppe-stateless
```

The chapms options can take a + sign at the beginning, which means they must be used for authentication. The mppe options, unfortunately, do not work this way. However, if you compiled ppp-mppe with the patches we suggested earlier in this chapter in the section "Patching ppp-mppe Sources," you also have the following options available:

```
require-mppe
require-mppe-stateless
chapms-strip-domain
```

If your system logs suggest that proper encryption could not be established, try removing any require options and be sure that all mppe-* and chapms* options are selected. If the VPN establishes correctly, there is an incompatibility of allowed authentication or encryption between the two endpoints. Compare the options on each end to make sure they specify compatible settings.

General PPP Problems

We discussed two different methods of establishing a VPN with PPP in Chapters 3 and 4. If you find that you are having generic PPP difficulties, you might want to refer to these chapters for ideas about PPP options that might be required. The troubleshooting section of these chapters also includes common PPP errors that can affect you when using PPTP.

Inbound Connections to PPTP Server Denied

If you are running the Linux PPTP server and have compiled it with --with-libwrap, TCP Wrappers may be rejecting the incoming connections. Check your entries in /etc/hosts.allow and /etc/hosts.deny. See man hosts.allow for information on how to configure TCP Wrappers. You might want to temporarily add ALL: ALL to the top of /etc/hosts.allow and see if the connection is established. If so, then TCP Wrappers are certainly misconfigured.

PPTP VPNs Still Aren't Working

PPTP requires both a single TCP channel (port 1723) and GRE packets in order to function. Reread the section "PPTP, Packet Filters, and Firewalls" to make sure you've properly configured your host or network equipment to allow these packets through. GRE is often not easily supported, and the packets are normally dropped on the floor without any error message whatsoever.

You might want to watch where the packets are flying using `tcpdump` at your PPTP endpoint and firewall. Run the following commands, one in each window:

```
root@firewall# tcpdump -n proto 47 or port 1723 -i INTERFACE1
root@firewall# tcpdump -n proto 47 or port 1723 -i INTERFACE2
root@pptp-machine# tcpdump -n proto 47 or port 1723
```

Replace *INTERFACE1* and *INTERFACE2* with your actual ethernet/ppp interface names. If all is going well, you should see the same packets on each side. If not, there is interference by the ruleset on your firewall. You might want to explicitly log any denied packets by adding the `-l` option to your `ipchains` rules to help see where packets are being dropped.

If you already have extensive `ipchains`/`iptables` rulesets, you are going to have a potentially annoying couple of days ahead of you while you try to get everything tweaked just right to support your PPTP VPN. Good luck.

The PPTP VPN Isn't Encrypted

One of the biggest flaws of the software we describe here is that it could be used to successfully establish a 100% functional network connection between client and server that doesn't encrypt the packets at all. This is because the `mppe-*` encryption algorithms are not *required* by `pppd` and thus might not be negotiated if not supported by the remote end.

The only way to be sure you have encryption on your VPN is to apply the `require-mppe` patch (described in the section "Patching ppp-mppe Sources" earlier in this chapter) and make sure you have the following in your `pppd` options file:

```
require-mppe
require-mppe-stateless
```

Make sure you check the VPN packets using `tcpdump` or other tools to verify that the packets are in fact encrypted, lest you implement a very insecure VPN.

Summary

PPTP is an annoying beast. Though it is a generic protocol, the only version in wide use is the one created by Microsoft. Though this version has been improved, it still has intrinsic and documented flaws that make most cryptographers and security professionals alike distrust it and recommend against its use.

We recognize that there are times when you must support PPTP, either because you are forced to connect to a server that only runs PPTP or because you need to support remote Windows client machines. In either of these cases, we offer our deepest sympathies.

In any case in which both endpoints support stronger VPN technology, such as IPSec, we recommend that you avoid PPTP entirely.

Implementing Nonstandard
VPN Protocols

8

VTun

VTun, or virtual tunnel, is a VPN solution written by Maxim Krasnyansky. A VPN built with VTun uses tunnel interfaces in which data is encrypted as it passes into the tunnel and is decrypted as it exits the far side of the tunnel. The next section provides an overview of VTun. Sections on compiling, configuring, troubleshooting, and compatibility of VTun round out the rest of the chapter.

Overview of VTun

A tunnel is a logical connection through which two devices appear to be directly connected. Tunnels work on the principal of packet encapsulation. *Packet encapsulation* is the process of placing a packet within another packet. In the case of VTun, the encapsulation is done on packets that are routed through the tunnel interface. VTun encapsulates packets within IP packets and uses IP networks to route these encapsulated packets from one side of the tunnel to the other. Tunnel interfaces are logical entrances into a tunneled connection and are created on both sides of a tunnel connection.

Each side of a tunnel has some information about the opposite end, such as a reachable network address and what networks lie beyond it. This way, when a packet comes into the server destined for a network beyond the far side of the tunnel, it is routed through the local tunnel interface. As mentioned earlier, the kernel then encapsulates this packet and forwards this new packet to the known address at the far side of the tunnel. Upon reaching the far side of the tunnel, the packet is inspected, de-encapsulated, and then forwarded to its original destination.

Figure 8.1 illustrates the process of packet encapsulation for tunnel transport. Host 192.168.1.10 sends a packet to the VTun machine 280.8.8.8. The VTun server then encapsulates the packet into another packet, with 280.8.8.8 as the source IP address and 270.7.7.7 as the destination IP address. When the client at 270.7.7.7 receives the packet, it is inspected and de-encapsulated. This returns the packet to its original state—that is, the source IP is again 192.168.1.10, and the destination IP reverts back to 192.168.2.15.

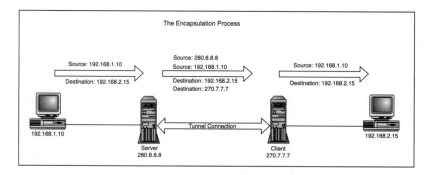

Figure 8.1 VTun using packet encapsulation.

VTun enables two servers to establish connections, negotiate tunnel parameters, and maintain the tunnel for as long as necessary. VTun enables the two servers to create a tunnel using TCP or UDP for the underlying transport.

In addition to normal tunnel behavior, VTun also introduces some new enhancements. VTun supports encryption of data so that any eavesdroppers will not be able to determine the contents of the encapsulated packet. VTun also supports compression so that packets are compressed as they enter the tunnel and are decompressed as they reach the tunnel endpoint. Finally, traffic shaping is a feature implemented by VTun to enable the throttling of tunnel connections to preserve bandwidth for prioritized traffic.

VTun supports several different types of tunnels. More information on specific configuration tasks for each tunnel type will be discussed later in the "VTun Configuration" section of this chapter.

VTun Components and Their Functions

VTun has two primary components: the Linux kernel TUN/TAP driver and the daemon `vtund`. The TUN/TAP kernel driver is used for creating the tunnel interfaces, whereas `vtund` is used for setup and maintenance of the local-to-remote tunneled connection.

The TUN/TAP Driver

The TUN/TAP driver is used as a logical access point to a tunnel. In other words, packets routed to the driver are sent to the opposite end of the tunnel. The inverse is also true; packets read from the driver have been sent from the opposite end of the tunnel to the local side. The driver has two parts: the virtual interface and the device files.

The virtual interface serves as an entrance to the tunnel. As packets are sent to the Linux server, routing decisions are made based on the destination field of each packet. vtund listens for packets sent to these interfaces and encapsulates or de-encapsulates the packet as appropriate. If the packet is destined for the far end of the tunnel, VTun will encapsulate the packet in IP and will forward it off to the tunnel endpoint. If the packet is destined for the local network, the packet is de-encapsulated and then forwarded the appropriate local interface. For IP tunnels (that is, tunnels that transport only IP traffic), the TUN driver is used. The TUN driver uses an interface named in the format of tunX, where X is some number that uniquely identifies each tunnel interface. For the rest of this chapter, the convention of referring to an IP tunnel virtual interface as tun will be used.

The IP address configured for the TUN/TAP interface also allows routing to point traffic destined to remote networks toward that local interface. The local tunnel interface is logically connected to the next hop toward the remote network.

To create a routing table entry for the networks on the far side of the tunnel, each tunnel interface must be configured with an IP address. For every tunnel connection, the remote and local tunnel interfaces are configured to be on the same network as point-to-point links. This further perpetuates the illusion that the network across the tunnel is only one hop away.

This sample routing table shows the routing used to send packets over the tunnel interface. Using this routing table, we will examine the process of routing packets over the tunnel interface.

```
[root@vpn-clnt /root]# netstat -nr
Kernel IP routing table
Destination     Gateway         Genmask         Flags  MSS Window irtt Iface
10.3.0.1        0.0.0.0         255.255.255.255 UH     40  0       0    tun1
10.3.0.0        10.3.0.1        255.255.255.252 UG     40  0       0    tun1
192.168.2.0     0.0.0.0         255.255.255.0   U      40  0       0    eth1
192.168.1.0     10.3.0.1        255.255.255.0   UG     40  0       0    tun1
127.0.0.0       0.0.0.0         255.0.0.0       U      40  0       0    lo
```

In the routing table, 192.168.2.0/24 is the local network, and 192.168.1.0/24 is the remote network. In other words, packets that are sent to 192.168.1.0/24 should be sent across the tunnel. In the routing table, the lines that are important to our tunnel-routing decisions are as follows:

```
192.168.1.0     10.3.0.1            255.255.255.0   UG      40 0
➥0 tun1
```

```
10.3.0.1          0.0.0.0          255.255.255.255   UH      40 0
➥0 tun1
```

The first line points traffic for the network 192.168.0/24 to the IP for the tunnel interface. The second line states that the IP address 10.3.0.1 is directly connected and is assigned to the interface tun1. When these packets are routed to the tun1 interface, they are placed in the queue for processing. vtund will then be able to read the interface queue and process the packets.

The TAP driver is for tunnels that transport ethernet frames. The TAP driver is also used to create a virtual interface for transport of those frames. The TAP virtual interface uses the naming convention tapX, where X is a number to uniquely identify each tap interface. For the rest of this chapter, each tap interface will be referred to simply as tap.

Because in the case of the TAP driver we are dealing with layer 2 traffic, creating layer 3 routes will not enable two separate ethernet networks to communicate. Instead, we will need to bridge the ethernet frames. Bridging is a method for transporting ethernet traffic from one collision domain (sometimes referred to in this text as a *segment*) to another.

Recent Linux kernels include support for the TUN/TAP driver, but most distributions do not by default support it. It is therefore likely that you will need to recompile your kernel to add support for TUN/TAP.

The *vtund* Daemon

The vtund daemon is responsible for initiating and receiving tunnel connections, as well as maintenance of any currently established tunnels. vtund reads vtund.conf for tunnel configuration parameters and configures vtund's mode of operation—client or server.

vtund is responsible for packet input and output for the TUN/TAP interface. When packets are routed to the TUN/TAP interface, VTun reads the packets from the interface queue and encapsulates them for transport across the tunnel.

vtund configured as a server will wait for incoming client connections and then send configured tunnel parameters back to the client. In server mode, vtund can also be configured to run in standalone mode or inetd mode. This will be discussed more later in this section.

In client mode, vtund will attempt to initiate a tunnel connection with the server. Users on the road or telecommuters are good examples of when vtund would be configured in client mode. Another good example would be remote offices connecting to the company headquarters.

The vtund.conf configuration file also contains any other commands necessary to establish a tunnel connection. Common commands include ifconfig commands for bringing up tunnel interfaces and routing statements for the remote network.

The vtund daemon supports several command-line options. A few of the more useful options are listed in Table 8.1.

Table 8.1   **Some Useful *vtund* Command-Line Options**

Option	Description
-f file	Causes vtund configuration information to be read from file
-s	Runs vtund in standalone server mode
-i	Causes vtund server to run in inetd mode
-p	Causes vtund client to attempt to reconnect to the server after the tunnel connection has terminated (persistent mode)
session server	Causes vtund client to establish the session specified in the configuration file to server

inetd vs. *Standalone Server Mode*

vtund in server mode can run in standalone server mode or in inetd mode. In standalone server mode, vtund runs continuously and waits for incoming connections. In inetd mode, vtund is actually spawned from the super server inetd.

The benefit to running in inetd mode is that it provides an extra level of security with the use of TCP Wrappers. TCP Wrappers are a form of access control filter. inetd uses TCP Wrappers to set access control to the server based primarily on traffic source address and destination port number.

Standalone mode is designed for servers that will be handling a large amount of traffic. In inetd mode, the VTun traffic must first pass through the inetd daemon, which introduces a small bit of latency into the connection. This at first might seem like a negligible amount of time, but if your VPN server is handling a large number of VTun connections, the latency will increase. The increase in load might eventually cause timeouts and other problems for remote users.

Distribution Differences

Some newer Linux distributions use xinetd, not inetd. They are functionally similar in that they are both super-server type daemons, but xinetd allows for a greater amount of flexibility in configuring services. Regardless of what is bundled with your distribution, the command-line option for vtund to run in inetd mode is the same whether you are running xinetd or inetd.

Supported Encryption Methods

In any VPN implementation, it is important that both data encryption and data authentication be present to ensure the highest level of security and data integrity. Data encryption makes it difficult to intercept traffic and get the user data being sent across the tunnel. Integrity Protection ensures that the data has not been tampered with after it enters the tunnel.

To implement encryption and authentication, VTun uses OpenSSL. Although OpenSSL supports several types of encryption, VTun currently uses only the Blowfish algorithm.

Blowfish was developed by Bruce Schneier of Counterpane Software. The source code for Blowfish is not patented and can be downloaded from many sites on the Internet. Blowfish was designed to be very fast and efficient. This makes it ideal for VTun because packets must be encrypted and decrypted quickly to ensure that additional latency is not introduced into a network conversation.

Blowfish is a symmetric algorithm, meaning the same key used to encrypt the data is used to decrypt the data. Although VTun uses a key length of 128 bits, Blowfish supports a key length of up to 448 bits. The 128 bits provides a key space of 3.4×10^{38} keys, making it sufficiently difficult to perform a brute force attack on encrypted data.

VTun uses Blowfish in Electronic Code Book (ECB) mode. ECB mode breaks the data into 64-bit blocks and then encrypts each of these blocks one by one. This means that two identical blocks of plain text would produce two identical blocks of cipher text. Because of this, ciphers that use ECB mode are susceptible to attacks that analyze patterns of cipher text. It should be noted, however, that even though ECB is susceptible to this type of attack, it is still fairly difficult for an attacker to successfully crack a given block of cipher text in this way. In this case, "susceptible to attack" does not mean "easy to crack."

For Integrity Protection, VTun uses md5 to create a 128-bit key hash from a key phrase (the data). Md5 is a hashing algorithm used to produce an irreversible value for a given set of data. This value is very nearly unique, and it is extremely unlikely that two different sets of data would produce the same md5 hash value. In short, md5 is a method for fingerprinting data. By including this value in the packet, it is possible for the computer receiving the packet to perform another md5 hash on the data received and compare the value with the one sent along with the packet. If they are the same, the packet passes the integrity check. If they are different, the packet must have been tampered with.

Challenge-Based Authentication

For additional security, when the client is authenticating itself to the server, it uses challenge-based authentication. Challenge-based authentication is a more secure method by which two parties can exchange passwords because plaintext passwords are not sent over the network.

For the client to authenticate itself to a server, challenge-based authentication uses this sequence of events:

1. The client initiates connection with the server.

2. The server issues a challenge. The challenge consists of encrypting some random data with the secret key that both the client and server share. This encrypted data is then sent to the client.

3. The client receives the challenge and decrypts it with the secret key that the client and server both share. The client then calculates a hash for the random data and sends it to the server.

4. The server receives the hashed data from the client and compares it with a hash of the random data originally sent. If the two values match, the client is authenticated. If the two values are different, the client fails to authenticate.

If the client authenticates itself, VTun will continue to the next step in the process for creating a tunnel. The server will pass encryption and compression settings back to the client. If the client supports these options, the tunnel will be established.

Supported Tunneling Modes

VTun supports four different types of tunnels. Depending on the type of VPN you need to design, any one of the four might be the right solution for you. Additionally, your VTun configuration need not be limited to only one type of tunnel. A single VTun daemon process can handle all four types of connections if it has been configured to do so.

Tunnels can use either TCP or UDP for tunnel transport. For more reliable delivery, TCP should be used. Although TCP has more overhead, tighter compression can be used to make up for lost bandwidth.

UDP tunnels require less bandwidth and in general are quicker than TCP tunnels. UDP tunnels can be used when bandwidth is tight.

IP Tunnels

IP tunnels are tunnels that transport only IP traffic. IP tunnels can be used for both network-network and host-network connectivity. For office-to-office connectivity, IP tunnels provide a way to create a virtual topology between two IP networks. IP tunnels use the TUN device driver in the Linux kernel. The configuration is similar for user-to-office VPNs, but the client network to be tunneled is generally a single IP.

IP tunnels use the TUN interface to create tunnel virtual interfaces. These interfaces serve as a logical entryway for IP packets into the IP tunnel. Statements in the routing table are used to determine whether packets are sent across the tunnel or not. Figure 8.2 illustrates the steps the kernel takes to route a packet out the tunnel interface.

Ethernet Tunnels

Whereas IP tunnels are used to handle IP packets, ethernet tunnels are used to create tunnels that transport ethernet frames. Although ethernet tunnels can forward IP packets just like IP tunnels, they can also forward other protocols that use ethernet, such as IPX. Any other protocol that runs natively over ethernet can be transmitted across a tunnel. Ethernet tunnels use the TAP device driver included with the kernel.

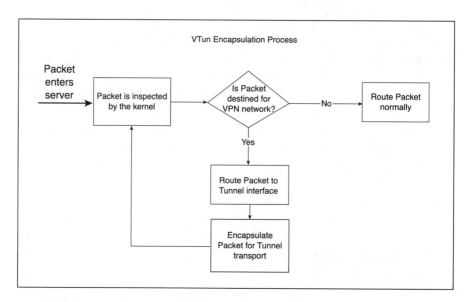

Figure 8.2   The routing process for VPN traffic.

Ethernet packets are forwarded to the tap interface by creating a bridge with the tap interface and an ethernet interface.

Bridging can be used to forward all ethernet packets from one network segment to another. Bridging will be discussed in more detail in the "Ethernet Bridging Support" section later in this chapter.

Serial Tunnels

Serial tunnels use PPP or SLIP to provide a virtual PPP connection from one side of the tunnel to the other. Because PPP and SLIP provide their own network interfaces, it is possible to use VTun without compiling TUN/TAP support into the kernel.

Aside from the interface differences, PPP tunnels act in much the same way as the TUN/TAP driver. The PPP interface serves as the entrance to the tunnel.

Pipe Tunnels

In some situations, in which network connectivity is unwanted or not available, VTun can be used to create a secure connection where output from a command is directed. A pipe tunnel gets its name from where the tunnel gets its input—a UNIX pipe. A pipe tunnel is very similar to the `pipe` option used from the command line. When output from a command is passed to a pipe symbol, the output is directed to the command following it.

Pipe tunnels work in a similar fashion. Essentially, when the client activates the tunnel, the command will execute on one side, and the other side will receive its output. Pipe tunnels are a good way to transport files or data directly between two VTun machines.

Other Supported Features

In addition to common VPN features, VTun also supports several uncommon features.

Compression

VTun supports traffic compression. This allows for more efficient use of the tunnel and provides more bandwidth for user traffic. Depending on the underlying tunnel connection, TCP or UDP, different types of compression can be used.

TCP tunnels can use Zlib for compression. Zlib provides the best compression available to VTun but can only be used by TCP tunnels because it requires that packets be processed in a reliable manner.

Zlib uses a modified version of the LZ77 compression, called deflation. Zlib was designed to be portable to any platform and is included with most distributions of Linux. Zlib's compression format is similar to the one used by `gzip`.

UDP tunnels can use LZO for compression. LZO does not compress as well as Zlib, but it is faster and works with UDP packet delivery better.

Compression is available only for IP and ethernet tunnels. For pipe and serial tunnels, no data compression is supported.

Traffic Shaping

The capability to define bandwidth limits for each tunnel is important so that one tunnel does not take any bandwidth from other tunnels. VTun supports traffic shaping by rate-limiting the amount of bandwidth a tunnel can use. Traffic shaping is a good idea for VTun servers with a limited amount of bandwidth.

Dependencies

All of the following procedures can be used to install packages that are prerequisites for VTun. The commands listed should be useable on Linux kernel versions greater than or equal to 2.4.0.

IP Forwarding

IP forwarding enables a VPN server to route packets to the appropriate destination, based on the server's routing table. If IP forwarding is not enabled, packets coming into the VPN server that are destined for the opposite end of the tunnel will simply be discarded.

To enable the routing of packets on your Linux machine, you will need to enable IP forwarding. The kernel will check the file for /proc/sys/ipv4/ip_forward to find out if it should route packets or not. There is a single number in this file: 0 or 1. If the value is 1, IP forwarding will be set to true, and the kernel will route packets. If it is 0, IP forwarding will be set to false, and the kernel will not route packets.

To start forwarding packets, run the following command:

```
[root@vpn-serv /root]# echo "1" > /proc/sys/ipv4/ip_forward
```

To enable IP forwarding at boot time, place the preceding command at the end of the file /etc/rc.d/rc.local.

OpenSSL

OpenSSL is needed by VTun to implement encryption. OpenSSL can be downloaded from www.openssl.org. As of this writing, OpenSSL's current version is 0.9.6b.

To compile OpenSSL from source code, follow these steps:

1. Download the source code from www.openssl.org.

2. To uncompress the source code, use the following command:

   ```
   gzip -cd openssl.tar.gz | tar -xvf -
   ```

3. Run the config command included with the OpenSSL package to generate a Makefile.

   ```
   cd .openssl-0.9.6b
   ./config
   ```

   The system will attempt to resolve the location of all header files and libraries needed to build OpenSSL.

   The config script supports several command-line options that allow for a more flexible installation. To see the options that config supports, run config with the -help option.

4. Install the newly compiled binaries by running the following:

   ```
   make install
   ```

   Once make install has finished running, the OpenSSL libraries and headers will be installed either in /usr/local/ssl or in the directory specified with the -prefix argument while running config.

Kernel Sources

First, make sure you have the kernel sources installed. The kernel source is usually installed in /usr/src/, so check in this directory. If the sources are not installed, you will need to obtain the kernel sources either in the rpm package or tar'ed and gzip'ed from your favorite Linux mirror.

To install the kernel sources on an rpm-based system, follow these steps:

1. Download the kernel rpm from your favorite distribution mirror.

2. Install the rpm with the following command.

```
rpm -ivh kernel-source-2.4.2-2.i386.rpm
```

To install the kernel source from a tar package, use the following steps:

1. Download the kernel source from your favorite mirror.

2. Extract the tar file.

```
gzip -cd linux-2.4.2.tar.gz | tar -xvf -C /usr/src -
```

After running either of these commands, the kernel source will now be installed in /usr/src.

TUN/TAP Driver

As previously mentioned, the TUN/TAP driver is bundled with all recent versions of the Linux kernel source. Support for the TUN/TAP driver is not installed by default in most distributions, so you will probably need to recompile the kernel. The TUN/TAP driver can be compiled directly into the kernel or as a dynamically loadable module.

To enable TUN/TAP support, you can use the make menuconfig command while in the kernel source directory. This will enable you to configure the kernel with a menu interface. Once the menu comes up, select Network Device Support, Universal Tun/TAP Driver Support. This will add the TUN/TAP driver to your kernel.

After you have selected this option, configure, build, and install your kernel normally. After rebooting, you will be able to use the TUN/TAP driver to create tunnel interfaces.

Once the TUN/TAP driver has been enabled, a device file must be created in the /dev/net directory. You must use the mknod command to create a character device file with a major number of 10 and a minor number of 200. The major is used to link a device file to a specific type of device. The minor number is used to link a device file to a specific device. To do this, type the following command:

```
mknod /dev/net/tun c 10 200
```

This will create the /dev/net/tun device file, which is used to read and write data to a tunX virtual interface.

To create the device files for that tap interface, you must create the device file with a major number of 90 and a minor number of 128.

```
mknod /dev/net/tap c 90 128
```

The TUN/TAP driver can be loaded as a module, or the driver can be statically placed in the kernel. To use modules, once you have configured the kernel, make sure to build the modules and install them. To do this, run these commands:

```
cd /usr/src/linux
make modules
make modules_install
depmod -a
```

The modules will be installed in /lib/modules/*kernel version*. Finally, to enable automatic loading of the TUN/TAP module, add the following lines to /etc/modules.conf:

```
alias char-major-10-200 tun
alias char-major-90-128 tap
```

After these lines have been added, when the tun device file is accessed, the tun modules will be loaded.

Ethernet Bridging Support

To send your ethernet LAN traffic from one VTun server to another, you will need to add support for ethernet bridging in your kernel. Ethernet bridging will allow the Linux server to bond two ethernet interfaces so that they appear to be on the same segment. Specifically, we will bond a tap interface to an ethernet interface.

Bonding, Bridging, and Broadcasts

By bonding two interfaces together in a bridge, any ethernet frame received on one interface is copied to the other. LANs with a large amount of broadcast traffic (which by definition is processed by every interface) can significantly degrade the performance of an ethernet tunnel.

You will also need to download the bridge-utils package, which is used to create ethernet bridges. While the kernel configuration will enable ethernet bridging, the bridge-utils package will create and register bridges with the kernel.

To enable ethernet bridging support, change to the directory where your Linux kernel sources are installed.

```
cd /usr/src/linux
make menuconfig
```

Select the option 802.1d Ethernet Bridging from the Networking Options section. When finished, save your configuration changes and exit to the command prompt. Then rebuild the kernel.

Once this has completed, you will need to reboot for bridging support to become active.

Bridge-utils can be downloaded from http://bridge.sourceforge.net. Bridge-utils contains the program used to register ethernet bridges with the kernel, brctl.

After you have downloaded the package, follow these steps to build bridge-utils on your system.

1. Download the source from `http://bridge.sourceforge.net`.

2. Unpack the source.

   ```
   gzip -cd bridge-utils-0.9.3.tar.gz | tar -xvf -
   ```

3. Build the binaries.

   ```
   cd bridge-utils
   make
   ```

4. Install the binaries on your system.

   ```
   cp brctl/brctl /usr/local/bin/.
   ```

`brctl` is now installed on your system in `/usr/local/bin`. Using `brctl` to create ethernet bridges will be discussed in the "Ethernet Tunnel" section later in this chapter.

PPP

To enable PPP for serial tunnels, you need to have `pppd` compiled and installed on your system. Most distributions include PPP by default. However, if for some reason the PPP package is not installed on your system, these steps will take you through getting PPP in place on your system.

To install PPP on RPM-based systems, follow these steps:

1. Download the PPP RPM.

2. Use the `rpm` command to install the package.

To install PPP from source code, use the following steps:

1. Configure PPP support in the kernel.

   ```
   cd /usr/src/linux
   make menuconfig
   ```

2. Select Network Device Support, PPP (Point-to-Point Protocol) support.

3. Select Network Device Support, PPP support for async serial ports.

These can be selected as modules or compiled directly into the kernel. Note that you can select to install PPP support either as a module or built directly into the kernel. If you select to add support for PPP as a module, you will need to make changes to `/etc/modules.conf` if you want PPP to be loaded automatically. PPP in some distributions has been built to use kernel modules, so you might need to add PPP support as a module.

To install PPP from source code, follow these steps:

1. Download from `ftp://cs.anu.edu.au/pub/software/ppp/`.

2. Unpack the tar file.

   ```
   gzip -cd ppp-2.4.1.tar.gz | tar -xvf -
   ```

3. Create a Makefile using the `configure` command.

```
cd ppp-2.4.1
./configure
```

4. Build the binaries.

```
make
```

5. Install the binaries.

```
make install
```

6. Create the proper device files.

```
mknod /dev/ppp c 108 0
```

7. If you have installed PPP support as a module, add the following lines to `/etc/conf.modules`:

```
alias /dev/ppp          ppp_generic
alias char-major-108    ppp_generic
alias tty-ldisc-3       ppp_async
```

PPP should now be installed on your system. No system configuration for PPP is needed because VTun will pass options to PPP directly.

zlib

For RPM-based systems, these steps will install `zlib` on your system.

1. Download the `zlib` rpm from a distribution mirror.

2. Install the `rpm` package.

```
rpm -ivh zlib-1.1.3-22.rpm
```

For systems that do not have `zlib` installed, the following steps can be used to configure and build `zlib`:

1. Download the tarball from `www.gzip.org/zlib`.

2. Unpack the source code with the following command:

```
gzip -cd zlib-1.1.3.tar.gz | tar -xvf -
```

3. Run the `configure` command to build a Makefile for your system.

```
cd zlib-1.1.3
./configure
```

`configure` supports several command-line options for specifying how `zlib` will be built. To list which options `configure` supports, use the command-line option `-help`.

4. Run `make install` to install `zlib`.

```
make install
```

Building LZO Libraries

LZO libraries are necessary for VTun to support compression over UDP tunnels. LZO is not included by default with most distributions. LZO can be downloaded from `http://wildsau.idv.uni-linz.ac.at/mfx/lzo.html`. The current version of LZO (as of this writing) is 1.07.

To build the LZO libraries, follow these steps:

1. Download the tarball from `http://wildsau.idv.uni-linz.ac.at/mfx/lzo.html`.

2. Unpack the source code.

   ```
   gzip -cd lzo-1.07.tar.gz | tar -xvf -
   ```

3. Run the `configure` script to build a Makefile for your system.

   ```
   cd lzo-1.07
   ./configure
   ```

   The `configure` script supports several command-line options to customize your LZO build. To list these options, run the following:

   ```
   ./configure -help
   ```

4. Build the binaries.

   ```
   make
   ```

5. Finally, install the libraries.

   ```
   make install
   ```

As with the other packages, the `make install` command will install the library and header files in a default directory unless another location has been specified with the `configure` script.

Compiling VTun

VTun source code is available from `http://vtun.sourceforge.net`. The most current stable version of VTun is 2.4. The `vtun-2.4.tar.gz` package contains source code for the `vtund` daemon.

1. Download the source code from `http://vtun.sourceforge.net`.

2. Unpack the source code.

   After downloading the source code, the next step is to uncompress and untar the packaged file.

   ```
   gzip -cd vtun-2.4.tar.gz | tar -xvf -
   ```

3. Configure the VTun build.

   Paths for libraries and other features used by VTun are enabled by the use of the `configure` script included with the VTun package. Several options supported from the command line will allow a more flexible build of VTun. Running `./configure` with these options produces the results listed in Table 8.2.

Table 8.2   **Options and Results from the *configure* Script**

Option	Result
`--disable-shaper`	Disables traffic shaper support
`--disable-ssl`	Disables support for SSL
`--disable-zlib`	Disables support for compression over TCP tunnels
`--disable-lzo`	Disable support for compression over UDP tunnels
`--with-ssl-headers`	Enables you to specify the location of the SSL header files
`--with-ssl-libs`	Enables you to specify the location of the SSL libraries
`--with-lzo-headers`	Enables you to specify the location of the LZO header files
`--with-lzo-libs`	Enables you to specify the location of the LZO library files
`—bindir=directory`	Enables you to specify the location of the files when they are installed

If no command-line options are specified, `configure` will attempt to guess system settings and generate a Makefile based on its findings. If `configure` is unable to find required libraries, you will need to use the command-line options to specify the locations.

4. Once `configure` has been executed and a Makefile has been generated, the `make` command is used to build the `vtund` binary.

   `make`

5. Install the software.

   Once the `make` command has finished building `vtund`, `make install` is used to install the compiled binaries into either the default directory `/usr/local/sbin` or the directory specified by the `-bindir` command-line option for `configure`.

   `make install`

Now VTun should be completely installed. By default, it is installed in `/usr/local/sbin`.

VTun Configuration

The following section covers the configuration options available for VTun.

Overview of *vtund.conf*

The VTun configuration file `vtund.conf` is used to specify options for each virtual tunnel. The following section will list configuration options and explain how they are used. The default location of the configuration file is `/usr/local/etc/vtund.conf`.

The configuration file is formatted in the following way:

```
Section {
        SettingX    value;
        SettingY    value;
}
```

`Section` can be `options`, `default`, or *tunnel name*. The `options` section contains general setup information for `vtund`, such as program paths and port settings. The `default` section contains settings that are to be considered the default for all tunnels. The values can be overwritten on an individual tunnel basis. To do so, simply change the setting in the specific tunnel section. The *tunnel name* settings define the characteristics for individual tunnels. Note that each *tunnel name* must be unique because it is meant to define only a single tunnel.

Options Section

Table 8.3 presents the options available for the options portion of the `vtund.conf` file.

Table 8.3 **Options for *vtund.conf***

Option	Description
port	Enables you to configure on which port `vtund` listens. Value must be a valid port number. On the client, this value is used to contact the server on the specified port.
Ifconfig	Specifies the path to the `ifconfig` command.
Ppp	Specifies the path to the `pppd` command.
Route	Specifies the path to the `route` command.
Firewall	Specifies the path to the `firewall` command (generally ipchains or iptables).
Type	Enables you to specify whether `vtund` runs standalone or is spawned from `inetd`. This setting is either `stand` for standalone or `inetd` if it is spawned from `inetd`. Only the server uses this setting.
Persist	This setting causes a client to attempt to reconnect to a server in the event of a disconnect.

Tunnel and Default Sections

Table 8.4 lists the options for the tunnel and default sections of the `vtund.conf` file.

Table 8.4 **Options for the Tunnel and Default Sections of *vtund.conf***

Option	Description
Passwd	Specifies the password used to authenticate and begin tunnel negotiation. Passwords must contain both numeric and alphabetic characters. If one does not, this will generate an error and the connection will fail.
Type	Enables the user to define the tunnel type, either IP, ethernet, serial, or pipe. The values are `tun`, `tap`, `tty`, and `pipe`, respectively. If not specified, it will default to a serial tunnel. Only the server uses this.
Proto	Indicates the protocol used for the underlying tunnel transport. This can be either `tcp` or `udp`. If not specified, it defaults to `tcp`. Only the server uses this.
Compress method:[1-9]	Used to specify the compression method (if any) used on the tunnel. The method can be either `zlib` or `lzo`. The number listed after the method sets the level of compression. A setting of 1 is less compression, more speed. A setting of 9 is more compression, less speed. Note that the compression method used is dependent on the protocol defined in the `proto` setting. Only the server uses this.
Encryption	Turns encryption on and off for the tunnel. This is set to either `yes` or `no`. This is sent from the VTun server to the client.
Speed X:Y	Enables rate limiting of the tunnel. Two values can be included, one for inbound traffic (`X`) and one for outbound traffic (`Y`). If only one value is set, it is assumed to be the same for both. Values are in kilobits/second. A value of 0 turns off rate limiting. Only the server uses this.
Up { command1; command2 }	List the commands (`command1`, `command2`, and so on) to be executed after the connection has been established. These commands should include tunnel interface configuration (`ifconfig`), routing table changes, and any firewall rule changes to allow tunnel traffic. Note that `%%` in the `Up` section is used to refer to the interface name used by that tunnel.

Option	Description
Down {command1; command2; }	Same as Up, only the commands are executed when the tunnel connection is brought down.
Stat	Enables the tracking of tunnel traffic statistics. Statistics are logged every five minutes.
Srcaddr { iface value; addr value; port value; }	Configures vtund to use a specific local IP address as its source address. iface is used to specify the name of a local interface, addr is used to bind to a specific IP address, and port configures vtund to use a specific source port.

There are several options that only the VTun server uses, such as proto and type. This is because the VTun server sends details for the tunnel connection back to the client. It is up to the client to match the server's parameters; otherwise, a connection will not be established.

Also, several types of parameters are dependent on each other. For example, if a connection is configured as UDP but the compression method specified is Zlib, this will cause an error because only LZO compression can be used with UDP. It is important to check the dependencies of each parameter before rolling a configuration into production.

The up setting is one of the most important configuration options. It is within this section that the tunX or tapX interface is configured and IP routing information is entered into the routing table.

Just as it is important to make sure that all intradependencies are taken into account in the configuration file (as in the example earlier with UDP and LZO compression), it is also important to match the capabilities of the client and the server. If a server has configured a tunnel for options that the client cannot support, there is no "fallback" support for a less secure connection. The tunnel simply fails to connect. Ideally, the vtund daemons on both sides of the tunnel are configured and built identically so that there can be no capabilities mismatch.

IP Tunnel Configuration

This section will cover an implementation of an IP tunnel, (that is, a tunnel that supports IP traffic). We will build our VPN using the network introduced earlier in the book. Our goal will be to create a tunnel between the private networks 192.168. 1.0/24 and 192.168.2.0/24. Additionally, we will also configure our VPN to use Blowfish encryption and compression. The VPN that will be configured is illustrated in Figure 8.3.

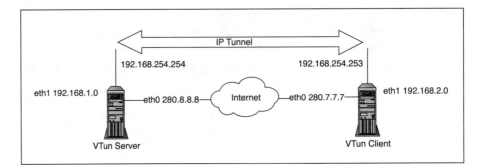

Figure 8.3   IP tunnel.

IP Tunnel Server Configuration

Because the server passes all tunnel attributes to the client, it is in the server configuration that we will define all tunnel settings. For the client to connect properly, it is only necessary that it support all the options sent to it by the server.

In this particular case, the server is directly connected to the network 192.168.1.0/24. From our network diagram, we see that the tunnel interface on the server side will be configured as 192.168.192.254, on the network as 192.168.254.252. Also, we will presume in this scenario that we want to use maximum compression.

The following are the contents of the /usr/local/etc/vtund.conf file.

```
options {
      port 5000;
      ppp            /usr/sbin/pppd;
ifconfig     /sbin/ifconfig;
      route        /sbin/route;
      firewall     /sbin/ipchains;
}
default {
      compress yes;
      speed 0;
}
IP-Tunnel {
  pass password1;
  type  tun;
  proto tcp;
  comp  zlib:9;
  encr  yes;
  keepalive yes;
  up {
      ifconfig "%% 192.168.254.254 pointopoint 192.168.254.253 mtu 1500";
      route "add -net 192.168.254.252/30 gw 192.168.254.253";
      route "add -net 192.168.2.0/24 gw 192.168.254.254";
  };
}
```

After the tunnel is brought up, the commands in the up section will be executed. Note that two routes are added: one for the point-to-point network and one for the remote network. Also note that the %% in the ifconfig line is used to refer to the interface name used by this tunnel.

Now lets examine some key elements to our vtund configuration. Because this is a tunnel for only IP traffic, we configure the type of connection as tun. Also, we have decided that maximum compression is one of our goals, so we will want to use Zlib compression. The configuration option comp zlib:9 instructs VTun to use Zlib compression with maximum supported compression, level 9. To use Zlib compression, we must also configure the tunnel to use TCP for transport. The configuration option proto tcp does this.

Finally, to enable encryption, simply turn it on with the line encryption yes.

Once we have finished writing our configuration file, we can start the vtund in server mode.

To run vtund in standalone mode, simply execute vtund with the command line options -s.

```
vtund -s
```

Running vtund in inetd mode is a bit more complicated. Because vtund will be spawned by the inetd super-server, we must update a few files to configure inetd properly. The first file we must modify is /etc/services. This file will map a service name to a port. We need to add a single line to identify the service. The line to add will depend on which port you want vtund to listen to for connections. For this example, we will assume we want to use port 5000. Additionally, we will assume that we want to map both UDP and TCP packets on this port to the service vtund. The following lines can be added to /etc/services to create this mapping.

```
vtund          5000/tcp
vtund          5000/udp
```

Choosing a Port

We have randomly chosen port 5000 for the VTun service. Before you make changes to your /etc/services file, you should verify that no other services are running on this port. You can use the netstat -a command to display which ports are in use on your system.

Once we have added these lines to /etc/services, we can add a line for vtund in the configuration file for inetd. Inetd reads its configuration from /etc/inetd.conf. Adding the following line to /etc/inetd.conf will correctly configure vtund to run in inetd mode:

```
vtund    stream  tcp     wait    root    /usr/local/sbin/vtund vtund -I -f
/etc/vtund.conf
```

If your system uses xinetd, a replacement for inetd with an enhanced feature set, you will need to create a service file named vtund in the directory /etc/xinetd.d. The contents of the file should be as follows:

```
service Vtun
{
        flags           = REUSE
        socket_type = stream
        wait            = no
        user            = root
        server          = /usr/local/sbin/vtund -i
        disable         = no
}
```

Once the connection has been brought up, you should be able to see your tunnel
interface with the `ifconfig` command.

```
[root@vtun-serv ~]# ifconfig tun0
tun0      Link encap:Point-to-Point Protocol
          inet addr:192.168.254.254  P-t-P:192.168.254.253  Mask:255.255.255.255
          UP POINTOPOINT RUNNING NOARP MULTICAST  MTU:1450  Metric:1
          RX packets:16 errors:0 dropped:0 overruns:0 frame:0
          TX packets:16 errors:0 dropped:0 overruns:0 carrier:0
          collisions:0 txqueuelen:10
```

You should also verify that your routing is correct. Use the `netstat` command make
sure your routing table is correct.

As your final test, you should try to `ping` IP addresses on the remote network.

```
[root@vtun-serv ~]# ping -c 3 192.168.2.15
PING 192.168.2.15 (192.168.2.15) from 192.168.254.254 : 56(84) bytes of data.
64 bytes from 192.168.2.15: icmp_seq=0 ttl=127 time=260.758 msec
64 bytes from 192.168.2.15: icmp_seq=1 ttl=127 time=380.958 msec
64 bytes from 192.168.2.15: icmp_seq=2 ttl=127 time=285.275 msec
```

IP Tunnel Client Configuration

For our client configuration, there are fewer options to be configured. Because all of
the parameters for the tunnel are passed from client to server, this configuration file
will be much smaller.

The essential settings in a client file are a `port` setting, a `passwd` setting, and an `up`
section that correctly brings up the tunnel interface and configures routing on the
client side. The `port` setting defines on which port the server is listening for the VTun
connections. This should match the server's `vtund.conf`. The `passwd` option provides
the key with which to authenticate to the server. This also must match the server configuration. The `up` section must mirror what is on the server, meaning that the IP for
the tunnel interface must be configured for the other end of the server's point-to-
point link. Also, the routes added will point to the internal network connected to the
server.

We will include the `persist` option so that if a tunnel connection drops, the client
will attempt to reconnect to the server.

Our client configuration looks like the following:

```
Default {
    Port 5000;
        }

IP-Tunnel {
  pass  password1;
  persist yes;
  up {
        ifconfig "%% 192.168.254.253 pointopoint 192.168.192.254 mtu 1500";
        route "add -net 192.168.254.252/30 gw 192.168.254.254";
        route "add -net 192.168.1.0/24 gw 192.168.254.254";
  };
}
```

Passwords

Although we have used the password password1 in our configuration examples, this is just to make it easier for the reader. In reality, these passwords should be as strong as possible.

To bring up this connection, on the client computer, type the following:

```
vtund IP-Tunnel server.ip.address
```

Just as with the server, you will now be able to see the tun interface.

You will also be able to see the routes to the server's network on the client with the netstat command.

```
[root@vtun-clnt /root]# netstat -nr
Kernel IP routing table
Destination Gateway        Genmask          Flags MSS Window irtt Iface
10.3.0.1    0.0.0.0        255.255.255.255  UH    40  0      0    tun1
10.3.0.0    10.3.0.1       255.255.255.252  UG    40  0      0    tun1
192.168.2.0 0.0.0.0        255.255.255.0    U     40  0      0    eth1
192.168.1.0 10.3.0.1       255.255.255.0    UG    40  0      0    tun1
127.0.0.0   0.0.0.0        255.0.0.0        U     40  0      0    lo
0.0.0.0     65.24.226.1    0.0.0.0          UG    40  0      0    eth0
```

As your final test, you should try to ping IP addresses on the far side of the tunnel.

```
[root@vtun-serv ~]# ping -c 3 192.168.254.254
PING 192.168.254.254 (192.168.254.254) from 192.168.254.254 : 56(84) bytes of
➥data.
64 bytes from 192.168.254.253: icmp_seq=0 ttl=255 time=729.680 msec
64 bytes from 192.168.254.253: icmp_seq=1 ttl=255 time=338.135 msec
64 bytes from 192.168.254.253: icmp_seq=2 ttl=255 time=366.829 msec
```

Finally, to test complete end-to-end connectivity, you should be able to ping an address on the remote network.

```
[root@vtun-serv ~]# ping -c 3 192.168.1.10
PING 192.168.1.10 (192.168.1.10) from 192.168.254.253 : 56(84) bytes of data.
```

```
64 bytes from 192.168.1.10: icmp_seq=0 ttl=127 time=312.129 msec
64 bytes from 192.168.1.10: icmp_seq=1 ttl=127 time=230.238 msec
64 bytes from 192.168.1.10: icmp_seq=2 ttl=127 time=342.838 msec
```

Ethernet Tunnel

For our next VPN, we will configure an ethernet tunnel between our two sites. An ethernet tunnel will enable us to forward not only IP traffic but also any other layer 3 traffic that runs over ethernet.

Because a few extra commands are needed to set up ethernet tunnels, they are a bit more complicated than IP tunnels. Aside from the VTun configuration, you will also need to have the `brctl` command, included in the bridge-utils package, installed and working. Figure 8.4 shows the relationship between the bridge interface, `tap` interface, and Ethernet Tunnel.

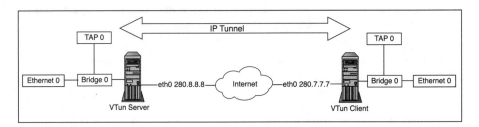

Figure 8.4   The ethernet tunnel.

Ethernet Tunnel Server

Most of the configuration for our ethernet tunnel will be the same as our IP tunnel configuration mentioned earlier. One of the changes that will need to be made is to the `device` setting. Because Ethernet tunnels use the TAP driver and thus a `tap` interface, this will need to be reflected in the configuration. The second change needs to be made to the `up` section, to add routes for any protocols you want to forward across your tunnel.

In this example, the `up` section will create a bridge interface that will bond the internal ethernet interface and the `tap` interface. After the interfaces are bonded, their IP address will be zeroed out, and we will reassign the IP address of the ethernet interface to the bridge interface. This will allow IP connectivity for devices that use the IP address of the ethernet interface as their gateway, while at the same time bridging all ethernet traffic that the ethernet sees to the tap interface.

Note that, for this example, IP connectivity between 192.168.1.0/24 and 192.168.2.0/24 is not the goal. This is designed purely to tunnel ethernet traffic.

A sample configuration file looks like this:

```
Ether-tunnel {
    pass  password1;
    type  ether;
    proto tcp;
    comp  zlib:9;
    encr  yes;
    keepalive yes;

    up {
        ifconfig "%% 192.168.254.253 netmask 255.255.255.252";
        brctl addbr bridge0
        brctl addif bridge0 eth1
        brctl addif bridge0 %%
        ifconfig "eth1 0.0.0.0"
        ifconfig "%% 0.0.0.0"
        ifconfig "bridge0 192.168.1.254 netmask 255.255.255.0"
    };
     down {
        brctl delbr bridge0
        ifconfig "eth1 192.168.1.254 netmask 255.255.255.0";

            };
        };
}
```

If you wanted to add support for another protocol on ethernet, you could add the appropriate protocol routing information in the up section.

Broadcasts

Note that, in this configuration, all broadcast traffic will be forwarded across the tunnel. Although this might be desirable in some cases, it can also significantly degrade the performance of your VPN.

In the up section, `brctl` commands have been added to create a bridge named `bridge0`. Once the bridge has been created, we add the `eth1` and the newly created tap interface (referenced by the `%%`) to the bridge. Adding these two interfaces to the bridge will mirror ethernet frames between them. Any frame that `eth1` receives, the tap interface will also receive. Once the `tap` interface receives a frame, it is forwarded to the VTun client.

Once the bridge has been created, interfaces added to the bridge will lose IP connectivity. So that clients using 192.168.1.254 as a gateway address will still be able to reach it, the IP is assigned to the `bridge0` interface.

After the bridge has been created, the `brctl show` command is used to view the status.

Aside from protocol-routing information, the other change that needs to be made is to the `type` field. Changing this to `ether` configures the connection to be ethernet.

Ethernet Tunnel Client

The ethernet tunnel client is configured in much the same way as the IP tunnel client. A few configuration options are different.

```
Default {
  Port 5000;
      }
Ether-Tunnel {
    pass password1;
    type ether;
    proto tcp;
    keepalive yes;
    up {
        ifconfig "%% 192.168.254.253 netmask 255.255.255.252";
        brctl addbr bridge0
        brctl addif bridge0 eth1
        brctl addif bridge0 %%
        ifconfig "eth1 0.0.0.0"
        ifconfig "%% 0.0.0.0"
        ifconfig "bridge0 192.168.1.254 netmask 255.255.255.0"
    };
    down {
        brctl delbr bridge0
        ifconfig "eth1 192.168.1.254 netmask 255.255.255.0";

            };
}
```

As with the ethernet tunnel server, the up section contains statements that enable ethernet bridging. In this example, we still want to have IP connectivity to the server, so we assign the IP address of eth1 to bridge1.

To start the ethernet tunnel, on the client machine, run the following:

```
vtund Ether-tunnel host-server
```

The client machine will then attempt to connect to the ethernet tunnel server. Note that as with the other tunnels, the capabilities of each machine must match. For example, if the server will only establish tunnels compressed with the LZO algorithm, make sure that vtund on the client machine has been installed with LZO support.

Depending on the needs of the end user, there are several ways to test that the tunnel is functioning. For our sample network, let's presume that our end users use NetBIOS traffic to share files. In this case, when NetBIOS users browse for other computers, they should be able to see computers on both the local and remote sides of the tunnel.

Also, to check the status of our bridge, we can use the command brctl to show the status of our bridge interface.

```
[root@vtun-serv ~]# brctl show
bridge name     bridge id            STP enabled     interfaces
```

```
bridge0        8000.002078102dc4              yes          eth1
                                                           tap0
```

Note from the output of this command that both `eth1` and `tap0` belong to `bridge0`.

Serial Tunnel

For scenarios in which you are not able to use a `tun` or `tap` interface, you can set up a serial tunnel. As previously mentioned, a serial tunnel creates a virtual serial link, which acts as a tunnel. For this example, we will create a PPP tunnel. PPP is designed for point-to-point links, which is how tunnel interfaces are configured.

Figure 8.5 is a high-level picture of the VPN to be built with the PPP tunnel.

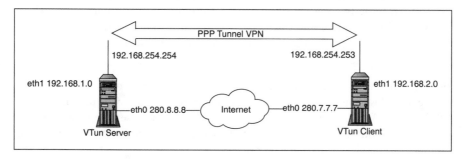

Figure 8.5 The serial tunnel.

Serial Tunnel Server

The serial tunnel server will use PPP in server mode to pass out IP information to the client.

```
PPP-tunnel {
pass  password1;
comp  yes;
  encr  yes;
  up {
      ppp "192.168.254.254:192.168.254.253 proxyarp";
      route "add -net 192.168.2.0/24 gw 192.168.254.253";
  };
}
```

The `ppp` statement in the `up` section specifies the local and remote IP addresses. The IP for the local PPP interface will be 192.168.254.254, and the IP for the remote PPP interface will be 192.168.254.253. The `proxyarp` option tells PPP to add an entry to the system's ARP table with the IP address of the remote PPP interface and the hardware address of the local interface. This creates the illusion that the remote PPP interface is connected to the local network because the local server will respond to the `arp` requests with its own address.

Serial Tunnel Client

As with the other tunnel types, tunnel options are passed from server to client. PPP is also given its address from the PPP server, so there will be few statements in the up section.

```
PPP-tunnel {
  pass  password1;
  up {
      ppp "noipdefault";
      route "add -net 192.168.1.0/24 gw 192.168.254.254";
  };
}
```

In the up section, as we have done before, a route is added for the remote VPN network. Alternatively, because the IP address for the PPP interface is not configured locally, the route could be added using the device name instead of the IP address. The command to add a route by device would look like the following:

```
route add -net 192.168.1.0/24 dev ppp0
```

Also, note that serial tunnels take a bit longer than other tunnel types to establish a connection. This is due to the extra time taken for the PPP daemons to negotiate the PPP protocol. Because the connection is slower, this might cause statements in your up section to fail. You should double-check your serial tunnel after it has been established to ensure that all proper routing is in place.

To start the PPP tunnel, on the VTun client, type the following command:

```
vtund PPP-tunnel 270.8.8.8
```

As was mentioned in the "PPP" section, the IP address for the local interface will be received from the server. The `noipdefault` setting tells the PPP client to not configure the PPP interface as the default route. Once the link has been established, the routing table should have an entry with the following line:

```
Destination     Gateway        Genmask        Flags  MSS Window  irtt Iface
192.168.254.253 0.0.0.0        255.255.255.255 UH      40 0          0 ppp0
```

This PPP tunnel configuration works in much the same way as the IP tunnel detailed earlier in the chapter. Because it is similar, we will be able to use the same techniques to test and verify that the PPP tunnel is functioning properly.

To test the PPP connection itself, we can test that the remote side is reachable. If we are on the client, we can use `ping` to verify that the two PPP interfaces are communicating.

```
PING 192.168.254.254 (192.168.254.254) from 192.168.254.253 : 56(84) bytes of
➥data.
64 bytes from 192.168.254.254: icmp_seq=0 ttl=255 time=196.615 msec
64 bytes from 192.168.254.254: icmp_seq=1 ttl=255 time=352.150 msec
64 bytes from 192.168.254.254: icmp_seq=2 ttl=255 time=274.243 msec
```

If the interface responds to `pings`, we can continue our testing and use `ping` to test remote network reachability. From the client, we should be able to `ping` a host on the network 192.168.1.0.

```
[root@vtun-clnt ~]# ping -c 3 192.168.1.10
PING 192.168.1.10 (192.168.1.10) from 192.168.254.253 : 56(84) bytes of data.
64 bytes from 192.168.1.10: icmp_seq=0 ttl=127 time=175.704 msec
64 bytes from 192.168.1.10: icmp_seq=1 ttl=127 time=150.991 msec
64 bytes from 192.168.1.10: icmp_seq=2 ttl=127 time=264.362 msec
```

Real Testing

To really test that routing for the tunnels has been done correctly, the remote address on the 192.168.1.0 network should not be the IP of the VTun server. If either side of the tunnel is able to `ping` the remote PPP interface, it will also be able to `ping` every interface on the VTun machine. To truly test routing, reachability testing should be done to machines behind the VTun server.

Pipe Tunnel Example

For this example, the goal will be to securely transfer our logs to another server, where they will be archived. Because security is a concern, we will use VTun to encrypt the traffic to keep unwanted third parties from viewing the log files. The log file server where logs are archived will be the VTun server. VTun clients will be the machines sending the log files.

The first step with pipe tunnels is deciding which program to use to transfer the information across. If we were archiving log files on the same machine, we would probably use the `tar` or `cpio` command to create the backups. As an example, if we wanted to create a `tar` archive of all the files in the `/var/log` directory, we would type the following:

```
tar -cvf log_backup.tar /var/log/*
```

This would create a `tar` archive named `log_backup.tar`.

Once we have decided on the command to use, we need to break the command up into a client and server section. For this example, the client section will create the output; the server section will store the output. Note that the client and server roles can be reversed—the server can produce the output, the client can receive it. It all depends on how you configure your solution.

To redirect `tar`'s output to the screen, use the `f -` option. The ' option gives `tar` the name of the file to store the archive in. The - option passes standard out as the filename to use. We can then use a redirect, or a >, to send the output of the `tar` command to a file.

```
tar -cvf - /var/log/* > backup.tar
```

Here, the `tar -cvf - /var/log/*` portion is the client section because it will be producing the data. The `> backup.tar` portion is the server section, which will be storing the data.

Figure 8.6 shows the output from the VTun client being directed to the VTun server. The VTun server uses the `cat` command to receive the input and direct it to a file.

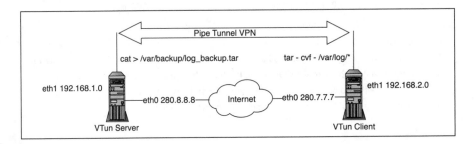

Figure 8.6   The pipe tunnel.

Pipe Tunnel Server

The pipe tunnel server will be the machine where log files are archived. For a pipe tunnel, this means it will have to "receive" the files and place them into a directory. From the preceding sample command, we want to run the `> backup.tar` command on this side to receive the data.

```
options {
  port 5000;
}
default {
  compress      no;
  speed         0;
}
Pipe-tunnel {
  type pipe;
  pass password1;
  encrypt yes;
        up {
  prog /bin/bash "-c 'cat > /var/backup/backup.tar'";
        };
}
```

From our configuration example, the `type pipe` setting configures VTun to create a pipe tunnel. The `encrypt yes` line turns on Blowfish encryption. Finally, the `prog` and `args` settings are the program and arguments to be used to receive the output from the client. Because this example is doing a simple redirect, we can use `/bin/bash` to receive the output and redirect it to `/var/backup/backup.tar`. The `-c` option tells bash to run the program following the `-c` and then exit.

Pipe Tunnel Client

The configuration for the pipe tunnel client will be similar to the configuration for the pipe tunnel server.

```
options {
  port        5000;
  persist     no;
  timeout     60;
}
Pipe-tunnel {
  passwd      password1;
        up {
  prog  /bin/bash "-c 'tar -cvf - /var/log/*'";
        };
}
```

Because we are using the client to create the output, we will use the `tar` command here to send the output across the tunnel. The setting `prog /bin/bash` uses the bash. The arguments passed to `/bin/bash` are specified by the `args` setting. The `-c` in the `args` setting tells `bash` to run the command following the `-c` and then exit. The client runs the `tar` program and redirects output to standard out, which is received by the VTun and is passed to the far side of the tunnel.

As with the other tunnel types, the pipe tunnel is initiated by the VTun client. To start the pipe tunnel, use the following command:

```
vtund Pipe-tunnel 270.8.8.8
```

To test connectivity, once the VTun client has established the tunnel, the file `/var/backup/backup.tar` should exist on the VTun server.

As is shown from this example, VTun is an extremely flexible solution for securing just about any type of traffic you can imagine.

Troubleshooting

Here is a list of common error messages and how to fix them. Error messages will be found in the logfile where syslog sends messages of the **info** priority. This is generally the file /var/log/messages.

Can't allocate tun device. No such file or directory.

The tunnel device files have not been created correctly, or the TUN/TAP driver has not been installed in the kernel. See the TUN/TAP installation section on how to create device files. Also, make sure you have compiled the TUN/TAP driver into the kernel. This can be verified by checking your boot messages for an initialization message. Use the following command:

```
[root@vtun-serv log]#  grep TUN /var/log/dmesg
Universal TUN/TAP device driver 1.3 1999-2000 Maxim Krasnyansky
```

ZLIB compression is not supported.

This message indicates that VTun was compiled without Zlib support. To correct this, download and compile Zlib. The other options are to use LZO compression (if it is installed) or to disable compression entirely.

LZO compression is not supported.

This error is generated when VTun attempts to initialize LZO compression on a tunnel when LZO support was not added at compile time. To correct, disable compression or use Zlib.

Session network timeout.

An established tunnel has lost connectivity to the remote end. Make sure the remote end is still reachable and that VTun is running on it.

Encryption is not supported.

VTun was compiled without OpenSSL support. To correct this, you will need to download and install the OpenSSL libraries.

Traffic shaping is not supported.

VTun was compiled without traffic shaping support. Traffic shaping is disabled by running the `configure` script with the command-line option `-disable-shaper`. To correct this problem, rerun the `configure` script and recompile VTun.

No hosts defined.

No tunnels are defined within your configuration file. Define a tunnel (using the examples listed earlier in this chapter as guidelines) and restart `vtund`.

Connection timed out.

The client timed out while attempting to connect to the server. Make sure the server is reachable by pinging it. If you were attempting to connect by name, make sure DNS resolves to the correct IP address. Also, make sure the port settings on the client and the server are the same.

Denied connection from *host*.

The server has denied a connection to a client. Make sure the passwords are the same on both machines.

Compatibility

Although VTun is based on several standards, it is not compatible with any other tunneling protocols. This is because of the way the VTun client and server initiate connections.

VTun itself, however, is supported on several different platforms. In addition to Linux, VTun is also supported on the following operating systems:

- The BSD family: FreeBSD, OpenBSD, NetBSD
- Solaris

The steps for installing the VTun on these platforms are similar to the installation on Linux. When possible, the commands listed in this text have been written to be useful on other platforms.

Summary

In this chapter, you learned about using VTun as a VPN solution. VTun provides a flexible method for creating secure tunnels across untrusted networks. With the variety of tunnels that VTun supports, it is a much more capable VPN solution than that provided by many competing products.

For more information on VTun, see the VTun web site at `http://vtun.sourceforge.net`.

9

cIPe

WHEN YOU WANT TO BUILD A VPN, especially if you are using UNIX frequently, you often tend to use simpler, more lightweight packages as low-level tools on which to build. Later you might want to add scripts, cron jobs, and other neat things, so it is important for the package you select to be highly customizable and simple.

Many of the lightweight packages designed to fill this niche end up leaving important features behind in trying to trade functionality for simplicity. However, many are providing more or less the necessary minimum of functions you need to build a secure private network. In this chapter, we will describe one such package called cIPe.

Overview of cIPe

Crypto IP Encapsulation (cIPe) is a simple, lightweight package that provides for tunneling of encrypted IP packets over UDP. The package is available under GNU's GPL and can be downloaded freely. The examples in this chapter will be based on the version 1.5.1 of the package, which supports Linux kernel v2.{2, 3, 4}.* and primarily focuses on the i386 platform. Although there is a port of cIPe to Windows NT, given the focus of this book, we will concentrate on the Linux implementation.

cIPe Components and Their Functions

The cIPe package (in the rest of this chapter we will refer to it as "CIPE" or "the package") consists of a kernel module and a user-level managing utility implemented as a daemon (`ciped`).

Kernel Module

The *kernel module* performs various operations pertaining to the handling of IP packets, such as transceiving as well as encrypting them using a symmetric cipher. The module realizes a virtual network device that can be configured and used for routing, just like all other network devices such as `eth0`, `ppp0`, and so on.

The name of the device depends on the protocol version as well as the algorithm used; typically, it is `cipcbX`. The last three letters of the device name represent version 3 of the CIPE protocol (a, b, c = 3), Blowfish symmetric cipher (b), and the index of the network device (0, 1, …, n), respectively. The kernel module is named the same way except for the device number, which is not present. For example, the default name of the kernel module is `cipcb`.

User-Level Managing Utility

The *user-level* `ciped` utility uses similar naming principles and is often called `ciped-cb`, for that matter. This is done so that the utility can co-exist with other CIPE implementations that use different versions of CIPE and encryption protocols. The primary task of the utility is to perform key exchange and configuration of the CIPE package.

Note that CIPE always operates on point-to-point links. A simple analogue of this setup would be a PPP connection. If you have ever tried to set `pppd` up, you probably know that both sides have interfaces associated with them, and each interface must be assigned an IP address, MTU, and so forth; indeed, it would look something like the following:

```
# ifconfig -a

ppp0 Link encap:Point-to-Point Protocol
inet addr: xxx.xxx.xxx.1 P-t-P:xxx.xxx.xxx.2 Mask:255.255.255.255
UP POINTOPOINT RUNNING NOARP MULTICAST MTU:576 Metric:1
RX packets:156 errors:0 dropped:0 overruns:0 frame:0
TX packets:0 errors:14836 dropped:135 overruns:0 carrier:0 coll:0

cipcb0 Link encap:IPIP Tunnel Hwaddr
inet addr: yyy.yyy.yyy.1 P-t-P:yyy.yyy.yyy.2 Mask:255.255.255.255
UP POINTOPOINT NOTRAILERS RUNNING NOARP MTU:1442 Metric:1
RX packets:0 errors:0 dropped:0 overruns:0 frame:0
TX packets:0 errors:0 dropped:0 overruns:0 carrier:0 collisions:0
```

Conversely, `ciped` is similar to `pppd` in many ways. First, there is one copy of `ciped` per active `cipecb` device. Second, `ciped`'s `/etc/cipe/options` configuration file syntax somewhat resembles `/etc/ppp/options`. Finally, both `ciped` and `pppd` execute `ip-up` and `ip-down` scripts when links go up and down, respectively.

By drawing a parallel between `pppd` and `ciped`, we are trying to instill a mental picture of CIPE as a point-to-point concept. You will need this to better understand the sample VPN configuration we are going to introduce later in this chapter.

Public-Key Configuration Utility

Starting with version 1.5, CIPE supports a public-key exchange algorithm (Diffie-Hellman) as well as RSA signatures. To configure and perform an initial key exchange, an additional security utility called `pkcipe` is included in CIPE distribution.

The `pkcipe` utility establishes a TCP connection between two endpoints of a CIPE point-to-point link, exchanges public keys, and then determines a shared key to be used by the `ciped` utility to symmetrically encrypt the data. After the public-key exchange is done, `pkcipe` generates a configuration file that contains the secret key it negotiated and then executes `ciped` with the new configuration file.

Thus, `pkcipe` is aimed at facilitating the life of a network administrator and eliminating the need to manually distribute shared keys as described earlier. CIPE still supports the old way of manually disseminating shared keys, however, should you decide to use it.

Supported Cryptographic Algorithms and Protocols

In the following subsection, we will provide an overview of the cryptographic protocols and algorithms you can use with CIPE.

Blowfish, IDEA, Diffie-Hellman

Originally, CIPE was designed to be very lightweight, so it relied on a network administrator to add a 128-bit static *secret* key to CIPE configuration files on both sides of a point-to-point link. This key was then used to negotiate a dynamic *session* key that could be changed repeatedly and used as a key with the supported symmetric cipher schemes CIPE could employ to encrypt tunneled data. This mechanism is still employed by CIPE, although a special add-on utility is now included, as mentioned earlier, that performs Diffie-Hellman–based key exchange.

As of version 1.5.1, CIPE supports two *symmetric ciphers*, namely *Blowfish* and *IDEA*, both of which use 128-bit keys. Which one of these ciphers should be selected? It depends on your goals. When making a decision, however, you might want to consider that IDEA is patented to ensure there are no legal problems.

The Default Cipher is Blowfish

CIPE will use Blowfish by default unless you specify `--enable-idea` when configuring the package. See the section "Compiling CIPE" later in this chapter.

If you are looking for an industry-level solution, we recommend that you look at the packages that support more recent symmetric ciphers such as AES (Rijndael), Twofish, RC6, MARS, Serpent, and so on.

CIPE's Transfer Protocol

CIPE uses this protocol to transmit data encrypted using the two ciphers described earlier. CIPE currently supports versions 3 and 4 of its transfer protocol.

Version 3 is the default protocol. It should generally be enough, although it only supports IP over IP and no other formats of data to be encapsulated. If you want to use CIPE to tunnel OSI Layer 2 packets (Ethernet, for example) or other protocols, use version 4.

Version 4 is more flexible and can be used to encapsulate multiple protocols. In most cases, this version of the CIPE protocol is used to make CIPE act as an encrypting bridge, tunneling Ethernet frames. See the section "Compiling CIPE" for more information on how to tell CIPE to use this version of the protocol.

Implications of Using CIPE as an Encrypting Bridge

If you want to use CIPE as an encrypting bridge, you should be aware of possible security and performance issues associated with this choice.

If you tunnel all Ethernet traffic in and out of your intranet, then all the higher level protocols encapsulated in the Ethernet frames that were not recognized by your firewall rules (ipx/spx, for example) will pass through. To stay in control of what goes in and out of your network, you will need to either set up your firewall to look into each Ethernet frame or filter traffic before the tunneling occurs. In addition, analyzing each packet can also be costly from a performance viewpoint.

Note that the performance of your system might also decrease significantly if broadcast traffic is tunneled. Because the CIPE machine is going to act as a bridge, its Ethernet interface will be put in promiscuous mode, and the interface will see all the traffic on the media, including broadcast frames. Sometimes there can be a lot of such frames, particularly with Microsoft domain protocols, which are known to generate huge amounts of broadcast traffic. These frames can easily clog your tunnel and slow your tunneling machine down because of the additional cycles required to encrypt and decrypt broadcast traffic.

Installation

We will now go through a detailed description of CIPE installation. Remember that you will need to execute all commands in a superuser mode, as follows:

```
[root@fox /root]# id
uid=0(root), gid=0(root), groups=0(root),1(bin),2(daemon),10(wheel)
```

You will also need the latest version of the CIPE package. See http://sites.inka.de/ sites/bigred/devel/cipe.html.

Dependencies

To install CIPE, you will need to have the following components on your system: kernel sources, the OpenSSL library, the `modutils` package, and the `/dev/urandom` device. In addition, make sure IP forwarding is enabled. A detailed description of the dependencies is given in the following sections.

Kernel Sources

First, you need to make sure you are running the supported version of the Linux kernel. CIPE supports the majority of the popular Linux kernel releases, namely 2.1.★ (since 2.1.103), 2.3.★, and 2.4.★ (since 2.3.48), so it will probably support yours. Just in case, here is how to check:

```
[root@fox /root]# uname -r
2.2.17-14smp
```

You also need to ensure that the version of the running kernel exactly matches the version of the source tree you have in the `/usr/src` directory. See Chapter 5, "IPSec," if you need instructions on updating the source tree and installing a new version of the kernel.

It is necessary to recompile CIPE along with other external modules after you rebuild the kernel. This will take care of any discrepancies caused by source changes and will decrease the chances of cipe kernel module crashing.

IP Forwarding

Next, do not forget to enable IP forwarding. For example:

```
[root@fox /root]# echo 1 > /proc/sys/net/ipv4/ip_forward
```

/dev/urandom

CIPE needs a good source of entropy, particularly for dynamic keys generation, so the `/dev/urandom` device must be present:

```
[root@fox /root]# ls -l /dev/urandom
crw-r--r--   1 root     root       1,   9 Jan 20  2001 /dev/urandom
```

If the device does not exist, you can recreate it using the following:

```
[root@fox /root]# mknod -m 0644 /dev/urandom c 1 9
```

modutils

You will also need to have the `modutils` package installed.

```
root@fox /root]# rpm -qai | egrep modutil
Name: modutils Group: System Environment/Kernel
Source RPM: modutils-2.3.14-3.src.rpm
```

The `modutils` package will be utilized later to load the CIPE's kernel module that implements a virtual network device.

OpenSSL (Required by *pkcipe*)

Finally, if you want to use `pkcipe` for public-key exchanges and initial link configuration, it is necessary to add the OpenSSL package (version 0.9.6 and later). Visit `www.openssl.org` for the latest copy of the OpenSSL.

Compiling CIPE

The recommendations we provide in this section are based on our testbed running RedHat Linux v7.1 with 2.2.16-SMP kernel. We encourage you to read the following section even if you are using a different Linux flavor or kernel version because most of the ideas and recommendations will still apply.

Running *configure*

By now, you should have all the previously described prerequisites installed. The next step is to configure and compile CIPE. Generally, untarring the CIPE package and running `./configure` should suffice, as follows:

```
[root@fox 1] tar xzvf cipe
[root@fox 1]# cd cipe-1.5.1
[root@fox cipe-1.5.1]# ./configure
```

Now you can skip to building CIPE unless `configure` complains about something or you want to fine-tune it. If you are running into problems, walk through the following steps:

1. Look at the kind of error `configure` stops at. Usually there is something missing. For example, if you happen to play with different kernel versions, you might have several kernel source directories available in `/usr/src`.

   Which one to use? The one that has the same version as the kernel you are using, of course. In this case, your configure command line should look like this:

   ```
   [root@fox cipe-1.5.1]# ./configure --with-linux=/usr/src/linux-x.y.z
   ```

   The argument specifies the directory where the kernel source you want to use is installed.

2. There are about a dozen arguments that CIPE's `configure` script supports to assist you with troubleshooting. Here are some of the arguments you might find useful:

   ```
   --with-ssl-includes=<path_to_OpenSSL_includes>
   --with-ssl-libs=<path_to_OpenSSL_libs>
   ```

You can manually specify a path to the OpenSSL includes and libs if CIPE fails to find them. You might need this if you had an earlier version of OpenSSL and messed things up while trying to upgrade it.

```
--enable-idea
```

For those of you who want to use IDEA cipher to encrypt data:

```
--enable-protocol={3,4}
```

Specify which version of encapsulation protocol to use. CIPE v1.5.1. supports versions 3 and 4. Version 3 is used by default.

```
--disable-send-config
```

Use this to prevent CIPE from sending config information between peers upon startup to detect configuration mismatches. Keep in mind that the information is sent in plaintext.

3. If everything goes smoothly and the `configure` script does not complain, you can proceed to building CIPE.

Building CIPE

To compile and install CIPE, use the following:

```
[root@fox cipe-1.5.1]# make all install
```

This command should install `ciped-*` binary. The last two characters of the binary name will be set accordingly to the selected CIPE protocol version and encryption. The binary will be copied to `/usr/local/sbin` by default. If you do not like the defaults, use the following:

```
[root@fox cipe-1.5.1]# make BINDIR=<where_to_install> install
```

The command also copies the CIPE kernel module to `/lib/modules/`uname -r`/misc` so that you are able to load the module afterward.

If the package was compiled with `pkcipe`, the latter will also be installed along with the `rsa-keygen` utility. This utility will also generate a host key on the fly, if none was found.

/etc/cipe

For some reason, CIPE's developers decided not to create the `/etc/cipe` directory automatically in the install target of CIPE's Makefile. Instead, they're relying on the system administrator to do that. In addition, the admin needs to copy the config files, namely `ip-up`, `ip-down`, and `options`, from the `samples/` directory of the CIPE package.

The only intelligent explanation that we could come up with is that CIPE gives the administrator a chance to decide where to keep the configuration files, but how often does that happen? In addition, if administrators want to move the configuration files from /etc/cipe, they can always do that.

So why can this not be done automatically, you might ask? We are completely with you on this. In any case, here is the process:

```
[root@fox cipe-1.5.1]# mkdir /etc/cipe ; chmod 755 /etc/cipe
[root@fox cipe-1.5.1]# cp samples/ip-* /etc/cipe
[root@fox cipe-1.5.1]# chmod 644 /etc/cipe/ip-*
[root@fox cipe-1.5.1]# cp samples/options /etc/cipe
[root@fox cipe-1.5.1]# chmod 600 /etc/cipe/options
```

The /etc/cipe/options file should *only* be readable by root because it usually contains a secret key used when establishing connections.

Strangely, pkcipe's installation routines do create /etc/cipe/pk, and that is definitely a step in the right direction.

Troubleshooting

The following sections address problems we encountered when building CIPE.

'sysconf@GLIBC'   Here is one of the problems we faced when building CIPE. First, configure complained about missing OpenSSL, so we had to upgrade OpenSSL from version 0.9.5 to 0.9.6a. This seemed to be okay but only for configure. When trying to compile pkcipe, we received the following error:

```
[make's output is omitted]
gcc  -o pkcipe proto.o negotiate.o main.o packet.o lock.o p_sha1.o
-L/usr/lib -lcrypto -ldl  -L../lib -lcipe
/usr/lib/libcrypto.so: undefined reference to `sysconf@GLIBC_2.2'
```

We fixed the problem by completing the following steps:

1. Download and compile the latest version of OpenSSL. For this demonstration, we will assume that a freshly built OpenSSL is in the directory /usr/tmp/openssl-0.9.6a.

2. Run CIPE's configure with the following parameters:

```
[root@fox cipe-1.5.1]# ./configure --with-ssl-libs=/usr/tmp/openssl-0.9.6a
```

3. Replace the following line in pkcipe/Makefile:

```
LIBS := -L/usr/lib -lcrypto -ldl  -L$(lib) -lcipe
```

with

```
LIBS := -L/usr/lib -L/usr/tmp/openssl-0.9.6a -lcrypto -ldl -L$(lib) -lcipe
```

After we did this, everything compiled and installed without a hitch. We suspect that pkcipe still being in its early beta is one of the causes for this problem.

ip_select_ident()   In Linux kernel version 2.4.2 and higher, an additional parameter was added to the `ip_select_ident()` function, and some versions of CIPE happen to use the old format. If you have this problem, you can either get the latest version at `http://sites.inka.de/sites/bigred/devel/cipe.html` or browse through the mailing list on the CIPE site and find a patch.

#ifdef SO_BINDTODEVICE **and** *HAVE_DEVNAME_ARRAY*   On various 2.0.★ prereleases, it is possible that the `output.c` file does not compile. If you happen to have a 2.0.★ kernel, replace the line

```
#ifdef SO_BINDTODEVICE
```

in `output.c` with `#if 1` or `#if 0`, whichever is helpful with your release.

Another possible problem pertains to 2.3.99 prereleases, where you might have problems with `device.c` compilation. Usually it is enough to simply change the line

```
#ifdef HAVE_DEVNAME_ARRAY
```

to either `#if 1` or `#if 0`, as with versions 2.0.★.

According to CIPE's authors, all the problems mentioned here are fixed with kernel version 2.4.0 and higher, so if you are using 2.0.★, you might be better off upgrading the kernel anyway.

CIPE Configuration

You have at least two options when it comes to configuring CIPE. One is to manually set and distribute shared keys. Another is to use the `pkcipe` utility to do key generation and distribution automatically. This section will provide a detailed description of both options. Additionally, we will explain the options you will need to use for static and dynamic peers.

Static Key–Based Configuration (Default)

The following subsections will provide an overview of CIPE configuration files, methods used to generate keys, and scripts you need to have to run CIPE.

/etc/cipe/options

Here is an example of a minimal /etc/cipe/options file:

```
# Without a "device" line, the device is picked dynamically
# device cipcb0

# peer's interface IP address
ptpaddr        10.1.2.1

# our CIPE device's IP address
ipaddr         10.1.1.1
```

```
# Remember that CIPE tunnels over UDP so you need to
# define IP addresses and ports
#
# The following are real IP addresses with ports
# that CIPE will use for tunneling.
#
# Note: if you set port 0 here, the system will pick
# one and tell it to you via the ip-up script.
# Same with IP=0.0.0.0
#
me               self.sandybeach.florida.com:9100

# the UDP address we connect to.
# Of course no wildcards here.
#
peer             office.detroit.company.com:30000

ipup=/etc/cipe/ip-up.detroit
ipdown=/etc/cipe/ip-down.detroit

# The shared key. Must be secret.
# This is why we do not want anybody except for root
# to see this file. The key is 128 bits in hexadecimal notation.
#
key              3248fd20adf9c00ccf9ecc2393bbb3e4
```

As you can see from the configuration file, you need to specify IP addresses of both interfaces forming your CIPE point-to-point connection: `ipaddr` for your side of the connection and `ptpaddr` for your peer's side.

You should also set the two real IP addresses that will be used to build your tunnel that will support the point-to-point connection. You will also need to set up port numbers that will be used to differentiate between UDP packets that belong to different tunnels.

Mirroring Configuration

Naturally, each CIPE peer must have a mirrored version of the other side's `/etc/cipe/options`. For example, `ip` and `ptpaddr`, as well as `me` and `peer` parameters, *must be inverted* for each side of the point-to-point link.

The `ipup` and `ipdown` options specify paths to two scripts that will be executed when the point-to-point link associated with the options file comes up and goes down, respectively. These scripts are very similar to those used by `pppd` and are typically used to add routing records. We will examine these files in one of the following subsections.

The key options specify a 128-bit shared key that will be used to determine a temporary dynamic key that is utilized to encrypt tunneled data.

Initializing a Secret Key

To initialize the CIPE secret key in /etc/cipe/options, you can come up with 16 bytes of data or, for example, use a hash of the pseudo random data provided by /dev/urandom, as follows:

```
[root@fox /root]# dd if=/dev/urandom count=4 2>/dev/null | md5sum | awk '{print
➥$1}' >> /etc/cipe/options
```

It is up to you to decide which one of these is safer. However, it is not as important as making sure the key is delivered to your peer *securely*.

The problem of distributing keys is more of a challenge than it might seem, especially when you operate a VPN with a large number of gateways. Also, remember that using ssh /, stunnel /, and so on to distribute the keys is better than Telnet and FTP, but it is not a panacea and you must always consider the risks involved.

Man-in-the-Middle Attacks Are More Serious Than You Think

Regardless of how secure the package you use for your VPN is, if an attacker captures keys while you are distributing them, your VPN is no longer secure. Have you already thought about how you plan to distribute your shared keys? Are you going to use FTP or NFS? You probably know that these protocols do not encrypt packets, so by using them, you are literally handing your keys out to attackers.

However, we want to warn you that even if you use SSH or SSL, you are still likely to be vulnerable to active attacks, including man-in-the-middle. The problem is fundamental, and stealing the keys you distribute using SSH or SSL can be almost as easy as capturing FTP and NFS traffic in the previous example.

So what can you do to decrease the chances of an active attack? One of the most important things you should know is to beware of messages about changed keys and new certificates—you could be under attack. In practice, it is also important to know how the attack works in order to prevent it. To see examples of active attacks and to find out more about the problem as well as ways to deal with it, see www.cc.gatech.edu/~ok/mitm.

Also, for older versions of CIPE (before 1.4.0), you will need to use keys that only consist of decimal digits. This is a bug, not a feature. It is described for compatibility reasons because if your peer is using an older version of CIPE, your shared key will be interpreted differently on the peer's side.

To circumvent the problem, you can use a variation of the preceding command that filters out nondecimal characters. For example:

```
[root@fox /root]# dd if=/dev/urandom count=4 2>/dev/null | md5sum | tr -d a-f >>
➥/etc/cipe/options
```

Static vs. Dynamic Peer IP Addresses

Sometimes it is desirable for one (or both) of the peers to use dynamic IP addresses. For example, Internet service providers often use a pool of addresses to assign to their users. You might have a DSL line or a cable modem that obtains its IP address via DHCP, and the IP address can change at any time.

How does CIPE remedy this situation? Two basic scenarios are described here.

The first scenario takes places when one side has a static IP address and the other a dynamic one. In this scenario, the static IP side must simply set its peer address to 0.0.0.0 and set the maxerr option to -1. The latter prevents CIPE from exiting when it determines that it is not able to connect to the dummy address of the peer. A sample server (static IP) side configuration is given here:

```
ptpaddr      10.1.2.1
ipaddr       10.1.1.1
me           self.sandybeach.com:9999
peer         0.0.0.0:9999
maxerr       -1
key          3248fd20adf9c00ccf9ecc2393bbb3e4
```

On the dynamic IP side, the configuration looks as follows:

```
ptpaddr      10.1.1.1
ipaddr       10.1.2.1
me           0.0.0.0:9999
dynip        1
peer         self.sandybeach.com:9999
ping         60
maxerr       3
key          3248fd20adf9c00ccf9ecc2393bbb3e4
```

Note that two additional options were added at the dynamic IP side: dynip and ping. The dynip option is needed for the ciped on the dynamic IP side to be able to register IP address changes. The ping option tells the dynamic side to contact the other side immediately upon determining its own current dynamic IP address.

Now let's zoom out and look at the way both sides interact.

The static IP side waits for incoming UDP packets on the port 9999. The dynamic IP side sends a UDP packet from its current IP to the static IP side, port 9999. The dynamic IP side makes three attempts (specified by the maxerr option), and if all three are unsuccessful, it exits. Keep in mind that the static IP might be behind a firewall or SOCKS5 proxy, and that should still work just fine.

The second scenario takes place when both sides have dynamic IP addresses. Obviously, one of the sides has to tell the other its IP address to break the loop. This can be achieved by using a dynamic DNS service, such as DynIP or DNS2GO, to associate a domain name with a dynamic IP address. Thus, this scenario will be similar to the static-dynamic one previously described. The only difference is that the static IP side would actually use a static domain name, not IP. The following is a sample configuration for this scenario.

This is the side with dynamic IP and a static domain:

```
ptpaddr      10.1.2.1
ipaddr       10.1.1.1
me           sb.dynip.com:9999
peer         0.0.0.0:9999
maxerr       -1
key          3248fd20adf9c00ccf9ecc2393bbb3e4
```

This is the side with dynamic IP:

```
ptpaddr      10.1.1.1
ipaddr       10.1.2.1
me           0.0.0.0:9999
peer         sb.dynip.com:9999
dynip        1
ping         60
maxerr       3
key          3248fd20adf9c00ccf9ecc2393bbb3e4
```

ip-up *and* ip-down *Scripts*

The `ip-up` and `ip-down` scripts are executed whenever a point-to-point link handled by a CIPE daemon comes up or goes down, respectively. These scripts are usually used to set up routes, perform logging, and so on.

When a point-to-point connection has been established, the appropriate CIPE interface comes up, and the `ip-up` script for that interface is called. The name of the script can be specified in the options file or in a `ciped` command line.

The script is called with a number of parameters, such as the CIPE interface name, the `ciped` daemon's process ID, the IP address of the local side of the interface, the IP address of the remote side, and so on.

A simple `ip-up` script is as follows:

```
#!/bin/sh
# ip-up <interface> <myaddr> <daemon-pid> <local> <remote> <arg>
#
# This script is called whenever the CIPE interface comes up/is opened.
# Arguments:
#  $1 interface     the CIPE interface
#  $2 myaddr        our UDP address
#  $3 daemon-pid    the daemon's process ID
#  $4 local         IP address of our CIPE device
#  $5 remote        IP address of the remote CIPE device
#  $6 arg           argument supplied via options
#
# This script can: set up routes, set up proxy arp records,
# start daemons, perform logging.
umask 022
PATH=/sbin:/bin:/usr/sbin:/usr/bin

# add a route to the network passed in the arg (from the options file)
route add -net $6 gw $5 netmask 255.255.255.0

# just a logging example
now=`date "+%b %d %T"`
echo "$now - interface $1 is up. parameters: $*" >> /var/log/cipe.log
```

The preceding script adds routing to the network that has just become available via the remote-end IP address. The script also performs simple logging of the connection time and parameters. The appropriate `options` file looks as follows (note the `arg` parameter/option):

```
ptpaddr          10.1.2.1
ipaddr           10.1.1.1
me                sb.dynip.com:9999
peer             0.0.0.0:9999
maxerr           -1
arg              10.1.2.0
key              3248fd20adf9c00ccf9ecc2393bbb3e4
```

The special `arg` option, in this case, is used to pass the number of the network that the remote IP has access to; thus, all the packets for that network can be routed via the remote IP.

Now we are going to discuss the "opposite" of the `ip-up` script, called `ip-down`. It is called whenever a point-to-point link is disconnected (goes down). Accordingly, the purpose of the `ip-down` script is to clean up after the `ip-up` script, remove routes, and so on. Here is an example of a basic `ip-down` script:

```
#!/bin/sh
# ip-down <interface> <myaddr> <daemon-pid> <local> #<remote> <arg>

# Sample of the ip-down script.
# This is called with the same arguments as ip-up after the device was
# closed. It can be used for removing proxyarps, or (like here)
# for logging purposes, etc.

umask 022
PATH=/sbin:/bin:/usr/sbin:/usr/bin

# Logging example
now=`date "+%b %d %T"`
echo "$now - interface $1 is down: $*" >> /var/log/cipe.log

# remove the daemon PID file
rm -f /var/run/cipe/$6.pid /var/run/cipe/$1.pid

route del -net $6 netmask 255.255.255.0

# If the system runs gated, tell it what has happened
#gdc interface

exit 0
```

This script simply logs the fact that the CIPE point-to-point link went down and then removes routing for the remote network that was accessible via the link.

Using CIPE with gated

Note that if you run gated (the gateway routing daemon), you should put the static routing entries associated with CIPE tunnels that you have in /etc/gated.conf. An easier way of doing this is to notify gated of the changes in interface configuration by directly invoking a user-interface utility for gated called gdc. The last four lines of the preceding ip-down script show a simple command that will tell gated to recheck the interface configuration. Simply remove the comment mark (#) in front of the gdc interface command to enable it.

Using Multiple Configuration Files

If you want to use a number of CIPE connections, you will need a way to select different options, ip-up, and ip-down files on a per-connection basis. You can do this by assigning a unique name to each connection and creating a set of configuration files for each name.

For example, if you have three CIPE tunnels named bbone, telework, and v42b, you can create a directory for each one and copy options, ip-up, and ip-down files to those directories. Then you should modify each options file to refer to the right ip-up script. For example, the options file for bbone might look as follows:

```
ptpaddr     10.1.3.1
ipaddr      10.1.3.2
me          bbone.rtr-1.uucp-nonex.net:9999
peer        bbone.rtr-2.europe-nonex.com:9999
ipup        /etc/cipe/bbone/ip-up
ipdown      /etc/cipe/bbone/ip-down
key         45890020adf9c00ccf9ecc2393bbb3e4
```

As you can see, the ipup and ipdown options refer to the appropriate ip-up and ip-down scripts specifically tailored to accommodate the bbone interface.

Subsequently, whenever you want to run ciped, you should inform it which options file you want to use. For instance:

```
[root@fox cipe-1.5.1]# ciped-cb -o /etc/cipe/options
```

List of Supported Parameters for /etc/cipe/options

Here we describe the parameters/options supported by CIPE version 1.5.1. The list of parameters consists of two parts: The first part describes the parameters that are required, and the second gives a list of optional parameters. Table 9.1 runs down each parameter option.

Table 9.1   **Required and Optional Parameters for** */etc/cipe/options*

REQUIRED PARAMETERS

Parameter/Option	Format	Description
ipaddr	*IP*	IP address of the local side of a point-to-point CIPE link.
ptpaddr	*IP*	IP address of the peer's side of a point-to-point CIPE link.
me	*IP:port*	Local CIPE IP address.
peer	*IP:port*	CIPE peer's IP address.
key	*Hexadecimal string*	128-bit shared key.

OPTIONAL PARAMETERS

Parameter/Option	Format	Description
device	*String*	Name of the CIPE device. If not provided, the system picks a free one.
debug	*Bool*	Do not switch background; use stderr instead of the syslog.
mask	*IP*	Netmask of the CIPE device. Used with protocol 4.
bcast	*IP*	Broadcast address of the CIPE device. Used with protocol 4.
mtu	*Int*	Device MTU (default: ethernet standard MTU minus all necessary headers).
cttl	*Int*	Carrier TTL value. If not specified or 0, use the payload packet's TTL. Default recommendation is 64.
nokey	*Bool*	Do not encrypt at all; just encapsulate in UDP. Only with this option, 'key' is not needed.
socks	*TCP*	Address and port of the SOCKS5 server.
tokxc	*Int*	Timeout (in seconds) for key exchange. Default: 10.
tokey	*Int*	Dynamic key lifetime. Default: 600 seconds (10 minutes).
ipup	*String*	Script to run instead of /etc/cipe/ip-up.
Ipdown	*String*	Script to run instead of /etc/cipe/ip-down.
arg	*String*	Argument to supply to ip-up, ip-down.

OPTIONAL PARAMETERS (CONTINUES)

Parameter/Option	Format	Description
maxerr	*Int*	Maximum number of errors before ciped exits.
tokxts	*Int*	Key exchange timestamp timeout. Default: 0 (no timestamps). Set this to 30 to prevent key exchange replay attacks, but only if the peer runs CIPE 1.2 or later and both system clocks are reasonably synchronized.
ping	*Int*	Frequency (in seconds) for keep-alive pings. Default is to not send any pings. The "ping" used here is internal to CIPE, not ICMP ping.
toping	*Int*	Timeout for pings. If no answer is received on a keep-alive ping in this time, it counts as an error. Default is to not check for answers.
dynip	*Bool*	Assume the carrier is on a dynamic IP address.
hwaddr	*String*	Set the dummy MAC address used in Ethernet mode (protocol 4).
ifconfig	*Bool*	Require an external ifconfig call to configure the interface.
checksum	*Bool*	Use checksummed UDP carrier packets. Only necessary if the network does not like unchecksummed packets.

pkcipe-Based Configuration

This section will explain how to set up configuration files used by pkcipe. You will also learn how to generate public keys and start pkcipe up both automatically and manually.

Setting up Host Keys and Identities

As you remember, pkcipe makes it possible for a network administrator to avoid manually setting up shared keys on both sides of a CIPE link via /etc/cipe/options.

The pkcipe utility currently uses Diffie-Hellman key exchange and public-key cryptography to verify the other side's identity and then negotiate a secret key. After the secret key has been negotiated, CIPE creates a temporary configuration file for ciped in /var/run/cipe and executes ciped with that configuration file.

To configure `pkcipe`, several files need to be present. Do not get bored just yet. It is very simple, and if you have a clear picture in your head, you can set everything up in 15 minutes.

/etc/cipe/identity{.priv}

First of all, each host that is going to use `pkcipe` *must* have an identity.

The identity consists of two files: `identity` and `identity.priv`. These files represent public/private keys, respectively. The files are generated by the `rsa-keygen` script (CIPE's wrapper around the `openssl` command-line utility) that is included in the `pkcipe` part of the CIPE package.

Restricted Access to /etc/cipe/identity.priv

Note that `/etc/cipe/identity.priv` (a host's private key) must only be readable by root. For example, you verify the following:

```
[root@fox cipe]# chmod 400 /etc/cipe/identity.priv
[root@fox cipe]# ls -l /etc/cipe/identity.priv
-r--------   1 root     root          887 May  6 23:27 /etc/cipe/identity.priv
```

If you did `make install` as we described earlier, the identity files should already be in `/etc/cipe` for you. If they are not there for some reason, you can just type the following command to generate a new identity:

```
[root@fox pkcipe]# rsa-keygen /etc/cipe/identity 1024
warning, not much extra random data, consider using the -rand option
Generating RSA private key, 1024 bit long modulus
.++++++
..++++++
e is 65537 (0x10001)
read RSA key
writing RSA key
Private key in /etc/cipe/identity.priv, Public key in /etc/cipe/identity
```

/etc/cipe/pk/*

Remember that *you must have a public key for each host to which you want to establish a tunnel.* These public keys are stored in `/etc/cipe/pk` and are nothing more than `/etc/cipe/identity` files from all the hosts you interact with.

For example, if you want to establish a connection to a host named `juno.testbed.com`, you need to copy that host's `/etc/cipe/identity` to your `/etc/cipe/pk` directory and simply call that file `/etc/cipe/pk/juno`. The other side must copy your `identity.pub` into its `/etc/cipe/pk` and call it whatever your hostname is.

Naming Public Key Files

Does it matter how your public key/identity file is named at peer hosts? Actually, it does. This is because your pkcipe will transmit its identity to the remote side, and that name will be used to search for a public key/identity file in /etc/cipe/pk. pkcipe currently uses the gethostname() call to obtain the name of your host. Alternatively, you can pass the name to pkcipe as the last parameter on the command line invoking pkcipe. Just use the following:

```
[root@fox pk]# hostname -s
fox
```

Thus, you might end up having a number of public keys of different hosts in your /etc/cipe/pk director. For instance:

```
[root@fox pk]# ls -l /etc/cipe/pk
total 28
-rw-r--r--   1 root     root          272 May  6 23:17 aleste
-rw-r--r--   1 root     root          272 May  6 23:13 bravo
-rw-r--r--   1 root     root          272 May  6 23:15 centipede
-rw-r--r--   1 root     root          272 May  6 23:13 dexter
-rw-r--r--   1 root     root          272 May  6 23:16 goonies
-rw-r--r--   1 root     root          272 May  6 23:16 metal-gear
```

Keeping Options in Public-Key Files

With pkcipe you only add *global* options that will affect all connections to the /etc/cipe/options file. If you want to add *connection-specific* options, you can add them directly to the public keys in /etc/cipe/pk on a per-peer basis. To illustrate, the following is a sample public-key file with added options for one of the remote hosts we use (/etc/cipe/pk/dexter):

```
-----BEGIN PUBLIC KEY-----
MIGfMA0GCSqGSIb3DQEBAQUAA4GNADCBiQKBgQC5Qt2TvBJvdZe2ek67kK0+t6dR
agz5CAcvPgsD206UQEKQ/pgbc0Ub4yOGnx0lcJ7duRfLh5CFTAtQeCaiHJDQiDVm
6shBtoltXdN5wrVbkLukor3IUjTVzvNdwKC16d7WMgiQT+kAZc3VcX/lxCCTtDZZ
UphAOQQyRpQd4ZrBTwIDAQAB
-----END PUBLIC KEY-----

ptpaddr        10.1.1.5
ipaddr         10.1.1.6

me             zyxel.eerie.nonex.com:9999
peer           peer.eerie.nonex.com:3001

debug          1
maxerr         3

ipup           /etc/cipe/dexter/ip-up
ipdown         /etc/cipe/dexter/ip-down
```

As you can see, the preceding file consists of a public key on the remote side and the options pertaining to the link with the remote side. These options override any global options specified in /etc/cipe/options. Thus, in each public-key file, you can define peer-specific configuration.

> **Adding a Line to ip-up Script to Accommodate pkcipe**
>
> Make sure the ip-up script you refer to in the options file previously described contains the following line (from the default ip-* scripts located in the pkcipe/ directory of the CIPE distribution):
>
> ```
> # Create/update PID file.
> echo "$3 $1" >/var/run/cipe/${6:-$1}.pid
> ```

pkcipe and Incoming Connections

Having set up all the necessary keys as previously explained, you need to decide how you are going to run pkcipe. When making the decision, you need to remember that pkcipe uses TCP to exchange keys, and one of the sides must act as a server and the other as a client, respectively.

Option 1: Spawning pkcipe *from* inetd *or* xinetd

There are several possible setups. Possibly, the most elegant one is to use inetd (or xinetd) to run pkcipe as a service that is spawned when incoming connections arrive. In this case, you do not have to worry about executing a number of ciped processes, each with a different options file and so on. Instead, pkcipe takes care of authentication and shared key negotiation; it then spawns ciped for each connection if everything is okay.

In this case, what you need to do is designate a single port for pkcipe on your system (you do it only once) and add it to inetd/xinetd configuration. Thus, whenever a client pkcipe process connects to the server pkcipe via TCP, it transmits its identity (dexter, for example), which is then verified by pkcipe by using the client's public key in the /etc/cipe/pk directory. Subsequently, pkcipe spawns ciped.

Here is a detailed description of how you can add pkcipe as a service to be executed by inetd. First, look in /etc/services and add the following line to the file (9950 is the port number that will be associated with pkcipe service):

```
pkcipe 9950/tcp
```

Then add a line at the end of the /etc/inetd.conf file, as follows:

```
pkcipe stream tcp nowait root /usr/local/sbin/pkcipe pkcipe
```

If you prefer to use a wrapper by Wietse Venema, here is another option:

```
pkcipe stream tcp nowait root /usr/sbin/tcpd /usr/local/sbin/pkcipe
```

Briefly, the preceding line tells inetd to listen on the TCP port for pkcipe specified in /etc/services; when an incoming connection is established, inetd will execute

/usr/sbin/tcpd as root, passing it /usr/local/sbin/pkcipe as a parameter. If you want to find out more about inetd, we recommend that you look at inetd(8) and inetd.conf(8) man pages.

Identity Names

Note that, by default, pkcipe uses the hostname returned by the gethostname() function as the name of your identity. However, note that you can pass any host identity name to pkcipe, and it will be used by the remote side to search for your public key in the /etc/cipe/pk directory, as mentioned in the previous section. It can be done by appending an identity name (a one-word hostname without adding a domain name, for example) as a parameter to /usr/local/sbin/pkcipe in any of the two additional lines for inetd.conf previously described. For example,

```
pkcipe stream tcp nowait root /usr/sbin/tcpd /usr/local/sbin/pkcipe hostId
```

Some systems use xinetd in place of the good ol' inetd. The setup is still straightforward, though. You just need to add a file called pkcipe to the /etc/xinetd.d directory. Put the following information in the file:

```
service pkcipe
{
        socket_type     = stream
        protocol        = tcp
        wait            = no
        user            = root
        port            = 9950
        type            = UNLISTED
        server          = /usr/local/sbin/pkcipe
        log_on_failure  += USERID
}
```

In this case, we were lazy and did not add a service for pkcipe to /etc/services, so we had to use the type UNLISTED, port 9950, and protocol tcp options to compensate. If you add a service to /etc/services, you can skip these three additional options.

Also, you might want to add command-line options to pkcipe. Do not add them at the end of the server option. Use server_args on a separate line instead and make sure you do not start it with the name/path to pkcipe, as you would do in /etc/inetd.conf (that is, no argv[0] needed here).

Finally, do not forget to send a signal to inetd or xinetd to reread its configuration. With inetd, it is enough to do the following:

```
[root@fox /root]# ps -ax|egrep inetd
600 ?         S      0:00 inetd
32009 pts/0   S      0:00 egrep inetd
[root@fox /root]# kill -1 600
```

In contrast, xinetd requires that a different signal be sent to make it a little bit more challenging and keep system administrators busy reading manual pages. Here is how to "hup" xinetd:

```
[root@fox xinetd.d]# ps -ax¦egrep xinetd
621 ?        S      0:00 xinetd -reuse -pidfile /var/run/xinetd.pid
32009 pts/0   S      0:00 egrep xinetd
[root@fox xinetd.d]# kill -SIGUSR1 621
```

Using Signals Under UNIX

Although we assume that most of our readers are familiar with the idea of using signals under UNIX, here is a brief explanation for those of you who would like to understand what is happening. When xinetd is first executed (usually during system startup), it sets up handlers for basic signals such as SIGHUP, SIGUSR1, SIGUSR2, and so on. Subsequently, when you pass a -SIGHUP argument to kill a utility, as in the preceding example, the utility calls a kernel function that informs inetd's signal handler that a signal was sent. It is up to the handler to decide what it will do in response. Typically, sending a SIGHUP signal causes daemons to reread their configuration.

Option 2: Manually Starting pkcipe *on a Given Port*

Although the pkcipe authors do not presently mention this feature in the documentation, an additional command-line argument to pkcipe makes it possible to manually specify the TCP port number on which it will be listening. We accidentally found this option when going through pkcipe source code, so there is no guarantee that it will work in the next releases. It seems quite useful, though, so we believe it will still be present in the newer releases.

If you manually start pkcipe (as root) using the following command:

```
[root@fox xinetd.d]# pkcipe -s 9950
```

This will cause pkcipe to bind to the specified TCP port and wait for incoming connections. Therefore, it is not necessary to add anything to either inetd or xinetd. The disadvantage of this method is that the command needs to be executed from somewhere, either during system startup or by some initialization script. However, it is invaluable for manually testing the system.

Using CIPE

You can use CIPE in different ways. The following sections will cover the details of CIPE usage as well as several basic scenarios you might want to utilize.

Scenarios

In this section, we will describe several popular configurations and provide practical examples of using CIPE with each one. We will also briefly comment on the possible

scenarios in which you might find CIPE useful. A scenario describing the use of
`pkcipe` to build a CIPE VPN will be provided at the end of this section.

Before we start with the scenarios, here is a recommendation. If you are using
RFC1918 private networks—10.0.0.0/8, 172.16.0.0/12, and 192.168.0.0/16—it is
considered good practice to add the following rules to disable routing for all the private networks first and then add routes one by one, as necessary:

```
route add -net 10.0.0.0/8 gw 127.0.0.1 reject
route add -net 172.16.0.0/12 gw 127.0.0.1 reject
route add -net 192.168.0.0/16 gw 127.0.0.1 reject
```

Rule of Least Privilege (ROLP)

The practice of enabling routing for only those private networks that are in use is based on the so-called
Rule of Least Privilege. The rule states that to achieve better security, an entity should only have the
privileges it needs to perform the tasks assigned to it.

Later, when you want to add a route for a private network (for example, 10.1.1.0/24),
you can use the following:

```
route add -net 10.1.1.0/24 gw 172.16.1.1
```

This command will override the three rules we specified earlier and will be used by
the system to route packets for a 10.1.1.0/24 network. The rest of the private network
space will not be routable. Thus, you improve the security of your system because only
the private networks that you know of pass through. This is because you need to add
an explicit rule for each private network that you want your machine to route. The
primary reason for adding the reject rules with higher metric is that, when a CIPE
link goes down, the default route will be used to send packets to the addresses that
were used for the CIPE link. Because the default route is usually unencrypted, the
traffic could potentially be revealed to a third person.

Generally, many people believe it is more secure to follow the "deny everything,
enable specific" rule (similar to ROLP) than to "allow everything, deny specific," and
routing is not an exception.

Static Peers

For this set of scenarios, all peers are assumed to have static IP addresses that do not
change from session to session and that can be referred to in CIPE and gated configuration files as constants. Additionally, it is assumed that statically configured `ciped` is
used.

Should you decide to use `pkcipe`, you need to simply append the contents of the
`/etc/cipe/options.<name>` file to the appropriate public key of <name> in `/etc/cipe/`
`pk`, set up `pkcipe` as described in the previous section, and establish a connection
between two peers using `pkcipe`.

Network–Network CIPE Tunneling

In this scenario, two networks are connected using a CIPE tunnel between their respective gateways, and a static route is set up between these gateways whenever a connection is established. In our example, 192.168.1.0/24 and 192.168.2.0/24 are the networks that need to be connected using a CIPE point-to-point tunnel. 172.16.1.1/24 and 172.17.3.5/16 are the IP addresses of the interfaces on the two gateways, A and B. We also assume that the link between the two networks is called "soho." Our example is depicted in Figure 9.1.

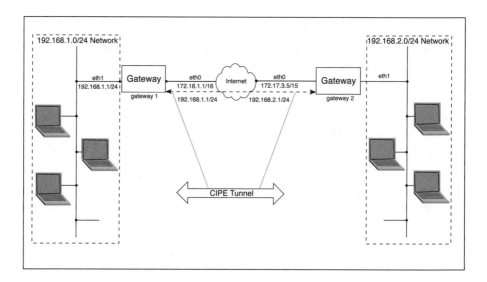

Figure 9.1 Network-network CIPE tunneling example.

As you can see from Figure 9.1, workstations that belong to both networks do not need to know anything about the fact that tunneling occurs.

Whenever a workstation from the 192.168.1.0/24 network wants to send an IP packet destined to, say, 192.168.2.10/24, the workstation applies the appropriate netmask, determines that 192.168.2.10/24 is not on the local network, and sends the packet to the default gateway. The default gateway for machines on 192.168.1.0/24 is, as you might have already guessed, 192.168.1.1. It knows about the tunnel and forwards the packet via the secure tunnel to the other side, which is directly connected to 192.168.2.0/24.

> **Netmask: /24 = 255.255.255.0**
> For 192.168.2.10/24, 24 bits are used to specify a network, so the netmask would be 255.255.255.0.

Based on the configuration previously described, the /etc/cipe/options.soho file on
gateway A might look like this (in other words, setting up Gateway A as
eth0=172.16.1.1/24, eth1=192.168.1.1/24):

```
Ipaddr          192.168.1.1
ptpaddr         192.168.2.1
peer            172.17.3.5:9500
me              172.16.1.1:9500
key             258feab39293177fc7f9e1273f19015f
ipup            /etc/cipe/soho/ip-up
ipdown          /etc/cipe/soho/ip-down
debug           true
maxerr          -1
```

The next two listings show the contents of the /etc/cipe/soho/ip-up and /etc/cipe/
soho/ip-down scripts on the gateway A.

The /etc/cipe/soho/ip-up looks like this:

```
#!/bin/sh
# ip-up <interface> <myaddr> <daemon-pid> <local> <remote> <arg>

umask 022
PATH=/sbin:/bin:/usr/sbin:/usr/bin

# route packets for 192.168.2.0/24 to our peer
route add -net 192.168.2.0/24 gw $5

# or let gated know
# gdc interface

# no logging. feel free to add, if necessary.
exit 0
```

The /etc/cipe/soho/ip-down file looks like this:

```
#!/bin/sh
# ip-down <interface> <myaddr> <daemon-pid> <local> <remote> <arg>
# This script is called with the same arguments as ip-up
# after the interface goes down.

umask 022
PATH=/sbin:/bin:/usr/sbin:/usr/bin

# remove the daemon PID file
rm -f /var/run/cipe/$6.pid /var/run/cipe/$1.pid

# remove routing for 192.168.2.0
route del -net 192.168.2.0/24

# or let gated know
#gdc interface

exit 0
```

For gateway B, all three configuration files previously mentioned will look similar. Just make sure you do not forget to exchange `ipaddr` with `ptpaddr` and `me` with `peer` in the `/etc/cipe/options.soho` file. Additionally, you will have to use 192.168.1.0/24 instead of 192.168.2.0/24 in both `/etc/cipe/soho/ip-up` and `/etc/cipe/soho/ip-down`.

You can start `ciped` on both machines using the following:

```
[root@fox cipe]# ciped-cb -o /etc/cipe/options
```

Host-Network CIPE Tunneling Using Proxy ARP

Sometimes you might want to fool computers on a local network into thinking that your workstation is directly connected. On the other hand, you might simply need to remotely access the local network resources yourself while away on vacation or working from home.

In both cases, you can accomplish your goals by using CIPE tunneling along with the Proxy Address Resolution Protocol (ARP). Whether it is your machine or another machine on the local network, you can make it appear as if all the machines are directly interconnected.

How can this possibly work? The idea is that a gateway capable of tunneling packets to a remote workstation will "pretend" to be that workstation on the local network.

More specifically, the gateway will answer to ARP queries on behalf of the remote workstation, which will cause other workstations on the local network to update their ARP caches and direct their OSI Layer 2 frames to the gateway.

Generally, the ARP protocol is used to map between Layer 2 MAC addresses and Layer 3 IP addresses for *directly* connected networks. On Linux, it is implemented by the kernel ARP module.

Consider the following configuration, for instance:

A private network 192.168.1.0/24 has several workstations and a gateway A.

Gateway A's IP address on the private network is 192.168.1.1. The CIPE's interface on A has the same IP. Gateway A also has an external interface with a public routable IP address IP1.

Mobile workstation B's CIPE interface IP address is 192.168.1.3. Mobile workstation B also has a public routable IP address for its external interface, namely IP2.

The configuration is shown in Figure 9.2. When mobile workstation B is not physically present and wants to make itself appear to all the workstations on network B as if it were directly connected, B establishes a secure CIPE tunnel to gateway A. The gateway, in turn, serves as a proxy for all the packets directed to and from workstation B.

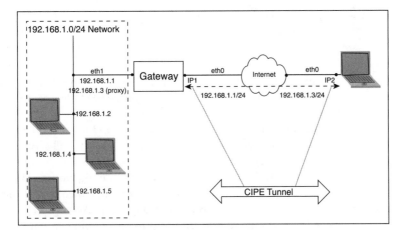

Figure 9.2 Host–network CIPE tunneling using Proxy ARP.

Let us call the configuration for this scenario "arp." Then the /etc/cipe/options.arp file for the mobile workstation B will contain the following:

```
peer            IP1:9500
me              IP2:9500
ipaddr          192.168.1.3
ptpaddr         192.168.1.1
key             611bb02f9293177fc7f9e1273f02dd19
ipup  /etc/cipe/arp/ip-up
ipdown /etc/cipe/arp/ip-down
debug           true
maxerr          -1
```

The /etc/cipe/options.arp on the gateway side will look similar. Again, make sure you switch ip/ptpaddr, peer/me, as before.

The important difference pertaining to the Proxy ARP configuration scenario is an additional line in /etc/cipe/arp/ip-up on the gateway side. Here is what the file should have:

```
#!/bin/sh
# ip-up <interface> <myaddr> <daemon-pid> <local> <remote> <arg>

umask 022
PATH=/sbin:/bin:/usr/sbin:/usr/bin

# just a logging example
now=`date "+%b %d %T"`
echo "$now UP   $*" >> /var/log/cipe.log

# Create/update PID file. Note: PKCIPE needs this.
echo "$3 $1" >/var/run/cipe/${6:-$1}.pid
```

```
# Proxy-ARP the peer's address on eth0
arp -i eth1 -Ds $5 eth1 pub

exit 0
```

Note the line that begins with `arp`. It tells the kernel to modify its ARP cache and add a proxy entry for workstation B. The second argument, - `eth1`, denotes the name of the device with which the proxy entry is associated.

The name of the device used in the preceding `arp` command line should correspond to the device that is connected to the local network and that will serve as a proxy for workstation B's address.

Conversely, because gateway A cannot reach any networks using workstation B's IP address, there is no need for A to add routing for B. Even though there will be no routing added, A will still be able to "see" B and exchange IP packets with it because B is directly connected to A and its address represents the other end of a point-to-point CIPE link.

As far as B is concerned, it needs to know how to get to 192.168.1.0/24. This means B can make an assumption that because the other end of the CIPE interface is an IP address that belongs to 192.168.1.0/24, the network can be reached via the CIPE interface. On older versions of Linux this does not always seem to work right, so you will need to add a routing entry manually, as in the following command:

```
[root@fox cipe]# route add -net 192.168.1.0/24 dev cipcb0
```

Simply add the preceding command to the `ip-up` script and routing will be updated automatically every time your CIPE link goes up.

Host-Host CIPE Tunneling

This scenario is probably the simplest one of the three scenarios we describe. You do not have to worry about routing or Proxy ARP entries. The only thing you need to set up is a CIPE tunnel. As soon as both peers that form the tunnel are able to interact and the appropriate CIPE interface comes up, you should be able to exchange data between peers using the tunnel.

In our example of a host-host CIPE tunnel, we will use two hosts, A and B. Both of them will have static IP addresses, namely 172.16.1.5/12 and 172.16.1.6/12. We assume that these addresses can be used to communicate between the hosts and tunnel CIPE packets.

Routable vs. Nonroutable Addresses in our Example

If you want to use this scenario and communicate via the Internet, you will need a pair of public routable IP addresses instead (172.16.0.0/12 are nonroutable private IP addresses that were chosen merely to illustrate the scenario).

In addition, hosts A and B will have two addresses that are used as the addresses of the two sides of the CIPE host-host tunnel: 192.168.1.1/24 and 192.168.1.2/24. The sample configuration we use is depicted in Figure 9.3.

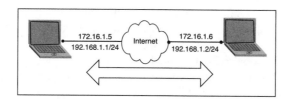

Figure 9.3   Host-host CIPE tunneling example.

In our example, the `ciped` configuration file for host A contains the following information:

```
peer            172.16.1.6:9990
me              172.16.1.5:9990
ipaddr          192.168.1.1
ptpaddr         192.168.1.2
key             974ba02f9293177fc7f1e1273f02dd21
debug           true
maxerr          -1
```

The configuration for host B should be an inverse of the host A's configuration and might look like this:

```
peer            172.16.1.5:9990
me              172.16.1.6:9990
ipaddr          192.168.1.2
ptpaddr         192.168.1.1
key             974ba02f9293177fc7f1e1273f02dd21
debug           true
maxerr          -1
```

As long as you have the previously specified configuration on both A and B, you can run `ciped` and try to ping the addresses of the CIPE tunneling interface (192.168.1.{1,2}). Use `ifconfig` to find out the remote address of the CIPE point-to-point tunnel and use `ping` to test the tunnel. Make sure you do not use any routes that might refer to the addresses of the CIPE tunnel chosen for the `ipaddr` and `ptpaddr` parameters.

So what would be a "killer app" for the host-host scenario? There can be a number of such "killer apps" because the data you transmit using the CIPE tunnel is encrypted; thus you can secure many kinds of applications that otherwise are insecure. Examples include sending and receiving mail (SMTP and POP3/IMAP), reading news (NNTP), downloading files (FTP), remote access (Telnet, r* services), and so forth. You can also prevent sniffing that is widely used by attackers.

What makes CIPE different from other tunneling and VPN packages is that it uses UDP as an underlying transport, which means you no longer have problems associated with stacking TCP over PPP over TCP. No, this is not a typo. A typical example of such a situation would be trying to tunnel PPP over SSH connections that use TCP. If you then run TCP on top of the tunneled PPP connection, you will find out that this setup has a serious problem. The problem sometimes manifests itself in an "internal meltdown" effect caused by the higher TCP layer queuing up retransmissions faster than the lower TCP layer can transmit. You can read more about why TCP over TCP is discouraged at `http://sites.inka.de/sites/bigred/devel/tcp-tcp.html`.

Securing Applications That Use UDP

You can also use the host-host scenario to secure applications that work over UDP. Such applications usually cannot be tunneled by the protocols that work over TCP. For instance, one of the protocols that could definitely be made more secure using host-host CIPE scenario is the Simple Network Management Protocol (SNMP). It is notorious for its very basic security protection in the form of community strings transmitted in cleartext.

This issue is especially important for versions 1 and 2 of the SNMP protocol that are widely used. Because the information sent in cleartext can easily be sniffed and revealed, many SNMP devices and applications are vulnerable to attacks. CIPE can help you solve this problem by tunneling SNMP over an encrypted CIPE link.

Dynamic Peers

Since version 0.5, CIPE has been capable of picking up peers' addresses based on the first packet received. This makes it possible to establish CIPE tunnels even if one or both of the peers have dynamic IP addresses.

We have already briefly commented on one of the possible configurations in the earlier section "Static vs. Dynamic Peer IP Addresses." This section will be different in that we will consider dynamic IP versions of the scenarios described for static IPs earlier.

Dynamic DNS Service

For some of the configurations we are going to describe, you will need to use a dynamic DNS service that will enable you to have a static domain name associated with your dynamic IP. There are both free and commercial dynamic DNS providers. If you need to get a domain name associated with a dynamic IP, the following links might be helpful: `http://dnsq.org/`, `http://ddns.nu/`, `http://dyndsl.com`.

Before we proceed, it is important to note that there is no way we know of to get CIPE tunnels to work when there is absolutely nothing static about peers and the information is not propagated between them in some way.

For example, if both peers are behind a firewall doing network address translation (NAT) or masquerading, they do not know how to contact each other unless there is something static they can use, such as a specific port allocated on the firewall.

Network-Network CIPE Tunneling Using Dynamic IPs

It often happens that one of the peers in the network-network setup has a dynamic IP address. In this case, the configuration files for the network-network CIPE tunnel will look different than those used for the tunnel with static IPs.

If only one of the peers has a dynamic IP address (dynamic peer), it is not necessary to use dynamic DNS. You just need to use the same configuration files as with the static network-network connection, with a few additional options as follows:

1. The dynamic peer initiates a connection, and its `options` file for the tunnel, in addition to other options, contains the following:

   ```
   ping 60
   dynip 1
   maxerr 3
   me    0.0.0.0:9999
   ```

2. The static peer adds the following lines to its `options` file for the tunnel:

   ```
   maxerr -1
   peer  0.0.0.0:9999
   ```

The additional options for the dynamic peer will tell it to initiate a connection as soon as possible. The dynamic peer will also ping the static peer every 60 seconds, making it possible to reflect any changes in the dynamic peer's IP address.

If the static peer cannot be reached or there is an error, the dynamic peer will give up after three attempts (effectively 3 minutes because of the 60-second ping options).

As for the static peer, it will assume that the other end has a dynamic IP address and will wait for it to initiate a CIPE connection.

If both sides use dynamic IP addresses, there is no easy way for one side to find out the address of the other side unless a static component is added to the system. A common way of solving this problem is to use a static domain name that is associated with one of the peers' dynamic IP addresses. This domain name serves as the static component necessary for one of the peers to contact the other.

When using static domain names with dynamic IPs, it is crucial to ensure that whenever an IP address changes, the domain is updated to reflect the changes before the other side uses the domain to reestablish a CIPE tunnel. You should choose update and ping intervals carefully to ensure that they are balanced.

The problem is making update intervals large enough to minimize overhead associated with changing domain information and yet small enough to decrease the risks of a remote CIPE getting the wrong address, failing, and eventually exiting.

Using maxerr −1 to Ignore Errors

Setting the maxerr option to -1 on the initiating side should remedy the situation, but it is not a good idea if there is a high chance of other kinds of errors that should not be ignored.

Two factors work in your favor, though. First, dynamic IP addresses are usually not updated very frequently unless you use a dial-up connection that is not stable. Second, you can probably tolerate some downtime. Choose carefully based on what is more important to you. If overhead associated with updating a static domain is significant, use larger update intervals. If downtime is a problem, ping more frequently and inform ciped each time a new address is obtained.

Host-Network CIPE Tunneling Using Dynamic IPs

To use network-host tunneling with Proxy ARP and dynamic IPs, simply use the configuration from the scenario described for static IPs and add extra parameters as explained in the previous section.

The main difference between this scenario and the network-network scenario is that typically less emphasis is placed on link downtime. Indeed, it's often expected that the mobile user will just manually reinitiate a connection.

In addition, there is only one workstation for which packets are tunneled, and the workstation's IP address is assumed to be changing frequently anyway. In the network-network scenario, however, the connectivity between two *networks* with *multiple* workstations is at stake, and downtime can be more important.

Ping Intervals and Downtime

If downtime *is* important to you, you can set ping intervals to be smaller on the workstation side. If both peers are dynamic, make sure ping values and domain updates are balanced, as discussed in the previous section.

Host-Host CIPE Tunneling Using Dynamic IPs

This scenario will be a limited version of the network-network scenario described earlier. The difference is that host-host does not require adding routing. Refer to the "Network-Network CIPE Tunneling" section for more information.

CIPE with NAT/Masquerading Firewalls and SOCKS5 Proxies

In this section, we will first describe using CIPE with firewalls that do network address translation (NAT), sometimes also referred to as masquerading firewalls. Then we will explain how to use CIPE with SOCKS5 proxies.

SOCKS5 and NAT

The SOCKS version 5 Protocol, also referred to as authenticated firewall traversal (AFT), is an open Internet standard specified in RFC1928 that defines proxy functions at OSI Layer 4 (Transport). Among other things, version 5 supports strong authentication, message security, integrity protection, as well as UDP forwarding.

One of the main differences between SOCKS5 and NAT is that SOCKS5 enables return data paths and incoming connections to be requested by applications. NAT, in contrast, provides only unidirectional translation because it was designed to work at OSI Layer 3 (IP). NAT does not allow applications to specify which incoming connections need to be forwarded; to circumvent the problem, firewall rules are usually used.

NAT and Masquerading

So what if one or both CIPE peers have private IP addresses and are behind a firewall that uses IP masquerading/NAT?

Before moving on, stop for a second and think. Have you considered connecting the firewalls instead of connecting the peers behind the firewalls? If yes, go to the static scenarios described earlier. This will save you some effort so you will have time to enjoy a cup of freshly brewed coffee or tea.

If that is not an option and you absolutely have to have peers behind the firewall, there are two possibilities. If only one of the peers is behind a firewall, it should be sufficient to use the same techniques as with the dynamic IP addresses, namely:

1. Use a dummy peer IP address and disable errors on the static peer side, as follows:

   ```
   peer      0.0.0.0:0
   maxerr   1
   ```

2. Add the following options to the configuration of the peer behind a firewall (the peer can use its private IP address in the me parameter of the configuration; it will be changed by the firewall anyway):

   ```
   ping 60
   maxerr 3
   me   192.168.1.1:9999
   ```

Note that the static peer should not be specific about the remote port number. This is because the NAT module on the other peer's firewall replaces the port number with a randomly chosen port, and it is not known in advance.

You might have noticed that the source of all the packets from the peer behind a firewall will be the IP address of the firewall. So, why not use it with the peer parameter in the static peer configuration? The reason is that we need to know the firewall's address at any given time. If we have no control over the firewall, statically specifying the IP address can be risky because any changes in the IP address of the firewall would deprecate our configuration.

SOCKS5 Proxies

As we mentioned earlier, SOCKS5 supports UDP proxying, which is used by CIPE to exchange encrypted data between peers. SOCKS5 proxies can select both IP addresses and port numbers at their discretion. Their choices are returned to the peer that requested a connection, but the peer does not have any means to affect the selection of the address and port numbers. Therefore, the CIPE peer that will be accepting connections *must support dynamic IP addresses.*

SOCKS4 is Not Supported

CIPE currently only works with SOCKS version 5 because version 5 is capable of UDP proxying. Earlier versions of SOCKS, such as SOCKS4, cannot be used with CIPE because they do not support UDP.

Here is a sample scenario. There are two peers. One of them has a static public IP and will be accepting connections. The other peer has a static private IP and is working through a SOCKS5 server.

The peer with a static public IP must add the following lines to its configuration files to support dynamic IP addresses:

```
peer        0.0.0.0:0
maxerr -1
```

The peer that works through a SOCKS5 proxy must have the following option configured (we assume that 192.168.1.5 is the address of the interface SOCKS5 machine):

```
socks       192.168.1.5:1080
```

This will tell the `ciped` of the peer that works through the SOCKS5 proxy to establish a control connection and use SOCKS5 for all communications.

You need to also make a decision as to whether the peer that works through the SOCKS5 proxy is going to use a password to authenticate itself. CIPE currently implements two authentication methods of those defined by SOCKS5, namely password and none.

If you want to use a password for the peer to authenticate to SOCKS5 proxy, you should set the `SOCKS5_USER` and `SOCKS5_PASSWD` environment variables to the username and password, respectively. For example:

```
[root@fox /usr/local/s5]# export SOCKS5_USER="cipes5"
[root@fox /usr/local/s5]# export SOCKS5_PASSWD="s5cpe4_s"
```

By now, you should have all the necessary configurations in place so that you can try to start `ciped` on both peers and get everything working. Note that if the SOCKS5 server goes down, it closes the control connection. You will need to restart `ciped` in this case to recover from the failure.

Using *pkcipe*

Before you start using `pkcipe`, you should understand that it is nothing more that just a front end to `ciped` that was designed to facilitate key distribution.

Where would `pkcipe` fit well? For instance, you might want to use it when there are a large number of peers and it is difficult to securely distribute keys to all of the peers. Another example is when you do not want to trust a single peer to generate a shared key. Because `pkcipe` uses the identities of both peers and then allows them to participate in the selection of a key, the decision is made collaboratively, and no single peer can deliberately generate a weak key.

How do you use `pkcipe`? First, you should configure each `pkcipe` peer. You need to generate an identity (private/public key) for every peer, distribute public keys between peers that are going to be connected, and add options associated with each peer at the end of its public key. We described the process of `pkcipe` configuration in detail earlier, so for this section, we will assume that you are familiar with the basics of `pkcipe` configuration.

Example of Using pkcipe *to Configure Three Peers*

For our sample scenario, we will use three peers: A, B, and C. We will go through `pkcipe` options on each peer and show how to use `pkcipe` to configure the peers so that A is connected to B and B is connected to C. For each pair of peers, you will need to select one of the scenarios we showed earlier: network-network, host-network, host-host, static vs. dynamic IPs, and so on.

For example, if A and B both use static IP addresses and you want to use network-network CIPE configuration, you should determine which options are needed for the scenario. When determining the options, take into account that `pkcipe` uses TCP connections. This means you should address the problem of incoming connections for firewalled peers. You will use your choices later in the `pkcipe` configuration.

The first step is to run `rsa-keygen` scripts on A, B, and C to generate identities for all the peers using the following:

```
[root@{A,B,C} /etc/cipe]# rsa-keygen /etc/cipe/identity 1024
```

To distribute public keys, copy A's `/etc/cipe/identity` (it contains A's public key) to B as `/etc/cipe/pk/A`. Copy B's `/etc/cipe/identity` to A as `/etc/cipe/pk/B`. Do the same for B and C. As a result, all the peers will have each other's public keys.

pkcipe Requires Root Privileges

The pkcipe command *must* be run as root.

Then, for each pair of peers (such as A and B, B and C), decide which side is going to be the initiator of a TCP connection and which side is going to accept connections. For the accepting side, you can run `pkcipe` as a server:

```
[root@A xinetd.d]# pkcipe -s 9950
```

Or you can add it to `inetd/xinetd` configuration as explained earlier in the `pkcipe` configuration section.

After you have determined how the accepting side is going to work, you should use the options for the scenario you have chosen for each pair of peers and add the options to the exchanged public files on each side. For instance, if you selected a network-network scenario for A and B and they both use static addresses, the public key file for B on A, namely `/etc/cipe/pk/B`, might contain the following:

```
·····BEGIN PUBLIC KEY·····
MIGfMA0GCSqGSIb3DQEBAQUAA4GNADCBiQKBgQDQEKca1ga24Yx5Vp5SiMS0DKc2
8Pr0SIgOvFoOty/hhu3BDCjTktnFm8R/ICKbYSAMhBZJyidHO16jFZEDXP33ajvk
xjdDAiNZqYrA792a5ypedNj6VEIeJChQhLrRVgx3jKfnKRkeBQ3IvO+VMleCHWY6
V3uOUrdc1fwNIMwlaQIDAQAB
·····END PUBLIC KEY·····

ipaddr 192.168.1.1
ptpaddr    192.168.2.1
peer  172.17.3.5:9500
me    172.16.1.1:9500
ipup  /etc/cipe/B/ip-up
ipdown /etc/cipe/B/ip-down
debug true
maxerr -1
```

In this configuration file, we assume that A and B's IP address is 172.17.3.5.

The public key file for A, namely `/etc/cipe/pk/A`, on B's side should consist of the following parameters:s IP address is 172.16.1.1

```
·····BEGIN PUBLIC KEY·····
MIGfMA0GCSqGSIb3DQEBAQUAA4GNADCBiQKBgQChw/uQDPm09zmIP7eaNuLVYvMh
VQRY+qmA2380Roh2iCmU+3sN/O8mHos3W8KHmKQNi7PNFHS2n0K5W9NMdZZU2UE8
ce6+MpnbjAGWi9F4CaZFhe8S1aFuBBY0Ummp2MnR6t4TFJVOUULOpwPLmheRKNcB
4A0CFtsWtVa4EJKapwIDAQAB
·····END PUBLIC KEY·····

ipaddr 192.168.2.1
ptpaddr    192.168.1.1
peer  172.16.1.1:9500
me    172.17.3.5:9500
ipup  /etc/cipe/A/ip-up
ipdown /etc/cipe/A/ip-down
debug true
maxerr -1
```

If you did everything correctly, `pkcipe` on A's side should now be listening for incoming connections. If you set `pkcipe` up to listen on port 9900, `pkcipe` on B's side can be started as follows:

```
[root@B /etc/cipe]# pkcipe -c 172.16.1.1:9900
```

Consequently, `pkcipe` should be able to generate an `options` file with a key it has negotiated and run `ciped` for you. You should still add routing and any other options you might need to have in your `ip-up` and `ip-down` scripts on both peers.

Finally, don't forget to keep the following line in your `ip-up` script (`pkcipe` needs it):

```
echo "$3 $1" >/var/run/cipe/${6:-$1}.pid
```

The `ip-down` file must also contain the following lines:

```
# remove the daemon PID file
rm -f /var/run/cipe/$6.pid /var/run/cipe/$1.pid
```

The other two peers, B and C, will use `pkcipe` in a similar way. You might want to add different options to the public key files, according to the scenario you have.

Command-Line Arguments

Table 9.2 provides a list of command-line arguments supported by `pkcipe` as of version 1.5.1.

Table 9.2 **Command-Line Arguments Supported by *pkcipe* 1.5.1**

Argument	Description
`-c host:port`	Connect to the given host and port using TCP.
`-s port`	Listen for incoming TCP connections on the given port.
`-t timeout`	Timeout used when reading data from the network.
`-r host`	Useful with SOCKS5 when you want to specify where you want CIPE's UDP packets to be routed.
`-k keyfile`	By default, `pkcipe` uses `/etc/cipe/identity` and `/etc/cipe/identity.priv`. You can override the default settings by using this option.
`-D debug`	Use this option to specify logging flags. See the section "Debugging" later in this chapter for more details.
`-E`	Output errors to standard error, not syslog.

Pros and Cons of Using pkcipe

One of the most important advantages `pkcipe` has is that you no longer have to distribute shared secret keys. Instead, you distribute public keys. Also, there is no need for you to come up with a different shared key for each tunnel you want to use. Finally, you only need to distribute public keys once, and `pkcipe` will automatically renegotiate shared keys for you from time to time.

These advantages do not come for free, however, and `pkcipe` has its weaknesses. In particular, a closer look reveals that although `pkcipe` might improve security, it is vulnerable to active attacks. For example, active adversaries interfering with Diffie-Hellman key exchange can mimic identities of peers and gain access to the data that CIPE tunnels. See `www.cc.gatech.edu/~ok/mitm` for more information.

As for decreased amount of work, do not forget that `pkcipe` needs to be configured too and that takes time. In addition, the distribution of public keys with `pkcipe` requires more work because it takes two copy operations for each pair of peers to exchange keys as opposed to only one operation with the old scheme, although in the long run it will probably be worth it because shared keys will be renegotiated automatically.

Overall, we consider `pkcipe` to be a useful addition although it has its problems.

Debugging

How do you determine what is wrong if one of the CIPE components does not work? You will need to use different techniques to elicit debug information from different CIPE components. In this section, we will consider the techniques you can use with each component as well as a general tool you can use with most components (`strace`).

CIPE Mailing List

If you feel stranded and have tried everything without any success, try the CIPE mailing list available via `http://sites.inka.de/bigred/archive/cipe-l/`. If you want to ask a question, you will need to subscribe to the mailing list and then email `cipe-l@inka.de`.

strace *Tool*

You can use this tool to get a detailed overview of the system functions that a component is calling. This might give you an idea what specific function call causes the component to crash. Here an example of `strace` output:

```
[root@nyquist /root]# strace -f -o/tmp/out ciped-cb
[root@nyquist /root]# tail -20 /tmp/out
12472 write(1, "me=199.77.128.173:30001\n", 24) = 24
12472 write(1, "peer=128.61.33.81:30500\n", 24) = 24
12472 write(1, "key=(secret)\n", 13)    = 13
12472 write(1, "nokey=no\n", 9)         = 9
12472 write(1, "socks=\n", 7)           = 7
12472 write(1, "tokxc=0\n", 8)          = 8
12472 write(1, "tokey=0\n", 8)          = 8
12472 write(1, "ipup=(none)\n", 12)     = 12
12472 write(1, "ipdown=(none)\n", 14)   = 14
12472 write(1, "arg=(none)\n", 11)      = 11
12472 write(1, "maxerr=-1\n", 10)       = 10
12472 write(1, "tokxts=0\n", 9)         = 9
12472 write(1, "ping=0\n", 7)           = 7
12472 write(1, "toping=0\n", 9)         = 9
12472 write(1, "dynip=no\n", 9)         = 9
12472 write(1, "hwaddr=(none)\n", 14)   = 14
12472 write(1, "ifconfig=no\n", 12)     = 12
12472 write(1, "checksum=no\n", 12)     = 12
```

```
12472 rt_sigaction(SIGHUP, {0x804c154, [HUP INT ALRM TERM CHLD], 0x4000000}, NULL,
➡8) = 0
12472 rt_sigprocmask(SIG_UNBLOCK, [HUP], NULL, 8) = 0
12472 rt_sigaction(SIGINT, {0x804c154, [HUP INT ALRM TERM CHLD], 0x4000000}, NULL,
➡8) = 0
12472 rt_sigprocmask(SIG_UNBLOCK, [INT], NULL, 8) = 0
12472 rt_sigaction(SIGTERM, {0x804c154, [HUP INT ALRM TERM CHLD], 0x4000000},
➡NULL, 8) = 0
12472 rt_sigprocmask(SIG_UNBLOCK, [TERM], NULL, 8) = 0
12472 rt_sigaction(SIGPIPE, {0x804c154, [HUP INT ALRM TERM CHLD], 0x4000000},
➡NULL, 8) = 0
12472 rt_sigprocmask(SIG_UNBLOCK, [PIPE], NULL, 8) = 0
12472 rt_sigaction(SIGUSR1, {0x804c154, [HUP INT ALRM TERM CHLD], 0x4000000},
➡NULL, 8) = 0
12472 rt_sigprocmask(SIG_UNBLOCK, [USR1], NULL, 8) = 0
12472 open("/dev/urandom", O_RDONLY)     = 3
12472 socket(PF_INET, SOCK_DGRAM, IPPROTO_IP) = 4
12472 setsockopt(4, SOL_SOCKET, SO_RCVBUF, [65536], 4) = 0
12472 bind(4, {sin_family=AF_INET, sin_port=htons(30001),
➡sin_addr=inet_addr("199.77.128.173")}}, 16) = 0
12472 connect(4, {sin_family=AF_INET, sin_port=htons(30500),
➡sin_addr=inet_addr("128.61.33.81")}}, 16) = 0
12472 getsockname(4, {sin_family=AF_INET, sin_port=htons(30001),
➡sin_addr=inet_addr("199.77.128.173")}}, [16]) = 0
12472 ioctl(4, 0x89f4, 0xbffff960)       = -1 EINVAL (Invalid argument)
12472 write(2, "opendev: alloc", 14)     = 14
12472 write(2, "\n", 1)                  = 1
12472 close(4)                           = 0
12472 munmap(0x40018000, 4096)           = 0
12472 _exit(1)
```

In this case, the sixth line from the bottom causes ciped to abort and display an error message: opendev: alloc. You can use this information when you pose your question(s) to the CIPE mailing list if the solution is not obvious to you.

cipcb *Kernel Module*

To find out where the problem is, the first thing you can do is look at the syslog output (that is, the /var/log/messages file) for errors and status information written by the cipcb kernel module:

```
[root@fox pkcipe]# tail -5 /var/log/messages
```

You can also set the logging level when loading the module, as follows:

```
[root@fox pkcipe]# modprobe cipcb cipe_debug=5
```

The higher the value of the debug argument, the more verbose cipcb will be in the syslog.

ciped

You can set the debug option in /etc/cipe/options as shown here:

```
debug 1
```

Note that it is a Boolean option that can be either true (1) or false (0). If the debug option is set to 1, ciped will not go into the background. Instead, it will stay interactive and display error messages to the standard error.

Alternatively, you can set this option via ciped command line, as follows:

```
[root@fox cipe]#ciped-cb -o /etc/cipe/options debug=1
```

This will have the same effect as putting the debug option to /etc/cipe/options. However, make sure you use name=value and not name value if you want to specify options on the command line.

If you decide not to set the debug option to 1, you can always look in the syslog, as with the kernel module:

```
[root@fox pkcipe]# tail -10 /var/log/messages
```

pkcipe

Use the -D debug command-line option to tell pkcipe to display debug messages pertaining to its elements. As of version 1.5.1, the following values are defined in the pkcipe source:

```
#define DEB_PROTO       1
#define DEB_KEY         2
#define DEB_BNUM        4
#define DEB_PKT         8
#define DEB_PKTERR      16
#define DEB_LOCK        32
#define DEB_SIGN        64
#define DEB_PDUMP       128
#define DEB_PSHA1       256
```

As you can see, DEB_SIGN will log any messages related to signatures, DEB_PKTERR will log whenever an error occurs in pkcipe packets, and so on. Note that this is an internal option and that CIPE authors do not elaborate on it in the documentation. Use at your own risk.

Another option to use is -E. Use it if you want to log to standard error instead of syslog.

Limitations

In our opinion, the major limitation of CIPE is its level of usability. CIPE is a great tool to play with, especially if you are a geek; however, there's quite a bit of work involved, and it's not a very friendly option for those who are new to Linux.

Another limitation is that CIPE only implements two symmetric algorithms, of which one is patented. This effectively leaves a broad user base without a great deal of choice. If the CIPE authors added support for more ciphers, such as the new AES (Rijndael), 3DES, and so on, it would make the package much more appealing to the broadest possible audience.

Yet another important limitation that CIPE has is its documentation. Unfortunately, CIPE's documentation is very scarce and does not provide nearly as much information as many users would need to successfully troubleshoot and use it. The documentation clearly lacks examples. In particular, there is almost nothing available on using CIPE protocol version 4 in a bridging mode.

CIPE is also limited in that it does not provide any performance evaluation in the documentation. Although CIPE seems to be lightweight and not very resource consuming, qualitative performance measurement is important. We feel that this fact, as well as the fact that CIPE's overall security has not been carefully evaluated by a broadly qualified base of professionals, might limit CIPE's acceptance.

Summary

Overall, we believe that CIPE is a valuable package that can be successfully used to build VPNs under Linux. Whether it is going to be your ultimate solution or not, it is definitely worth trying.

10

tinc

NO SINGLE SOFTWARE PACKAGE IS CAPABLE of addressing all possible problems and requirements you might have when building a VPN. Fortunately, Linux provides several alternative VPN packages. Although in principle the majority of the packages work very similarly, in reality, the differences between them are significant enough for you to prefer one over another. In particular, there are differences in key generation and distribution, underlying transport protocols, available ciphers, performance, and so forth. Thus, it is important to know your alternatives.

This chapter describes a package called tinc, another tool designed for building VPNs under Linux. The package has been in development since 1999 and is now quite stable. Before proceeding to the package details, take a look at the overview in the next section to get a better idea of tinc's features.

An Overview of *tinc*

tinc is a lightweight package providing basic VPN functionality. It is currently available for Linux, FreeBSD, and Solaris. The package is distributed freely under GNU's GPL and is maintained by Guus Sliepen and Ivo Timmermans.

The following sections will focus on the version 1.0pre4 of the tinc package running on an i386-based Linux platform. You can download the latest version of tinc from http://tinc.nl.linux.org.

Features

The following sections outline the characteristics of tinc.

Designed to Work in Userspace

tinc was designed to work completely in userspace. For users, this means that errors in implementation will not lead to kernel crashes. It also means that you need not worry about having a part of the package you can't compile if its version does not closely match the kernel's version.

Uses Blowfish and RSA

Currently, tinc uses Blowfish in CBC mode as a symmetric cipher. To obtain keys to be used by the symmetric cipher, asymmetric public-key algorithms (such as RSA) are utilized.

Note that you need to have the OpenSSL library installed for the cryptographic functions tinc uses. This makes changing ciphers easier because the interfaces supplied by the library are similar for different ciphers.

Keep in mind that because tinc uses asymmetric. algorithms, it relies on the fact that you can distribute public keys in a fashion that prevents active attacks and replacement of the keys. Whether you can do it securely or not, it is ultimately your responsibility to perform key distribution.

Uses Both TCP and UDP

The underlying transport protocols used by tinc are TCP and UDP. These protocols are utilized to transmit control information and data, respectively. For masqueraded machines, it is possible to use TCP exclusively, although this scheme might cause problems because of the TCP-over-TCP meltdown effect explained earlier in the book (in the "Host-host CIPE Tunneling" section of Chapter 9, "cIPe").

Contains Embedded Support for Routing

One of the features that makes tinc stand out is its embedded support for routing. tinc automatically propagates routes for various subnets comprising a VPN, thus saving you all the additional work you would otherwise do to set up routing.

To illustrate, if your VPN consists of M peers and you want to add a new peer, typically you would make M-1 modifications to configuration files of all the peers, except for the one to which the new peer is connected, to reflect new routing. In contrast, if you use tinc, you will not need to make any changes to routing tables on any of the peers. As soon as the new peer is connected, routing information will be propagated automatically by tinc.

Requires Ethertap or a Universal TUN/TAP Driver

As previously described, the tinc package is available for several platforms, including FreeBSD, Linux, and Solaris. Because tinc depends on ethertap (Linux kernel versions prior to 2.4) or the universal TUN/TAP driver, the platforms for which it is available need to provide support for either of these drivers.

The use of the ethertap or universal TUN/TAP drivers means higher portability for tinc because there is nothing in the package that is bound to a particular kernel version. Accordingly, as soon as support for the ethertap or TUN/TAP driver is included by an unsupported platform, tinc can be ported to such platform fairly quickly.

Installation

You have at least three options when choosing the kind of installation you want to perform:

1. Use an RPM or DEB package containing a set of precompiled, dynamically linked binaries.

2. Download tinc source and compile it yourself.

3. Use a set of precompiled, statically linked tinc binaries.

Note
Do not forget that you will need root privileges to install and run tinc.

If you want to avoid compilation, the first option would probably be the easiest way of installing tinc. Simply add tinc as a package to the system and you are all set. Beware, however, that binary packages are typically slightly out-of-date in comparison to the source distribution. In addition, you will probably need to install other packages on which tinc depends, such as OpenSSL, for instance. Go to http://tinc.nl.linux.org or http://rpmfind.net to find the latest version of the RPM/DEB tinc package.

The second option involves building a fresh set of binaries from the tinc source code. This option comes in handy when you want to ensure that everything is built properly from the bottom up and that all the dependencies are in place. A detailed description of what you need to do will be provided in a moment. Meanwhile, you can download the latest version of tinc source from http://tinc.nl.linux.org.

The third option is useful when you are experiencing problems with the libraries on which tinc depends and find it difficult to compile. Because the binaries are statically linked, you do not need to worry about having all the libraries on your system. We recommend that you use this option as your last resort.

Dependencies

This section describes installation and configuration of the components on which tinc relies, namely ethertap or the universal TUN/TAP driver and the OpenSSL library.

Ethertap or Universal TUN/TAP Driver

Typically, the way to add support for ethertap or the TUN/TAP driver is to enable it in your kernel. The exact steps required to do this will depend on the version of the operating system you are using.

Use Ethertap for Kernel Versions up to 2.4.0

For Linux kernel versions from 2.1.60 up to—but not including—2.4.0, you will need to enable ethertap. You can check whether an ethertap module is already available in your system using the following command:

```
[root@fox /etc]# ls -l /lib/modules/`uname -r`/net/ethertap.o
-rw-r--r--   1 root      root          4628 Jun  1 20:24
/lib/modules/2.2.16-22smp/net/ethertap.o
```

If you do have `ethertap.o`, you should also try to load the ethertap module and check the updated module list for ethertap as shown here:

```
[root@fox /etc]# modprobe -vd ethertap
===========================================
Module ethertap
kname ethertap
objkey ethertap
names: ethertap
mode: NORMAL
Module matching ethertap: /lib/modules/2.2.16-22smp/net/ethertap.o
===========================================

[root@fox /etc]# lsmod
Module                  Size  Used by
ethertap                2516  0  (unused)
lockd                  31656  1  (autoclean)
sunrpc                 54116  1  (autoclean) [lockd]
eepro100               16664  3  (autoclean)
es1371                 29988  0
soundcore               2980  4  [es1371]
usb-ohci               13072  0  (unused)
usbcore                44392  1  [usb-ohci]
aic7xxx               137528  2
```

> **Note**
> You should have the `modutils` package installed to be able to perform operations on loadable modules.

If you are able to load the module, it is likely that the following final test will also succeed:

```
[root@fox linux]# ifconfig tap0
tap0      Link encap:Ethernet  HWaddr FE:FD:00:00:00:00
          BROADCAST NOARP MULTICAST  MTU:1500  Metric:1
          RX packets:0 errors:0 dropped:0 overruns:0 frame:0
```

```
        TX packets:0 errors:0 dropped:0 overruns:0 carrier:0
        collisions:0 txqueuelen:0
        Interrupt:5
```

If you were able to obtain `tap0` device information, you can skip the rest of this section; if not, you should reconfigure your kernel (see Chapter 2, "VPN Fundamentals" for more information on reconfiguring a kernel) and turn on the following options: In the Code maturity level options menu:

[★] Prompt for development and/or incomplete code/drivers

In the Networking options menu:

[★] Kernel/User netlink socket

[M] Netlink device emulation

In the Network device support menu:

[M] Ethertap network tap

You should then recompile and install both your new kernel and modules. With that out of the way, there is one additional change to be made. Look in `/etc/modules.conf` and add one or more extra lines to it as shown here:

```
alias char-major-36 netlink-dev

alias tap0 ethertap
options tap0 -o tap0 unit=0

alias tap1 ethertap
options tap1 -o tap1 unit=1

[…]

alias tapN ethertap
options tapN -o tapX unit=N
```

As you can see, you should add two lines for each tap device (read: `tinc` daemon) that you want to use simultaneously.

In addition, you should ensure that all the tap devices you are going to use exist in the `/dev` directory. For instance, here is the contents of `/dev` on our system:

```
[root@fox linux]# ls -l /dev/tap?
crw-r--r--  1 root     root     36,  16 Jun  1 01:21 /dev/tap0
crw-r--r--  1 root     root     36,  17 Jun  1 01:22 /dev/tap1
crw-r--r--  1 root     root     36,  18 Jun  1 01:22 /dev/tap2
crw-r--r--  1 root     root     36,  19 Jun  1 01:22 /dev/tap3
crw-r--r--  1 root     root     36,  20 Jun  1 01:22 /dev/tap4
crw-r--r--  1 root     root     36,  21 Jun  1 01:22 /dev/tap5
```

If you need to create several tap devices, you can do it by using the following series of commands:

```
[root@fox linux]# mknod /dev/tap0 c 36 16
[root@fox linux]# mknod /dev/tap1 c 36 17
```

```
[root@fox linux]# mknod /dev/tap2 c 36 18
[root@fox linux]# mknod /dev/tap3 c 36 19

[...]

[root@fox linux]# mknod /dev/tapN c 36 16+N
[root@fox linux]# chmod 600 /dev/tap*
[root@fox linux]# chown 0.0 /dev/tap*
```

Use the Universal TUN/TAP Driver for Kernel Version 2.4.0 and Higher

Start by configuring a new kernel to support the universal TUN/TAP driver as shown here:

In the Code maturity level options menu:

[*] Prompt for development and/or incomplete code/drivers

In the Network device support menu:

<M> Universal TUN/TAP device driver support

If you decide to use the TUN/TAP driver as a module, make sure you also add the following information to /etc/modules.conf:

```
alias char-major-10-200 tun
```

Note that you can also choose to compile the TUN/TAP driver into the kernel. In this case, no changes other than those to the kernel configuration previously described are necessary.

In both cases, however, you will need to create a device file to be used by the universal TUN/TAP driver, unless the device file already exists on your system. For example:

```
[root@fox linux]# ls -l /dev/tun
crw-------   1 root     root      10, 200 Jun  6 01:18 /dev/tun
```

Your system might also have /dev/net/tun automatically created. Therefore, also check for the following file:

```
[root@fox linux]# ls -l /dev/net/tun
crw-------   1 root     root      10, 200 Jun  6 01:18 /dev/net/tun
```

If you determine that there is no tunneling device on your system, the device can be created as follows:

```
[root@fox linux]# mknod /dev/tun c 10 200
[root@fox linux]# chmod 600 /dev/tun
[root@fox linux]# chown 0.0 /dev/tun
```

OpenSSL Library

There is a good chance that your Linux system already comes with the OpenSSL library installed. For example:

```
[root@fox linux]# rpm -qa|egrep openssl
openssl-0.9.6-3
```

If you do not have the OpenSSL library installed, you can either download the latest version of its source from `www.openssl.org` or just find a packaged version of the library at `http://rpmfind.net`.

Building *tinc* from Source Code

To build `tinc` from source code, you will need to have all of the dependencies previously specified in place. Then you can try to run `./configure` followed by `make all check install`. Both commands should be run from `tinc`'s source directory.

Before you do that, there are some options you might want to pass to the `configure` script so that everything is handled the way you want it to be. By default, `tinc` will use `/usr/local/etc/tinc` as its configuration directory. You might want to change it to `/etc/tinc` by specifying an appropriate parameter on the command line. Look at the output of the following command for additional options:

```
[root@fox tinc]# ./configure --help
```

Here is the sequence of commands used to build and install `tinc`:

```
[root@fox]# cd tinc-src
[root@fox]# ./configure --sysconfdir=/etc --with-openssl=/usr/local/ssl
[root@fox]# make all check install
```

If everything compiles and installs without a hitch, you can proceed to the "Installing Configuration Files" subsection. Otherwise, read on for help in solving the problem. The next subsection considers some of the possible issues that might arise when compiling `tinc`.

Troubleshooting

One of the most frequent problems with `tinc` is failing to detect the OpenSSL library even if you have the library installed on your system. If you have this kind of problem, the `configure` script probably stops and displays a message similar to the following:

```
checking for evp.h... no
checking for openssl/evp.h... no

It seems like OpenSSL is not installed on this system.  But perhaps
you need to supply the exact location of the headers and libraries.
You can try running configure with the --with-openssl=/DIRECTORY
parameter.  If you installed the headers and libraries in a different
location you can use --with-openssl-include=/DIR and
--with-openssl-lib=/DIR.

configure: error: OpenSSL not found.
```

You might try to run configure using –with-openssl-* options referring to the appropriate directories. The way we usually do it is as follows (the exact paths will depend on your configuration):

```
[root@fox tinc]# ./configure --sysconfdir=/etc --with-openssl=/usr/local/ssl
```

Alternatively, it is possible to be even more specific and tell `configure` about the exact paths to OpenSSL includes and libraries. You can do it by running the following:

```
[root@fox tinc]# ./configure --sysconfdir=/etc --with-openssl=/usr/local/ssl --
➥with-openssl-lib=/usr/local/ssl/lib/lib –with-openssl-
➥include=/usr/local/ssl/include
```

Generally, this should take care of the problem. We have found, however, that `tinc`'s `configure` script will often continue complaining about OpenSSL includes.

Our solution might seem a little bit harsh, but it is effective. Using root privileges, create the `/usr/include/openssl` directory and copy OpenSSL include files to that directory. For example:

```
[root@fox tinc]# mkdir -m 755 /usr/include/openssl
[root@fox tinc]# chown 0.0 /usr/include/openssl
[root@fox tinc]# cp /usr/local/openssl/include/openssl/*
/usr/include/openssl
```

In the event that you are unable to determine why `tinc` is failing to compile, we recommend that you check `config.log` for a detailed explanation.

Finally, you can always ask for help on `tinc`'s mailing list by sending an email with your questions to `tinc@nl.linux.org`. To view responses to your inquiry, you can either subscribe to the `tinc` mailing list or browse an online copy via `http://tinc.nl.linux.org`.

Installing Configuration Files

As of version 1.0pre4, `tinc` does not set up a directory with configuration files as a part of a standard `make install` sequence. Therefore, unless you are using a prepackaged `tinc` RPM or DEB archive, you will need to create directories and copy configuration samples manually.

Here is what you need to do (this assumes that the name of your VPN is *shattuck*):

```
 [root@fox tinc]# mkdir -m 700 /etc/tinc /etc/tinc/shattuck
➥/etc/tinc/shattuck/hosts
[root@fox tinc]# chown 0.0 /etc/tinc /etc/tinc/shattuck /etc/tinc/shattuck/hosts
[root@fox /]# cd <your_tinc_source_directory>
[root@fox tinc]# cp doc/sample-config/* /etc/tinc/shattuck/
[root@fox tinc]# cp doc/sample-config/hosts/* /etc/tinc/shattuck/hosts
```

Note

You might find it useful to also take a look at the prepackaged `tinc` archive in RPM or DEB format. The archive contains additional samples of both configuration files and `rc.d` scripts to start `tinc` as a daemon on system initialization.

Adding *tinc* to */etc/rc.d*

You can skip this section if you installed `tinc` from an RPM or DEB package.

We will now describe how to manually set up `tinc` to be run automatically upon reboot as one of the `init` scripts on a RedHat Linux system. To perform the setup, you should run the commands described here.

First, verify `/etc/rc.d/init.d`. Then go to your `tinc` source directory and copy the startup script for RedHat while adding correct permissions.

```
[root@fox /root]# mkdir -p /etc/rc.d/init.d/
[root@fox /root]# cd <your_tinc_source_directory>
[root@fox ~tinc]# cp redhat/tinc /etc/rc.d/init.d/
[root@fox ~tinc]# chown 0.0 /etc/rc.d/init.d/tinc
[root@fox ~tinc]# chmod 755 /etc/rc.d/init.d/tinc
```

The next step is to use `chkconfig` to add links to the `tinc` startup script. To do that, type the following:

```
[root@fox ~tinc]# /sbin/chkconfig --add tinc
```

At this point, the `tinc` startup script should be ready to be run by `init(8)` next time you reboot your system.

Modifying /etc/services

The official port number used by `tinc` is 655. This number is registered with Internet Assigned Numbers Authority (IANA) and can be added to a system-wide `/etc/services` file. The addition is not mandatory, but it can be useful if you prefer to use symbolic names instead of port numbers. Simply insert the following lines into `/etc/services`:

```
tinc   655/tcp
tinc   655/udp
```

Configuration

In the following sections, you will learn about `tinc` configuration files, modifying firewall rules to support `tinc`, and different ways to run `tinc`.

Overview of Configuration Files

Normally, all configuration files that `tinc` uses are located in the `/etc/tinc` directory and its subdirectories. If you only use one VPN, you might want to put all your configuration files directly into the `/etc/tinc` directory. However, a substantial part of `tinc` functionality is based on the notion of multiple daemons working concurrently and servicing different VPNs. Such orientation comes in handy when you need your hosts to support several VPNs.

If you were to keep all the configuration files for multiple VPNs in the same directory, you would probably lose track of which file belongs to which VPN fairly quickly, especially if you do not work with the configuration files every day. To avoid such chaos, `tinc` can associate a separate subdirectory of `/etc/tinc` with a different VPN.

We recommend that you use this feature if you want to have multiple tinc VPNs on your machine. Simply create a subdirectory for each VPN that your machine belongs to and keep configuration files for the appropriate VPN there.

Now you have an idea where to put tinc configuration files. It is time to take a closer look at the files themselves.

tinc.conf

This is a main configuration file. You should have this file for each VPN you use. The file contains configuration information for your machine as a member of the VPN. For example, if the name of your VPN is *shattuck* and the name you assigned to your machine is *kitaro*, your /etc/tinc/shattuck/tinc.conf file might look as follows:

```
Name = kitaro
TapDevice = /dev/tap0
PrivateKeyFile = /etc/tinc/shattuck/kitaro.priv
ConnectTo = deepblue
```

The Name option specifies the name under which your machine is known to members of the *shattuck* VPN.

The ConnectTo option instructs tinc to connect to its peer named *deepblue*. For this to work, you should have a /etc/tinc/shattuck/hosts/deepblue file containing contact information for the peer. If you do not specify the ConnectTo option, tinc will start waiting for incoming connections.

/etc/tinc/<vpn>/hosts/*

This directory contains configuration files for hosts that belong to a VPN <vpn>. The directory should consist of at least one file that contains configuration for your machine. In the preceding example, you will need to create /etc/tinc/shattuck/hosts/kitaro. You can also use the directory to store configuration files for the peers to which your machine is going to connect.

tinc-up and tinc-down Scripts

If the name of your VPN is *shattuck*, when you start tinc for the VPN, it will execute the /etc/tinc/shattuck/tinc-up script. The script should set up an appropriate tinc interface and perform some additional configuration required for normal operation. Note that you will need to use different tinc-up scripts for ethertap and the universal TUN/TAP driver.

For the ethertap driver, you can use the following script:

```
#!/bin/sh
# bring interface down first
ifconfig tap0 down

# required by tinc
# sets up tap0 MAC address to a special value
```

```
# to ensure that tinc tunneling works
ifconfig tap0 hw ether fe:fd:00:00:00:00

# a.b.c.d should be replaced with the interface's IP address
ifconfig tap0 a.b.c.d netmask 255.255.255.0

# make sure you have this line to disable ARP on
# the tinc interface
ifconfig tap0 -arp
```

If you are using the universal TUN/TAP driver, you should replace the name of the
interface in the preceding example with $NETNAME. For example:

```
#!/bin/sh
ifconfig $NETNAME down
ifconfig $NETNAME hw ether fe:fd:00:00:00:00
ifconfig $NETNAME a.b.c.d netmask 255.255.255.0
ifconfig $NETNAME -arp
```

Note

Normally, you will not need to add routing commands to the tinc-up script because the kernel and tinc
will take care of that for you. If you still think you might have to add routing, consider the following:

- The kernel normally adds routing for the directly connected interfaces, among which is tinc's
  tunneling interface, and

- for more complex routes, tinc will propagate routing information automatically.

Before exiting, your tinc daemon will call the /etc/tinc/shattuck/tinc-down script
to perform cleanup work. This script is provided merely for the users' convenience,
and tinc does not require the script to be present. You might find the script useful
when you want to add log entries, reconfigure devices, add firewall rules to divert traffic, and so on.

Configuring *tinc*

At this point, we will assume you have performed all the necessary installations, in particular installing packages and creating directories and device files. If you have not yet
done so, read the previous sections.

For simplicity, our configuration will be based on the following scenario:

1. You want to connect your host to a VPN called *shattuck*.

2. The name of your host is *kitaro*, as in the earlier example, and the name of the
   host you will be connecting to is *bancroft*.

3. You have a simple VPN consisting of only two hosts. The network address of the
   VPN is 192.168.1.0/24. The real IP address of the *kitaro* host is 172.16.1.1, and
   the real IP address of the *bancroft* host is 172.16.20.1.

Sketching Configuration

Before getting into details and showing contents of files, we would like you to have a clear picture of what exactly you need to do to configure the VPN in our test scenario.

For the first peer, *kitaro*, you will need to do the following:

1. Modify the main configuration file for *kitaro* (/etc/tinc/shattuck/tinc.conf).

2. Generate keys and put the public key into the /etc/tinc/shattuck/hosts/kitaro file.

3. Modify the host configuration file for *kitaro* (/etc/tinc/shattuck/hosts/kitaro) and copy the file to *bancroft's* /etc/tinc/shattuck/hosts directory.

For the second peer, *bancroft*, you will need to perform a mirrored set of steps, namely:

1. Modify the main configuration file for *bancroft* (/etc/tinc/shattuck/tinc.conf).

2. Generate keys and put the public key into the /etc/tinc/shattuck/hosts/bancroft file.

3. Modify the host configuration file for *bancroft* (/etc/tinc/shattuck/hosts/bancroft) and copy it to *kitaro's* /etc/tinc/shattuck/hosts directory.

Contents of the */etc/tinc* Directory

At this point, the /etc/tinc directory on both peers should contain the following information:

```
[root@fox tinc]# ls -lR /etc/tinc
/etc/tinc:
total 4
drwx------    3 root     root          4096 Jun  1 21:24 shattuck

/etc/tinc/shattuck:
total 12
drwx------    2 root     root          4096 Jun  1 21:24 hosts
-rw-r--r--    1 root     root           473 Jun  1 17:20 tinc.conf
```

It does not matter what you currently have in the tinc.conf file because we will completely rewrite it while configuring the VPN.

Main Configuration File

In the following sections, we will describe basic and extended options supported by tinc's main configuration file.

/etc/tinc/shattuck/tinc.conf

The file that contains the main configuration options for the *shattuck* VPN on both peers is /etc/tinc/shattuck/tinc.conf. Let's go ahead and edit that file now.

If you are using the ethertap driver, the configuration file for *kitaro* should contain the following lines:

```
Name = kitaro
ConnectTo = bancroft
Hostnames = no
KeyExpire = 3600
PingTimeout = 60
PrivateKeyFile = /etc/tinc/shattuck/rsa_key.priv
TapDevice = /dev/tap0
```

For the universal TUN/TAP driver, use the same configuration except you need to replace the preceding `TapDevice` line with one of the following lines, depending on which of the devices exists on your system:

```
TapDevice=/dev/tun
```

or

```
TapDevice=/dev/net/tun
```

For *bancroft*, `/etc/tinc/shattuck/tinc.conf` should be created similarly. If you are using the ethertap driver, the configuration file should be as follows:

```
Name = bancroft
Hostnames = no
KeyExpire = 3600
PingTimeout = 60
PrivateKeyFile = /etc/tinc/shattuck/rsa_key.priv
TapDevice = /dev/tap0
```

Change the `TapDevice` option, as previously described, if you are using the TUN/TAP driver.

Basic Options

This section provides a description of the basic options to be used in the main configuration file.

The first option, `Name`, sets a symbolic name by which your host will be known in the VPN. This can be any unique string you might come up with, although it might be a good idea to associate the name with the name of your host as stated in the DNS.

The second option, `ConnectTo`, denotes that `tinc` should connect to a host called *bancroft*, such that the `/etc/tinc/shattuck/hosts/bancroft` file should contain the public key, IP address, and other information for the host.

The next option, `Hostnames`, tells `tinc` not to resolve IP addresses to hostnames. This option is especially useful if your hostname is not present in the DNS, if it takes a while for a DNS server to respond, or if you do not want the performance of the VPN to be dependent on the availability of DNS.

The `KeyExpire` option defines the time in seconds during which the shared encryption keys used by `tinc`'s symmetric cipher are valid. In our configuration, the encryption keys will be renegotiated every hour.

The PingTimeout option stipulates the time interval in seconds that the link needs to be inactive for tinc to send a keep-alive packet. If the other end does not respond within the same number of seconds, tinc aborts the connection and updates routing information.

The PrivateKeyFile option defines the name of the RSA private-key file that tinc should use. We will show how to generate this file in a moment. For now, do not worry about this option.

Extended Options

Here is a list of options that can be used in the main configuration file in addition to the ones already described:

- Interface = <device_name>. By default, tinc will be listening for incoming connections on all network interfaces that are up. With this option, you can specify an interface name on which you want tinc to listen, such as eth0, ppp0, sl0, and so on.

- InterfaceIP = <local_IP_address>. When you are using IP aliases, you might have more than one IP address associated with an interface. This option lets you define to which IP addresses you want tinc to bind. The default behavior is to listen on all the addresses associated with the interface.

- PrivateKey = <hexadecimal_key_string>. This option enables you to provide a private key as a string. For safety reasons, however, we recommend that you use the PrivateKeyFile option instead.

Generating Keys

Run the following command on both peers to generate an RSA keypair for each peer:

```
[root@fox /root]# tincd -n shattuck -K

Generating 1024 bits keys:
...............++++++ p
................++++++ q
Done.

Please enter a file to save public RSA key to [/etc/tinc/shattuck/hosts/{kitaro |
➡bancroft}]: <_press_enter here>

Please enter a file to save private RSA key to [/etc/tinc/shattuck/rsa_key.priv]:
➡< press_enter here>
```

As you probably noticed, if you just press Enter, your public key will be saved in /etc/tinc/shattuck/hosts/kitaro if you specified Name=kitaro in the /etc/tinc/shattuck/tinc.conf file. For *bancroft*, the name of the file with the public key should be /etc/tinc/shattuck/hosts/bancroft accordingly.

As for the private key, it will be written out to /etc/tinc/shattuck/rsa_key.priv on both hosts. You should refer to this file using the PrivateKeyFile option of tinc.conf and keep the private-key file secret. Note that it is better to use absolute pathnames. This will ensure that there is no ambiguity as to where the key is saved.

Host Configuration Files

Peers that form a VPN need to know about each other. First, they need to know each other's IP addresses or at least the IP address of the host to which they will be connecting. Second, each peer needs to know the other side's public key to negotiate a shared key used by the symmetric cipher. Third, they need to know what VPNs or subsets of addresses are associated with each peer. All this information is stored on a per-peer basis in each peer's /etc/tinc/<vpn>/hosts/ directory.

We will provide examples of host configuration files used by our sample VPN in a moment. Note that because the VPN in our scenario consists of only two hosts, the following subnet options will actually be the IP addresses of the two members of the VPN. In addition, the number of network bits will be defined as /32—an equivalent to a 255.255.255.255 netmask.

/etc/tinc/shattuck/hosts/kitaro

On *kitaro*, the /etc/tinc/shattuck/hosts/kitaro file should now contain a freshly generated public key. Add the following lines to the beginning of the file:

```
# Subnet on the virtual private network that is local to this host
#
# * In our example, a subnet with netmask 255.255.255.255, essentially
# * a degenerate case consisting of the virtual IP address of our host
Subnet = 192.168.1.1/32

# The real IP address of this tinc host
# (not really a routable address in our example)
Address = 172.16.1.1
```

In addition to modifying the file, you will also need to copy the file to the *bancroft*'s /etc/tinc/shattuck/hosts directory.

/etc/tinc/shattuck/hosts/bancroft

When modifying /etc/tinc/shattuck/tinc.conf on *kitaro* earlier, you specified the name of the peer to which the tinc daemon on *kitaro* is going to connect. However, the daemon only knows the symbolic name of the peer, and that is not enough to establish a connection. To address this problem, you should copy *bancroft*'s information to the /etc/tinc/shattuck/hosts directory on your host.

On *bancroft*, the /etc/tinc/shattuck/hosts/bancroft configuration file might look as follows:

```
# Subnet on the virtual private network that is local to this host
Subnet = 192.168.1.2/32
```

```
# The real IP address of this tinc host
# (not really a routable address in our example)
# Can be used by other hosts to connect to tinc, if this host
# does not have a ConnectTo option in tinc.conf
Address = 172.16.20.1

# 655 is the default port so you can omit or change this, if you want
Port = 655

# this key should be your peer's public key
-----BEGIN RSA PUBLIC KEY-----
MIGJAoGBAL0KkKFvDAGM2UpsydUI6wtefgnzSD3vi0SJSYEuC+/Bb2dMQz32vSTZ
++K/4XkKk8OV8FC8xFKBItplIgiNiBr9usaFFJ3RkPpv4qFmIbmkanVvBZB1yn+f
ST1TDkt4Z26g0CfS/o22BcX0YhKYfQaSfn+VssJcJEan0Oy4D8oFAgMA//8=
-----END RSA PUBLIC KEY-----
```

As you can see, the configuration file tells tinc on our side that it will be able to connect to its peer called *bancroft* using the IP address of 172.16.20.1 on port 655 as well as the public key specified in the configuration file.

All Host Configuration Options

Host configuration options include the following:

- Address = <IP address | hostname>   This option is only required if you want to be able to connect to the host you are configuring. The IP address you specify here must be a routable IP address at which the host can be reached, not the address of the host in a VPN.

- IndirectData = <yes | no>   This option indicates whether other tinc daemons besides the one you specified with the ConnectTo option in tinc.conf can make a direct connection to the host. By default, connections from outside are disabled.

- Port = <port>   Using this option, you can select a port on which to accept incoming connections. The port number will be used for both TCP and UDP transports. The default value for the *port* is 655, which is officially registered with IANA. The value can be specified as a decimal (by default), an octal (when preceded by a single zero), or a hexadecimal (prefixed with "0x" tuple, as in "0xFF") number.

- Subnet = <IP address/netbits>   This option determines the range of IP addresses that will be accepted by the host for which the option is defined. The range must be a subset of the VPN network specified for the tap device, not of the real network to which the host is connected.

  The *netbits* part of the option details the length of the network part of the IP address. For instance, if your netmask is 255.255.0.0, the number of network bits is /16. For a netmask of 255.255.255.240, the number of network bits should be /28. This notation is the same notation used by Classless Interdomain Routing (CIDR), defined in RFC 1519.

- TCPonly = <yes | no>   If you are behind a firewall or are having problems with tinc sending data over UDP as underlying transport, you might want to restrict tinc to only using TCP. As of version 1.0pre4, this option is experimental, but it is likely to be present in the subsequent versions of tinc. If the option is set to *yes*, tinc will tunnel packets over a TCP connection and refrain from using UDP. Setting this option also implicitly sets the IndirectData option.

tinc-up and *tinc-down* Scripts

For both peers in the sample scenario, you can skip tinc-down and use only tinc-up. The contents of a /etc/tinc/shattuck/tinc-up script on *kitaro* are given here:

```
#!/bin/sh
# bring interface down first
ifconfig tap0 down

# required by tinc
# sets up tap0 MAC address to a special value
# to ensure that tinc tunneling works
ifconfig tap0 hw ether fe:fd:00:00:00:00

# tinc interface's IP address
ifconfig tap0 192.168.1.1 netmask 255.255.255.255

# make sure you have this line to disable ARP on
# the tinc interface
ifconfig tap0 -arp
```

Note
If you are using the universal TUN/TAP driver, do not forget to replace tap0 with $NETNAME.

To create tinc-up for *bancroft*, use the same file as with *kitaro*. The only difference is that you will need to change the IP address specified on line 11 from 192.168.1.1 to 192.168.1.20.

Adding Firewall Rules

It is fairly common to create all configuration files and forget to enable packets to and from the tunneling interface. If you have already configured your tinc VPN but still do not see responses when pinging the opposite side of the tunneling interface, one possible cause might be your firewall rules. We will now describe how to check for this problem and modify the existing firewall rules to support tinc.

Be aware that some firewalls along the path from one of your peers to the other might filter out tinc traffic. If you have tried everything and still do not see tinc packets going through, we recommend that you select a different port number by using the *Port* option in the host configuration file.

ipchains and Forwarding

First, check whether your kernel supports `ipchains`:

```
[root@fox /]# ls -l /proc/net/ip_fwchains
-rw-------    1 root root    0 Mar 5 17:19 /proc/net/ip_fwchains
```

If there is no such file, you can exclude `ipchains` from the list of possible reasons why `tinc` does not work and move on. Make sure, however, that if you have other machines using your `tinc` tunnel, you enable IP forwarding:

```
[root@fox /]# echo 1 > /proc/sys/net/ipv4/ip_forward
```

Second, look for the `ipchains` package itself, as follows:

```
[root@fox /]# rpm -qvh | egrep ipchains
ipchains-1.3.9-5
```

Again, if you do not have the package installed, you can skip this section and move on because you do not have to have `ipchains` for `tinc` to work. However, we recommend that you install `ipchains` because it enables you to improve your security by providing increased control over the traffic going in and out of your system.

If you determine that `ipchains` *is* installed, the following section will describe how to view and adjust it.

Modifying *ipchains* Rules

You can list all existing `ipchains` rules using the following:

```
[root@fox /]# ipchains -L
```

Here is what you need to do to enable `tinc` traffic on port 655 to and from your host:

```
[root@fox /]# ipchains -A input -j ACCEPT -d <local_tinc_ip> 655 -p udp
[root@fox /]# ipchains -A output -j ACCEPT -d <peer_tinc_ip> 655 -p udp
[root@fox /]# ipchains -A input -j ACCEPT -d <local_tinc_ip> 655 -b -p tcp
[root@fox /]# ipchains -A output -j ACCEPT -d <peer_tinc_ip> 655 -b -p tcp
```

Running *tinc*

Given that the configuration for both peers in our scenario is in place, `tinc` should not complain, and you should be able to run it on either peer using the following command line:

```
[root@fox tinc]# tincd -n <vpn_name>
```

Or, in our specific example, you should use the following:

```
[root@fox tinc]# tincd -n shattuck
```

This is a fairly common way of running `tinc`. By specifying a VPN name on the command line, you are telling `tinc` to look for configuration files in the /etc/tinc/ *<vpn_name>*/ directory.

Note that if you do not specify the `-n` option when executing `tinc`, it will look in `/etc/tinc` or `/usr/local/etc/tinc` by default, depending on the options you used during installation.

You can also run `tinc` as a service. Typically, if you installed `tinc` as a package, you should be able to simply type the following:

```
[root@fox /root]# /etc/init.d/tinc start
```

After `tinc` is started, you can find its process ID in the `/var/run/tinc.<vpn_name>.pid` file. You can use the `pid` to send various kinds of signals described in the following section.

Note that there are a number of additional command-line options that `tinc` supports. In the following section, we will describe some of the options we found useful. If you want to learn more, you can obtain the most recent list of options from the `tincd(8)` man page.

Useful Options and Signals

This section describes various command-line options you can use when running `tinc`. It also gives a description of signals you can send to the `tinc` daemon to affect its execution.

Options

The information in both this and the following sections is taken from the `tinc-1.0pre4` man page. Many of the comments were rewritten and expanded in Table 10.1 in an effort to provide a concise description of the options we found useful.

Table 10.1   *tinc* **Options**

Option	Description
`-c, --config=PATH`	Read configuration options from the directory *PATH*. The default is `/etc/tinc/<vpn_name>/`. This is useful when you decide not to keep configuration files in `/etc/tinc/<vpn_name>`.
`-D, --no-detach`	Don't fork and detach. This will also disable the automatic restart mechanism for fatal errors.
`-d`	Increase debug level. The higher it gets, the more gets logged. Everything is output via syslog. See the "Troubleshooting" section below for more information.
`-k, --kill`	Attempt to kill a running `tincd` and exit. A TERM signal (15) gets sent to the daemon that has its PID in `/var/run/tinc.pid`. Because it kills only one `tinc` daemon, you should use `-n` here if you started it that way. It will then read the PID from `/var/run/tinc.NETNAME.pid`.

continues

Table 10.1 **continued**

Option	Description
-n, --net=<vpn_name>	Work with a VPN called <vpn_name>. Determines a path where tinc looks for configuration files.
-K, --generate-keys[=BITS]	Generate RSA public/private keypair of BITS length. If BITS is not specified, 1024 is the default. tinc will ask where you want to store the files but will default to the configuration directory. Note that you can use the -c or -n option in combination with -K.

Signals

Knowing the process ID of the appropriate tinc daemon from the /var/run/tinc.<vpn_name>.pid file, you can send signals to the daemon. The signals will be interpreted as characterized in Table 10.2.

Table 10.2 **Signals That Can Be Sent to the** *tinc* **Daemon and Their Results**

Signal	Description
HUP	Causes tinc to close all connections, reread the configuration file, and restart.
INT	Forces tinc to close all connections and quit.
USR1	Causes tinc to output the current list of connections to syslog.
USR2	Causes tinc to output the current list of subnets to syslog.
ALRM	Forces tincd to try to connect to its peer immediately. tincd usually attempts to do this itself, but it increases the waiting time between two consecutive attempts each time a failure occurs. If an attempt to connect to an uplink the first time after tinc is started is not successful, the waiting time is set to the maximum time of 15 minutes.

Using *tinc*

Regardless of how complex a VPN is, it can always be deconstructed into basic scenarios that are fairly easy to set up. Most of these basic scenarios deal with only two peers and thus can be represented by a point-to-point link. As in previous chapters, the scenarios are categorized as either *host-host*, *host-network*, or *network-network*. This section will discuss how to use tinc to handle each category so that you can use it to assemble your own VPN.

Because, for each point-to-point link, one of the peers originates and the other waits for incoming connections, it is important to understand that there must be something static about the waiting peer. When both peers have static IP addresses, we use the addresses. When one or both peers have dynamic IP addresses or reside behind a masquerading/NAT firewall, we still need to use a static property for one of the peers, such as dynamic DNS or an explicit firewall rule forwarding packets from a certain port to the peer behind the firewall.

How can you make use of the preceding ideas? Think point-to-point. Determine which one of your peers is going to be the originator and which one is the receiver. Think how you are going to refer to the receiver: Does it have a constant IP address or domain name? Maybe you should add a firewall rule that forwards all the packets from port 9000 to the receiving peer. Ultimately, figure out which category your needs fit in and follow the appropriate scenario described here.

The following examples assume you use the ethertap driver. If you are using the universal TUN/TAP driver, you should replace `/dev/tap0` with either `/dev/tun` or `/dev/net/tun`, whichever exists on your system.

Static Peers

For this set of scenarios, we assume that all peers have constant routable IP addresses and are not behind a Masquerading/NAT firewall.

> **Note**
>
> Note that `tinc` was developed with the idea of a VPN that might consist of a number of different subnetworks. Therefore, for each peer, you will need to specify a subnetwork to which the peer is directly connected.

The following first scenario is the most generic one. It enables you to connect two networks. The next two scenarios use a partial case of the first scenario, with one or both peers using a network address with the netmask of 255.255.255.255, which corresponds to a single IP address.

After each peer has been configured, you can run `tincd` as follows:

```
[root@fox tinc]# tincd -n abcd
```

Network-Network Tunneling

To illustrate tunneling between several networks using `tinc`, we will use four peers—A, B, C, and D—such that:

1. Each peer will be directly connected to one network: 192.168.1.0/24, 192.168.2.0/24, 192.168.3.0/24, and 192.168.4.0/24, respectively.

2. A will be connecting to B; B will be connecting to D; C will be connecting to B.

We will assume that the real IP addresses of A, B, C, and D's interfaces are 172.16.1.1, 172.16.2.1, 172,16.3.1, and 172.16.4.1, respectively. Note that although in our examples we use public RFC1918 addresses as real IP addresses, you will most likely have to use routable IP addresses, such as 194.44.100.1, 198.133.219.25, and so on. See Chapter 2 for more details on the conventions used in this book.

1. The VPN addresses for A, B, C, and D will be 192.168.1.1, 192.168.2.1, 192.168.3.1, and 192.168.4.1, respectively.

2. The name of the VPN comprising A, B, C, and D will be *abcd*.

This example is further explained in Figure 10.1.

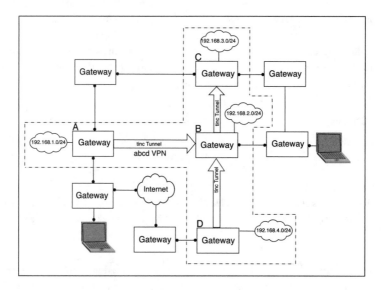

Figure 10.1   A network–network tinc tunneling example.

/etc/tinc/abcd/tinc.conf

All four peers in our sample scenario will have a similar tinc.conf file. The first two lines will be different for each peer, and the rest of the file will be the same for all peers.

The following are the contents of the tinc.conf file for peer A:

```
Name = A
ConnectTo = B
Hostnames = no
KeyExpire = 3600
PingTimeout = 60
PrivateKeyFile = /etc/tinc/abcd/rsa_key.priv
TapDevice = /dev/tap0
```

Peer B will be configured as follows:

```
Name = B
ConnectTo = D
Hostnames = no
KeyExpire = 3600
PingTimeout = 60
PrivateKeyFile = /etc/tinc/abcd/rsa_key.priv
TapDevice = /dev/tap0
```

The configuration file for peer C should contain the following:

```
Name = C
ConnectTo = B
Hostnames = no
KeyExpire = 3600
PingTimeout = 60
PrivateKeyFile = /etc/tinc/abcd/rsa_key.priv
TapDevice = /dev/tap0
```

Peer D will not be connecting to any other peers. Therefore, the `ConnectTo` option should be omitted, and the configuration file for D should look as follows:

```
Name = D
Hostnames = no
KeyExpire = 3600
PingTimeout = 60
PrivateKeyFile = /etc/tinc/abcd/rsa_key.priv
TapDevice = /dev/tap0
```

Host Configuration Files: /etc/tinc/abcd/hosts/{A,B,C,and D}

First, generate a pair of keys for each peer using the following:

```
[root@fox tinc]# tincd -n abcd -K
```

The public key for host A will be saved in /etc/tinc/hosts/A, for host B in /etc/tinc/hosts/B, and so on.

The host configuration file for peer A is as follows:

```
Subnet = 192.168.1.0/24
Address = 172.16.1.1
Port = 655

# here you should have the public key generated by tincd -K
-----BEGIN A's RSA PUBLIC KEY-----
[...]
-----END A's RSA PUBLIC KEY-----
```

For peer B, the host configuration file should contain the following:

```
Subnet = 192.168.2.0/24
Address = 172.16.2.1
Port = 655
```

```
# here you should have the public key generated by tincd -K
-----BEGIN B's RSA PUBLIC KEY-----
[…]
-----END B's RSA PUBLIC KEY-----
```

For peer C, the host configuration file should contain the following:

```
Subnet = 192.168.3.0/24
Address = 172.16.3.1
Port = 655

# here you should have the public key generated by tincd -K
-----BEGIN C's RSA PUBLIC KEY-----
[…]
-----END C's RSA PUBLIC KEY-----
```

Finally, peer D's host configuration file is as follows:

```
Subnet = 192.168.4.0/24
Address = 172.16.4.1
Port = 655

# here you should have the public key generated by tincd -K
-----BEGIN D's RSA PUBLIC KEY-----
[…]
-----END D's RSA PUBLIC KEY-----
```

Copy host configuration files between peers that will be connected to each other. The host configuration files should be put in the /etc/tinc/abcd/hosts directory.

For instance, because A will be connecting to B, A should have B's host configuration file, and B needs to have A's host configuration file. Similarly, make sure B and C as well as B and D have each other's host configuration files.

/etc/tinc/abcd/tinc-up

The tinc-up script will also be very similar on all four peers. The line that will be different is the tinc interface's IP address. The following is a commented version of a tinc-up script. Copy the file to each peer's /etc/tinc/abcd directory and uncomment the appropriate ifconfig line.

```
#!/bin/sh
#
# Note:
# Replace tap0 with $NETNAME, if you are using universal TUN/TAP driver
#
# bring interface down first
ifconfig tap0 down

# required by tinc
# sets up tap0 MAC address to a special value
# to ensure that tinc tunneling works
ifconfig tap0 hw ether fe:fd:00:00:00:00

# tinc interface's IP address
#
```

```
# For peer A, use:
# ifconfig tap0 192.168.1.1 netmask 255.255.255.0
#
# For peer B, use:
# ifconfig tap0 192.168.2.1 netmask 255.255.255.0
#
# For peer C, use:
# ifconfig tap0 192.168.3.1 netmask 255.255.255.0
#
# For peer D, use:
# ifconfig tap0 192.168.4.1 netmask 255.255.255.0

# make sure you have this line to disable ARP on
# the tinc interface
# (should not be necessary anymore in tinc v1.0)
ifconfig tap0 -arp
```

Host-Network Tunneling

The host-network sample scenario is a subset of the network-network scenario in which one of the networks consists of a single host. To explain how tinc can be used in the host-network scenario, lets take two peers, A and B, from the network-network scenario and assume that B does not have a separate network. Instead, B will be on A's 192.168.1.0/24 network. The provisions for this scenario are defined as follows:

1. The name of the VPN is *ab*.
2. A initiates a connection and B listens.
3. A's network is 192.168.1.0/24; A's real IP address is 172.16.1.1; A's VPN IP Address is 192.168.1.1.
4. B's VPN IP address is 192.168.1.2; B's real IP address is 172.16.5.1.

Figure 10.2 provides an overview of this scenario.

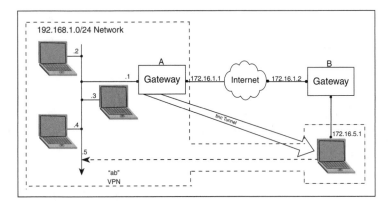

Figure 10.2 A host-network tinc tunneling example.

/etc/tinc/ab/tinc.conf

The contents of the main configuration file, `tinc.conf`, on A are as follows:

```
Name = A
ConnectTo = B
Hostnames = no
KeyExpire = 3600
PingTimeout = 60
PrivateKeyFile = /etc/tinc/ab/rsa_key.priv
TapDevice = /dev/tap0
```

For B, as with peer D in the network-network scenario, the main configuration file will be different in that it does not contain the `ConnectTo` option, which will cause B to wait for incoming connections:

```
Name = B
Hostnames = no
KeyExpire = 3600
PingTimeout = 60
PrivateKeyFile = /etc/tinc/ab/rsa_key.priv
TapDevice = /dev/tap0
```

Host Configuration Files: /etc/tinc/ab/hosts/{A,B}

As in the network-network scenario, make sure you generate RSA keypairs for A and B by running `tincd -n ab -K` on both hosts. Then switch to your favorite editor and insert the following information into `/etc/tinc/ab/hosts/A` and `/etc/tinc/ab/hosts/B` on A and B, respectively:

```
# /etc/tinc/ab/hosts/A
Subnet = 192.168.1.0/24
Address = 172.16.1.1
Port = 655


# here you should have A's public key generated by tincd -K
-----BEGIN A's RSA PUBLIC KEY-----
[…]
-----END A's RSA PUBLIC KEY-----

# /etc/tinc/ab/hosts/B
Subnet = 192.168.1.2/32
Address = 172.16.5.1
Port = 655


# here you should have B's public key generated by tincd -K
-----BEGIN B's RSA PUBLIC KEY-----
[…]
-----END B's RSA PUBLIC KEY-----
```

Copy A's `config` to B's `/etc/tinc/ab/hosts` and copy B's to A's `/etc/tinc/ab/hosts`. You are now done with host configuration files.

> **Note**
>
> As you've probably noticed, for B we used a subnet that consisted of only one IP address because the netmask was set to 255.255.255.255 (32 bits specified for the network part of the IP). This trick is known to cause `tinc` version 1.0-pre4 and older to hiccup, so don't be surprised if that happens. Download the latest version of `tinc` if you encounter something like this in your syslog:
>
> Jun 10 12:10:08 alvarez ab[1002]: Cannot route packet: unknown destination address
> ➥172.16.1.1

/etc/tinc/ab/tinc-up

Use the following file as a `tinc-up` script on both A and B. Don't forget to uncomment the appropriate `ifconfig` line on each of the peers.

```
#!/bin/sh
#
# Note:
# Replace tap0 with $NETNAME, if you are using universal TUN/TAP driver
#
ifconfig tap0 down
ifconfig tap0 hw ether fe:fd:00:00:00:00

# tinc interface's IP address
#
# For peer A, use:
# ifconfig tap0 192.168.1.1 netmask 255.255.255.0
#
# For peer B, use:
# ifconfig tap0 192.168.1.2 netmask 255.255.255.0

# Should not be necessary in tinc v1.0
ifconfig tap0 -arp
```

Host–Host Tunneling

By further limiting the network-network scenario, it is possible to make each of the interconnected networks consist of only one host. This is achieved, as before, by using 32 bits to specify the network address (adding /32 in the `Subnet` option), which corresponds to the netmask of 255.255.255.255.

Fundamentally, the configuration for this scenario will be very similar to the one for the host-network scenario. Therefore, we will take the host-network scenario as a baseline from which to start and will focus on the modifications you need to make to get the host-host example up and running.

Let's examine the provisions we use in our host-host example:

1. The name of a VPN is *ab*.

2. The VPN comprises two peers: A and B.

> **Note**
>
> Note that we *reversed* the roles of A and B such that A is now the listener and B the originator.

3. Peer A's VPN IP address is 192.168.1.1 and its real IP address is 172.168.1.1.

4. Peer B's VPN IP address is 192.168.1.2 and its real IP address is 172.168.5.1.

Although our sample host-host scenario is fairly simple, you might still find it useful to have a picture in front of you delineating main elements, addresses, and interfaces to better understand what's really happening. Figure 10.3 shows a sketch of the sample scenario.

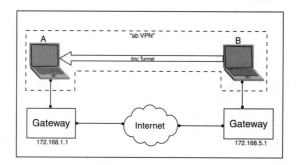

Figure 10.3   A host-host tinc tunneling example.

/etc/tinc/ab/tinc.conf

For peer A, you should omit the `ConnectTo` option because A is going to be listening for incoming connections. Accordingly, for peer B, this option should be added to make it connect to A. Here is A's `tinc.conf`:

```
Name = A
Hostnames = no
KeyExpire = 3600
PingTimeout = 60
PrivateKeyFile = /etc/tinc/ab/rsa_key.priv
TapDevice = /dev/tap0
```

For B, *tinc.conf* should have the following options:

```
Name = B
ConnectTo = A
Hostnames = no
```

```
KeyExpire = 3600
PingTimeout = 60
PrivateKeyFile = /etc/tinc/ab/rsa_key.priv
TapDevice = /dev/tap0
```

Host Configuration Files: /etc/tinc/ab/hosts/{A,B}

As before, generate keys for both peers using tincd -K. Then set the number of network bits in the Subnet option on both peers to 32. This will cause tinc to interpret the subnet address as a single IP. Host configuration files for peers A and B are as follows:

```
# /etc/tinc/ab/hosts/A
Subnet = 192.168.1.1/32
Address = 172.16.1.1
Port = 655

# here you should have A's public key generated by tincd -K
-----BEGIN A's RSA PUBLIC KEY-----
[...]
-----END A's RSA PUBLIC KEY-----

# /etc/tinc/ab/hosts/B
Subnet = 192.168.1.2/32
Address = 172.16.5.1
Port = 655

# here you should have B's public key generated by tincd -K
-----BEGIN B's RSA PUBLIC KEY-----
[...]
-----END B's RSA PUBLIC KEY-----
```

/etc/tinc/ab/tinc-up

Use the following tinc-up script on peer A without changes. For peer B, you will need to change the IP address to B's IP of 192.168.1.5.

```
#!/bin/sh
#
# Note:
# Replace tap0 with $NETNAME, if you are using universal TUN/TAP driver
#
ifconfig tap0 down
ifconfig tap0 hw ether fe:fd:00:00:00:00
ifconfig tap0 192.168.1.1 netmask 255.255.255.0
# Should not be necessary anymore in tinc v1.0
ifconfig tap0 -arp
```

Dynamic Peers

You might find scenarios described in this section useful when one or more of the peers that make up your VPN have dynamic IP addresses. For example, some ISPs allocate IP addresses to clients using DHCP. Another typical example is when you have dial-up PPP or SLIP access and your ISP dynamically selects an IP from a pool of addresses every time you log in.

Overview

If you are looking for basic ideas that you can use with dynamic peers, here is a brief overview of what we are going to describe in this section.

Use One Point-to-Point Link at a Time

Concentrate on the point-to-point links that form your VPN. Remember that tinc uses both TCP and UDP and that both of the protocols either use port 655 (by default) or the port you specified in the appropriate host configuration file.

Use the TCPonly Option to Disable UDP

If one of the peers in a point-to-point link is behind a Masquerading/NAT firewall and you are having problems with UDP traffic coming through, you can use the TCPonly option in both peers' host configuration files. This option will cause tinc to transmit everything over TCP and to completely disable UDP transport.

Use Dynamic DNS to Introduce a Static Property

If you can find (or create, for example, using dynamic DNS) something static about one of the dynamic peers, use that property to connect to that peer. For instance, use dynamic DNS to assign a static hostname to a dynamic peer and then use the hostname with the ConnectTo option.

Use Triangulation or Changing Network Topology

If both peers are dynamic and it is hard to find or create something static about them, use *triangulation*. This implies that at least one of your peers is static. If that's the case, simply redefine the topology of your network and set up dynamic peers to connect to the static peer. The idea is illustrated in Figure 10.4.

As you can see, given peers A and B that are behind a firewall, you replace one connection between A and B with two connections to a third peer C that has a static IP (that is, AC and BC; AB = AC + BC), hence triangulation.

Now lets zoom in on your VPN. Lets consider each point-to-point link that is a part of your VPN independently. Are any of the peers behind a Masquerading/NAT firewall? Are both peers dynamic or just one of them? If one of the peers has a static IP, you can move on to configuration; otherwise, you will need to figure out something static about one of the peers so that the other peer can connect to it.

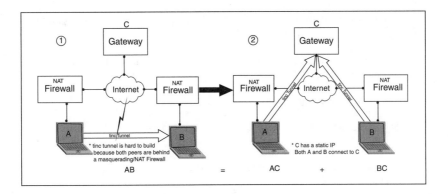

Figure 10.4 Triangulation: changing network topology to accommodate dynamic peers.

Here are a couple of resources you might find helpful to create a static property for a peer that has a dynamic IP. The easiest way to do it is to utilize the dynamic DNS service (see Chapter 9 for a list of dynamic DNS providers available online), which assigns a static domain name to the IP address of a dynamic peer. You can also try using a forwarding rule within a firewall configuration. Presumably, this rule would be updated every time the IP address of the appropriate dynamic peer changes.

The following sections explain two typical scenarios that you might have with dynamic peers.

Network-Network Tunneling with Dynamic Peers

As a basis for the scenario in this section, we will consider the network-network scenario with four peers—A, B, C, and D—that was described in detail earlier in the "Network-Network Tunneling" section. The original scenario is depicted in Figure 10.1.

To illustrate how to deal with dynamic peers, we will assume that peers A and D in the original scenario are dynamic. We will then list the changes you would need to make in the original network-network scenario to accommodate that.

Changes to the Original Network-Network Scenario

As you remember, peer A connects to peer B, and peer B connects to peer D. If we make peers A and D dynamic (so that they both have dynamic IP addresses), the change will only affect D's configuration because D is the one to which other peer (B) connects. You will not need to change A's configuration because A is connecting to another peer. Simply omit A's IP address in its host configuration file.

For D, you should change its host configuration file, (/etc/tinc/abcd/hosts/D) and specify D's *domain name,* not IP address, in the file. Use one of the dynamic DNS service providers to obtain a domain name for D and set up D so that it sends an update to the appropriate dynamic DNS provider whenever D's IP address changes. There is usually an FAQ for each provider detailing the process for IP address updates.

Assuming the domain name you've registered for D is `D.dyndns.org`, here is what D's modified host configuration file should look like:

```
# Subnet on the virtual private network that is local to this host
Subnet = 192.168.1.2/32

Address = D.dyndns.org

# 655 is the default port so you can omit or change this, if you want
Port = 655

# this key should be your peer's public key
-----BEGIN RSA PUBLIC KEY-----
[…]
-----END RSA PUBLIC KEY-----
```

Make sure you copy the updated file to the peers that are going to be connecting to D (in our scenario, there is only one such peer, B).

The PingTimeout *Option*

The configuration for the preceding scenario is more complex than just signing up for a dynamic DNS domain and modifying the host configuration files. Think, for instance, about the situation when D goes down, comes back up, and updates dynamic DNS. Obviously, B should be notified in some way about the need to reconnect and reload the DNS record for D.

Of course, B might be able to sense that a TCP connection to D was closed, but in many cases, D will not be able to exit gracefully and close the TCP connection by sending a TCP_FIN packet, so B will have to time out. Timing out can often be undesirable because, although B is timing out, the tinc tunnel is down even if D comes back up quickly.

Therefore, you might find it helpful to look at the `PingTimeout` option used in B's main configuration file. If you adjust the value of this option, you might be able to minimize the downtime of the connection. You should be careful, though, because setting the option to a small value on slow or overloaded links might lead to problems.

You need to also think about how you are going to restart tinc on B and D if the link goes down. Sometimes it is enough to use tinc and its /etc/rc.d/init.d script as is. You can also solve this problem by writing a simple shell wrapper for tincd that will restart it and possibly notify peers in the event of a failure.

Changing Network Topology

So, why are we connecting from B to D? Would it not be easier to simply reverse the direction and make D connect to B because B has a static address? The answer to this question will depend on your specific configuration. For example, it will work if one of your peers is static, but what if *both* peers are dynamic?

The question brings up the idea of *changing network topology to accommodate dynamic peers*. Refer to Figure 10.4 for a scenario in which dynamic DNS service and port forwarding are unnecessary. Of course, changing network topology is not always acceptable, and this is why we described the preceding scenario. In many cases, however, it will save you a lot of time.

Masquerading/NAT Gateways and UDP

We will now describe two basic scenarios: one is when you want to connect *to* a peer behind a masquerading/NAT firewall and the other is when you want to connect *from* such a peer.

Keep in mind that if *both* peers are behind a NAT gateway or firewall, it might be better to use triangulation (if you can find a third peer with a static IP address), as was shown in Figure 10.4. Thus, for peers A and B behind a masquerading/NAT firewall, you replace one tinc connection between A and B with two connections to a third peer, C, that has a static IP—AC and BC.

Connecting to a Peer Behind a Firewall

If one of the peers is behind a masquerading/NAT firewall, it can be quite difficult to get tinc to connect to that peer unless the firewall is set up to forward all traffic on a certain port to the peer behind the firewall. You can achieve this, for example, by using ssh. Run the following command on the firewall:

```
[root@fox tinc]# ssh -L 9000:172.16.1.1:650 localhost
```

This will tell ssh to redirect local TCP port 9000 to port 650 of the firewalled tinc peer whose IP address is 172.16.1.1.

Forwarding a TCP port is not enough, however, and you also need to take care of the fact that tinc uses UDP. Most NAT firewalls do not do address translation for stateless protocols, so you will need to either tell tinc to disable UDP or force your firewall to NAT UDP packets.

Disabling UDP is easier and, on recent versions of tinc, can be done by utilizing the TCPonly option on both peers. Be aware that the code for this option is experimental as of version 1.0pre4 of tinc and is not present in some of the earlier versions of tinc.

Connecting from a Peer Behind a Firewall

As previously mentioned, because tinc uses TCP and UDP, a masquerading/NAT firewall needs to forward both protocols. If your firewall cannot do network address translation for UDP packets, you will need to configure tinc to use TCP as the only transport. To do that, you should use the TCPonly option as described earlier.

The next problem you might need to resolve is when the source port for all tinc packets sent through the firewall is replaced by the NAT function of that firewall (if the port address translation [PAT] feature is enabled) so that the port number becomes dynamic. In such a case, you need to make sure you do not specify the Port option in the host configuration file of the peer from which you want to establish a connection. Also, if you have removed the `Port` option, do not forget to copy the modified host configuration file for a peer to all its peers.

Troubleshooting

We already have described a number of the errors that might occur during configuration. In this section, we will focus on the errors that occur when you try to run `tinc`. The description of options and messages in this section is based on `tinc-1.0pre4` documentation. If you want to get the most recent information, go to the `tinc` web site at `http://tinc.nl.linux.org`. However, most of the ideas we describe here are generic enough to be useful regardless of which version of `tinc` you are using.

> **Note**
>
> If you have no idea why your `tinc` VPN does not work, remember that you can always get answers on the `tinc` mailing list. To ask a question, send an email to `tinc@nl.linux.org`. Our experience with this list has been positive. The responses are usually prompt and adequate. Note, however, that unless you are subscribed to the mailing list, you will need visit `tinc`'s web site to view responses to your question.

Using the *tinc* Log for Troubleshooting

To effectively troubleshoot `tinc`, you will need to be able to view `tinc` messages in the syslog, set debug levels, and interpret various runtime error messages. These elements will be described in the following three sections.

Viewing *tinc* Log Messages

Because `tinc` logs its messages using syslog, you can view the messages on most systems simply by typing the following:

```
[root@fox tinc]# egrep tinc <your_vpn_name> /var/log/messages | tail --lines=80 -f
➡..
```

If your system has a modified `/etc/syslog.conf`, the log information might reside in a file different from `/var/log/messages`, so you will need to adjust the preceding command accordingly.

Alternatively, you can simply try to visually browse through the syslog file, as follows:

```
[root@fox tinc]# more /var/log/messages
```

Note that the amount of data written out to the syslog by `tinc` depends on the debug level you specified when starting `tincd`. A detailed description of the debug levels is given in the next section.

Debug Levels

You can specify different debug levels when starting `tincd`.

Literally, the more `-d` options that are given to `tincd`, the more messages it will log. Each level inherits all messages of the previous level.

If you do not specify any debug options, `tinc` will do basic logging, such as connection attempts, start/stop messages, and any serious errors.

Table 10.3 provides a detailed description of each logging level you can request if you run `tinc` with the appropriate option.

Table 10.3 **Logging Levels for *tinc***

Option	Description
`-d`	Causes `tinc` to log all connections made to other `tinc` daemons
`-dd`	Causes `tinc` to log status and error messages from other `tinc` daemons
`-ddd`	Causes `tinc` to log all requests that are exchanged with other `tinc` daemons, including authentication, key exchange, and connection list updates
`-dddd`	Causes `tinc` to log a copy of everything received on the TCP link (called the meta socket in `tinc`'s documentation)
`-ddddd`	Log all network traffic over the virtual private network

Error Messages

The following is a list of the most common error messages you can see when running `tinc`. Most of these messages are visible only in the syslog. See the syslog viewing section discussed earlier for information on how to view `tinc`-related messages there.

- `Could not open /dev/tap0: No such device`. You forgot to `modprobe netlink_dev` or to `modprobe ethertap`. You forgot to compile `Netlink device emulation` in the kernel.

- `Can't write to /dev/net/tun: No such device`. You forgot to `modprobe tun` or forgot to `compile Universal TUN/TAP driver` into the kernel.

- `Packet with destination 1.2.3.4 is looping back to us!` Note that you will only see this message if you specified a debug level of 5 or higher.

  This error indicates that packets are being sent out to the `tap` device, but according to the `Subnet` directives in your host configuration file, those packets should be accepted by your host.

  It is likely that the `Subnet` line in your host configuration file is wrong. You probably specified a netmask that is just as inclusive as the netmask of the `tinc`'s tap device set in the tinc-up script. The latter netmask should in almost all cases be more inclusive, so you will need to rethink your configuration. Change it to a subnet that is accepted locally by another interface or, if that is not the case, try changing the prefix length to /32.

- **Network doesn't work, syslog shows only packets of length 46.** This problem usually manifests itself in the following messages:

```
Jan 1 12:00:00 host tinc.net[1234]: Read packet of length 46 from tap device
Jan 1 12:00:00 host tinc.net[1234]: Trying to look up 0.0.192.168 in connection
➥list failed!
```

  Add ifconfig $NETNAME -arp to your /etc/tinc/<*your_vpn*>/tinc-up script.

- **Network address and subnet mask do not match!** The Subnet field must contain a network address. If you only want to use one IP address, set the netmask to /32, which corresponds to 255.255.255.255 (an example of a least-inclusive mask).

- **This is a bug: net.c:253: 24: <Some error>.** This is something that, according to tinc authors and developers, should not have happened, so they strongly encourage users to report such errors. You can go to tinc's web site and use the contact info from the site to email the details of the error.

- **Error reading RSA key file `rsa_key.priv': No such file or directory.** Make sure you specify a complete pathname for the RSA key in tinc.conf. Specifying a relative path will not work because tinc changes its directory to / when starting to avoid keeping a mount point busy.

Using *tcpdump* to Capture *tinc*'s Traffic

Because most of the traffic transmitted by tinc over the unprotected network is encrypted, one of the few reasons you might still want to use tcpdump on regular network interfaces is simply verification of the existence of traffic from or to specific IP addresses and ports.

For instance, if tinc is having problems establishing a connection or traffic is not coming through, run the following command to see what is actually transmitted:

```
[root@fox tinc]# tcpdump -i eth0 'src host <peer's_real_ip> and src port 655 and
➥dst host <local_ip> and dst port 655 and tcp'
```

Make sure you adjust port numbers in the preceding example to reflect the numbers you used in host configuration files of both peers. Replace the tcp option with the udp option to see the data transmitted over UDP.

You can also run tcpdump on a tinc tunneling interface. In this case, you should be able to see the decrypted traffic tunneled through the tinc interface:

```
[root@fox tinc]# tcpdump -i tap0 'src host <local_tinc_ip> and dst host
➥<peers_tinc_ip> and tcp'
```

Note

For the universal TUN/TAP driver, replace `tap0` with the name of the VPN for which you want to capture traffic (there should be a tunneling interface with the same name).

Limitations

In our opinion, there are several areas in which `tinc` could benefit from increased functionality. In particular, it would be useful if `tinc` could tunnel different kinds of traffic, such as ethernet frames or Novell's IPX/SPX. There is also a lack of policy control. This is especially important for extranets. Additionally, there is an absence of concrete integrated performance and throughput measurement tools, an essential function for determining how scalable a VPN solution is.

Because of the first limitation, `tinc` cannot forward lower-layer protocols as a bridge and is only capable of handling IPv4 traffic as a router. Many people request this feature because they want to use NetBEUI, which is utilized by Windows Network Neighborhood. The good news is that the code for this feature is in development as of version 1.0-pre4 and should be available soon.

The second limitation has two sides to it. On one side, `tinc` developers want to make the package as lightweight and easy-to-use as possible. On the other side, it is important not to exclude useful features. Striking a balance can be difficult, but `tinc` developers seem very responsive to user comments, so there is a chance they might include policy management mechanisms in future versions. For now, your best bet is either to use a commercial solution such as Check Point's Policy Editor or to define and enforce a policy using such tools as `ipchains`, `DiffServ`, and so on.

Finally, what is missing (in our opinion) is a concise and thorough study of `tinc` performance. It is unclear what the overhead is, how `tinc`'s performance degrades when additional hosts are added, what bottlenecks are introduced with the automatic propagation of routing, and so forth. Some of these limitations, however, are common to the majority of open-source products. `tinc` is not an exception.

Summary

We started this chapter by arguing that understanding your alternatives is an important step in selecting a VPN package appropriate to your needs. By now, you should have an idea of `tinc`'s strengths and weaknesses. From our experience with `tinc`, we can say that it is a great tool with common limitations. Plus, `tinc` is not administratively demanding. It is well supported, relatively easy to use, and more importantly, free. Decide for yourself.

IV

Appendices

Commercial Solutions

ALTHOUGH WE GENERALLY ADVOCATE THE USE of open-source software, sometimes an open-source solution is not adequate. For instance, you might need extensive user support for your VPN, which is usually limited in open-source products. Alternatively, you might want a VPN solution for a large corporation; in this situation, you might be better off buying a product off the shelf. Finally, you might decide to buy a specialized piece of hardware without even bothering to install anything. For all of the above-mentioned cases, you will need to find a vendor and then choose. To assist you in choosing the solution that is right for you, we have compiled a list of companies offering commercial VPN products (see Table A.1).

Table A.1 **Companies Offering Commercial VPN Products**

Firm	**Commercial VPN Product Description**
Symantec Enterprise Solutions `http://enterprisesecurity. symantec.com`	IPSec-based Symantec Enterprise VPN. Also offers Symantec Enterprise Firewall, which supports a number of user-authentication methods, including Digital Certificates, Radius, and so on.

Table A.1 **Continued**

Firm	Commercial VPN Product Description
Enterasys Networks www.enterasys.com	Aurorean VPN client software that uses IPSec to establish secure tunnels. Both IP and IPX are supported for encapsulation.
Certicom Corp. www.moviansecurity.com www.certicom.com	MovianVPN Wireless VPN client for portable devices. Tunnel mode ESP/IPSec and IKE are supported.
Alcatel www.cid.alcatel.com/ doctypes/product/html/ n230.jhtml	Alcatel 713x Secure VPN products. The products support IPSec and are certified by ICSA.
Cisco www.cisco.com	Cisco VPN clients, Cisco PIX firewall, and Cisco VPN 300x concentrators. The latter also supports IPSec through NAT, which is one of its distinct features.
CheckPoint Software www.checkpoint.com/products/	CheckPoint VPN-1/Firewall-1 suite as well as a number of other VPN products such as VPN-1 Gateway, VPN-1 SecuRemote, VPN-1 Secure Client, VPN-1 Secure Server, High Availability for VPN-1, QoS for VPN-1, and VPN-1 Accelerator Card.
Intel www.intel.com/network/idc/ products/vpn_gateway.htm	Intel Netstructure VPN Client, VPN Deployment Tool, and 31xx VPN Gateway. The solution is certified by ICSA and supports IPSec and L2TP, offloading of intensive en/decryption to external hardware, X.509v3 certificates, and so on.
BorderWare Technologies www.borderware.com	Firewall Server Product with optional VPN Client and Server, both supporting IKE/IPSec.
Entrust www.entrust.com/products/ vpn/index.htm	VPN solutions: Remote-User VPN and Office-Office VPN suites. Among products are Enrollment Server for VPN, Entrust Authority Self-Administration Server, Entrust Authority Roaming Server, Entrust Entelligence.
Lucent www.lucent.com	VPN Firewall Brick Hardware Solution as well as Lucent Security Management Server (LSMS). ICSA and NSA certified; supports IPSec.
SafeNet www.safenet-inc.com	SafeNet SoftRemote VPN package.
Lasat SafePipe www.lasat.com	Linux-based box that can be used for a VPN. IPSec is supported.

Table A.1 **Continued**

Firm	Commercial VPN Product Description
Linux Magic www.linuxmagic.com/vpn/	VPN/Firewall product using FreeS/WAN.
Merilus www.merilus.com	Firecard, a PCI card with firewall, VPN, and network management functionality embedded.
SSH Communications Security www.ssh.com/products/vpn/ index.cfm	SSH Complete VPN solution. Consists of three parts: a physical SSH VPN gateway, SSH Sentinel VPN Client, and SSH VPN Central Manager. Provides support for IPSEC and PKI. Advanced feature: SSH NAT Traversal for VPNs.
F-Secure VPN+	VPN+ Client and Server versions. The Server version currently (2001) costs around $700. F-Secure VPN+ works over IPSec, is capable of forwarding, filtering, and authenticating VPN traffic. The package uses a centralized, policy-based management to implement corporate security policy.
PGPvpn/PGPnet www.f-secure.com	IPSec-based VPN tool. Supports X.509v3 certificates; Ciphers: 3DES, AES, Twofish, IDEA, CAST ciphers. See also PGPfire—a firewall solution from PGP.

B

Selecting a Cipher

I F YOUR VPN PACKAGE SUPPORTS MULTIPLE ciphers, you might wonder whether the cipher used by default is good enough for you. To determine the cipher that is adequate for your needs, you might find it helpful to learn about popular ciphers and the criteria you can use to select them. In addition, it is essential to understand what parameters ciphers might have and what those parameters mean.

Note that selecting an adequate cipher is only one piece of the puzzle. For example, one of the other pieces is key distribution. If you have not solved the problem of distributing keys, even the most advanced cipher will not help you. If security is a big concern, we recommend that you conduct a detailed risk assessment of various components of your VPN. It should give you an idea of what other elements you might need to adjust in addition to selecting a different cipher.

In this appendix, we will focus on six popular symmetric ciphers: 3DES, AES Rijndael, RC4, Blowfish, IDEA, and CAST. We will briefly evaluate these ciphers based on each of the following criteria: security, performance, and availability. We will also describe the generic parameters that these and other ciphers can have, such as key length, block size, and mode (ECB, CBC, OFB, CFB, and so on).

The other goal we have for this appendix is to discuss the selection of parameters for asymmetric ciphers. We will not talk about choosing an asymmetric cipher because currently there are not many to choose from. (RSA and DSA are the two algorithms that dominate.) Instead, we will explain to you how different parameters affect security and performance of an asymmetric cipher.

The examples in this section will be based on the OpenSSL v0.9.6b, a free cryptographic library used by many open-source VPN packages as well as other popular software, such as Apache, OpenSSH, sendmail, and Samba.

Essential Cipher Parameters

This section provides a description of several important cipher parameters, such as key length, key lifetime, and cipher modes, as well as our recommendations for how to choose the parameters.

Key Length and Lifetime

We will begin by describing typical key lengths. Key lengths used these days are usually 128–256 bits as well as 1024–4096 for symmetric and asymmetric ciphers, respectively. The maximum number of attempts that an attacker would need to break the ciphers with such key lengths using brute force is 2^{128}-2^{256} for symmetric and 2^{1024}-2^{4096} for asymmetric. Note that even a 128-bit key (2^{128} keys to try) can keep the attacker capable of one terabyte of attempts per second busy for a quite a while—close to 10^{20}, which is longer than the age of the universe. So what is the best way for you to choose a key length?

There are several important points you need to consider when deciding on key length for both symmetric and asymmetric ciphers.

First, do not rely on key length by itself to guarantee security. In principle, the strength of a cipher should be determined by its key length; in practice, the cipher's design is just as important. Increase key length if you want more security, but do not underestimate the importance of other factors such as key distribution and the cryptographic strength of the cipher you are using.

Second, many packages use both symmetric and asymmetric ciphers as a method to increase the security of the overall solution. However, the security of a system is only as great as the security of its weakest link. If you use RC4 with 40-bit keys as your symmetric cipher and 2,048-bit RSA as your asymmetric cipher, there is a good chance that RC4 is your weakest link. In this case, you have at least two options. One is to improve the security of the system by increasing the RC4 keysize or switching to a different symmetric cipher with bigger keys. The other option is to stick with 40-bit symmetric keys and decrease the RSA keysize to 512-bit. It probably will not make the level security of your system any lower because it is already low enough. For medium security, we recommend 128-bit symmetric with 2,048-bit asymmetric keys. For high security, 256-bit symmetric and 4,096-bit asymmetric keys should suffice at this time. This might entail additional planning, however, particularly because many symmetric ciphers only support 128-bit keys.

Third, the lifetime of a key is important. If you can select it when selecting a cipher, we definitely encourage you to do so. A corollary is that the frequency of key change can be crucial as well, particularly for symmetric ciphers. Nonetheless, the rapidly growing availability of centralized and distributed computing power will always have a tidal effect on the operational decision-making processes of those who desire to protect information with any cryptographic measures.

Note

Note that some packages, such as tinc or clPe, renegotiate symmetric keys for you automatically. Usually this happens after a certain number of packets have been transmitted. Thus, you might not even need to change keys yourself if you turn this option on in the package you are using.

Modes

You might have already heard about different modes in which block ciphers can work. You can use modes to make your system more secure, efficient, and fault tolerant. Here is an example:

```
OpenSSL> enc ?
[…]
-des-ecb    -des-cbc      -des-cfb      -des-ofb      -des  (des-cbc)
-des-ede    -des-ede-cbc  -des-ede-cfb  -des-ede-ofb  -desx-none
-des-ede3   -des-ede3-cbc -des-ede3-cfb -des-ede3-ofb -des3 (des-ede3-cbc)
-idea-ecb   -idea-cbc     -idea-cfb     -idea-ofb     -idea (idea-cbc)
-rc2-ecb    -rc2-cbc      -rc2-cfb      -rc2-ofb      -rc2  (rc2-cbc)
-bf-ecb     -bf-cbc       -bf-cfb       -bf-ofb       -bf   (bf-cbc)
-cast5-ecb  -cast5-cbc    -cast5-cfb    -cast5-ofb    -cast (cast5-cbc)
-rc5-ecb    -rc5-cbc      -rc5-cfb      -rc5-ofb      -rc5  (rc5-cbc)
```

In this example, we obtained a list of supported symmetric ciphers for OpenSSL. As you see, each of these ciphers has a three-letter mode name appended to it. There are four commonly supported modes: Electronic Codebook (ECB), Cipher Block Chaining (CBC), Cipher Feedback (CFB), and Output Feedback (OFB).

If a cipher runs in Electronic Codebook mode, it means the cipher will encrypt each block independently. The advantage of this mode is its simplicity. Operations on blocks can be done in parallel as well, and this might make your system more efficient. The major problem of this mode is that an attacker can detect patterns and change a secure message by rearranging, repeating, or removing blocks without knowing the key.

If a cipher uses Cipher Block Chaining, encrypted blocks depend on each other. More specifically, the plaintext of the current block is XORed (that is, exclusively added so that the resulting bit is 1 only if either the current bit of the block or the current bit of the XOR mask is 1) with the ciphertext of the previous block and then is encrypted. The advantage of this mode is that an attacker can't change one block (except for the last one) without affecting the others. The drawback is that very long messages will still have patterns.

The other two modes—Cipher Feedback and Output Feedback—are similar to each other. In CFB mode, the current plaintext is XORed with the encrypted ciphertext of the previous block. In OFB mode, the current plaintext is XORed with a value that does not depend on plaintext or ciphertext.

One of the advantages of CFB mode is that it makes it possible for a block cipher to encrypt less data than a block size. This way, for example, 1 byte of data can be encrypted immediately without waiting for the other 7 bytes (for a 64-bit block cipher) to arrive. The disadvantage of CFB is that bit errors that occur during transmission are propagated and affect the decryption of subsequent blocks. OFB addresses this issue and is considered to be more fault tolerant; however, OFB has its problems also. In particular, if attackers know one of the plaintext blocks, they can replace it with a false one. There are other problems with OFB, so an additional mode was proposed to fix them (Counter mode).

This is by no means a comprehensive overview, but by now, you at least have a basic idea of what different cipher modes actually mean. We prefer using CBC or CFB because ECB is probably not the most secure of the four and OFB has its own problems. There is no universal solution, so we recommend that you take a closer look at each mode and decide which one is best for you based on your priorities and the results of a risk analysis. In short, weigh the options based on cost, long-term support options, and functionality. Note that the cost of protecting your information should always be quantifiably less than the cost of its compromise.

Selection Criteria

In this subsection, we consider six popular symmetric ciphers in light of three selection criteria: security, performance, and availability.

Security

Although all six of the popular symmetric ciphers we are considering (3DES, AES Rijndael, RC4, Blowfish, IDEA, and CAST) are relatively secure, some of them are believed to provide a higher level of security than others. In the paragraphs that follow, we will select our top three ciphers out of the six symmetric ciphers.

First, it is our belief that, all things being equal, one of the best tests of a security solution is time. If a cipher has been known and used for years with its details openly published, there is a good chance that if it had any major flaws, they already would have been found. There is no guarantee of this, of course. However, it is likely that the flaws would have been found. Therefore, it is generally a good idea to stick with older, well-tested ciphers.

Coming from this point of view, a typical example of such a cipher would be 3DES. 3DES itself is not old, but it is based on DES, which has been known for several decades. One of the major problems with DES is its key size; it uses 56-bit keys (with the remaining 8 bits being used for error detection) that can be attacked using brute force in a matter of days, sometimes even hours. To fix the problem, the 3DES cipher uses either two 56-bit keys combined into one 112-bit key or three 56-bit keys combined into one 168-bit key. Thus, if you prefer the time-test argument, use 3DES. On that basis, we will put it as number one on our list.

Recently, an Advanced Encryption Standard algorithm designed to replace DES was finally selected after several years of analysis and competition. The winner is called Rijndael. The cipher has undergone a lot of scrutiny by leading security experts throughout the world and has been competing with a number of other highly appraised ciphers. As a direct result of the comprehensive analysis and comparison, we decided to put AES Rijndael as number two on our list.

Finally, many experts, including the famed author of *Applied Cryptography*, Bruce Schneier, believe that IDEA is currently one of the most secure ciphers available (too bad it is patented). Because of its strong mathematical basis, we make IDEA our third choice.

In addition to selecting the top three ciphers, the following is a list of the supported parameters for each cipher we are considering:

- **3DES**. 112- or 168-bit keys, 64-bit blocks.
- **AES Rijndael**. 128-, 192-, or 256-bit keys; 128-, 192-, or 256-bit blocks.
- **IDEA**. 128-bit keys, 64-bit blocks.
- **Blowfish**. Up to 448-bit keys, 64-bit blocks.
- **RC4**. 40- or 128-bit keys, stream cipher (no blocks).
- **CAST**. 40- or 128-bit keys, 64-bit blocks.

Performance

To determine the performance of our six symmetric ciphers, we used a PC with two 750Mhz Intel Processors and 1GB of RAM. The PC was running Linux with 2.4.3-SMP kernel. The following is the performance chart we obtained using the OpenSSL library interface (YMMV):

```
[root@fox] # openssl
OpenSSL> speed
[...]
OpenSSL 0.9.6b 9 Jul 2001
built on: Mon Jul  9 22:39:13 PDT 2001
options:bn(64,32) md2(int) rc4(idx,int) des(ptr,risc1,16,long) idea(int)
blowfish(idx)

compiler: gcc -fPIC -DTHREADS -D_REENTRANT -DDSO_DLFCN -DHAVE_DLFCN_H -DL_ENDIAN -
DTERMIO -O3 -fomit-frame-pointer -m4
86 -Wall -DSHA1_ASM -DMD5_ASM -DRMD160_ASM
```

```
The 'numbers' are in 1000s of bytes per second processed.

blk size(bytes) 8          64         256        1024      8192
rc4            56622.25k  78368.26k  83119.45k  84258.47k 84555.09k
des3           5841.83k   6162.79k   6200.32k   6210.56k  6215.00k
idea cbc       8335.61k   9087.53k   9199.79k   9228.97k  9262.42k
blowfish cbc 22650.41k   26011.43k  26582.95k  26670.08k 26796.03k
cast cbc     22178.06k   25689.28k  26240.68k  26422.61k 26462.89k
```

From this chart, you can see that the two leaders are RC4 and Blowfish, with maximum speeds of 84.5 and 26.7 MB/sec, respectively. CAST is also fairly close with 26.4 MB/sec. The slowest of the five tested ciphers was 3DES with 6.2 MB/sec.

The current version of OpenSSL did not have support for the AES Rijndael's cipher, so we were not able to test it. However, the data from AES specifications suggests 27, 22, and 19 Mb/sec (for some reason the specs say Mbits, not MBytes, which makes Rijndael much slower, but there is probably a typo in the specs) for an ANSI C implementation with 128-, 192-, and 256-bit keys.

We also have tested RSA and DSA with different key sizes. The results of our tests are as follows:

```
sign    verify    sign/s verify/s
rsa  512 bits  0.0018s  0.0002s  555.2   6409.8
rsa 1024 bits  0.0091s  0.0005s  109.9   2157.9
rsa 2048 bits  0.0548s  0.0016s   18.3    637.5
rsa 4096 bits  0.3668s  0.0055s    2.7    180.2
                 sign    verify   sign/s verify/s
dsa  512 bits  0.0016s  0.0019s  631.0    531.6
dsa 1024 bits  0.0046s  0.0057s  217.7    176.3
dsa 2048 bits  0.0153s  0.0185s   65.2     54.2
```

Note

A number of factors affecting performance might be different in your case (such as cache sizes, system bus, processing power, and so on), so you might find it useful to perform similar tests on your machine to get an idea of the performance of the ciphers you are going to use.

Note that for asymmetric algorithms, the performance for the four common key sizes differs significantly for both RSA and DSA. As you can see, the trade-off between security and performance of asymmetric algorithms becomes critical. Decide which one is more important for you and choose the key length accordingly.

Availability

By availability, in this case we mean whether you need to pay for using a cipher as well as whether the use of the cipher is restricted in any way. Of the six symmetric ciphers we are considering, two are patented. Those are IDEA and CAST.

The details on the availability of all six ciphers are as follows:

- **IDEA.** The IDEA cipher is patented by ETH/Ascom-Tech of Switzerland. If you want to use it for commercial use, you need to obtain a license. For non-commercial use, however, the IDEA cipher is free.

- **CAST.** The CAST cipher is patented by Entrust, but it is free for both commercial and noncommercial use.

- **AES Rijndael, 3DES, RC4, and Blowfish.** These are free for both noncommercial and commercial use.

C

Glossary

Access Control List (ACL)   A set of data associated with a resource that defines entities that are allowed or denied access to the resource.

Advanced Encryption Standard (AES) Rijndael   A new symmetric cipher officially selected by NIST to replace DES. The cipher supports 128-, 192-, and 256-bit keys with varying block sizes.

asymmetric/public-key cipher   A cryptographic algorithm that uses different keys for encryption and decryption. The algorithm uses a keypair that consists of a private and a public key so that it is computationally infeasible to derive a public key from a private one.

authentication   The action of verifying information such as an identity, a credential, or ownership of something.

Authentication Header (AH)   The part of the IPSec protocol suite that provides authentication service to IP packets.

Authoritative   Can be used to describe either a type of a DNS server or a response to a DNS query. An authoritative DNS server contains a "master" copy of a DNS zone that is generated based on the server's local configuration, possibly with the help of another name server. Authoritative response is the response from an authoritative DNS server.

authorization   The act of determining what an entity is allowed to do or have access to; this usually occurs after authentication and relies on it.

Certificate Authority   A trusted entity whose credentials (a private key, for example) are used to bind the identity of a person to some data, such as the person's public key.

Classless Inter-Domain Routing (CIDR)   Allows the IP address space to be divided into portions of variable length, different from standard /8, /16, or /24 (class A, B, and C respectively). For example, if you have a small network that consists of 10 hosts, without CIDR you would have to request either /24, /16, or /8 networks, all of which have much more addresses that you need. With CIDR, in contrast, you can simply use /28 (28 bits to define network), which will give you (2**(32-28))-2=(2**4)-2=14 addresses.

ciphertext   Encrypted plaintext.

Collision Domain   Represents an area of an Ethernet's CSMA/CD network in which data sent from/to a connected network device may collide with data from other network devices.

Customer Premise (or Provided) Equipment (CPE)   Usually refers to equipment a subscriber should have in order to make use of telecommunications. Common types of CPE include telephones, modems, routers, and PCs.

digital certificate   Used to bind a public key to an identity by signing both with a trusted third party's private key (see *Certificate Authority*). In practice, a digital certificate can be a block of data containing DER encoded ASN.1 representations of an identity, the public key associated with the identity, the certificate's validity period, the certificate's issuer, and additional information.

ESP (Encapsulating Security Payload)   The part of the IPSec protocol suite that provides confidentiality and authentication services to IP packets.

hash or message digest   A one-way function that generates a digest based on an arbitrary block of data. The digest is typically 128 (MD5) or 160 (SHA-1) bits. One of the important properties of the hash function is that it should minimize collisions (that is, when different blocks of data result in the same digest).

Hash-based Message Authentication Code (HMAC)   A Message Authentication Code that uses cryptographic hash functions, for example, MD5, MD4, SHA-1 and so on. See also message authentication code (MAC).

integrity   A property that guarantees that data has not been tampered with.

kernel modules   Code that can be added to the kernel without stopping or rebooting a system. Examples include modules to support different file systems, device drivers, and so on. Modules usually have a `.o` extension. You can list, add, and remove modules using the `modutils` package (make sure it is installed). For instance, you can get a list of currently installed modules using `lsmod(8)`, install a new module using `insmod(8)` or `modprobe(8)`, and remove the module using `rmmod(8)`.

Major/Minor number   On Unix systems, devices usually have associated major and minor numbers. The major number identifies the type of a device. The minor number is used to distinguish devices of the same type.

Message Authentication Code (MAC) A hash that also depends on a key. The key is required to verify the hash.

Message Digest Algorithm (MD5) One-way cryptographic hash function generating 128-bit message digests.

.NET Microsoft's initiative to provide comprehensive web services through a collection of scripting, user management, and e-commerce tools.

nonrepudiation Prevents users from denying the actions they have performed. Examples include real senders unable to deny that a message was sent by them or real receivers unable to deny that the message was received by them.

OpenSSL An open-source library implementing secure sockets layer (SSL)/transport layer security (TLS) protocols as well as a full-strength crypto library providing access to a number of ciphers, hashes, encoding routines, and so on.

Pipe A colloquial term referring to the abstract concept of a direct logical connection between entities (for example, devices, processes).

plaintext Unencrypted data.

Pre-Shared Key (PSK) The secret that parties may need to share in order to communicate securely.

Public-Key Cryptography Standards (PKCS) A series of documents published by RSA Data Security to accelerate the deployment of public-key cryptography applications. The documents describe entities related to public-key cryptography, such as protocols, message formats, and so on. For instance, PKCS#1, #2, and #4 describe RSA; PKCS#3 describes Diffie-Hellman key agreement; PKCS#7 describes general syntax for data with cryptography applied to it (such as digital signatures and envelopes). See www.rsasecurity.com/rsalabs/pkcs/ for the detailed list.

Public-Key Infrastructure (PKI) A system designed to solve the public-key management problem by reliably and securely distributing, binding to identities, and revoking public keys.

runlevel A compound system state that allows only a selected group of processes to run. The details of each state are defined in the configuration file of init(1) (often it is /etc/inittab). Examples: Switching to level 0 leads to a system being halted, level 1 is single-user mode, level 3 is a multiuser mode at which most systems typically run, and level 6 is rebooting. You can change runlevels on Linux using telinit(1) by running it as a superuser. If you changed init's configuration file, don't forget to run telinit q to make sure init rereads the file.

Secure Hashing Algorithm (SHA-1) One-way cryptographic hash function generating 160-bit message digests.

segment An abstract part of a network, defining a continuous part of a network not interrupted by a network device that changes the protocol properties of that network. Usually only used when referring to LANs.

shared key A key used by a symmetric cipher to encrypt or decrypt data (also called a symmetric or private key).

signals   A form of interruption on a UNIX system. When a signal is received, the process that received the signal is temporarily suspended, and its signal handler is run (either the default or the one installed by the process). The signal handler then takes action based on the type of signal received. Signals can be sent using the `kill(1)` utility; signal handlers can be installed using the `signal(2)` system call.

symmetric/private–key cipher   A cryptographic algorithm that uses the same key (usually called a symmetric, shared, or private key) for encryption and decryption. Symmetric ciphers can operate on blocks (fixed, usually 64 or 128 bits) or streams (as small as 1 bit) of data and are called block or stream ciphers, respectively.

Total cost of ownership (TCO)   The cumulative cost of owning or operating something. This includes purchase costs, leasing costs, support costs, depreciation, personnel, and so on.

Virtual Network Computing (VNC)   Virtual Network Computing is a free remote display system developed at AT&T that allows remote control of desktops on other hosts.

War Dialing   With a modem, war dialing is the process of dialing numbers at random looking for another modem with which to connect.

Index

G-H

Q-R

W-Z

HOW TO CONTACT US

VISIT OUR WEB SITE

WWW.NEWRIDERS.COM

On our web site, you'll find information about our other books, authors, tables of contents, and book errata. You will also find information about book registration and how to purchase our books, both domestically and internationally.

EMAIL US

Contact us at: **nrfeedback@newriders.com**

- If you have comments or questions about this book
- To report errors that you have found in this book
- If you have a book proposal to submit or are interested in writing for New Riders
- If you are an expert in a computer topic or technology and are interested in being a technical editor who reviews manuscripts for technical accuracy

Contact us at: **nreducation@newriders.com**

- If you are an instructor from an educational institution who wants to preview New Riders books for classroom use. Email should include your name, title, school, department, address, phone number, office days/hours, text in use, and enrollment, along with your request for desk/examination copies and/or additional information.

Contact us at: **nrmedia@newriders.com**

- If you are a member of the media who is interested in reviewing copies of New Riders books. Send your name, mailing address, and email address, along with the name of the publication or web site you work for.

BULK PURCHASES/CORPORATE SALES

If you are interested in buying 10 or more copies of a title or want to set up an account for your company to purchase directly from the publisher at a substantial discount, contact us at 800-382-3419 or email your contact information to corpsales@pearsontechgroup.com. A sales representative will contact you with more information.

WRITE TO US

New Riders Publishing
201 W. 103rd St.
Indianapolis, IN 46290-1097

CALL/FAX US

Toll-free (800) 571-5840
If outside U.S. (317) 581-3500
Ask for New Riders
FAX: (317) 581-4663

New Riders

WWW.NEWRIDERS.COM

VOICES THAT MATTER

RELATED NEW RIDERS TITLES

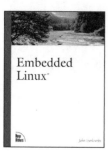

ISBN: 073570998X
224 pages
US$34.99

Embedded Linux

John Lombardo

Embedded Linux provides the reader the information needed to design, develop, and debug an embedded Linux appliance. It explores why Linux is a great choice for an embedded application and what to look for when choosing hardware.

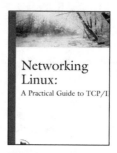

ISBN: 0735710317
400 pages
US$39.99

Networking Linux: A Practical Guide to TCP/I

Pat Eyler

This book goes beyond the conceptual and shows step-by-step the necessary know-how Linux TCP/IP implementation. Ideal for programmers and networking administrators in need of a platform-specific guide in order to increase their knowledge and overall efficienc

ISBN: 0735710015
572 pages
US$49.99

Vi IMproved (Vim)

Steve Oualline

Real Linux users don't use GUIs. No matter how popular, slick, and sophisticated the interfaces become for Linux and UNIX, you'll always need to be able to navigate in a text editor. The vim editor contains many more features than the old vi editor including help, multiple windows, syntax highlighting, programmer support, and HTML support. *Vi IMproved* is a concise reference for the vim editor.

ISBN: 0735710996
592 pages
US$49.99

Linux Firewalls, Second Edition

Robert Ziegler

"*I've spent countless hours digging through other Linux security books trying to find firewall setup information (particularly ipchains configuration info). This book is fa and away the best one I've come across. It felt like it was written specifically for me... I read about half of it in one sitting and was immediately able to debug my firewall setup afterwards.*"

—An online reviewer

ISBN: 073570970X
750 pages
US$49.99

PHP Functions Essential Reference

Graeme Merrall,
Landon Bradshaw, et al.

Co-authored by some of the leading developers in the PHP community, the *PHP Functions Essential Reference* is guaranteed to help you write effective code that makes full use of the rich variety of functions available in PHP 4.

ISBN: 1578702674
300 pages
US$39.99

Linux Routing

Joe Brockmeier
Dee Ann LeBlanc, and
Ronald McCarty

The administrator's guide to understanding Linux routing systems and techniques. *Linux Routing* explains and demo strates routing solutions for com mon network types, using variou types of hardware, and then explores the inner workings of t daemons and commands used fo routing in Linux.

olutions from experts you know and trust.

www.informit.com

New Riders has partnered with **InformIT.com** to bring technical information to your desktop. Drawing on New Riders authors and reviewers to provide additional information on topics you're interested in, **InformIT.com** has free, in-depth information you won't find anywhere else.

- **Master the skills you need, when you need them**

- **Call on resources from some of the best minds in the industry**

- **Get answers when you need them, using InformIT's comprehensive library or live experts online**

- **Go above and beyond what you find in New Riders books, extending your knowledge**

As an **InformIT** partner, **New Riders** has shared the wisdom and knowledge of our authors with you online. Visit **InformIT.com** to see what you're missing.

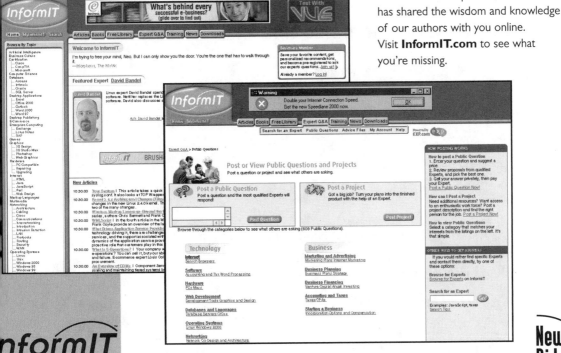

www.informit.com ▪ **www.newriders.com**

New Riders

Publishing
the Voices
that Matter

OUR BOOKS

OUR AUTHORS

SUPPORT

▦ web development ▦ graphics & design ▦ server technology ▦ certification

NEWS/EVENTS

PRESS ROOM

EDUCATORS

ABOUT US

CONTACT US

WRITE/REVIEW

You already know that New Riders brings you the Voices that Matter.

But what does that mean? It means that New Riders brings you the

Voices that challenge your assumptions, take your talents to the next

level, or simply help you better understand the complex technical world

we're all navigating.

Visit **www.newriders.com** to find:

▶ Never before published chapters

▶ Sample chapters and excerpts

▶ Author bios

▶ Contests

▶ Up-to-date industry event information

▶ Book reviews

▶ Special offers

▶ Info on how to join our User Group program

▶ Inspirational galleries where you can submit your
own masterpieces

▶ Ways to have your Voice heard

New
Riders

WWW.NEWRIDERS.COM

Colophon

On the cover of this book is an image of the River Clyde winding through the City Center of Glasgow, Scotland. Glasgow is the largest city in Scotland, and the third largest city in the United Kingdom. It is located in the Clyde Valley 64 km west of Edinburgh, and is a short distance from lochs and mountains that provide some of the most beautiful countryside in Britain.

Glasgow is home to half the population of Scotland, and is the country's cultural capital. The city was officially founded in 1180, but its history can be traced back to the founding of a church in the sixth century. The name "Glasgow" is said to be derived from a Gaelic word meaning "dear green place."

Glasgow has a mixture of Medieval, Georgian, and Victorian architecture, the oldest remaining home being Provand's Lordship, built in 1471. The pedestrian-friendly City Center is the main shopping and nightlife area, boardered by Trongate and the Merchant City to the East, motorways to the North and West, and the River Clyde to the South.

This book was written using Microsoft Word, and laid out in QuarkXPress. The fonts used for the body text are Bembo and MCPdigital. It was printed on 50# Husky Offset Smooth paper at VonHoffman Graphics, Inc., in Owensville, Missouri. Prepress consisted of PostScript computer-to-plate technology (filmless process). The cover was printed at Moore Langen Printing in Terre Haute, Indiana, on Carolina, coated on one side.